Archaeology

The discovery of material remains from the recent or the ancient past has always been a source of fascination, but the development of archaeology as an academic discipline which interpreted such finds is relatively recent. It was the work of Winckelmann at Pompeii in the 1760s which first revealed the potential of systematic excavation to scholars and the wider public. Pioneering figures of the nineteenth century such as Schliemann, Layard and Petrie transformed archaeology from a search for ancient artifacts, by means as crude as using gunpowder to break into a tomb, to a science which drew from a wide range of disciplines - ancient languages and literature, geology, chemistry, social history - to increase our understanding of human life and society in the remote past.

Prehistoric Man

The Scottish archaeologist and anthropologist Daniel Wilson (1816–92) spent the latter part of his life in Canada. Published in 1862, this is a seminal work in the study of early man in which Wilson utilises studies of native tribes 'still seen there in a condition which seems to reproduce some of the most familiar phases ascribed to the infancy of the unhistoric world'. He believed that civilisations initially developed in mild climates and judged the Mayans to have been the most advanced civilisation in the New World. Twentieth-century anthropologist Bruce Trigger argued that Wilson 'interpreted evidence about human behaviour in a way that is far more in accord with modern thinking than are the racist views of Darwin and Lubbock', and it is in this light that this two-volume work can be judged. Volume 2 covers topics ranging from ceramic arts to the influence of interbreeding and migration upon civilisations.

Prehistoric Man

*Researches into the Origin of Civilisation
in the Old and the New World*

VOLUME 2

DANIEL WILSON

CAMBRIDGE UNIVERSITY PRESS

Cambridge, New York, Melbourne, Madrid, Cape Town,
Singapore, São Paolo, Delhi, Mexico City

Published in the United States of America by Cambridge University Press, New York

www.cambridge.org
Information on this title: www.cambridge.org/9781108054850

© in this compilation Cambridge University Press 2013

This edition first published 1862
This digitally printed version 2013

ISBN 978-1-108-05485-0 Paperback

PREHISTORIC MAN.

VOLUME II.

CAW WE LITCKS

A FLATHEAD WOMAN AND CHILD.

Drawn by D. Wilson, L.L.D. — from sketches by Paul Kane.

PREHISTORIC MAN

RESEARCHES INTO THE ORIGIN OF CIVILISATION
IN THE OLD AND THE NEW WORLD.

BY

DANIEL WILSON, LL.D.,

PROFESSOR OF HISTORY AND ENGLISH LITERATURE IN UNIVERSITY COLLEGE, TORONTO ;
AUTHOR OF THE "ARCHÆOLOGY AND PREHISTORIC ANNALS OF SCOTLAND," ETC.

IN TWO VOLUMES.

VOLUME II.

Cambridge:

MACMILLAN AND CO.,

AND 23, HENRIETTA STREET, COVENT GARDEN,

London.

1862.

EDINBURGH : T. CONSTABLE,
PRINTER TO THE QUEEN, AND TO THE UNIVERSITY.

CONTENTS.

PREHISTORIC MAN.

CHAPTER XVI.

AMONG the native products of the American continent, there is none which so strikingly distinguishes it as the tobacco-plant, and the purposes to which its leaf is applied ; for even could it be proved that the use of it as a narcotic, and the practice of smoking its burning leaf, had originated independently in the Old World, the sacred institution of the peace-pipe must still remain the peculiar characteristic of the Red Indian of America. Its name—derived by some from the Haîtian *tambaku,* and by others from *Tabaco,* a province of Yucatan, where the Spaniards are affirmed to have first met with it,—appears to have been the native term for the pipe, and not for the plant, which was variously called *kohiba, petun, qutschartai, uppówoc, apouκe,* and indeed had a different name from almost every ancient and modern tribe and nation. The *tabaco,* or implement originally used by the Indians of Hispaniola for inhaling the smoke of the *kohiba,* or tobacco-plant, is described by Oviedo as a hollow, forked cane like the letter Y, the double ends of which were inserted in the nostrils, while the single end was applied to the burning leaves of the herb. This, however, was a peculiar insular custom, and a mere local name, though since brought into such universal use as the designation of the plant; while the pipe, which plays so prominent a part among the traces of the most ancient arts and rites of the continent, is now common to every quarter of the globe. Nothing, indeed, more clearly proves the antiquity and universality of the use of tobacco throughout the whole continent of America, than the totally distinct and diverse names by which it is designated in the various languages of the Indian tribes.

So far as we can now infer from the evidence furnished by native arts and relics connected with the use of the tobacco-plant, it seems to have been as familiar to most of the ancient tribes of the North-west, and the aborigines of the Canadian forests, as to those of the American tropics, of which the *Nicotiana tabacum* is believed to be a native. No such remarkable depositories indeed have been found to the north of the great chain of lakes as those disclosed to the explorers of the tumuli of " Mound City," in the Scioto Valley; but even now the tobacco-pipe monopolizes the ingenious art of many of the wild forest-tribes of the continent, and some of their most curious legends and superstitions are connected with the favourite national implement. Among them it retains the dignity of a time-honoured institution, the sacredness of which still survives with much of its ancient force; and to this accordingly the student of America's primeval antiquities is justified in turning, as an important link connecting the present with that ancient past. When referring to the miniature sculptures procured from the mounds of the Ohio and Scioto valleys, Messrs. Squier and Davis remark :—" From the appearance of these relics it is fairly inferable that among the Mound-Builders, as among the tribes of North American Indians, the practice of smoking was very general, if not universal. The conjecture that it was also more or less interwoven with their civil and religious observances is not without its support. The use of tobacco was known to nearly all the American nations, and the pipe was their grand diplomatist. In making war and in concluding peace it performed an important part. Their deliberations, domestic as well as public, were conducted under its influences ; and no treaty was ever made unsignalized by the passage of the calumet. The transfer of the pipe from the lips of one individual to those of another was the token of amity and friendship, a gage of honour with the chivalry of the forest which was seldom violated. In their religious ceremonies it was also introduced with various degrees of solemnity." But it is worthy of note that the form of the mound-pipes is altogether peculiar, and differs essentially from the endless varieties of form and pattern, wrought by Indian ingenuity from the most diverse materials pertaining to the native localities of tribes of the forest and prairie. Some consideration, therefore, of the arts of the modern pipe-sculptor, and of the native customs and traditions associated with the use of tobacco, is necessary, as a means of comparison between the ancient and the modern nations and tribes of the New World. Nor will it be out of place to consider here whether America was indeed the sole originator of the practice of smoking, and consequently how far its introduction into Europe and the Old World at large may be justly reckoned as one of the results of Columbus's adventurous daring.

In the Old World most of the ideas connected with the tobacco-pipe are homely and prosaic enough ; and though we associate the chibouk with the poetical reveries of the oriental day-dreamer, and the hookah with the pleasant fancies of the Anglo-Indian reposing in the shade of his bungalow, nevertheless, its seductive antique mystery, and all its symbolic significance, pertain alone to the New World. The tobacco-pipe, indeed, constitutes the peculiar and most characteristic symbol of America, intimately interwoven with the rites and superstitions, and with the relics of ancient ·customs and historical traditions of its aborigines. If Europe borrowed from it the first knowledge of its prized narcotic, the gift was received unaccompanied by any of the sacred or peculiar virtues which the Red Indian still attaches to it as the symbol of hospitality and amicable intercourse ; and Longfellow, accordingly, with no less poetic vigour than fitness, opens his *Song of Hiawatha* with the institution of "the peace-pipe" by the Great Spirit. The Master of Life descends on the mountains of the prairie, breaks a fragment from the red stone of the quarry, and, fashioning it with curious art into a figured pipe-head, he fills it with the bark of the red willow, chafes the forest into flame with the tempest of his breath, and kindling it, smokes the calumet as a signal to the nations, and the tribes of the ancient aborigines gathering from river, lake, and prairie, assemble at the divine summons, listen to the warnings and promises with which the Great Spirit seeks to guide them ; and this done, and the warriors having buried their warclubs, they smoke their first peace-pipe, and depart :—-

> " While the Master of Life, ascending,
> Through the opening of cloud-curtains,
> Through the doorways of the heaven,
> Vanished from before their faces,
> In the smoke that rolled around him,
> The pukwana of the peace-pipe !"

It is no mean triumph of the poet thus to redeem from associations, not only prosaic, but even offensive, a custom which so peculiarly pertains to the usages and

the rites of the American continent from the remotest
times of which its historic memorials furnish any trace ;
and which was no sooner practically introduced to the
knowledge of the Old World than that royal pedant,
King James, directed against it his world-famous
Counterblast to Tobacco, describing its use as "a custom loathesome to the eye, hateful to the nose, harmful
to the brain, dangerous to the lungs, and in the black
stinking fume thereof nearest resembling the horrible
stygian smoke of the pit that is bottomless !" In those,
however, as in other passages of his national epic, the
American poet has only embodied in forms of modern
verse the cherished legends of the New World : placing
the opening scene of *Hiawatha* on the heights of the
great red pipe-stone quarry of Coteau des Prairies,
between the Minnesota and Missouri rivers, in the
Far West.

On the summit of the ridge between these two tributaries of the Mississippi rises a bold perpendicular cliff,
beautifully marked with distinct horizontal layers of light
grey and rose or flesh-coloured quartz. From the base
of this a level prairie of about half a mile in width runs
parallel to it, and here it is that the famous red pipe-
stone is procured, at a depth of from four to five feet
from the surface. Numerous traces of ancient and modern
excavations indicate the resort of the Indian tribes of
many successive generations to the locality. "That this
place should have been visited," says Catlin, "for centuries
past by all the neighbouring tribes, who have hidden the
war-club as they approached it, and stayed the cruelties
of the scalping-knife, under the fear of the vengeance of
the Great Spirit who overlooks it, will not seem strange
or unnatural when their superstitions are known. That
such has been the custom there is not a shadow of doubt,
and that even so recently as to have been witnessed by

hundreds and thousands of Indians of different tribes
now living, and from many of whom I have personally
drawn the information; and, as additional and still more
conclusive evidence, here are to be seen the *totems* and
arms of the different tribes who have visited this place
for ages past, deeply engraven on the quartz rocks."[1]
The enterprising traveller who narrates this, speaks elsewhere of the thousands of inscriptions and paintings
observed by him on the neighbouring rocks; while the
feeling in which they originate was thus illustrated by
an Indian whose portrait he painted when in the Mandan country. " My brother," said the Mandan, "you
have made my picture, and I like it much. My friends
tell me they can see the eyes move, and it must be very
good; it must be partly alive. I am glad it is done,
though many of my people are afraid. I am a young
man, but my heart is strong. I have jumped on to the
Medicine Rock; I have placed my arrow on it, and no
Mandan can take it away. The red stone is slippery,
but my foot was true; it did not slip. My brother, this
pipe which I give to you I brought from a high mountain; it is towards the rising sun. Many were the pipes
we brought from thence, and we brought them away in
peace. We left our totems on the rocks; we cut them
deep in the stones, they are there now. The Great Spirit
told all nations to meet there in peace, and all nations
hid the war-club and the tomahawk. The Dahcotahs,
who are our enemies, are very strong; they have taken
up the tomahawk, and the blood of our warriors has run
on the rocks. We want to visit our medicines. Our
pipes are old and worn out."

The Medicine or Leaping-Rock, here referred to, is a
detached column standing between seven and eight feet

[1] *Illustrations of the Manners, etc., of the North American Indians.* By
Geo. Catlin. Eighth edition. Vol. ii. p. 167.

from the precipitous cliff; and the leap across this chasm is a daring feat which the young warriors are ambitious of performing. It was pointed out to Catlin by a Sioux chief, whose son had perished in the attempt. A conical mound marked the spot of his sepulture; and though the sanctity of this ancient neutral ground has been invaded, and the powerful nation of the Sioux now refuse to permit other tribes to have access to it, this is of quite recent occurrence. Alike by the evidence of the belief of many independent tribes, the memorials of their presence on the graven rocks, and the numerous excavations, sepulchral mounds, and other earthworks in the vicinity : the Indian tradition receives confirmation, that from time immemorial this has been the sacred neutral ground of all the tribes to the west, and of many of those to the east of the Mississippi, and the place whither they have made their regular pilgrimages to renew their pipes from the rock consecrated by the footprints of the Great Spirit. These marks of his footsteps are pointed out, deeply impressed in the rock, and resembling the track of a large bird! Nor is it without a special interest for us to note a Mandan tradition respecting this sacred spot; for the migrations of that once powerful Indian nation have been traced from the country lying between Cincinnati and Lake Erie, down the valley of the Ohio, over the graves of the ancient Mound-Builders, and thence up the great western branch of the Mississippi, until their utter extinction, chiefly by the frightful ravages of the small-pox in the year 1838, at their latest settlements on the Upper Missouri. The site of their last homes, and the place of their extinction, lies to the north of the Sioux's country, in whose possession the area of the pipe-stone quarries is now vested by the law of the strongest; and they, accordingly, may be considered as the guardians of the traditions of the locality. For, although they have thus set at defiance its most sacred and universally recognised characteristic, and so slighted the mandate of the Great Spirit, they do not the less strongly hold by the other superstitious ideas associated with the spot.

One of these legends derives its form from some of the peculiar features of the scene. Near the base of the perpendicular cliff, already described, there lies on the level prairie, where the Indian pipe-stone quarries are opened, a group of five large granite boulders disposed in a row. The largest of them is about twenty-five feet in diameter, and the smallest from twelve to fifteen feet. These, as prominent objects on the level plain, have attracted the attention of the superstitious visitors of the spot, and are regarded with awful reverence by the Indians. Two holes under them are the abodes of the guardian spirits of the spot; and Catlin, who not only visited the quarry, but broke off and carried away with him fragments of these sacred boulders, remarks : " As for the poor Indian, his superstitious veneration of them is such, that not a spear of grass is broken or bent by his feet within three or four roods of them, where he stops, and, in humble supplication, by throwing plugs of tobacco to them, solicits permission to dig and carry away the red stone for his pipes." Here, according to the traditions of many independent tribes, not only took place the mysterious birth of the red pipe, but the postdiluvian creation of the human race.

The tradition of the institution of the peace-pipe varies among the different tribes, but its general form is that which Longfellow has embodied in his Indian epic. It is thus narrated by the Sioux of the Mississippi : " Many ages after the red men were made, when all the different tribes were at war, the Great Spirit called them all together at the Red Rocks. He stood on the top of the rocks, and the red nations were assembled in infinite numbers on the plain below. He took out of the rock a piece of the red stone, and made a large pipe. He smoked it over them all; told them that it was part of their flesh; that though they were at war, they must meet at this place as friends; that it belonged to them all; that they must make their calumets from it, and smoke them to him whenever they wished to appease him or get his goodwill. The smoke from his big pipe rolled over them all, and he disappeared in its cloud. At the last whiff of his pipe a blaze of fire rolled over the rocks and melted their surface. At that moment two Indian maidens passed in a flame under the two medicine rocks, where they remain to this day. The voices of Tsomecostee and Tsomecostewondee, as they are named, are heard at times in answer to the invocations of the suppliants, and they must be propitiated before the pipe-stone is taken away."

An offering of tobacco is almost invariably the propitiatory gift, and it appears to have been used in similar acts of worship and sacrifice from the earliest period of intercourse with Europeans. In the narrative of the voyage of Drake, in 1572, it is noted that the natives brought a little basket made of rushes, and filled with an herb which they called *tobak*. This, which was the tobacco-plant, was regarded by the voyagers as a propitiatory offering; as the writer subsequently notes, they "came now the second time to us, bringing with them, as before had been done, feathers and bags of *tobak* for presents, or rather, indeed, for sacrifices, upon this persuasion that we were gods." In all probability, as already suggested, the practice of smoking originated in the use of the intoxicating fumes for purposes of divination, or other superstitious rites; and the universality of the later use of the 'plant has not entirely divested it of its sacred character. Harriot, who formed one of the voyagers by whom Virginia was discovered, tells, in his

"Briefe and True Report of the New Found Land of Virginia," of a plant which has diverse names in the West Indies, according to the several places and countries where it is used. The Spaniards generally call it *tobacco*, but it is there named by the natives *uppówoc*. "This *uppówoc* is of so precious estimation among them, that they think their gods are marvellously delighted therewith, whereupon sometime they make halowed fires, and cast some of the powder therein for a sacrifice. Being in a storme upon the waters, to pacifie their gods they cast some up into the aire ; and into the water ; so a weare for fish being newly set up, they cast some therein and into the aire ; also, after an escape of danger, they cast some into the aire likewise ; but all done with strange gestures, stamping, sometime dancing, clapping of hands, holding up of hands, and staring up into the heavens, uttering therewithal and chattering strange words and noises." Such practices and ideas of propitiatory offerings among the more southern Indian tribes of the sixteenth century, abundantly prove that the offerings of tobacco still made by the Sioux to the spirits that haunt the pipe-stone quarry, are of no merely local origin, but were anciently as universal as the peace-pipe itself. Nor were such religious associations with the favourite narcotic confined to the northern continent. Among the Peruvians the cocoa plant took the place of tobacco in this as well as in other respects. Dr. Tschudi states that he found the cocoa still regarded by the Peruvian Indians as something sacred· and mysterious. "In all ceremonies, whether religious or warlike, it was introduced for producing smoke at the great offerings, or as the sacrifice itself. During divine worship the priests chewed cocoa-leaves ; and, unless they were supplied with them, it was believed that the favour of the gods could not be propitiated." Christianity, after an interval of upwards of three hundred years, has not eradicated the Indian's faith in the virtues of the sacred plant. In the mines of Cerro de Pasco, masticated cocoa is thrown on the hard veins of metal to propitiate the gnomes of the mine, who, it is believed, would otherwise render the mountains impenetrable ; and the leaves of the cocoa are secretly placed in the mouth of the dead, to smooth his passage to another world. Thus we find, in the superstitions perpetuated among the Indians of the southern Cordilleras, striking analogies to those which survive among the northern Sioux, and give character to the strange rites they practise at the red pipe-stone quarry, on the Coteau des Prairies.

From among the many Indian traditions connected with that interesting locality, one of those which seem to perpetuate the idea of a general deluge, may best illustrate its most ancient associations. It was narrated to Catlin, by a distinguished Knisteneaux on the Upper Missouri, on the occasion of presenting to him a handsome red-stone pipe. " In the time of a great freshet, which took place many centuries ago, and destroyed all the nations of the earth, all the tribes of the red men assembled on the Coteau des Prairies, to get out of the way of the waters. After they had all gathered here from every part, the water continued to rise, until at length it covered them all in a mass, and their flesh was converted into red pipe-stone. Therefore, it has always been considered neutral ground ; it belongs to all tribes alike, and all were allowed to get it and smoke it together. While they were all drowning in a mass, a young woman, Kwaptahw, a virgin, caught hold of the foot of a very large bird that was flying over, and was carried to the top of a high cliff not far off, that was above the water. Here she had twins, and their father was the war-eagle, and her children have since peopled the earth." The idea that the red pipe-

stone is the flesh of their ancestors is a favourite one
among different and entirely independent tribes. When
Catlin and his party attempted to penetrate to the sacred
locality, they were stopped by the Sioux, and one of
them addressing him, said : "This red pipe was given to
the red men by the Great Spirit. It is a part of our
flesh, and therefore is great medicine. We know that
the whites are like a great cloud that rises in the east,
and will cover the whole country. We know that they
will have all our lands ; but if ever they get our red-pipe
quarry they will have to pay very dear for it." Thus is
it that even in the farthest West the Indian feels the
fatal touch of that white hand ; and to the intrigues of
interested white traders is ascribed the encroachment of
the Sioux on the sacred neutral ground, where, within
memory of living men, every tribe on the Missouri had
smoked with their enemies, while the Great Spirit kept
the peace among his red children on that spot consecrated
by the traditions of ages.

Apart, then, from such indications of superior skill, and
a truly artistic power of imitation, by which the ancient
pipe-sculptors are distinguished, it becomes an object of
some interest with us to observe other elements, either
of comparison or contrast, between the memorials of the
Mound-Builder's skill, and the numerous specimens of
pipe-sculpture produced by modern tribes. Nor are the
distinctive points either slight or unimportant.

Notwithstanding the endless variety which characterizes the form of the ancient Mound-Builder's pipes, one
general type is traceable through the whole. "They are
always carved from a single piece, and consist of a flat
curved base, with the bowl rising from the centre of the
convex side. From one of the ends, and communicating
with the hollow of the bowl, is drilled a small hole, which
answers the purpose of a tube ; the corresponding opposite

division being left for the manifest purpose of holding the implement to the mouth." The authors of the *Ancient Monuments of the Mississippi Valley* express their conviction, derived from the inspection of hundreds of specimens which have come under their notice, during their explorations of the ancient mounds, that the instrument is complete as found, and was used without any such tube or pipe-stem, as is almost invariably employed by the modern Indian, and also by the modern perfume-loving oriental when he fills his chibouk with the odorous shiraz or mild latakia. It is otherwise with the examples of pipe-heads carved out of the beautiful red pipe-stone, and other favourite materials for the pipe-sculpture of the modern Indian. It would seem, therefore, that the pipe-stem is one of the characteristics of the modern race ; if, indeed, it does not distinguish the northern tribes from Aztec, Toltecan, and other essentially diverse ancient peoples.

The use of tobacco, from the earliest eras of which we can recover a glimpse, pertained both to the northern and southern nations ; but the pipe-head would appear to be the emblem of the one, while the pipe-stem gives character to the singular rites and superstitions of the other. The incremated pipe-heads of the ancient Mound-Builders illustrate the sacred usages of the one ; while the skill with which the Indian medicine-man decorates the stem of his medicine-pipe, and the awe and reverence with which the whole tribe regard it, abundantly prove the virtues ascribed to that implement of the medicine-man's art. May it not be, that in the sacred associations connected with the pipe by the Mound-Builders of the Mississippi Valley, we have indications of contact between the migrating race of Southern and Central America, among whom no superstitious pipe usages are traceable, and the tribes of the north where such superstitions are most intimately interwoven with all their sacred mysteries ?

The utmost variety of form and material distinguishes the pipes of the modern Indians ; arising in part from the local facilities they possess for a suitable material from which to construct them, and in part also from the special style of art and decoration which has become the traditional usage of the tribe. The favourite red pipe-stone of the Coteau des Prairies has been generally sought after, from the facility with which it can be wrought, and the beauty of its colour and texture, as well as for the mysterious virtues which the ancient superstitions of the tribes have attached to it. But the pipe-sculptures of many tribes can be distinguished no less certainly by the material, than by the favourite conventional pattern.

Among the Assinaboin Indians a fine marble is used, much too hard to admit of minute carving, but susceptible of a high polish. This is cut into pipes of graceful form, and made so extremely thin, as to be nearly transparent, so that when lighted the glowing tobacco shines through, and presents a singular appearance when in use at night, or in a dark lodge. Another favourite material is a coarse species of jasper, also too hard to admit of elaborate ornamentation. This also is cut into various simple but tasteful designs, executed chiefly by the slow and laborious process of rubbing it down with other stones. The choice of the material for fashioning the favourite pipe is by no means invariably guided by the facilities which the position of the tribe affords. A suitable stone for such a purpose will be picked up and carried hundreds of miles. Mr. Kane informs me that, in coming down the Athabaska river, when drawing near its source in the Rocky Mountains, he observed his Assinaboin guides select the favourite bluish jasper from among the water-worn stones in the bed of the river, to carry home for the purpose of pipe manufacture, although they were then fully five hundred miles from their lodges. Such traditional adherence to the choice of a material peculiar to a remote source, as well as the perpetuation of special forms and patterns among the scattered members of the tribe, may frequently prove of considerable value as a clue to former migrations.

Among the Cree Indians a double pipe is occasionally in use, consisting of a bowl carved out of stone without much attempt at ornament, but with perforations on two sides, so that two smokers can insert their pipe-stems at once, and enjoy the same supply of tobacco. This form would seem peculiarly adapted for sealing the new-born amity of ancient foes turned friends ; but I have not been able to learn that any special significance is attached to the singular fancy. The Chippewas, on the St. Louis river, at the head of Lake Superior, a branch of the great Algonquin nation, also carve their pipes out of an easily-wrought dark close-grained stone ; and frequently introduce groups of animals and human figures with considerable artistic skill, but generally with accompaniments which betray the influence of European intercourse on the development of native art.

One of the most celebrated Indian pipe-sculptors is *Pabahmesad*, or the Flier, an Old Chippewa, still living on the Great Manitoulin Island in Lake Huron ; but more generally known as *Pwahguneka*, the Pipe Maker, literally " he makes pipes." Though brought in contact with the Christian Indians of the Manitoulin Islands, he resolutely adheres to the pagan creed and rites of his fathers, and resists all the encroachments of civilisation. His materials are the *muhkuhda-pwahgunahbeck*, or black pipe-stone of Lake Huron, the *wahbepwahgunahbeck*, or white pipe-stone, procured on St. Joseph's Island,

and the *misko-pwahgunahbeck,* or red pipe-stone of the
Coteau des Prairies. His saw, with which the stone is
first roughly blocked out, is made by himself out of a
bit of iron hoop, and his other tools are correspondingly
rude; nevertheless the workmanship of Pabahmesad
shows him to be a master of his art. A characteristic
illustration of his ingenious sculpture is engraved here

FIG. 26.—Chippewa Pipe.

(Fig. 26), from the original, in the museum of the
University of Toronto.

It is impossible that a people manifesting such peculiar aptitude for artistic imitation, should fail to copy
some of the novel arts and objects brought under their
notice by European traders and settlers. But the unimpressible nature of the Indian, and the dormant state
of his mental faculties, appear in the fact of his imitation extending only to the transference of a few novel
forms to his carvings, while all the ingenious discoveries
and useful arts of the European remain unheeded or
despised. Here and there the manufactures of Europe,
bartered by the fur trader for Indian peltries, find acceptance. The copper kettle displaces in part the rude
and fragile clay caldron, and the blanket gradually takes
the place of the more graceful buffalo robe. But the
most characteristic and interesting objects of native
workmanship disappear in this process of exchange:

with no other effect on the poor Indian than to make
him more dependent on the civilisation which he despises,
and to rob him of the few simple arts which he has
inherited from his fathers.

The tendency to imitation, within the limited range
of native art-manufacture, shows itself more like an
unreasoning instinct, where the Indian is now frequently found laboriously reproducing the simple form
of the clay pipe in the hardest stones ; though here also
his taste is seen to break the bonds of fashion, and to
superadd incongruous, yet not ungraceful ornaments and
devices to the homely European model.   But the most
elaborate of all the modern specimens of pipe-sculpture
are those executed by the Babeen, or big-lip Indians,
so called from the singular deformity the females produce by inserting a piece of wood into a slit made in
the lower lip.   The frontispiece to vol. I. illustrates the
characteristic physiognomy of this tribe.   It is an accurate portrait of a Chimpseyan chief, from sketches taken
by Mr. Paul Kane during his travels in the North-west.
The Chimpseyan or Babeen Indians are found along
the Pacific Coast, about latitude 54° 40′, and extend
from the borders of the Russian dominions eastward
nearly to Frazer River.   Some of their customs are
scarcely less singular than that from whence their name
is derived, and are deserving of minute comparison
with the older practices which pertained to the more
civilized regions of the continent.   This is especially
the case in relation to their rites of sepulture, wherein
they make another marked distinction between the
sexes.   Their females are wrapped in mats, and placed
on an elevated platform, or in a canoe raised on poles,
but they invariably burn their male dead.

The pipes of the Babeen, and also of the Clalam
Indians occupying the neighbouring Vancouver's Island,

are carved with the utmost elaborateness, and in the most singular and grotesque devices, from a soft blue claystone or slate found in that region. The form is in part determined by the material, which is only procurable in thin slabs ; so that the sculptures, wrought on both sides, present a sort of double bas-relief. From this, singular and grotesque groups are carved, without any apparent reference to the final destination of the whole as a pipe. The lower side is generally straight, and in the specimens I have examined, the pipes measure from two or three to fifteen inches long ; so that in these the pipe-stem is included. A small hollow is carved out of some protruding ornament to serve as a bowl, and from the further end a perforation is drilled to connect with this. The only addition made to it, when in use, is the insertion of a quill or straw as a mouth-piece instead of the usual pipe-stem, which would be incompatible with the peculiar form, as well as with the weight, of such elaborate and somewhat brittle works

Fig. 27.—Babeen Pipe.

of art. The woodcut (Fig. 27) illustrates the simpler devices of the Babeen sculptor in decorating one of his smaller pipes. But large and complicated designs are of common occurrence. One of the largest brought back by Mr. Kane measures nearly fifteen inches long. It consists of a grotesque intermixture of figures, in which that of the frog predominates ; though accompanied with strange monstrosities intermingling human

and brutal forms, and presenting some analogy to
much of the sculpture on the temple-ruins of Central
America.

The more elaborate specimen of pipe-sculpture shown
in Fig. 28, may be regarded as the conventional repre-

FIG. 28.—Babeen Pipe-Sculpture.

sentation, by the Babeen artist, of a bear-hunt in the
vicinity of one of the Hudson's Bay Company's stations
or forts ; and possibly the swampy nature of the scene
of action is indicated by the frogs, though the latter are
favourite objects with the Babeen sculptors. The grotesque masks imitated here, are executed the size of
life, and brilliantly coloured ; and furnish a frequent
subject repeated in miniature on the claystone carvings.
From the costume, it is evident that the man who turns
his back on the bear is intended to represent one of the
Hudson's Bay Company's trappers. The group constitutes altogether an ingenious and spirited specimen of
native art, such as would be regarded as no discredit-
able product of conventional design if sculptured on
a Norman capital of the twelfth century.

Messrs. Squier and Davis conclude their remarks on
the sculptures of the Mounds by observing : " It is un-
necessary to say more than that, as works of art, they
are immeasurably beyond anything which the North
American Indians are known to produce, even at this
day, with all the suggestions of European art, and the

advantages afforded by steel instruments. The Chinooks, and the Indians of the north-western coast, carve pipes, platters, and other articles, with much neatness, from slate. We see in their pipes, for instance, a heterogeneous collection of pulleys, cords, barrels, and rude human figures, evidently suggested by the tackling of the ships trading in those seas. The utmost that can be said of them is, that they are elaborate, unmeaning carvings, displaying some degree of ingenuity." This descriptive comparison of the mound-sculptures with the arts of the Indians of the north-west coast, is based on deductions drawn from exceptional specimens very different from many brought from the same localities, or investigated in the hands of the native sculptors ; which obviously constitute the true illustrations of Indian skill and artistic design. In addition to such, however, among a varied collection of Indian relics from the north-west coast, now in the possession of the Hon. G. W. Allan, of Toronto, there is one of the ingenious examples of imitative skill referred to, which was procured on Vancouver's Island. But while this exhibits evidence of the same skilful dexterity as other carvings in the blue pipe-slate of the Clalam and Babeen Indians, it presents the most striking contrast to them, alike in design and style of art. It has a regular bowl, imitated from that of a common clay pipe, and is decorated with twisted ropes, part of a ship's bulkhead, and other objects—including even the head of a screw-nail,—all equally familiar to us, but which no doubt attracted the eye of the native artist from their novelty.

Another example procured by Professor Hind during his command of the exploring expedition to the Assinaboin and Saskatchewan rivers, is a representation of one of the Hudson's Bay Company's forts, with figures in European costume. These cannot for a moment be compared with the ancient mound-sculptures ; and, indeed, the human figures are greatly inferior to those of the Chippewa sculptures. Nevertheless, as evidences of the predominance of the imitative faculty even among this rude tribe of the native Indians of North America, they are well worthy of careful study. But these are not the works by which to judge of the art of the Babeen sculptor. His own genuine native designs exhibit the most varied, elaborate, and fanciful devices, including human figures, some of them with birds' and beasts' heads, and frequently presenting considerable accuracy of imitative skill. In some of the larger pipes, the entire group presents much of the grotesque exuberance of fancy, mingled with imitations borrowed directly from nature, which constitute the charm of ecclesiastical sculptures of the thirteenth century. The figures are grouped together in the oddest varieties of posture, and ingeniously interlaced, and connected by elaborate ornaments ; the intermediate spaces being perforated, so as to give great lightness of appearance to the whole. But though well calculated to recall the quaint products of the mediæval sculptor's chisel : so far are these Babeen carvings from

Fig. 29.—Tawatin Ivory carving.

suggesting the slightest resemblance to European models, that when first examining them, as well as specimens in bone and ivory from the same locality,—and still more

so, some ivory carvings executed by the Tawatin Indians
on Frazer River, of which an example is figured here
(Fig. 29),—I was struck with certain resemblances to the
peculiar style of ancient Mexican and still more of Central American art. In this they only confirm the traces
of some common relationship, or early intercourse between those rude savage tribes of the North-west and the
latest native civilized occupants of the Mexican plateau,
which noticeable peculiarities in language and customs
had already suggested. The ivory carving figured here
measures four and a half inches long, and is executed
with minute delicacy. On the reverse (Fig. 30) a whale

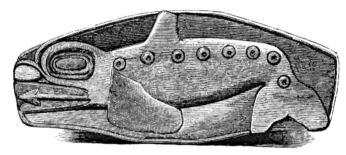

FIG. 30.—Tawatin Ivory carving.

is cut with considerable spirit ; and it is curious to find
in it the untutored sculptor of the Pacific coast giving
to the monster of the deep the same forked tongue which
formed the conventional attribute of the dragons and
leviathans of mediæval Europe.

   But there is another conclusion, of more general application, suggested by these Babeen sculptures. They are
deserving of special consideration, from illustrating, in
some respects, the just method of inductive history as
derived from ancient relics of primitive art. Impressed
with the discrepancy, which at first sight is apt to strike
even the least careful investigator, between the elaborate
art of the finer sculptures, and especially the pipe-heads

of the mounds, and other traces of skill and civilisation of their builders, Mr. Haven assumes a foreign origin for all such sculptures ; while others have inferred from them a native civilisation in the Mississippi and Ohio Valleys, corresponding in all respects to those isolated examples of art ; just as, from a rude but graceful Greek vase, we can infer the taste of a Callicrates or a Phidias. If, however, the conclusions adopted from the geometrical accuracy of the regular figures in their earthworks, the perfection of their execution on the largest scale, and the existence of definite standards of measurement, as implied in the recurrence of such large earthworks constructed of the same figures and precisely corresponding in size, are legitimate : then it cannot be said that we are without evidences of civilisation much more important and trustworthy even than their finest sculptures. Such geometrical construction and mensuration must have been accompanied with the use of instruments, a knowledge of figures, and other acquirements very far in advance of anything possessed by the most intelligent among the Indian tribes. What equivalent evidence, indeed, of our boasted civilisation would remain, if some of the newer cities, built on the site of the ancient mounds and enclosures, were abandoned to the same work of time which has buried the mounds of the Ohio in the depths of its ancient forest shadows? Whilst, however, we must guard against being misled by too sweeping deductions, on the one hand : it is important to note, in reference to such modern productions of native art, that while the Babeen sculptor executes a piece of pipe-carving so elaborate and ingenious as justly to excite our wonder and admiration, it furnishes no test of his general progress in arts or civilisation. On the contrary, he is ruder and more indifferent to the refinements of dress and decoration than many Indian tribes who produce no such special examples of ingenious skill. Some of the conclusions which such facts suggest will be found applicable to not a few deductions derived by European archæologists from isolated examples of primitive art.

Enough has been said to illustrate the endless variety of forms into which the favourite smoking implement of the New World has been wrought, in all ages, by the zealous devotees of the nicotian weed, working in such intractable materials, and supplied with the rudest and most imperfect tools. But the potter's art was not unknown, meanwhile, to the Indian smoker, and he also had his "clay," which indeed supplied the first models for some at least of the European pipes. Upon the sites of old Indian villages fragments of pottery occur in great abundance, and among these, clay pipes are of frequent occurrence. I have repeatedly dug them up in different Canadian localities ; and in nearly all such examples have found the bowl as small as the most diminutive of Scottish "Elfin pipes." They indicate the economic use of the tobacco among the older Indians, on whom it is well known to produce a highly intoxicating effect when indulged in to an excess which proves perfectly innocuous to the European ; and they help to throw some light on the question of the first introduction of the pipe to Europe.

The potter's art is among the most ancient practised by man, in every quarter of the globe, and it contributes its evidences of America's early ingenuity and skill. As applied, however, to the requirements of the smoker, its productions appear to belong chiefly to the later ages of the New World. In the vicinity of the city of Mexico large quantities of clay pipes have been dug up, in a variety of fanciful forms, one of which, given by Mr. Fairholt in his *Tobacco, its History and Associations,* represents a male figure with the characteristic features of the Mexican type. The right leg forms the tube of the pipe, while the other is bent so as to act as a handle. Clay pipes, with globular or trumpet-shaped bowls of a large size, have been repeatedly found in Canada and the Northern States, along with relics which indicate an era subsequent to the intercourse of the natives with Europeans. They are not therefore of any very great antiquity; but it is worthy of note, that they bear a nearer resemblance than any figured or described among American antiquities, to such as are introduced in ancient Mexican paintings;[1] nor are examples wanting of a more antique style of art. Many of the ancient clay pipes that have been discovered are described as having nearly the same form; and this presents so great a correspondence to that of the red clay pipe used in modern Turkey and Egypt with a cherry-tree pipe-stem, that it might be supposed to have furnished the model. The bowls of this class of pipes are not of the miniature proportions which, as it will be seen, induce a comparison between those of Canada and the early examples found in Britain; neither do the stone pipe-heads of the Mound-Builders suggest, by the size of the bowl, either the self-denying economy of the ancient smoker, or his practice of the Indian mode of exhaling the fumes of the tobacco, by which a small quantity suffices to produce the full narcotic effects of the favourite weed. They would rather seem to confirm the indications derived from other sources, of an essential difference in the ancient smoking usages of Central America and the Mound-Builders, from those which are still maintained in their primeval integrity among the Indians of the North-west.

The pipe, however, which among the ancient occupants

---

[1] Lord Kingsborough's *Mexican Antiquities*, vol. iv. plates 17, 57.

of the Mississippi Valley may have filled the place of the
golden censer in the gorgeous rites of Pagan and Christian
worship, and which presents so many and characteristic
forms among the Indian tribes of the far West, whatever may have been its importance in ancient times, is
no longer the special object of sacred associations. It
is to the pipe-stem that the modern Indian attaches all
his superstitious veneration. The medicine pipe-stem is
the palladium of the tribe, on which depends its safety
in peace and its success in war ; and it is accordingly
guarded with all the veneration, and surrounded with
the dignity befitting so sacred an institution ; while, in
its use in the war-council, or in the medicine dance, so
long as the proper and consecrated pipe-stem is employed, it matters not whether the pipe itself is of the
richest carving of which the red stone of the Coteau
des Prairies is susceptible, or be the begrimed stump of
a trader's English " clay."

The medicine pipe-stem carrier is accordingly an official of great dignity in the tribe, and is endowed with
special, though somewhat burdensome honours and privileges. A highly ornamental tent is provided for his
use, and frequently he is required to have so many
horses as renders the office even more onerous than
honourable. A bear-skin robe is set apart for wrapping
up the medicine pipe-stem, when carried, and for laying
it on while exposed to view. When wrapped up in its
covering, it is usually carried by the favourite wife of
the dignitary, while he himself bears the medicine-bowl,
out of which he takes his food. But though the sacred
pipe-stem is almost invariably borne by the wife of the
Indian dignitary, it is never allowed to be uncovered in
the presence of a woman ; and should one even by
chance cast her eyes on it when thus exposed, its virtues
can only be restored by a tedious ceremony, designed to

counteract the evil effects and propitiate the insulted spirit. If the stem is allowed to fall to the ground, whether designedly or from accident, it is in like manner regarded as an omen of evil ; and many elaborate ceremonies have to be gone through before it is reinstated in its former favour and beneficent influence. Mr. Kane met with a young Cree half-breed who confessed to him that, in a spirit of daring scepticism, he had once secretly thrown down the medicine pipe-stem and kicked it about ; but soon after, its official carrier was slain, and such misfortunes followed as left no doubt on his mind of the awful sanctity pertaining to this guardian and avenger of the honour of the tribe. The sacredness of the medicine pipe-stem attaches in part also to its bearer. Many special honours are due to him, and it is even a mark of disrespect, and unlucky, to pass between him and the fire.

At Fort Pitt, on the Saskatchewan river, Mr. Kane met with Kea-keke-sacowaw, the head chief of the Cree nation, then engaged in raising a war-party to make war on the Blackfeet. He had eleven medicine pipe-stems with him, gathered from the different bands of the tribe who had already enlisted in the cause, and each committed to him by the medicine-man of the band. Armed with such sacred credentials, he proceeds through the encampments of his nation, attended by a few of his own immediate followers, but without the pipe-stem bearers, whose rights and privileges pass for the time being to the chief. Whenever he comes to a village he calls on the braves to assemble, tells them he is getting up a war-party, recounts to them the unavenged wrongs of the tribe, recalls the names of those slain in former feuds with the Blackfeet, and appeals to them to join him in revenging their death. On such occasions the medicine pipe-stems are not uncovered ;

but Mr. Kane having persuaded the Cree chief to sit for his portrait, he witnessed the ceremony of " opening the medicine pipe-stem," as it is called, and during its progress had to smoke each of the eleven pipes before he could be allowed to commence his work. His spirited portrait represents the grim old chief, decorated with his war-paint, and holding in his hand a medicine pipe-stem, elaborately adorned with the head and plumes of an eagle.

All this ceremonial, and the peculiar sanctity attached to the pipe-stem, apart from the pipe, are special characteristics of the Red Indian of the North-west, of which no trace is apparent in the singular memorials of the ancient Mound-Builders, or in the sculptures and paintings of Mexico. The pipes of the Mound-Builders are complete, with their short flattened mouth-piece adapted to the lips ; and the same is the case with ancient Mexican examples. Throughout the whole elaborate illustrations of Lord Kingsborough's great work, the traces of Mexican usages connected with the tobacco-pipe are rare, and in no one can I discern anything which appears to represent a pipe-stem. In vol. iv. plate 17, of a series copied from a Mexican painting preserved at Pass, in Hungary, a figure coloured as a black, carries in his hand a plain white pipe, somewhat of the form of the larger clay pipes found in Canada and in the State of New York, and from the bowl rise yellow flames. On plate 57 of the same volume, copied from a Mexican painting in the Borgian Museum, in the College of the Propaganda at Rome, may be seen another figure, holding what seems to be a small clay tobacco-pipe, from whence smoke proceeds. One or two other pictures appear to represent figures putting the green tobacco, or some other leaf into the pipe, if indeed the instrument held in the hand be not rather a ladle or

patera. But any such illustrations are rare, and somewhat uncertain ; and only confirm the idea that the
tobacco-pipe was not invested in Mexico or Central
America with those singular and sacred attributes which
we must believe to have attached to it among the ancient
Mound-Builders of the Mississippi Valley ; and which,
under other but no less peculiar forms, are reverently
maintained among the native tribes of the North-west.

Having thus followed out with some minuteness the
native memorials of the American pipe, we cannot hesitate to infer from the varied evidence thus afforded that
the singular practice of smoking the burning leaves of
the tobacco plant reveals itself among the remotest
traces of human arts in the New World. When we turn
from archæological to philological evidence, it is only to
receive confirmation of this idea. The terms existing in
the widely diversified native vocabularies are as irreconcilable with the idea of the introduction of tobacco as
a recently borrowed novelty among the northern tribes
of the American continent, as the varied practices and
venerable legends and superstitions associated with its
use. We learn from the narrative of Father Francisco
Creuxio, that the Jesuit missionaries of the seventeenth
century found tobacco in abundant use among the Indians of Canada. So early as 1629 he describes the
Hurons as smoking immoderately the dried leaves and
stalks of the nicotian plant, commonly called *tobacco* or
petune. Another of the nations of Upper Canada received from the French the name of Petuns, from their
extensive cultivation of the same favourite plant, which
constituted an object of traffic with the Indians of the
lower St. Lawrence. This term appears to be of Flori-
dan origin, and was perhaps introduced by the missionaries themselves from the southern vocabulary. But the
Chippewa name for tobacco is *asamah,* seemingly a native

radical of onomatopœic origin, and having no other significance or application. So also the Chippewas have the word *butta* to express smoke, as the smoke of a fire ; but for tobacco fumes they employ a distinct term : *bucwanay*, literally, " it smokes," the *puckwana* of Longfellow's *Hiawatha.* *Opwahgun* is a " tobacco-pipe ; " and with the peculiar power of compound words and inflections, so remarkable in the languages of tribes so rude as those of the American forests, we have from this root *nipwahguneka*, " I make pipes ; " *kipwahguneka*, " thou makest pipes ; " *pwahguneka*, " he makes pipes ; " etc. So also *nisuggaswa*, " I smoke a pipe ; " *kisuggaswa*, " thou smokest ; " *suggaswa*, " he smokes," etc. While, therefore, Europe has borrowed the name of the Indian weed from that portion of the New World first visited by its Genoese discoverer : the language of the great Algonquin nation exhibits an ancient and entirely independent northern vocabulary associated with the use of tobacco, betraying none of the traces of compounded descriptive terms so discernible in all those applied to objects of European origin. The practice of smoking narcotics is interwoven with all their habits, so that they even reckon time by pipes, using such word-sentences as *ningopwahgun*, " I was one pipe [of time] about it."

The practice thus traceable through the languages, arts, and customs of America, has had a very precise date assigned to the first knowledge of it by Europeans ; though the opinion is far from being one of universal acceptance. In the first week of November 1492, two sailors landed from the caravel of Columbus to explore part of the coast of Cuba, and among others of the strange reports which they brought back to the great commander, they told him of having seen the natives carrying a lighted firebrand, and perfuming themselves by puffing from their mouths and noses a burning herb, which it would seem they used in the form of a cigar rolled up in the dried leaves of the maize or Indian corn. The story of its later introduction by Raleigh into England is well known ; and the famous *Counterblaste to Tobacco*, promulgated by King James, gives a marked prominence to the revival, if not to the origin of the custom in England so late as the seventeenth century.

The history of the custom thus dignified by the assaults of royalty, and against certain uses of which the supreme pontiff, Urban VIII., fulminated the thunders of the Church, has attracted considerable attention in modern times on various grounds, but especially in reference to the question, whether the practice of smoking narcotics, or the use and peculiar properties of tobacco, were known to the old world prior to the discovery of America. The green tobacco, *Nicotiana rustica*, cultivated in Thibet, western China, Northern India, and Syria, is a different species from the American plant ; and while it is affirmed by some to have been brought from America, and even the precise date of 1570 is assigned for its importation into Britain, high authorities in botany are still found to maintain the indigenous character of the *Nicotiana rustica*, in some parts of the Old World, as in Northern India, where it is stated to grow wild. Du Walde (1793) speaks of tobacco as one of the natural productions of Formosa, whence it was largely imported by the Chinese ; and Savary, Olearius, Chardin, and other writers, are all quoted[1] to show that the *Nicotiana Persica*, which furnishes the famous Shiraz tobacco, is not only indigenous to Persia, but that it was used for smoking from very early times. That all the varieties of the *Nicotiana* are not confined to the New World, is unquestionable. Of some fifty-eight admitted species, the great majority are indeed American, but a few

[1] A. C. M. Exeter. *Notes and Queries*, vol. ii. p. 154.

belong to the newer world of Australia, besides those
believed to be indigenous to Asia. It is not surprising,
therefore, that after all the attention which this subject
has latterly, on various accounts, attracted, writers should
be found to maintain the opinion that the use of tobacco
as a narcotic was known and practised by Asiatics
prior to the discovery of America. The oriental use of
tobacco may indeed be carried back to an era old enough
to satisfy the keenest stickler for the antiquity of the
practice, if he is not too nice as to his authorities. Dr.
Yates, in his *Travels in Egypt*, describes a painting
which he saw on one of the tombs at Thebes, containing
the representation of a smoking party. But this is modern compared with a record said to exist in the works
of the early fathers, and, at any rate, preserved as an old
tradition of the Greek Church, which ascribes the in-
ebriation of the patriarch Noah to the temptation of the
Devil by means of tobacco; so that King James was not,
after all, without authority for the black Stygian parentage he assigns to its fumes!

Professor Johnston—who marshals various authorities
on the Asiatic use of tobacco for smoking, prior to the
discovery of America, without venturing on any very
definite opinion of his own,—quotes Pallas as arguing
in favour of the antiquity of the practice from its extensive prevalence in Asia, and especially in China. It
would, indeed, be an important addition to the arguments in favour of a Mongol origin for the American
aborigines, if it could be shown that the most characteristic and universal of all their practices is derived from
an Asiatic and Mongol source. But the ethnological
bearings of the argument were not perceived when it
was thus advanced, and their very comprehensiveness
compels us to weigh with the more critical caution the
evidence by which it is sustained. "Among the Chi-

nese," says Pallas, "and among the Mongol tribes who had the most intercourse with them, the custom of smoking is so general, so frequent, and has become so indispensable a luxury ; the tobacco-purse affixed to their belt so necessary an article of dress ; the form of the pipes, from which the Dutch seem to have taken the model of theirs, so original ; and, lastly, the preparation of the yellow leaves, which are merely rubbed to pieces, and then put into the pipe, so peculiar : that they could not possibly derive all this from America by way of Europe, especially as India, where the practice is not so general, intervenes between Persia and China." But the opinions of Dr. Meyen, formerly Professor of Botany in the University of Berlin, are worthy of still greater weight, set forth as they are, alike on archæological and botanical grounds. In his *Geography of Plants*, he observes :—"It has long been the opinion that the use of tobacco, as well as its culture, was peculiar to the people of America, but this is now proved to be incorrect by our present more exact acquaintance with China and India. The consumption of tobacco in the Chinese empire is of immense extent, and the practice seems to be of great antiquity, for on very old sculptures I have observed the very same tobacco pipes which are still used. Besides, we now know the plant which furnishes the Chinese tobacco ; it is even said to grow wild in the East Indies. It is certain that this tobacco plant of eastern Asia is quite different from the American species."[1] To India, then, Dr. Meyen inclines, with others, to refer the native habitat of an Asiatic tobacco, which he thus affirms to have been in use by the Chinese as a narcotic, and consumed by inhaling its smoke through a pipe, altogether independent of the introduction of this luxury to Europe by the discoverers

[1] Meyen's *Outline of the Geography of Plants*, Ray Society, p. 361.

of America in the fifteenth century. When we call to remembrance that that strange people preceded Europe in wood-engraving, printing, the compass, and others of the most important of modern discoveries, there would be no just cause of surprise should it be proved that to them also we must ascribe such merit as pertains to the initiative in the uses to which tobacco is applied. Such evidence, however, must not be too hastily accepted; for a profoundly scientific botanist, though an altogether trustworthy authority in relation to the habitat of the plant, may be less qualified to pronounce an opinion on the value of such Chinese monumental evidence as Dr. Meyen loosely refers to under the designation of "very old sculptures."

The Koran has been appealed to, and its modern versions even furnish the American name. A traditional prophecy of Mahomet is also quoted by Sale, which, while it contradicts the assumed existence of tobacco in his time, foretells that, "in the latter days there shall be men bearing the name of Moslem, but not really such, and they shall smoke a certain weed which shall be called tobacco!"[1] If the prophecy did not bear on the face of it such unmistakable evidence of being the invention of some Moslem ascetic of later times, it would furnish no bad proof of Mahomet's right to the title of "the false prophet;" for Sale quotes, in the same preliminary discourse to his edition of the Koran, the Persian proverb, "coffee without tobacco is meat without salt." An appeal to the graphic pictures of eastern social habits in the *Arabian Nights' Entertainments* furnishes strong evidence against the ancient knowledge of a custom now so universal; and in so far as such negative evidence may be esteemed of any value, the pages of our own Shakspere might seem equally conclu-

[1] Sale's *Koran*, 8vo, London, 1812, p. 164.

sive : though, as will be seen, the practice had not only been introduced into England, but was becoming familiarly known in his later years, and is made the subject of frequent reference by his dramatic contemporaries in the reign of James I. When first introduced into England in the previous reign, it appears to have been chiefly favoured for its supposed medicinal virtues, and in this capacity it is referred to by Spenser in the third book of the *Faërie Queen*, which issued from the press in 1590, as "the soveraine weede, divine tobacco."[1]

In this character of a foreign medicinal herb, tobacco was no doubt known to Shakspere, and was even familiarly introduced on the stage when he was spending his last days at Stratford-on-Avon ; but no reference in his dramatic writings betrays an allusion to the "drinking" of its fumes as a fashion already so familiar as to admit of his employing it in illustration of the excesses of his day.

It is curious, indeed, to note how nearly we can approximate to a precise date for the literary recognition of the "Indian weed," which has been such a favourite of the student in later times. Warner, who wrote his once popular *Albion's England* in 1586, added to it three additional books in 1606, in the first of which (Book XIV. chap. 91) a critical imp inveighs against the decline of the manners of the good old times ; and among other symptoms of decay, misses the smoke of the old manor chimney, which once gave evidence of the hospitable hearth within. But in lieu of this, he notes a more perplexing smoke which "proceeds from nostrils and from throats of ladies, lords, and silly grooms," and exclaims astonished—

"Great Belzabub ! can all spit fire as well as thine ? "

[1] *Faërie Queen*, B. III. can. v. 32, 33.

But his fellow Incubus allays his fears by telling him that this novelty

> " Was an Indian weed,
> That fumed away more wealth than would a many thousands feed."

Tobacco, therefore, was not only in use, but already indulged in to an extravagant excess in Shakspere's later years. Though unnamed in his works, it repeatedly occurs in those of Lodge, Dekker, Middleton, and others of the early minor dramatists ; and still more familiarly in those of Ben Jonson, Beaumont and Fletcher, and others of later date. In Middleton's *Roaring Girl*, produced in 1611, five years before the death of Shakspere; and peculiarly valuable from the lively, though sufficiently coarse picture it furnishes of London manners in his day : we learn that " a pipe of smoak" was to be purchased for sixpence. In Ben Jonson's *Alchemist* of the same date, " Drugger, the tobacco man," plays a part ; and a similar character figures among the *dramatis personæ* of Beaumont and Fletcher's *Scornful Lady*. Moreover, the earliest of these notices not only refers to the costliness of the luxurious weed, with a pipe of which Drugger bribes the Alchemist ; but the allusions are no less distinct to the adulterations practised even at so early a date, and which were no doubt hinted at by Jonson in the name of his tobacconist.

Even thus early, however, Ben Jonson's allusions to the favourite " weed" are not to an unfamiliar novelty, though both with him, and in the later works of Beaumont and Fletcher, it is referred to invariably as a costly luxury. " 'Tis good tobacco, this !" exclaims Subtle ; " what is 't an ounce ?" and Savil, the steward in " The Scornful Lady," speaks ironically of " wealthy tobacco-merchants, that set up with one ounce and break for three !" It shares, indeed, with gambling, drinking, and other vices, in helping on the young spendthrifts of the drama to speedy ruin. In Beaumont and Fletcher's "Wit without Money," Valentine, "a gallant that will not be persuaded to keep his estate," picturing to his faithless rivals in his love-suit the beggary that awaits them, sums up a list of the slights of fortune with, "English tobacco, with half-pipes, nor in half a year once burnt." More quaint is the allusion with which Robin Goodfellow, in "The Shepherd's Dream" (1612), fixes the introduction of the novel luxury, where, reluctantly admitting the benefits of the Reformation, he bewails the exit of Popery and the introduction of tobacco as concurrent events!

From this date the allusions to the use and abuse of the Indian weed abound, and leave no room to question the wide diffusion of the practice of smoking in the seventeenth century. Burton, in his *Anatomy of Melancholy* (1621), prescribes tobacco as "a sovereign remedy to all diseases, but one commonly abused by most men;" while in Zacharie Boyd's *Last Battell of the Soule in Death,* printed at Edinburgh in 1629, the quaint old divine speaks of the backslider as one with whom "the wyne pint and tobacco pype with sneesing pouder, provoking sneuele, were his heartes delight!"

The term employed by Zacharie Boyd for snuff is still, in the abbreviated form of "*sneeshin*," the popular Scottish name for this preparation of tobacco. There are not wanting, however, abundant proofs of the ancient use of aromatic powders as snuff long before the introduction of tobacco to Europe. One familiar passage from Shakspere will occur to all, where Hotspur, describing the fopling lord "perfumed like a milliner," adds:—

> "And 'twixt his finger and his thumb he held
> A pouncet-box, which ever and anon
> He gave his nose, and took 't away again;
> Who, therewith angry, when it next came there
> Took it in snuff."

The illustration which this passage affords of the ancient
use of pungent and aromatic powders in one manner in
which tobacco was used by the natives of South America
in ante Columbian centuries, and in which it has been
so extensively employed since its introduction into
Europe, adds greatly to the force of the argument
against any older employment of narcotics in the way
of inhaling their fumes, based on the absence of earlier
notices of so remarkable a custom. The use, indeed, of
various narcotics, such as opium, bang, the leaf of the
hemp plant, and the betel-nut, the fruit of the Areca
palm, by the south-eastern Asiatics, appears to be traceable to a remote antiquity. Northern Europe has, in
like manner, had its ledum and hop, and in Siberia its
Amanita muscaria, or narcotic fungus. But the evidence fails us which should prove that in the case of the
pipe, as in that of the pouncet-box, the tobacco only
came as a substitute for older aromatics or narcotics,
similarly employed. Nor when the evidence is looked
into more carefully, are such direct proofs wanting as
suggest a comparatively recent origin, in so far as both
Europe and Asia are concerned, for the peculiar mode
of enjoying such narcotics by inhaling their fumes
through a pipe attached to the bowl, in which they are
subjected to a slow process of combustion.

When engaged in the preparation of the *Prehistoric
Annals of Scotland,* my attention was directed, among
various minor antiquities of the British Islands, to that
curious class of relics popularly known in Scotland by
the name of *Celtic* or *Elfin pipes,* in the north of England as *Fairy pipes,* and in Ireland, where they are more
abundant, as *Danes' pipes.* These objects have since then
become much less novel, and are now familiar as miniature pipes formed of white clay, with some resemblance
to the modern clay pipe, but variously ornamented, and

always of a very small size compared with any tobacco-pipe in modern use. Similar relics have been observed in England, found under circumstances calculated, like those attending the discovery of some of the Scottish examples, to suggest an antiquity for them long anterior to the introduction of America's favourite narcotic, with what King James, on finding its taxability, learned to designate its "precious stink!" The most remarkable of such discoveries are those in which pipes of this primitive form have been found on Roman sites alongside of genuine Roman remains. Such was the case, on the exposure in 1852, of part of the ancient Roman wall of London at the Tower postern; and along with masonry and tiles of undoubted Roman workmanship, a mutilated sepulchral inscription was found possessed of peculiar interest from supplying the only example, as is believed in Britain, of a Christian date of the second century. Only a few months later, similar discoveries were made on the site of the Roman town of Bremenium, and at one of the forts on the wall of Hadrian in Northumberland. The learned author of *The Roman Wall* refers to the discovery in the second edition of that work, and asks: "Shall we enumerate smoking pipes among the articles belonging to the Roman period? Some of them, indeed, have a mediæval aspect; but the fact of their being frequently found in Roman stations, along with the pottery and other remains undoubtedly Roman, ought not to be overlooked." Further investigation, however, removed all doubt on this subject from Dr. Bruce's mind; and in a communication on the subject, submitted to the Society of Antiquaries of Newcastle-upon-Tyne in 1857, after noting their rare and irregular occurrence on Roman sites, and the total absence of any reference to smoking either by classic authors or in ancient herbals, he adds: "These old pipes, laid together, exhibit a regular gradation in size, from the fairy bowl to the pipe of the present day. Elfin pipes were found some years ago at Hoylake in Cheshire, on the site where the troops of William III. were encamped previous to their embarkation for Ireland; on the battle-field of Boyne at Dundalk, and in other parts of Ireland where William's troops were quartered. With respect to the little tobacco-pipe bowls, their comparatively diminutive size may be well explained by the fact, that in the time of Queen Elizabeth, tobacco was sold at five guineas the ounce, and that, in after times, those who indulged in the expensive luxury of smoking tobacco, were accustomed, in buying it, to throw five-shilling pieces into the opposite scale."

But though the Anglo-Roman antiquary has renounced

Fig. 31.—Scottish Elfin Pipe.

the pleasant fancy, which accorded to his mural legionary the luxury of a pipe to beguile his dreary outlook from the bleak Northumbrian outposts of Imperial civilisation, the converts to his earlier opinion are loath to abandon an idea that seemed to evoke a new bond of sympathy between that ancient classic world and our own. The Abbé Cochet, in his work on Subterranean Normandy, mentions the discovery of the same class of miniature clay pipes in the Roman necropolis near Dieppe. He at first considered them to belong to the seventeenth century, or perhaps to the time of Henry III. and Henry IV. The Abbé, however, changed his opinions on reading the earlier remarks of Dr. Bruce in his *Roman Wall;* and the Baron de Bonstetten, who has since taken up the subject in the *Recueil des Antiquités Suisses*, publishes drawings of two objects in clay, which he regards as specimens of European smoking-pipes in use before the days of Columbus, if not indeed before those of Julius Cæsar!

The circumstances under which such objects have been occasionally met with are indeed perplexing enough, and must warn the enthusiastic antiquary against building comprehensive theories on one or two chance discoveries. They are affirmed to have been found by treasure-seekers at Cairney Mount in Lanarkshire, under an ancient standing-stone, alongside of a stone hatchet and "Elfin bolts," or flint arrow-heads;[1] and at Misk in Ayrshire, in sinking a pit for coal, after digging through many feet

Fig. 32.—Scottish Stone Pipe.

of sand.[2] The annexed woodcut (Fig. 32) represents a tobacco-pipe, cut in red sandstone, somewhat after an American model, in the form of an animal's head, with a perforation at one of the eyes, seemingly for the insertion of a reed or straw, as was commonly done by the early English smoker with a walnut shell. It was found a few years since, in digging a drain, at the village of Morningside, near Edinburgh, in a locality where numerous relics of Scottish prehistoric times have been dug up. To this unique example, may be further added the description of a curious old Scottish memorial of the luxury, which would seem at least to prove that we must trace the introduction of tobacco into this country to a date much

---

[1] *New Statistical Account*, vol. vi. p. 581.   [2] *Ibid.* vol. v. p. 430.

nearer the discovery of the New World by Columbus than the era of Raleigh's colonization of Virginia. The grim old keep of Cawdor Castle, associated in defiance of chronology with King Duncan and Macbeth, is augmented, like the majority of such Scottish fortalices, by additions of the sixteenth century. In one of the apartments of this latter erection, is a stone chimney richly carved with armorial bearings, and the grotesque devices common on works of the period. Among these are a mermaid playing the harp, a monkey blowing a horn, a cat playing a fiddle, and *a fox smoking a tobacco-pipe.*[1] There can be no mistake as to the meaning of the last lively representation, and on the same stone is the date 1510, the year in which the wing of the castle is ascertained to have been built, and in which it may be added Jamaica was settled by the Spaniards.

Considering how definite is the date of the intercourse of Europe with the New World, and how clearly the line of demarcation is defined, which separates what we may thus call the ante-Columbian and post-Columbian eras of the world, it seems strange indeed that there should be room for a moment's doubt on the question we have been considering. Yet the authors already referred to are by no means the first who have marshalled classical authorities in proof of the antiquity of smoking. In the *Anthologia Hibernica,*[2] for example, a learned treatise aims at proving, on the authority of Herodotus, Strabo, Pomponius Mela, and Solinus, that the northern nations of Europe were acquainted with tobacco, or an herb of similar properties, long before the discovery of America, and that they smoked it through small tubes. Pliny has also been produced to show that Coltsfoot (*Tussilago Farfara,* a mucilaginous and bitter herbaceous plant, the leaves of which were once in great

---

[1] Carruthers' *Highland Note-Book,* p. 54.   [2] Vol. i. p. 352.

favour for their supposed medicinal qualities), furnished a substitute for the American plant which superseded this and other fancied supplies of the ancients' pipes.

There is no question, however, that many plants have been substituted for tobacco since the introduction of the practice of smoking, and it is curious to note that coltsfoot appears to have been employed to adulterate it almost as soon as it came into use in England. Dame Ursula, in Ben Jonson's "Bartholomew Fair" (1614), addresses her dull tapster :—"Look too 't, sirrah, you were best ; threepence a pipe full, I will ha' made of all my whole half pound of tobacco, and a quarter of a pound of *coltsfoot* mix't with it too, to itch it out."

The libraries of Canada furnish very slender means for dallying with the bibliography of the nicotian art. But some of those references bear on the subject, and the very terms in which the royal author of the *Counterblaste* assails it as a novelty of such recent origin " as this present age can very well remember both the first author and forms of its introduction," seem sufficiently clear evidence that smoking was unknown to Europe before the discovery of the American continent. Spain doubtless first enjoyed the novel luxury ; probably not long after the commencement of the sixteenth century. The year 1559 is assigned for its introduction into France by Jean Nicot, French ambassador to the Court of Lisbon, from whom its generic name of *Nicotiana* is derived ; and most commonly that of 1586,—in which Admiral Drake's fleet returned from the attack on the West Indian islands,—is regarded as the date of its reaching England. But though in all probability only beginning at these dates to attract special attention, the custom of smoking tobacco can scarcely be supposed to have remained. unknown to the Spaniards long after the close of the fifteenth century, or to have failed to have come under the notice both of Frenchmen and Englishmen at an early period thereafter. When at length fairly introduced into England, it met with a ready welcome. So early as 1615, we find the popular poet, Joshua Sylvester, following in the wake of the royal counterblast, with his—" tobacco battered, and the pipes shattered about their ears that idly idolize so base and barbarous a weed, or at leastwise overlove so loathesome a vanity, by a volley of holy shot thundered from Mount Helicon,"—tolerable proof of the growing favour for the " weed." The plant itself was speedily brought over and cultivated in various districts, till prohibited by an Act of Parliament.

The costly nature of the luxury has been assumed as furnishing an ample explanation of the minute size of the original tobacco-pipe, which secured for it in later times its designation of " Elfin " or " Fairy Pipe." The circumstances, however, which render the rarer English literature of the sixteenth and seventeenth centuries inaccessible in Canada, have furnished resources of another kind which account for this on other, and no less probable grounds. During a visit to part of the Minnesota Territory, at the head of Lake Superior, in 1855, it was my good fortune to fall in with a party of Chippewa Indians, and to see them engage in their native dances, in footraces and other sports, and among the rest in the luxury of the pipe. But what struck me as most noticeable was, that they did not exhale the smoke from the mouth but from the nostrils ; and this, I have since learned from more than one traveller and Hudson-Bay trader, is the universal custom of the Indians of the North-west, from the Red River settlement to the shores of the Pacific. By this means the narcotic effects of the tobacco are greatly increased, in so much so that a single pipe of strong tobacco smoked by an Indian in this manner, will frequently produce complete giddiness and intoxication. The Indians accordingly make use of various herbs to mix with and dilute the tobacco, such as the leaf of the bearberry or the cranberry, the inner bark of the red willow (*Cornus sericea*), and of the dog-wood (*Cornus alternifolia*), to all of which the Indian word *kinikinik* is generally applied; and the leaves of the winterberry, which receives the name of *pahgezegun*.[1] The cranberry and winterberry leaves are prepared by passing them through the top of the flame, or more leisurely drying them over the fire, without allowing them to burn. Among the Creeks, the Chocktaws, and other Indians in the south, the leaves of the sumach, prepared in a similar manner, answer the like purpose. The leaf of the winterberry or teaberry (*Coltheria procumbens*) has a pleasant aroma, which may have had some influence on its selection. The Indians of the North-west ascribe to it the further property of giving them wind, and enabling them to hold out longer in running. A similar procedure is followed in the use of ardent spirits; and it is a frequent subject of remark by those who have had much intercourse with the Indians, how very small a quantity of whisky suffices to intoxicate them, although they dilute it largely in order to prolong the pleasure they derive from drinking.

The custom of increasing the action of the tobacco fumes on the nervous system by expelling them through the nostrils, though now chiefly confined to the Indians of this continent, appears to have been universally prac-

---

[1] The literal significance of *kinikinik* is "he mixes;" *kinikangun* is "a mixture;" and the words are applied by the Indians not to the diluent alone, but to the tobacco and diluents when mixed and prepared for use. So also *pahgezegun* is "anything mixed," and may be rendered, something to mix with tobacco. When, however, the Indian's supply of tobacco is exhausted, he frequently smokes the leaves of the bearberry or cranberry alone.

tised when the smoking of tobacco was introduced into
the Old World. It has been perpetuated in Europe by
those who had the earliest opportunities of acquiring the
native custom. The Spaniard still expels the smoke
through his nostrils, though using a light tobacco, and in
such moderation as to render the influence of the narcotic sufficiently innocuous. The Greek sailors in the
Levant very frequently retain the same practice, with
less moderation in its use. Melville also describes the
Sandwich Islanders, among whom tobacco is of such
recent introduction, as having adopted the Indian custom, whether from imitation or by a natural savage
instinct towards excess ; and evidence is not wanting to
prove that such was the original practice of the English
smoker. Paul Hentzner, in his *Journey into England*, in
1598, among other novelties describes witnessing at the
playhouse the practice, as then newly borrowed from the
Indians of Virginia : " Here," he says, " and everywhere
else, the English are constantly smoking of tobacco, and
in this manner : they have pipes on purpose made of
clay, into the further end of which they put the herb, so
dry that it may be rubbed into powder, and putting fire
to it, they draw the smoke into their mouths, which they
puff out again through their nostrils, like funnels, along
with it plenty of phlegm and defluxion of the head."

The minute size of the most ancient of the British
tobacco-pipes, which has led to their designation as those
of the elves or fairies, may therefore be more certainly
ascribed to the mode of using the tobacco, which rendered the contents of the smallest of them a sufficient
dose, than to economic habits in those who indulged in
the novel and costly luxury. This opinion is further confirmed by observing that the same miniature characteristics mark various specimens of antique native pipes of
a peculiar class found in Canada, and which appear to be

such as in all probability were in use, and furnished the models of the English clay pipes of the sixteenth century. But if the date thus assigned for the earliest English clay pipes be the true one, it has an important bearing on a much wider question ; and as a test of the value to be attached to popular traditions, may suggest the revision of more than one archæological theory based on the trustworthiness of such evidence. A contributor to *Notes and Queries*[1] quotes some doggrel lines printed in the *Harleian Miscellany* in 1624, where, speaking of the good old times of King Harry the Eighth, smoking is thus ludicrously described as a recent novelty :—

> " Nor did that time know
> To puff and to blow,
> In a piece of white clay
> As you do at this day,
> With fier and coale
> And a leafe in a hole !"

These lines are ascribed in the original to Skelton, who died in 1529 ; and by a course of reasoning which seems to run somewhat in a circle, it is assumed that they cannot be his, *because* tobacco was not introduced into England "till 1565 or thereabouts." Brand, in his *Popular Antiquities*, ascribes its introduction to Drake in 1586 ; while the old keep at Cawdor, already referred to, with its sculptured reynard and his pipe, would carry it back to 1510, and by implication still nearer the fifteenth century. So peculiar a custom as smoking would no doubt at first be chiefly confined to such as had acquired a taste for it in the countries from whence it was borrowed ; and until its more general diffusion had created a demand for tobacco, as well as for the pipe required for its use, the smoker who had not acquired an Indian pipe along with the "Indian weed" would have to depend on chance, or his own ingenuity, for the mate-

[1] *Notes and Queries*, vol. vii. p. 230.

rials requisite for its enjoyment. Hence an old diarist,
writing about 1680, tells us of the tobacco-smokers :—
"They first had silver pipes, but the ordinary sort made
use of a walnut shell and a straw. I have heard my
grandfather say that one pipe was handed from man to
man round the table. Within these thirty-five years
'twas scandalous for a divine to take tobacco. It was
then sold for its weight in silver. I have heard some of
our old yeoman neighbours say, that when they went to
market they culled out their biggest shillings to lay in
the scales against the tobacco ; now the customs of it
are the greatest his majestie hath." In the interval
between the primitive walnut-shell pipe, or the single
clay pipe for a whole company to partake of the costly
luxury, and this later era of its abundance, the supply
of pipes had, no doubt, kept pace with that of the tobacco, and they had undergone such alterations in form
as were requisite to adapt them to its later mode of use.
Their material also had become so uniform, and so well
recognised, that a clay pipe appears to have been regarded, in the seventeenth century, as the sole implement applicable to the smoker's art. An old string of
rhymed interrogatories, printed in *Wit's Recreations*, a
rare miscellany of 1640, thus quaintly sets forth this
idea :—

> " If all the world were sand,
>   Oh, then, what should we lack'o ;
> If, as they say, there were no clay,
>   How should we take tobacco ? "

Towards the latter end of the sixteenth, and in the
early years of the seventeenth century, under any view
of the case, small clay pipes, such as Teniers and Ostade
put into the mouths of their boors, must have been in
common use throughout the British Islands. They have
been dredged in numbers from the bed of the Thames,

found in abundance on various sites in England and Ireland, where the soldiers of the Parliament and Revolution encamped; and in Scotland in divers localities, from the Border northward even to the Orkneys. They have been repeatedly met with in old churchyards, and turned up in places of public resort. Occasionally, too, to the bewilderment of the antiquary, they are discovered in strange propinquity to primitive, Roman, and mediæval relics; but in a sufficient number of cases with such potters' stamps on them as suffice to assign these also to the sixteenth and seventeenth centuries. At a date so comparatively recent as that of the Revolution of 1688 they must have been nearly as familiar throughout Britain and Ireland as the larger clay pipe of the present day; and yet towards the end of the eighteenth century we find them described in Scottish statistical reports as "elfin pipes;" and when, at a later date, they attract a wider attention, it is found that, in total independence of each other, the peasantry of England, Scotland, and Ireland, have concurred in ascribing these modern antiques to the Danes, the elves, and the fairies! I must confess that a full consideration of all the bearings of this disclosure of the sources of modern popular belief has greatly modified the faith I once attached to such forms of tradition as memorials of the past. The same people who, by means of Welsh *triads*, genealogical poems, like the *Duan Albannach* and *Eire-annach*, and historical traditions, like the memory of the elder home of the Saxons in the *Gleeman's Song*, could transmit, by oral tradition alone, the chronicles of many generations, now depend so entirely on the printing-press, that they cannot be trusted with the most familiar traditions of a single century.

In one other point of view the present inquiry leads to results of some significance in their bearing on the favourite idea of American ethnologists relative to the indigenous origin of the red race. The principal varieties of the tobacco plant pertain to the flora of the New World, and it has been cultivated there from time immemorial in every variety of climate, from the tropical regions of the Northern and Southern continents to the country around the shores of Georgian Bay. Throughout the tribes and nations scattered over the same wide area of varied regions and climates, this plant has been used by the indigenous races as though guided by an instinctive perception of its adaptation to their peculiar constitution. Yet when the European discovers the New World, he exhibits no such inaptitude as might be conceived for the novel usage, so foreign to all his tastes and habits; but, on the contrary, he at once indulges in the intoxicating fumes with an impunity altogether beyond the capacity of the native smoker of the indigenous plant. Transferred to Europe, Asia, and Africa, the strange narcotic is speedily naturalized in all; and soon the pipe becomes as indissolubly associated in our minds with the dreamy luxuriousness of the oriental — with Egypt, India, Persia, and European Turkey,—as with the New World from whence it came. But in all, the constitutional power of the human frame to resist the intoxicating effects of the narcotic vapour, proves to be greater than in the native habitats of the *Nicotiana tabacum* and the indigenous races by whom its virtues were revealed to the world. Here, at least, we look in vain for that relation between the peculiar fauna and flora of American "realms," which has been supposed to constitute one of the strongest arguments for the indigenous origin of the Red Man on that western continent where alone his type now exists.

CHAPTER XVII.

PRIMITIVE ARCHITECTURE : MEGALITHIC.

THE primitive architecture of the American continent presents, in its gigantic earth-pyramids, hill-forts, and river-terrace enclosures, the familiar forms of earliest constructive skill, found wherever the footprints of infantile human progress remain uneffaced by the works of later intruders. There, however, such traces of the combined labour of man in the earlier stages of transition, from the nomade hunter to the settled claimant of the soil, present themselves to our study on a scale, as to number and magnitude, alike without a parallel among such earth-types of the walled cities of Nimrod, and the pyramids of Cheops or Cephrenes. They are the characteristic memorials of the partially developed but long extinct civilisation of that mysterious people, known from such remains as the race of the Mound-Builders. Their structures could not gather richness from the fretting tooth of time. They were truly builders, but not architects. Buried beneath their ancient mounds lie sculptures fit to vie with the most grotesque, and also with some of the most beautiful adornments of mediæval architecture ; but on the edifices themselves, so far as now appears, they expended none of that decorative design which elevates the constructive art of the builder into one of the fine arts, and blends together the ornamental and the useful into the most eloquent and

enduring of all national chronicles. To study the true
native architecture of the New World, we have to leave
behind us those monuments of old forgotten generations
of the Mississippi Valley, and, amid the tropical forests
of Central America and Yucatan, explore the silent
memorials of a no less mysterious but more eloquent
past. There that lamp of memory was lit which still
glows for us with the golden stains of time ; and its
ruined reliquaries rise amid a tropical vegetation so
luxurious, that the very air is oppressive from the fra-
grance of the banana, pine-apple, orange, lemon, and
plantain. There still tower above forests dense with
the growth of ages, ruined temples which stood before
the cocoa-nut, palm, and the gigantic ceiba encroached
on their abandoned courts and terraced walls ; and into
which the men of long-buried generations built their
love of power, their wealth of thought and strength, and
all their proudest aspirations of hope and faith.

It was at Copan that the enterprising explorer of the
historical antiquities of Central America first beheld
the forgotten memorials of its ancient civilisation ; and,
as he says, with an interest perhaps stronger than he
had ever felt in wandering among the ruins of Egypt,
he explored, amid the dense forest in which they were
buried, the remains of an ancient city, some of the
monuments of which, to his experienced eye, presented,
with more elegance of design, a workmanship equal to
the finest monuments of Egypt. Here at length were
not only traces of the obliterated history of an unknown
race, but " works of art, proving, like newly-discovered
historical records, that the people who once occupied
the continent of America were not savages." Toiling
onward through the tangled growth of tropical vegetation, intermingled with friezes and fragments of statuary,
and ascending the steps of a vast enclosure, terraced

with sculptured tiers perfect as those of the Roman Amphitheatre, he looked down from a height of a hundred feet on the silent evidence of ages once vital with a native energy and intellect not less wonderful than that which America has since borrowed from the nations of another continent. The traveller had himself stood in the silent shadows of Petra, and wandered amid the ruins of Egypt's cities of the dead. These have each their story, and awake the memories of a definite past; but when he asked the native Indians who were the builders of those ruins? they answered only " Quien sabe?" Who knows? And he had no wiser answer to substitute for their stolid reply. " There were no associations," he exclaims, " connected with the place ; none of those stirring recollections which hallow Rome, Athens, and

'The world's great mistress on the Egyptian plain ;'

but architecture, sculpture, and painting, all the arts which embellish life, had flourished in this overgrown forest ; orators, warriors, and statesmen, beauty, ambition, and glory, had lived and passed away ; and none knew that such things had been, or could tell of their past existence. Books, the records of knowledge, are silent on this theme. The city was desolate. No remnant of this race hangs round the ruins, with traditions handed down from father to son, and from generation to generation. It lay before us like a shattered bark in the midst of the ocean, her masts gone, her name effaced, her crew perished, and none to tell whence she came, to whom she belonged, how long on her voyage, or what caused her destruction ; her lost people to be traced only by some fancied resemblance in the construction of the vessel, and, perhaps, never to be known at all. The place where we sat, was it a citadel from which an unknown people had sounded the trumpet of war, or a temple for the worship of the god of peace? Or did the inhabitants worship the idols made with their own hands, and offer sacrifices on the stones before them? All was mystery, dark, impenetrable mystery, and every circumstance increased it. In Egypt, the colossal skeletons of gigantic temples stand in the unwatered sands, in all the nakedness of desolation; here, an immense forest shrouded the ruins, hiding them from sight, heightening the impression and moral effect, and giving an intensity and almost wildness to the interest."[1]

Such were the impressions produced on the mind of an intelligent explorer when first he gazed on one of the ruined cities of Central America. The existence of such remains had long before awakened attention, though, amid the circulation of vague and exaggerated rumours of their grandeur and extent, no very definite idea could be formed of the truth. So early as 1750, a party of Spaniards travelling in the province of Chiapas, suddenly found themselves in the midst of the ruins of a vast city, covering an area of some twenty miles in extent, and known to the Indians only by the descriptive designation of *Casas de Piedras.* It was the first stray waif of the wreck of an extinct Southern empire, which, with every fresh discovery, acquires increasing interest and mystery, as the great insignia of the North American continent. The empire of Mexico had been a province of Spain for nearly two centuries and a half, yet the existence of such a city had remained utterly unknown. Its ruins cover an area of greater extent than most of the capitals of Europe, and include remains of palaces and temples on a scale of vast magnificence, without a parallel among the most boasted modern structures; yet neither note of Spanish conquistador, nor vaguest native tradi-

[1] Stephens' *Travels in Central America*, vol. i. chap. v.

tion, indicates the knowledge that such had ever been. It received the name of Palenque, by which it is still known, from a rude Indian village in its vicinity ; and since then it has been explored by Royal Commissioners acting under the orders of Charles III. of Spain ; by a second Royal Commission, of which Dupaix was the leader, under the authority of Charles IV. ; by M. Baradere, the enterprising and zealous investigator, to whom we owe the publication of Dupaix's work ; and, finally, by the more modest, but far more effective labours of Messrs. Stephens and Catherwood. The results of those explorations have familiarized us with the remarkable sculptures, the mysterious hieroglyphic tablets, the paintings and bas-reliefs in stucco, and the ceiled halls and corridors inroofed by the overlapping stones of an architecture which wrought out edifices of magnificent extent without the use of the arch ; but to this day no more is known of the nameless city, or its builders, than of the significance of the hieroglyphics which mock its explorers with their tantalizing records.

But if the hieroglyphic inscriptions still defy every attempt at decipherment, the sculptures to which they are attached speak a language intelligible to all. Take, for example, one of the Palenque bas-reliefs, engraved by Stephens from the careful drawing of Catherwood, made from the original on one of the piers of the vast terraced building called the Palace. Its hieroglyphics convey no meaning to us, but we can be at no loss in deciphering the record it preserves of the physical characteristics, as well as of the intellectual and artistic capacity of the people by whom the great nameless city was reared. It supplies an unmistakable answer to the oft-renewed question,—" Were they the same race as the modern Indians ?" The bas-relief includes a group of three figures, with the strange costume and decorations, and the stranger physiognomy of the unknown people who once lorded it in the palaces of Palenque over the mighty city, and the regions which contributed the means whereby such proud structures were reared and maintained. The original, which had been modelled in a composition hard as stone, was found in a nearly perfect condition, and had been painted in elaborate colours, of which many traces remained. "The principal figure," Mr. Stephens notes, "stands in an upright position, and in profile, exhibiting an extraordinary facial angle of about forty-five degrees. The upper part of the head seems to have been compressed and lengthened, perhaps by the same process employed upon the heads of the Choctaw and Flathead Indians. The head represents a different species from any now existing in that region of country; and supposing the statues to be images of living personages, or the creations of artists according to their ideas of perfect figures, *they indicate a people now lost and unknown.*"[1] Bearing in remembrance that the intelligent traveller ultimately favoured the idea that the race of the Builders was the same as the degenerate Indians still occupying the villages around their ruined cities, it is important to separate his actual observations from theories subsequently made to harmonize with Morton's *Typical American Race.*[2] At Palenque he recognised the remains of a cultivated, polished, and peculiar people, who had passed through all the stages incident to the rise and fall of nations, reached their golden age and perished, without even a tradition of their name surviving. Cortes, in his march from Mexico to Honduras, by the Lake of Peten, must have passed within a few leagues of the city; but its ruins were already desolate as now, or it cannot be doubted that the conqueror would

---

[1] Stephens' *Travels in Central America*, vol ii. chap. xviii.
[2] *Travels in Yucatan*, vol. ii. chap. xxiv.

have made its name famous by a desolation like that
which illumines "the Venice of the Aztecs." But the American traveller saw in those regions, thus rich with the ruins
of an extinct golden age, not only the degraded and servile ·
Indian, but the scarcely less degraded descendant of the
Spanish conqueror ; and, therefore, he cherished the
belief that, with restored freedom, and the influences of
a native civilisation, uniting to cultivate the faculties of
the Indian, he might be elevated to the capacity of the
ancient builders ; and once more hew the rocks which he
quarried, and carve the timber that he felled, into sculptures and devices, as full of intellect, and as replete with
native originality of thought, as the carvings and reliefs
on the ruins of Palenque. Nor do we doubt the possibility of such an elevation for even more degraded races
than the Indians of Central America. But if once more
a race of native sculptors should hew out the representations of their civic and religious ceremonials in equally
skilful bas-reliefs, it is contrary to all past experience
that they would sculpture forms and features totally
different from their own. It is important, therefore, to
recall to mind an incidental and unheeded note of observations recorded by Mr. Stephens when leaving the ruins
of Palenque, with the character of its sculptures still
fresh in his memory. " Among the Indians," he observes,
" who came out to escort us to the village, was one
whom we had not seen before, and whose face bore a
striking resemblance to those delineated on the walls of
the buildings. In general, the faces of the indians were
of an entirely different character, but he might have
been taken for a lineal descendant of the perished race."[1]
Such a chance reappearance of the ancient type entirely
corresponds with the experience of the ethnologist in the
Old World. The ruined Alhambra is not the work of

[1] Stephens' *Travels in Central America*, vol. ii. chap. xxi.

the race to whom it now pertains, but the blood of the old Moors of Granada can still be traced among the rural population of Christian Spain. The population of modern Italy includes the descendants of Gaul, Lombard, Ostrogoth, Arab, Norman, and Austrian intruders; but among them all the observant traveller still detects, at times, the old native Roman type, essentially the same as he sees sculptured on the tomb of Scipio, or the column of Trajan: the descendants of the race by whom the marble palaces of Rome were reared, while yet the ancestors of Gaul and Goth, Arab, Norseman, and German, were but the rude mound-builders of Europe, or the nomades of Asiatic deserts.

It does not come within the purpose of this work to attempt to review in detail the characteristics of all the numerous monuments of ancient American art, which would be a mere repetition of narratives already familiar to the reader. It is only necessary to indicate the character of the architectural remains brought to light by the zealous enterprise of Mr. Stephens, and illustrated by the accurate pencil of Mr. Catherwood; for few modern works of travel have been more diligently studied than the volumes which embody their joint labours. In their first journey of nearly three thousand miles in the interior of Central America, Chiapas, and Yucatan, they visited eight ruined cities, the very existence of which was unknown, in most cases, to the inhabitants of the country in which they lie; and in the subsequent narrative of their journey in Yucatan, Mr. Stephens describes the results of visits to forty-four ruined cities, or architectural sites, still pregnant with eloquent memorials of the arts and civilisation of the New World. The materials thus contributed to the illumination of America's ancient native history, are rich and invaluable. Zealous antiquaries of the United States had been surveying the

mounds of the Ohio and Mississippi Valleys, exploring
the strange earthworks of Wisconsin, and diligently
searching for Phœnician characters or Scandinavian
runes on the Dighton rock, to give shape to their faith
in the existence of nations that had preceded them,
and substantiality to the dream of populous cities and
mighty confederacies, that had not so utterly passed
away from their ancient sites, but that some memorials
of their history remained. While the great tide of emigration swept westward, exterminating the Indian with
his forests, and effacing the feeble footprints on his trail,
the enterprising pioneer still sent back word from time
to time of ruined enclosures and fenced cities, which
gathered new features at every fresh narration, and filled
the imagination with vague and wondering faith in a
mighty past. But meanwhile the inhabitants of Spanish
America had been dwelling for centuries in the very
midst of ruins wonderful for their magnitude, rich variety, and beauty, with a stolid indifference even more
wonderful than the grand disclosures it so long withheld.
Of the forty-four sites of ancient edifices, some of them
the ruins of mighty cities, examined by Mr. Stephens
during his travels in Yucatan, few had ever been visited
by white men ; and when it is considered how small a
portion of the surface of Yucatan, or Central America,
has been explored, it is difficult for fancy to exaggerate
the wonders of native art and civilisation which have yet
to be revealed.

Among the various explorations by Mr. Stephens, a
peculiar charm attaches to his visit to the ancient
palaces of Utatlan, once the court of the native kings of
Quiché, and the most sumptuous city discovered by the
Spaniards in that region. Corn was growing among the
ruins, and the site was in use by an Indian family claiming descent from the royal line, while occupying a miser-

able hut amid the crumbling Quiché palaces. But the ruins, as described by Stephens, appear to be of Mexican rather than of Yucatan or Central American character. The principal feature now remaining, called El Sacrificatorio, closely corresponds to the Mexican teocallis; and in entire accordance with this, a figure of baked clay, found among the ruins, presents the modern Indian features, executed in a style of art greatly inferior to the totally diverse sculptures of Palenque and other ruins of unknown dates.[1]

The intermixture of the traces of two very distinct eras of art within the ancient Aztec dominions, is as clearly recognisable as that of Hellenic and Byzantine art in the later empire of Constantine. The general character of the terra-cottas and sculptured figures of Mexico is rude and barbarian ; yet in some of the ancient ruins, as at Oaxaca, terra-cotta busts and figures have been found which justly admit of comparison with the corresponding remains of classic art.[2] Such indications of two entirely distinct periods and styles accord with all the most ancient native traditions, which concur in the idea of successive migrations, foreign intrusion, and the displacement of an ancient and highly civilized people. Of these, Ixtlilxochitl gives a coherent digest, which, apart from his dates, seems to find some confirmation from the diverse characteristics of the predominant remains of art in Mexico and Central America. According to the old Tezcucan chronicler, on the intrusion of the Aztec conquerors, which he places in the middle of the tenth century, the Toltecs, who escaped their fury, spread themselves southward over Guatemala, Tecuantepec, Campeachy, Tecolotlan, and the neighbour-

[1] *Vide* Engraving, "Figures found at Santa Cruz del Quiché," Stephens' *Travels in Central America,* vol. ii.
[2] *Vide Antiquités Mexicaines,* tom. iii. pl. 36.

ing coasts and islands.[1] The architectural chronicles, however, would rather suggest that, in deserting Anahuac for the southern regions, where such abundant traces of ancient art have been found, the Toltecs migrated to a country already in occupation by a branch of the same highly civilized race.

There are manifestly two entirely distinct classes of ruins in Mexico, Central America, and Yucatan; and amid architectural remains so extensive and so varied, it may well be believed that there may be included relics of widely different periods. The one class consists chiefly of the relics of edifices reared as well as occupied by the races supplanted and enslaved by the conquering Spaniards; the other class finds its illustrations in Palenque, Quirigua, Copan, and other voiceless relics of cities, already in ruins before the intruding European mingled the descendants of native conquered and conquering races in one indiscriminate degradation. That these remains should have been found only in a few imperfect and scanty traces on the Mexican soil, accords with the transitional characteristics of its latest native conquerors, who appear to have played the same part there as the Tartar intruders on the southern sites of ancient Asiatic arts and civilisation. But as we descend from the Mexican plateau along the south-eastern slope of the Cordilleras, the remains of art, such as tradition ascribes to the genius and refinement of the peaceful and industrious Toltecs, multiply on every hand; and even mingle with the ruder arts of a remote antiquity recovered from the graves of Chiriqui and the Isthmus of Panama.

But a special interest attaches to the ruined capital of Quiché, though of a different and accidental character: for it was there that the indefatigable explorers first

---

[1] Ixtlilxochitl *Relaciones*, MS. No. 5, quoted by Prescott.

heard that, on the other side of the Great Sierra, was a living city, large and populous, occupied by the descendants of the ancient race of Builders, as in the days before the Conquest or the discovery of America. In earlier years the Padre, their informant, had climbed to the lofty summit of the Sierra, and from thence, at a height of ten or twelve thousand feet, looked over an immense plain, extending to Yucatan and the Gulf of Mexico, and beheld at a great distance, as had been told him, a large city, with turrets white and glittering in the sun. The Indian traditions tell that a native race, speaking the Maya language, guard there the marches of their land, and put to death every one of the race of strangers who approaches its borders. "That the region referred to," says Stephens, "does not acknowledge the government of Guatemala, has never been explored, and that no white man ever pretends to enter it, I am satisfied;" and—speculating on the possibility that there still live the Indian inhabitants of an Indian city, as Cortes found them, who can solve the mystery that hangs over the traces of native civilisation, and perchance even read the hieroglyphic inscriptions of Copan and Palenque,—he exclaims, "One look at that city was worth ten years of an everyday life!"[1] In the sober thoughts of a later period, the enthusiastic traveller held to the belief that the Padre had not only looked down on the white towers and temples of a vast city, but that the city might still be the abode of a native race, the descendants of the civilized nations of ante-Columbian centuries. As he draws his interesting narrative to a close, he once more turns "to that vast and unknown region, untraversed by a single road, wherein fancy pictures that mysterious city, seen from the topmost range of the Cordilleras, of unconquered, unvisited, and un-

---

[1] Stephens' *Travels in Central America*, vol. ii. chap. xi.

sought aboriginal inhabitants." Its exploration presented to the traveller's mind a noble field for future enterprise ; as unquestionably it is, even should the result only prove, as is most probable, another mysterious and magnificent pile of ruins.   He died in the belief that in the direction of that mysterious city lay discoveries for some future explorer, which would constitute a triumph to look back upon with delight through life.   Since then, numerous exploring expeditions have gone forth from the United States ; the mystery of a polar sea has been deemed object enough for brave men to face perils as great as any that such an enterprise could involve ; but the romance of the New World, this living city enshrining the mysteries of its strangely obscure yet significant past, has lapsed into dim forgetfulness, as a mere traveller's dream.

Referring, then, to the works of Stephens, Catherwood, and Waldeck for the details of native American architecture ; it may be noted, as a general characteristic of all the ruined cities of Central America, that they betray everywhere evidences of a barbaric pomp, wherein utility and convenience are alike sacrificed to architectural magnificence.   Though constructed, moreover, for the most part, of stones of moderate size, there is still that same laborious aim at vast and massive solidity which constitutes the essential characteristic of megalithic architecture.   Huge pyramidal mounds and terraces are reared as platforms for ponderous structures of massive grandeur, but only of a single storey in height ; and presenting, in the interior, a narrow and imperfectly-lighted vault, roofed in by the converging walls, which supplied to the unskilled builders the poor substitute for the arch.   It is the comparatively unintellectual civilisation of a nation only in the transitional state, where art and even science have been sufficiently developed to contribute to the sensuous cravings for pomp and magnificence, but are as yet of little avail for the mental and moral progress of the people at large. Such architectural display is the work of despotic power, controlled by the predominating influences of a priesthood, under whom pomp and oppressive magnificence take the place of the real power of the throne ; and the people are subjected to a despotism the more dread, because of its subtle direction of national festivities, no less than of fasts and sacrifices. But while we witness everywhere, among the ruins of Central America, the same evidences which are seen in the architecture of Egypt, Hindustan, Assyria, and Babylon, of a people's strength and ingenuity expended at the will of some supreme despotic authority, and working out results in which they could have no real interest or pleasure : it is vain to attempt to trace, to any such foreign sources, the models of those creations of native power and skill. They are in all respects essentially original and unique ; the pyramidal mound-structures are no more Egyptian than the earthworks of the Scioto Valley ; the hieroglyphics bear little more resemblance to those of the Nile than the rude carvings of the Indian on 'Dighton rock ; and the cornices, bas-reliefs, and architectural details of every kind, supply at most only some stray resemblances to ancient forms : cheating the eye like the chance notes of a strange opera, in which the ear seems to catch from time to time the illusive promise of some familiar strain. While, moreover, the architecture and sculpture are essentially native and original, they betray, amid their barbaric waste of magnificence, a wondrous power of invention, and frequent indications of a refined taste capable of far higher development. The elaborate ornaments of the Casa del Enano, at Uxmal, are described by Stephens as strange and incomprehensible in design, very elaborate, sometimes grotesque, but often simple, tasteful, and beautiful. " But," he adds, " the style and character of these ornaments were entirely different from those of any we had ever seen before, either in that country, or any other ; they bore no resemblance whatever to those of Copan or Palenque, and were quite as unique and peculiar." Again, the Casa del Gobernador supplies a wonderful evidence of ancient power, taste, and skill. It is the principal building of the ruined city of Uxmal. A terrace of cut stone, six hundred feet in length, forms the platform on which a second and third terrace of narrower bases are raised, to a height of thirty-five feet from the ground, and on this is reared the noble structure of the Casa del Gobernador, decorated, throughout its whole façade of three hundred and twenty feet, with rich, strange, and elaborate sculpture. Of this magnificent ruin Mr. Stephens remarks : " There is no rudeness or barbarity in the design or proportions ; on the contrary, the whole wears an air of architectural symmetry and grandeur ; and as the stranger ascends the steps and casts a bewildered eye along its open and desolate doors, it is hard to believe that he sees before him the work of a race in whose epitaph, as written by historians, they are called ignorant of art, and said to have perished in the rudeness of savage life. If it stood in Hyde Park or the Garden of the Tuileries, it would form a new order, I do not say equalling, but not unworthy to stand side by side with the remains of Egyptian, Grecian, and Roman art." It is untrue to say of such a people, though they have passed away leaving no name behind them, " They died, and made no sign !"[1] May we not rather exclaim, with Ruskin, " How cold is all history, how lifeless all imagery, compared to that

[1] Prescott's *Conquest of Mexico*, B. v. ch. iv.

which the living nation writes, and the uncorrupted marble bears! How many pages of doubtful record might we not often spare, for a few stones left one upon another!"[1]

There is historical evidence that some of the ruined cities were in occupation by the native population at the era of the Conquest, but the proof is no less conclusive that others were already ancient abandoned ruins ; and any inference therefore as to the modern date of the architecture already described is as fallacious as that which would assign the Colosseum to the builders of St. Peter's, because the modern Roman still vegetates under the shadow of both. The civilisation of Central America grew up on the soil where its memorials are still found, with as few traces of Asiatic as of European or African influences affecting it at any stage in its progress. It was, moreover, the growth of many generations, and is seen by us at a stage far removed from that in which it had its beginning. A national taste and style had been matured, so that we find a certain uniformity pervading the widely-scattered monuments of its intellectual development. But it had prevailed until the cultured artist had learned to work with freedom amid its prescriptive forms ; and it exhibits a rich exuberance of inventive fancy, akin to that of Europe's thirteenth and fourteenth centuries, rather than any archaic stiffness like that which marks the earliest Romanesque as it emerges from the slavish control of debased classic forms.

It is not therefore amid the expansive and long maturing civilisation of Central America and Yucatan that we can hope to recover the germs from whence it sprung ; nor, though we find the Aztec architecture of the country bounding them on the north of an inferior

[1] *Seven Lamps of Architecture,* p. 164.

character, are we tempted on that account to trace in this the evidence of a less matured stage. Its character seems rather to confirm the native traditions of an intruding race by whom the refined arts of the peaceful and industrious Toltecs were arrested in their progressive expansion, or partially borrowed and debased in their adaptation to the barbarous rites of the con querors. But there is still another remarkable people of the western hemisphere whose architectural remains, as well as other traces of their art and skill, embody records of an indigenous civilisation as remarkable as that which we have glanced at in the southern regions of the North American continent.

The ancient empires of Mexico and Peru are indissolubly associated together on the page of history in the melancholy community of suffering and extinction. Yet, while alike exhibiting extensive dominions under the control of a matured system of social polity, and vitalized by many indications of progress in the arts of civilisation: they present, in nearly every characteristic detail, elements of contrast rather than of comparison. Between the fifteenth and seventeenth degree south, the colossal mountain range of the Andes rises to a height varying from twenty-four to upwards of twenty-five thousand feet, from whence, as it sweeps northward across the tropical line, it gradually subsides into a line of hills as it enters the Isthmus of Panama, while its lofty chain extends nearly unbroken to the Straits of Magellan. Sheltered amid the lofty regions of the plateaus that rise step by step on the steep sides of the Andes, a gentle and industrious population found within the tropics all the effects of varying latitude in relative elevation ; while the narrow strip of coast land, rarely exceeding twenty leagues in width, gave them command of the burning regions of the palm and the cocoa-tree, fanned by the breezes of the Pacific ocean. Such a country, under the gradual development of a progressive civilisation, would have seemed fitted only for small, detached, and independent states, or a federation resembling in some degree that of the cantons of the Swiss Alps. But the most remarkable and enduring monuments of the civilisation of the Incas are the great military roads, fortresses, post-stations, aqueducts, and other public works; by means of which a coherent unity was maintained throughout dominions broken up by vast mountain ravines, narrow ocean-bounded lowlands, watered under a tropical sun only by a few scanty streams, and pathless sierras elevated into the regions of eternal snow. The Spanish conquerors, with all their boasted superiority, have allowed the great highways of the Incas to fall into ruin; yet, even after the lapse of three centuries, Humboldt recorded as his impression, on surveying one of them in its decay: "The great road of the Incas is one of the most useful, and at the same time one of the most gigantic works ever executed by man."[1]

Peruvian architecture betrays abundant evidence of the same all-pervading centralization which gave form and law to the institutions and arts of that singular people. Its masonry was for the most part as solid and ponderous as it was simple, though enriched by the munificence of the sovereigns, and the revenues of the sacerdotal order. The great temple at Cuzco, and other favoured sanctuaries of the national deities, were resplendent with gold and precious stones. In general, the walls were built of huge blocks of stone, or when of bricks, these were of large dimensions and an enduring composition which has well withstood the action of time. But the elevation was low, the doorways were

[1] *Vues des Cordillères*, p. 294.

the sole apertures for light, as well as for ingress and
egress ; and instead of the substantial approximation to
the arch, which confers durability as well as elevation
on the ruined cities of Central America, the roof appears
to have been of wood, with an imperfect concrete of
earth and pebbles, or even a thatch of straw. "It is
impossible," says Humboldt, "to examine attentively
one edifice of the time of the Incas, without recognising
the same type in all the others which cover the slopes
of the Andes. It seems as if one single architect had
constructed the greater number of the monuments."[1]
Simplicity, symmetry, and solidity, he adds, are the
three features which constitute the distinguishing characteristics of all the Peruvian edifices. The edges of
the stone are fitted to each other with the nicest care,
and the masonry is frequently polygonal, with the sur-
faces unhewn, except where the stones have been care
fully cut and fitted to each other. The Peruvian builder
appears to have wrought from choice with immense
masses of stone ; and though bas-reliefs and other
external ornaments are rare, there are not wanting
examples of elaborate sculpture in a style admitting
of comparison with those of the northern continent.
D'Orbigny gives an engraving of one doorway hewn
solidly out of a single mass of stone, and decorated with
sculptures in low relief, arranged in a series strikingly
suggestive of ideographic symbolism. It forms the
entrance to a ruined temple at Tiaguanaco, in the
Aymara country, which surrounds Lake Titicaca, with
its mysterious architectural remains, assigned by the
Peruvians themselves to an older date than the traditional advent of the Incas.[2] Dr. Tschudi has illustrated
and described some of the most remarkable specimens

---

[1] *Vues des Cordillères*, p. 197.
[2] D'Orþigny's *L'Homme Américain*, plate 10.

of cyclopean remains still to be met with on many ancient Peruvian sites. In some of these, as in a portion of the wall of the House of the Virgins of the Sun, in the city of Cuzco, the huge masses of polygonal masonry are of so striking a character as to have become objects of common wonder. One of these, prominent among the large blocks ingeniously dovetailed into each other, alike from its size and complicated figure, is popularly styled the stone of the twelve corners. The convent of the Dominican friars at Cuzco is built on the cyclopean remains of the temple of the sun. The ancient Spanish authors describe a fillet or cornice of gold, a span and a half in width, which ran round the exterior and was embedded in the masonry ; while, both externally and internally, it blazed with barbaric gems and gold, and was hung with costly hangings of brilliant hues. Now its remains only attract us by the solid masonry, constructed on a scale well calculated to suggest anew the art of the fabled Cyclops, to account for its massive and enduring strength.

Mr. J. H. Blake, to whose Peruvian researches I have already been indebted for interesting illustrations of ancient arts and customs, has favoured me with his notes on this department, in which his training and skill as an experienced civil engineer, render him peculiarly qualified to judge. "On the desert of Atacama, near the base of the Andes, in lat. 23° 40′ s., the walls of nearly all the buildings of an ancient town remain, remarkable for the peculiarity of the situation, admirably adapting it for defence. It lies on the side of a hill. On the one side is a natural ravine, and on the other an artificial one, intersecting each other at the summit of the hill, thus rendering it impregnable on all sides but one. This side presents an inclined plane in the form of an acute triangle, across which, extending from side to side, from the

base to the summit, are rows of buildings, each succeed
ing row being shorter than the one below it, till at the
top sufficient space is left only for a single building which
overlooks all the others. These buildings are all small,
and nearly of uniform size, each consisting of a single
apartment. The walls are constructed of irregular blocks
of granite cemented together, and the front walls. are all
pierced with loop-holes, both near the floor and about
five feet above. The floors are of cement, and are on a
level with the top of the wall of the building in front.
Each building is provided with a large earthen jar, sunk
below the floor, capable of holding from thirty to forty
gallons. These were probably used for storing water. A
short distance from this old town is a small fertile valley,
watered by streams from the Andes, while the rest of the
country for many leagues round is entirely destitute of
vegetation." Such, it is obvious, can only illustrate to
us the ruder arts and domestic habits of an outlying
settlement in an exposed situation remote from the centres of highest Peruvian civilisation. But the most enduring memorials of Inca sovereignty are those associated
with the construction and maintenance of the great public roads, post-houses, and telegraphic corps, by means
of which a coherent unity was preserved throughout the
singularly diversified regions of the vast empire. " Of
the great artificial roads," Mr. Blake notes, "that which
leads from Quito to Cuzco, and thence southward over
the valley of the Desaguadero, is the most extensive. It
is constructed of enormous masses of porphyry, and is
still perfect in many parts. Where rapid streams were
encountered, suspension bridges were constructed by
means of ropes formed of fibres of the maguey. Some
of these bridges exceeded two hundred feet in length,
and so well did this kind of bridge answer the purpose
for which it was designed, that it was adopted by the

Spaniards, and to this day affords the only means of crossing many rivers both in Peru and Chili. The remains of one of these great roads are still to be seen in the most barren and uninhabitable part of the desert of Atacama, as also the *tambos*, or houses for rest, erected at intervals throughout the whole length for the accommodation of the Inca and his suite. Numerous canals and subterranean aqueducts were formed to conduct the waters of lakes and rivers for irrigating the soil. Some of these have been preserved, and are still used by the Spaniards. One in the district of Condesuyer is of great magnitude, more than four hundred miles in length; but these great works, like the roads, were not confined to the more fertile parts of the country. In the southern part of Peru, and in the midst of the desert, extensive and numerous tunnels were excavated horizontally in sandstone rock, through which the water still runs, and is conducted into reservoirs from whence it is taken to the various gardens of Pica; producing in this arid and desert land one spot which, in the luxuriousness of its vegetation, is rarely found surpassed in places the most favourably situated for cultivation."

A diversity of construction is found in various of those aqueducts and other erections, indicating an intelligent skill in adapting the resources of the locality to the exigencies of the works. Some of the aqueducts, such as that in the valley of Nasea, are constructed of large blocks of masonry, while others, like the one which conveyed the waters of the spring of Amiloe to the city of Tenochitlan, are formed of earthen pipes. But such works not only exhibit diverse adaptations of engineering art to the special circumstances of the structure, they illustrate the skill of very different eras; and while they survive to shame the scepticism of modern critics as to the marvellous native civilisation of Peru, they also, as

in some of the ruined works around Lake Titicaca, point
to the memorials of centuries to which the Peruvians
themselves looked back as an ancient and half-forgotten
past in the days of the Incas. On the shores of Lake
Titicaca, extensive ruins still remain, which are believed
to have been in the same condition at the date of the
Conquest, and to have furnished the models of that
architecture with which the Incas covered their wide
domains. Valueless as much of the Mexican chronology
is, their mode of recording events gave some definite
hold on the chronicles of the nation ; whereas the system
of Peruvian quipus, under their quipucamayus, or keeper,
could have transmitted accurate records, at the most,
only to a few generations, and render valueless the pretended history of the dynasty of Manco Capac. In the
megalithic character of their architecture, however, the
elements of a self-originated and primitive art are strikingly apparent. It is one of the most characteristic
features pertaining to the development of human thought
in the earliest stages of constructive skill. There seems
to be an epoch in the early history of man, when what
may be styled the megalithic era of art develops itself
under the utmost variety of circumstances. In Egypt,
it was carried out with peculiar refinement by a people
whose mastery of sculpture and the decorative arts,
proves that it had its origin in a far deeper source than
the mere barbarous love of vast and imposing masses.
In Assyria, India, Persia, and throughout the Asiatic continent, this taste appears to have manifested itself among
many and widely severed races ; and in northern Europe
and the British Isles its enduring memorials are seen in
such rudely massive structures as Stennis and Stone-
henge. The same mental condition finds expression in
the pyramidal terraces and vast temple façades of Central
America and Yucatan, and is more fully present in the

massive solidity of Peruvian masonry. It is the uncon
scious aim at the expression of abstract power, which
attests its triumphs in such barbaric evidence of difficulties overcome ; and although it fails even to strive after
the beautiful, it not unfrequently impresses us with a
sense of sublimity in the very embodiment of that power
by which it was achieved.

In this respect the most ancient architectural remains
of the southern continent have a higher ethnological
value than those of Mexico, Central America, or Yucatan ; for they reveal to us the only truly primitive and
apparently self-originating architecture of the New
World : and, therefore, suggest a possible centre from
whence that intellectual impulse went forth, pervading
with its elevating and refining influences the nations
who were first discovered, by the European adventurers
of the sixteenth century, on the mainland of America ;
although at that date the distinct centres of Mexican and
Peruvian arts were in operation wholly independent of
each other, and had moved in opposite directions, unconscious of the rivalry thus carried on in the development
of a native civilisation for the nations of the Western
Hemisphere.

CHAPTER XVIII.

THE CERAMIC ART: POTTERY.

AMONG the primitive arts, in which the first rude requirements of primeval man were supplemented by evidences of taste and skill, the plastic or ceramic art merits, on many accounts, a foremost place. The plasticity of the potter's clay, which furnishes so many beautiful and striking metaphors of the Hebrew Scriptures, supplied a means whereby the varying phases of rudimentary national art, and the peculiar habits and tastes of diverse races, could perpetuate the minutest traits of intellectual development. The delicate shades of variation which give individuality and local character to tribes and national subdivisions, are scarcely more minute or expressive than those which the plastic clay has received from the potter's hand, to perpetuate local habits and tastes. On the plains of Shinar, the fathers of the un deluged world wrought and burnt the clay where still some of the most remarkable chronicles of early Asiatic civilisation are recovered, including their cuneatic bricks and cylinders, eloquent with a definite written history. Egypt, too, had her sun-dried bricks and pottery of diverse forms ; in working which the Egyptian taskmasters made the lives of their Hebrew serfs bitter with hard bondage, in mortar and in brick. These sun-dried bricks, which in the humid climates of temperate zones would perish in a few seasons, survive amid the sculp tured granite and limestones of ancient Egypt, with the still decipherable stamps of their makers, or with the historical cartouche of a Rameses or Thothmes unmistakably chronicling their antiquity. The Arabian conquerors who impressed new phases of art on the historical products of the Nile valley, carried with them into Spain the Egyptian fashion of building with sun-dried clay; and the Spanish term *adobe*, by which the Spanish American now designates the clay-built structures of Mexico and other parts of the New World, is the Arabic *cob* introduced into Spain by its African conquerors in the eighth century. But the simple art of building with sun-baked bricks was practised both in Mexico and Peru long before the Spaniard followed there the borrowed arts of the Saracen; and in no region of the world has the ingenuity of the potter been more curiously tasked than on the sites of the ancient Peruvian civilisation.

Few traces of antique art have proved more serviceable to the historian and ethnologist than those of the potter's handiwork. The graceful contour of the rudest Hellenic vase reflects the national genius that evoked the sculptures of the Parthenon; and reveals also, at times, the sensuous refinement that wrought its overthrow. The coarser, but more practical intellect of Rome gives character to her fictile ware; and the pottery, both of ancient and modern nations, reflects, as in a mirror, their salient mental characteristics. For it is an art, which, while it admits of all the perfection of form that a Phidias could impart, and all the exquisite beauty of adornment which a Raphael could design, is nevertheless allied to the homely duties and necessities of daily life. It does not therefore reflect the mere exceptional refinements of luxury, but also retains the impress of that prevailing standard of taste which suffices to satisfy the common mind. Hence the value of pottery as a material of history. Even its scattered fragments chronicle decipherable records; while from the more perfectly treasured sepulchral pottery, we recover minute traces of the manners and customs of long extinct nations, and trace the geographical limits of their conquests or their commerce, within well-defined periods of their history. Numismatic evidence is scarcely more definite, and much less comprehensive. The progress of Egypt and the many changes it has undergone through the long ages of its history, find striking illustrations in the pottery and porcelain accumulated on its historic sites.   Grecian colonization, and its æsthetic influence, are traced along the shores of the Mediterranean and the Euxine, by its beautiful fictile ware and its sepulchral pottery. Etruria's history is written. to a great extent in the same fragile, yet enduring characters. The footprints of the Roman conqueror are clearly defined to the utmost limits of imperial dominion by the same evidence; and sepulchral pottery is frequently the only conclusive evidence which enables the European ethnologist to discriminate between the grave of the intruding conqueror, and that of the aboriginal occupant of the soil.   Apart, therefore, from the exquisite beauty of many ancient remains of fictile art, which confers on them a high intrinsic value, the works of the potter have been minutely studied by the archæologist, and are constantly referred to as historical evidence, in proof of the geographical limits of the ancient empires of the Old World.   But nowhere has incipient civilisation given more distinctive characteristics to fictile art than in the New World.   Tried by this psychical test of æsthetic development, the unity of the American as a distinct race disappears as unequivocally as when fairly subjected to the physical proofs of cranial formation, from which such supposed homogeneous characteristics have been chiefly deduced.   The northern region lying around and immediately to the south of the great lakes, has its pecu-

liar fictile ware; the Southern States, bounded by the
Gulf of Florida, have their characteristic pottery and
terra-cottas; the ancient mounds of the Mississippi Valley
disclose other and diverse types of ceramic art; while
Mexico, Central America, Brazil, Chili, and Peru abound
in rich and wondrously varied memorials of skill and
exuberant fancy, wrought for many purposes from the
potter's clay. The site of every Indian town throughout
the North American continent, westward of the Rocky
Mountains, is marked as definitely by the fragments of
pottery scattered around it, as that of any Greek or
Roman city of the Old World; and the cemeteries of the
various tribes and nations abound with domestic and
sepulchral vases, inurning the ashes of the dead, or piously
deposited with food and gifts for their use.

The characteristics of those examples of American
ceramic art, are varied and expressive; and to the
ethnologist they are not less valuable than the characteristic fossils by which the geologist determines the relative
ages of the underlying strata. To one familiar with the
specialities of native American pottery there is as little
difficulty in discriminating between the manufactures of
the Northern Indian and Floridian, the Mound-Builder,
the Mexican, Yucateco, and Peruvian, as in noting the
well-defined characteristics of Hellenic and Roman art.
The pottery specially employed in Grecian funeral rites,
perpetuated the national character long after independence and political power had been swept away. For
probably not less than twelve hundred years, beginning
from the ninth century before the Christian era, the
Greek ceramic artist wrought his sepulchral pottery, and
decorated it with the most popular fancies of his gifted
race; and wherever the colonist wandered, or the conqueror forced his way, this invariable accessory of his
funeral rites chronicled the extent of his territorial influ-

ence. So too the boundaries of Roman dominion are traced out by Samian and other fictile ware; and no evidence more conclusively establishes the traces of the Roman stations and frontiers in Britain than the indelible fragmentary remains of Roman pottery. Beyond the Rhine, across the Irish Channel, or wherever the frontier lines of Roman dominion are defined, there also the traces of the Roman potter disappear; while the depth at which the fragments of fictile ware have been discovered in the alluvium of the Nile has been made the basis of profound speculations on the antiquity of civilisation, and even on the age of the human race. The value of pottery, therefore, as an aid to historical research cannot be questioned; and it only requires an equally minute study of that of the New World to define the limits of Aztec and Inca dominion, and trace out the wider influence over which their civilisation extended. The great variety of design, and the artistic excellencies frequently traceable in the higher class of native American pottery and terra-cottas, have not hitherto received the attention they deserve; and such results can only be effected by the labours of many observers; but towards this the present chapter may furnish one slight contribution.

The rude type of native American pottery which abounds on nearly every site of an old Indian village is not inferior to that of ancient Britain, and in its incised ornamentation frequently presents a curious correspondence to the simple patterns wrought by the allophylian potter of primeval Europe. The material is generally a compound of clay and pounded stone or shells, more or less modified according to the prevalent character of the soil in the localities where examples are found. The most common form of such vessels approximates to that of the gourd, having a rounded bottom, and either with

ears or holes perforated near the rim, or with projecting
knobs or a groove, to receive the withe or thong with
which they could be suspended over the fire ; some,
however, occur with flat bottoms, and considerable
variety is exhibited in the patterns of ornamentation.
Fragments of such vessels cover the site of every Indian
town, and are turned up in great quantities by the
plough, but perfect specimens of Indian pottery are
rare ; and the preservation of these is chiefly due to
the practice by the Indian of that almost universal
superstition of rude affection, which leads to the interment with the dead of the domestic utensil filled with
some favourite food or drink. Reference to a few examples will best illustrate this department of the subject.

A specimen of aboriginal pottery found in Pontiac
County, Lower Canada, and now preserved in the Museum of the Natural History Society of Montreal, is
a well-made example of the common type of gourd-
shaped Indian pottery ; and the fine lines which slightly
roughen its exterior, indicate its contact with the potter's
moulding tools, in a revolving motion, by means of
which it must have received its final form and finish.
It measures nearly twelve inches in height, and thirty-five
inches in greatest diameter, and was found on the first
clearing of the land for farming purposes. Underneath
a mound of stones over which the roots of a decayed
and fallen maple extended, a regularly walled but un-
cemented stone vault was found measuring eight feet
by six. The walls were about five feet high, and rose
two feet above the surface, over which a large unhewn
stone slab had been laid, and the whole covered with
earth. Within this two urns, of the same shape and
dimensions, were placed vertically, mouth to mouth,
and the lower one was filled with a brown powder,
which, on examination appeared to be the remains of

some farinaceous substance, probably Indian meal, or pounded parched corn. Other examples of Indian pottery found in various localities of the United States and Canada, and engraved in recent American publications, sufficiently illustrate its usual forms. It is generally from a half to three-quarters of an inch thick, coarse, imperfectly baked, and easily broken ; so that neither in material, workmanship, nor artistic design, does it admit of comparison with the pottery of the Mounds, or the ancient fictile ware of Central America, Yucatan, or Peru. Mr. Squier describes fragments of vessels found in the State of New York, which seem to indicate that they were originally moulded in forms nearly square, but with rounded angles. The ornamentation of this Indian pottery rarely partakes of any attempt at mimetic art ; and the rude implements of pointed bone with which its chevron, saltire, and other patterns were wrought on the soft clay, are of common occurrence alongside of the broken ware. Similar tools of the ancient Mound-Builders have been recovered, made of the bones of the deer and elk ; but they had been reduced with skilful art to a symmetrical form, and notwithstanding their decay, retain traces of having originally been highly polished. Some of the minuter examples have round, curved, and tapering points, whilst others are flat and chisel-shaped, indicating the more artistic and delicate processes of fictile ornamentation. Such tools and patterns as the Indian depositories disclose have pertained to the rude arts of primitive races in all ages ; and only serve to show how constantly the constructive instincts of man, when guided by the first impulses of intellectual expression, revert to closely assimilating forms.

This simple art of the native potter has obviously been practised by the north-eastern Indian tribes, with little or no variation, during many generations, and unquestionably before the intrusion of European arts into the New World ; nor has it even now been entirely superseded by the more serviceable manufactures which the fur-trader places within the reach of surviving tribes. Catlin, in describing a feast given to him by Mahtotohpa, the second chief of the Mandans, describes one of the dishes as an earthen vessel of native manufacture, somewhat in shape of a bread-tray, and filled with pemican and marrow fat. He then adds, " I spoke of the earthen dishes or bowls in which these viands were served out. They are a familiar part of the culinary furniture of every Mandan lodge, and are manufactured by the women of this tribe in great quantities, and modelled into a thousand forms and tastes. They are made by the hands of the women, from a tough black clay, and baked in kilns which are made for the purpose, and are nearly equal in hardness to our own manufacture of pottery ; though they have not yet got the art of glazing, which would be to them a most valuable secret. They make them so strong and serviceable, however, that they hang them over the fire as we do our iron pots, and boil their meat in them with perfect success. I have seen some few specimens of such manufacture which have been dug up in Indian mounds and tombs in the southern and middle States, placed in our eastern museums, and looked upon as a great wonder, when here this novelty is at once done away with, and the whole mystery ; where women can be seen handling and using them by hundreds, and they can be seen every day in the summer also, moulding them into many fanciful forms, and passing them through the kiln where they are hardened."[1] But such proofs of the practice by living tribes, of the ancient arts found in use by the

---

[1] Catlin's *Manners and Customs of the North American Indians,* Letter 16.

first European explorers of the New World, by no means
destroy either the interest or the mystery attached to
the older relics of the art. Man's capacity for progress
under certain favourable circumstances is not less remarkable than his unprogressive vitality at many diverse
stages of advancement : as shown in the forest Indian,
the Arab, the Chinese ; and in illustration of this we
find Mr. Squier remarking of the pottery of southern
areas of the American continent : "The ancient pottery
of Nicaragua is always well burned, and often elaborately
painted in brilliant and durable colour. The forms are
generally very regular, but there is no evidence of the
use of the potter's wheel ; on the contrary, there is
reason to believe that the ancient processes have undergone little or no modification since the Conquest. The
pottery now generally in use among all classes of Central
America is of the Indian manufacture, and is fashioned
entirely by hand."[1] But while we thus find the native
arts uninfluenced by contact with the matured civilisation alike of northern and southern Europe for upwards
of three centuries ; and discover the ancient processes
of the Indian potter still practised by his descendants
on the Yellow Stone River, near the head waters of the
Missouri : the evidence is no less distinct which proves
that the art was limited to certain tribes. The transition
in this respect is not a gradual one, like that which may
be supposed to connect the whole fictile manufactures
of the eastern tribes from the St. Lawrence to the Gulf
of Florida. To the west of the Rocky Mountains the
potter's art is superseded by manufactures and accompanying customs of a totally different kind.

Among the Chinooks, for example, inhabiting the tract
of country at the mouth of the Columbia river, their
domestic utensils include carved bowls and spoons of

[1] Squier's *Nicaragua*, vol. ii. pp. 337, 338.

horn, highly creditable to their ingenuity and decorative skill ; but their baskets and cooking-vessels are made of roots and grass woven so closely as to serve all the purposes of a pitcher in holding and carrying water. Similar vessels are found in use among the Indians of the Pacific coast as far south as Lower California, wrought in black and white grasses, in ornamental patterns, and frequently with representations of men and animals, in black, on a white ground. They are made in the form of bottles, bowls, and deep flower-pot-shaped baskets. Corresponding vessels, wrought from slips of coloured reed, were found in use by the Pah-Utah Indians, near the thirty-fifth parallel, in New Mexico, by the American exploring party of Lieutenant Whipple in 1854, and are described as exhibiting considerable taste as well as skill.[1]

In this curious application of a rude ingenuity, we find the perpetuation of arts which appear to have been practised amid the more advanced civilisation of the southern American continent. Among the varied objects obtained by the United States Naval Astronomical Expedition to the Southern Hemisphere, was a closely woven basket found in an ancient Peruvian tomb, along with pottery and numerous other relics ; but described as "used for holding liquids, and which it would still retain."[2] Many such indications suffice to confirm,— what the topography of the continent, and the sites of ancient civilisation on the Pacific would suggest à priori, —that the influence of social progress in Mexico and Central America, if not also in Peru, extended partially among the tribes to the west of the Rocky Mountains,

[1] *Reports of Explorations and Surveys of Route for a Railway from the Mississippi River to the Pacific Ocean, in 1853-54*, vol. iii. "Report upon the Indian Tribes," p. 51, plate 41, figs. 14, 15, 16.

[2] *United States Astronomical Expedition*, vol. ii. Append. E. p. 117.

even into high northern latitudes; while it was inoperative throughout the vast areas drained by the Mississippi and its tributaries, during any period of their occupation by the aboriginal Red Indian tribes.

The substitution of wicker or straw-work for pottery, however, cannot be assumed as any evidence of progress; though it might prove a highly convenient art for a nomade people to borrow from a sedentary population, as better suited to their wandering life than the fragile ware which ministers so largely to the convenience of settled communities. The mode of using such seemingly inadequate substitutes for the earthenware cooking-vessel is as simple as it is ingenious. The salmon which constitutes the principal food of the Chinooks along the Columbia River, is placed in one of those straw-baskets filled with water. Into this red-hot stones are dropped until the water boils; and Mr. Paul Kane informs me that he has seen fish dressed as expeditiously by this means as if boiled in the ordinary way in a kettle over a fire. Such grass baskets and cooking vessels possess obvious advantages to migratory tribes, over the more fragile pottery; but we do not find any indications of the use of the latter being in any degree confined to the more settled tribes; and the causes of a difference so obvious must be sought for in other sources pointing to essential distinctions in arts as well as in customs, between the flat-head tribes of California and the Columbia River, and the potters to the east of the Rocky Mountains. The frontispiece to volume II., drawn from sketches taken by Mr. Kane, represents Caw-we-litcks, a flat-head woman of the Cowlitz tribe engaged in making a waterproof grass basket, while her child lies beside her, undergoing the process of cranial deformation.

The ingenious arts of the pipe-sculptor were also expended by the modeller in moulding his clay pipe; and some examples of the latter are not unworthy to be placed alongside of the ancient sculptures of the mounds. These, however, are rare and exceptional specimens; though, as will be seen, the Mound-Builder was by no means deficient in the skill of the potter, but on the contrary manifested as much superiority in this, as in his other arts, to the ancient and modern forest tribes.

In later ages, alike in the Old World and the New, the seats of highest civilisation, and of most progressive enterprise, are found within the temperate zones. But it was not so with either of them in ancient times. The civilisation of Northern Europe is chiefly of a very recent period; and we look in vain along the region of the great lakes of the American continent, or in its wide North-west, for proofs of any ancient settled population practising arts of civilized life, unless we except from this the traces of the miners who first explored the mineral wealth of the copper regions of Lake Superior. It requires some considerable progress in civilisation to enable the hardy native of northern climates so to cope with their inclement seasons, as to command a residue of time for other than works of vital necessity; while in the sunny south nature spontaneously supplies so many wants, that the leisure required for the development of ornamental art and ingenious refinements of taste produces these, almost as luxuriantly as the endless variety of fruits and flowers with which the eye is gratified. When, however, the hardier sons of the north win for themselves by toil and self-denying perseverance the leisure which nature bestows freely on her more favoured children of the south, they develop a capacity for higher social achievements than all the luxurious civilisation of tropical climates. But such was not the destined fortune of the aboriginal tribes of the New World. Whether under more favourable circumstances the intelligent

Micmacs of New Brunswick, or the sagacious and politic
Iroquois along the southern shores of Ontario and the
St. Lawrence, would have won for the New World an
enduring civilisation of its own, can only now be subject
for conjecture. They had within them, unquestionably,
the elements with which to contend against all the
obstacles that climate or locality opposed to their national progress; but they were too far behind in the
march of civilisation to hold their ground in the critical
transitional stage, when brought into direct contact with
intruders armed with the accumulated momentum of
Europe's full maturity.

We find, accordingly, as we turn towards the south,
that the pottery wrought by the tribes along the Gulf
of Florida exhibits more art and a greater degree of
skill than can be traced in the best products of native
kilns on the upper waters of the Mississippi, or along
the shores of the Canadian lakes. Much greater care
appears to have been exercised by them in preparing
the clay to resist the action of fire, by mingling it with
finely-pounded quartz and shells. Their shapes are also
more fanciful, and both in the finer workmanship and
the style of ornament, they manifest a decided advancement when compared with the simpler arts of the
North-west. Many of their vessels were made of a
large size, and in constructing these a sort of mould
of basket-work appears to have been sometimes used,
which perished in the kiln, leaving the burnt clay impressed with the ornamental patterns wrought in the
osier frame. The smaller vessels were moulded over
gourds and other natural objects, and frequently decorated with graceful patterns wrought in relief, or painted.
Nevertheless, between such products of southern and
northern kilns, there is not any more essential difference than that which a slight progress in civilisation,

added to the greater leisure consequent on a more genial climate and productive soil, would educe. Though displaying, in some respects, more matured art and skill, their affinities with the pottery of the northern and western tribes are unmistakable; and their chief value for us consists in the capacity for manufacturing and artistic progress which they prove to have been inherent in the Red Indian.

Of the ancient ceramic art of the Mound-Builders we possess as yet a very limited knowledge. Unlike the durable sculptures in porphyry and limestone rescued from the ashes on their altar-hearths, the fragile pottery, though even less susceptible of the action of fire, is recovered with difficulty, and generally in fragments, even from the mounds in which it may have lain entire through unnumbered ages, until the invading axe or spade which brought it to light involved its destruction. But a sufficient number of examples have been recovered to prove alike their superiority in workmanship, and their essential diversity in character and style of ornament, from any known products of Indian manufacture. Among the varied objects discovered in the exploration of the remarkable group of sacrificial mounds on the banks of the Scioto river, called "Mound City," two of them were found to contain considerable remains of pottery, though unfortunately only a few nearly perfect vessels could be reconstructed out of the fragments. In the largest of these deposits pieces enough to have composed about a dozen vessels were found, from which two vases were restored; and alongside of these lay two chisels or graving tools of copper, a number of tubes of the same metal, arrow-heads of quartz, with one specimen formed of obsidian, and a large number of spear-heads skilfully chipped out of quartz and manganese garnet. But the whole deposit was closely in-

termixed with charcoal and ashes, and had been subjected to a strong heat, which had broken up or changed
every object liable to be affected by the action of fire.
The ornamental devices on the specimens of mound
pottery thus recovered are wrought by the hand with
modelling tools on the soft clay, the design being thrown
into relief by sinking the surrounding surface and
working it into a different texture.   The figures are
executed in a free, bold style ; and where the same
device is repeated, sufficient variations are traceable to
show that the artist modelled each design separately,
guided by the eye and the experienced hand.   Their
discoverers conceived that, from the delicacy of some of
the specimens recovered, and the amount of labour expended on them, they were not used for ordinary purposes ; and suggested their employment in the sacred
rites of the ancient priesthood.   Others of a coarser
texture have been designed for uses specially requiring
strength, and probably also the capability of withstanding fire.   The really important feature, however, is that
they differ essentially, alike in design and workmanship,
from any known class of Indian pottery.   In his latest
publication on the subject, Mr. Squier remarks : " In
the manufacture of pottery, the Mound-Builders attained
a considerable proficiency.   Many of the vases recovered
from the mounds display, in respect to material, finish,
and model, a marked superiority to anything of which
the existing Indian tribes are known to have been
capable, and compare favourably with the best Peruvian specimens.   Though of great symmetry of proportions, there is no good reason to believe that they
were turned on a lathe.   Their fine finish seems to have
been the result of the same process with that adopted
by the Peruvians in their manufactures.   Some of them
are tastefully ornamented with scrolls, figures of birds

and other devices, which are engraved in the surface, instead of being embossed upon it. The lines appear to have been cut with some sharp, gouge-shaped instrument, which entirely removed the detached material, leaving no ragged or raised edges. Nothing can exceed the regularity and precision with which the ornaments are executed. The material of which the vases are composed is a fine clay, which, in the more delicate specimens, was worked nearly pure, or possessing a very slight silicious intermixture. Some of the coarser specimens have pulverized quartz mingled with the clay, while others are tempered with salmon-coloured mica in small flakes, which gives them a ruddy and rather brilliant appearance, and was perhaps introduced with some view to ornament as well as utility. None appear to have been glazed, though one or two, either from baking or the subsequent great heat to which they were subjected, exhibit a slightly vitrified surface."[1]

The largest specimen of the pottery of the mounds hitherto recovered measures five and a half inches in height. It was found in detached fragments on one of the altar-mounds along with a few shell and pearl beads, convex copper disks, and a large deposit of fine ashes unmixed with charcoal: the sole relics of precious objects offered up, along with the beautiful vase, on the glowing fire of the altar. But besides these, a more precious sacrifice had been made : unless, contrary to all analogies in the mounds of this class, it be supposed to be sepulchral instead of sacrificial. Above the deposit of ashes in which the fragments of the broken vase lay entombed, and covering the entire basin of the altar, was a layer of silvery or opaque mica in sheets, overlapping each other ; and immediately over the centre a

---

[1] *Ancient Monuments in the United States, Harper's Magazine,* vol. xxi. p. 175.

heap of burnt human bones, apparently sufficient to have formed a single skeleton, was found, repeating the suggestion which other evidence supplies, that the artistic skill of the Mound-Builders may not have been incompatible with the hideous rites of human sacrifice.

It has been generally assumed that the ancient and widely-diffused lathe or wheel of the potter remained totally unknown to the most civilized nations of the New World ; and Mr. Squier has expressed his opinion very decidedly against the supposed knowledge of the lathe by the ingenious Mound-Builders. It may be doubted, however, if we are yet in possession of a sufficient number of specimens of their fictile ware to determine this interesting question. The example referred to is highly polished, and finished both within and without with a uniformity of thickness, not exceeding one-sixth of an inch, and with a smoothness of surface equalling the most perfect productions of the modern kiln. "Its finish," Messrs. Squier and Davis remark, " resembles in all respects that of the finer Peruvian pottery, and when held in certain positions towards the light, exhibits the same peculiarities of surface as if it had been carefully shaved and smoothed with a sharp knife." We must not, indeed, confound with the idea of the ancient potter's use of some simple process for giving a revolving motion to the mass of clay, while modelling it with his simple tools, his mastery of all the latest refinements of the wheel and the lathe. But the characteristics of some of the few specimens of mound-pottery already found, if confirmed by further discoveries, would go far to prove that he had discovered for himself some mechanical appliance involving the most essential elements of the potter's wheel ; and indeed, notwithstanding the opinion more recently expressed by Mr. Squier in his *Ancient Monuments of the*

United States, something nearly equivalent to the view
now suggested has already been admitted in the joint
production of Dr. Davis and himself, where it is remarked : "It is not impossible, but on the contrary
appears extremely probable from a close inspection of
the mound pottery, that the ancient people possessed
the simple approximation towards the potter's wheel,
consisting of a stick of wood grasped in the hand by the
middle, and turned round inside a wall of clay formed
by the other hand, or by another workman." The uniformity in the arrangement of the patterns wrought on
the exterior of the vases, and the precision with which
they are executed, alike accord with the idea of skilled
workmanship, and the aid of such mechanical appliances
as we know to have been among the earliest inventions
of man in every civilized nation of the Old World. A
few curious terra-cottas found in the mounds add further
illustrations to the proof of the progress achieved by
that singular people in different branches of ceramic art.
But such examples have not yet been met with in sufficient numbers to admit of any proper comparison with
the relics of the same class found in such quantities on
the sites of ancient Mexican population.

Thus far, then, we perceive that throughout the vast
region of the New World, lying between the Atlantic
sea-board and the Rocky Mountains, and bounded north
and southward by the great lakes and the Gulf of
Florida, certain common characteristics appear to have
pertained to the fictile ware of the aboriginal tribes
during the period subsequent to European discovery, or
embraced by the older centuries which sepulchral and
other ancient Indian depositories reveal to us. Among
the southern tribes, indeed, the potter's art was brought
to greater perfection, and an ingenious fancy was employed in diversifying its forms and multiplying its

decorations; so that curious specimens of southern pottery are frequently found bearing little or no resemblance to the common fictile ware of the northern and western Indians. Adair says of the Choctaws and Natchez, that " they made a prodigious number of vessels of pottery, of such variety of forms as would be tedious to describe, and impossible to name ;" and De Soto refers to the fine earthenware of the latter tribe in the seventeenth century as of considerable variety of composition and much elegance of shape, so as to appear to him little inferior to that of Portugal. Nevertheless, the prevailing forms of the Choctaw and Natchez pottery present unmistakable affinities to those of ruder northern tribes. In the valley of Zuñi in New Mexico, the American exploring party of 1854 had their attention drawn to a sacred spring near the table-land, on a branch of the river Zuñi, enclosed by a low circular stone wall, on which were vases or water-pots, deposited there as offerings to the spirit of the fountain. Specimens were brought away in spite of the superstitions of the Zuñians and their belief that whoever attempted to abstract one of the consecrated vessels was instantly struck dead with lightning. They are made of a light-coloured clay tolerably well burnt, and ornamented with devices painted on them with a dark brown or chocolate colour ; but though the decorations are novel, the form of the vessels is the same as that so frequently adopted by the Indian potter, and borrowed no doubt from the gourd, which it most nearly resembles. Other vases, restored from fragments found by the explorers on the Little Colorado, repeat the same familiar outline, and indicate affinities among the widely-extended Indian tribes, which so much other evidence tends to confirm.

But not so is it with the fictile ware recovered from the mounds of the Scioto Valley. In the very centre of

the vast area, which thus appears to have been occupied
throughout all known centuries by homogeneous tribes,
closely corresponding in many customs and simple arts,
we find the traces of a people of unknown antiquity,
essentially differing alike in arts, customs, sacred and
sepulchral rites and ceremonies, from all the modern
occupants of the Mississippi Valley. Though very partially advanced in civilisation, they have nevertheless
left behind them evidences of skill and acquired knowledge greatly in advance of any possessed by the forest
tribes that succeeded them ; and we must turn to the
seats of native American civilisation in search of any
parallel to those strange, extinct communities, that reared
their lofty memorial mounds on the river terraces of the
Ohio, and wrought their mysterious geometric problems
in the gigantic earthworks of High Bank and Newark.

The materials for illustrating the intellectual characteristics of the civilized nations of America, have as yet
been gathered only in the most partial and insufficient
manner. The celebrated Mexican collection of Mr. William
Bullock, if permanently secured, would have gone far
towards the completion of one important section of the
requisite historical illustrations ; but after being exhibited
both in America and Europe, it was allowed to be dispersed and lost. The valuable materials recovered by
the joint labours of Stephens and Catherwood from the
sites of a more matured civilisation in Central America,
perished by a worse fate even than the auctioneer's
hammer ; and no adequate collections exist to furnish
fully the means of studying the mental development of
the civilized or semi-civilized nations of the New World
by means of their artistic productions. Yet, next to
language, and its written evidences, what proof can equal,
in trustworthiness or value, that which exhibits the intellectual capacity, and degree of refinement and taste of

extinct generations, as expressed in sculptured, plastic, or pictorial art ? But though the materials within our reach are inadequate for fully mastering the details of inquiries thus comprehensive and important, they are nevertheless sufficient to furnish some exceedingly valuable data. In the British Museum, a collection both of Mexican and Peruvian pottery, statuettes, and reliefs in terra-cotta, supplies some interesting examples of the indigenous ante-Columbian art of America ; and one of the halls of the Louvre contains the nucleus of a valuable cabinet of American antiquities. The Society of Anti-quaries of Scotland has also a small collection, including specimens of the miniature terra-cottas of Mexico, so interesting from the illustrations they afford, both to the historian and the ethnologist, of the costume and the features of the ancient people by whom those ingenious works of art were modelled. From the latter collection the Egyptian-looking head figured here is selected ; and

FIG. 33.—Mexican Terra-Cotta.

may serve as an illustration of one of the most common head-dresses, as well as of the peculiar features perpetu-ated in those terra-cottas, so little resembling those of the modern Mexicans or the American Indians. In the United States, one important collection, chiefly of Mexican antiquities, has been formed by the zeal and liberality of two individuals, and is now preserved in the rooms of the American Philosophical Society at Philadelphia. It contains nearly two thousand objects, including numerous terra-cottas, specimens of pottery, and works wrought in stone and metal. These objects were collected by the Hon. J. Poinsett during a diplomatic residence of five years in Mexico, and by Mr. W. H. Keating; and were variously obtained within the area of the ancient city of Mexico, on the plains near the pyramids of St. Juan Teotihuacan, Cholula, Tezcuco, the Island of Sacrificios, and from the western side of the Sierra Madre of the Cordilleras.[1] It is impossible, indeed, to examine this interesting collection with any minuteness, without being convinced that it includes the artistic productions of diverse races, and probably of widely different periods. A few specimens, indeed, are unquestionably of Peruvian origin ; others correspond to the peculiar art of Central America, as distinguished from that of Mexico ; though it is probable that this distinction is one of periods rather than of locality : the arts of Central America having also been common to the Mexican plateau in that period to which so many of its traditions seem to point, when a higher native civilisation flourished there prior to the intrusion of the Aztecs. A Mexican skull of large and massive proportions, with a full, broad, but retreating forehead, and a predominance in the longitudinal diameter, conflicting with the assigned proportions of the typical American cranium, is engraved in Dr. Morton's *Crania Americana*, plate xvi. He remarks of it : "This is a relic of the genuine Toltecan stock, having been exhumed from an ancient cemetery at Cerro de Quesilas, near the city of Mexico, by the Hon. J. R. Poinsett, and by him presented to the Academy of Natural Sciences of Philadelphia. It was accompanied by numerous antique vessels, weapons, etc., indicating a person of distinction." This no doubt affords

[1] *Transactions of the American Philosophical Society*, N.S., vol. iii. p. 570.

a clue to one of the localities from whence the Mexican antiquities were recovered ; and probably points to some of those which, from their correspondence to the higher art of Central America, suggested the idea of a Toltecan origin. To the same period of an earlier and purer art, should probably be ascribed a fragment of bright red pottery (Fig. 34), wrought with one of the most familiar varieties of the classic frette ; and which, if found on

Fig. 34.—Mexican Frette.

any European site among fragments of Samian ware, would be unhesitatingly assigned to a Roman origin. Such, however, is no solitary example of the repetition of classic and other ancient patterns, in the ornamentation employed by the native artists of ante-Columbian America. Alike in the works of the Peruvian modeller and sculptor, we find evidences of their independent adoption of ornaments familiar to the artists of Etruria, Greece, and Rome, while the disciples of Plato were speculating on the lost Atlantis of the world's engirdling ocean ; and for eighteen centuries more, it was to be a canon of European faith that the eastern shores of the Atlantic constituted the uttermost limits of the world. To the ethnologist, the independent evolution by the human mind of the like forms and devices among nations separated equally by time and space, is replete with an interest and importance of a far higher kind than any that could result from tracing them to some assumed intercourse between such diverse nations. They are evidences of an intellectual unity, far more important in its comprehensive bearings than anything that could result from assumed Phœnician, Hellenic, or Scandinavian migrations to the New World. But while such is the conclusion forced on the mind when required to account for these recurring coincidences, it is otherwise when we find the ornamentation of Peruvian pottery reproduced as a prominent feature in the architectural decorations of Central America and Yucatan. The same argument might indeed satisfy the mind in reference to

Fig. 35.—Black Pottery, Berue.

the frette ornament, wrought in its simplest ancient form, but on a gigantic scale, as the principal decoration of the beautifully proportioned gateway of Labnà, or on the Casa del Gobernador at Uxmal ; but there is a variety of frette peculiar to the ceramic art of Peru, and the sculptured decorations of Yucatan, the correspondence of which is at least worthy of note. It is shown on one of the specimens of black Peruvian pottery brought from Berue (Fig. 35), with a monkey as the peculiar feature of the vessel. It has a step-like form in the first line of the frette; and the very same peculiarity plays a prominent part in the ruins of Mitla,[1] and again appears in Mr. Catherwood's drawings of the fine doorway at Chunhuhu, where it is introduced on a scale that specially attracted the notice of Mr. Stephens, from the bold and striking aspect of the details. It is not there one selected from amongst many ornaments, owing to its presenting an exceptional resemblance to Peruvian decorations, but constitutes the chief feature in the design, giving its character to the sideposts of the main doorway.

The plastic art is peculiarly valuable, alike on account of the facility with which it reproduces the costly decorations of the sculptor; and the many minute and simple indices of style and mode of thought which it perpetuates: such as lie entirely beyond the compass of architecture, in its ambitious aims and special adaptations to the sanctities of religion, or the sovereign majesty of the state. To those who have watched a skilful artist at work with his modelling tools, tracing his ideas almost as rapidly in the plastic clay as when sketching with the pencil, it is scarcely necessary to recall with what seeming ease thought is directly translated into expressive form. All the difficulties of perspective, colour, and light and shade, which perplex the inexperienced draughtsman, are unconsciously solved in the first process of the modeller or sculptor; and it is no doubt due to this that the severer art of the sculptor appears, under very diverse circumstances, to have attained its perfect development, while the painter is still painfully labouring at mere deceptive imitation. Among the Mexicans, modelling in clay appears to have been extensively practised: and numerous terra cotta idols, statuettes, models of animals and other objects, have been recovered from the debris

---

[1] Brantz Meyer's *Mexican History and Archæology*, plate ii.

of the ancient canals of Mexico; and may therefore be ascribed, with little hesitation, to the period of the Conquest. Considerable freedom is manifest in the modelling, but as works of art they claim no high rank; and in the contrast they present in this respect to the best fictile art and sculpture, both of Central America and Peru, they may be accepted as the truest exponent of the ruder intellectual development assigned both by tradition and history to the Aztec conquerors of the older nations of the Mexican plateau.

But the modeller's art becomes most interesting and valuable to the historian and ethnologist, when it furnishes the representations of the human face and figure. In the vicinity of some of the ancient teocallis, and on other sacred sites, small terra-cottas, chiefly representing the heads of men and animals, abound. Collections of such brought from Mexico, are preserved in the British Museum, the Museum of the Society of Antiquaries of Scotland, and in the cabinet of the Historical Society of New York; while in that of the American Philosophical Society at Philadelphia they number about one thousand: illustrating the artificial malformations of the human head, the prevailing national features, and a great variety of head-dresses and ornaments for the hair. Dr. E. H. Davis has in his collection a small Mexican terra-cotta, exhibiting the head under the process of compression, precisely in the same manner as is still practised by the Chinooks and other tribes of the Northwest. But besides such small terra-cottas, which would require a volume devoted specially to them, fully to illustrate their interesting details, the collections of the American Philosophical Society include a series of large clay masks of the human face, twenty-eight in all, and varying in dimensions from about half life-size to somewhat larger than life. These are executed with great

freedom and very considerable artistic skill, and are in
a totally different and very superior style to the terra-
cotta Mexican idols and other figures already referred to.
They exhibit great variety of expression, and manifest
details of individual portraiture.   Others have the features exaggerated into caricature with equal life and
spirit.[1]   Few objects of art could present features of
higher interest to the ethnologist.   Mr. Francis Pulszky,
in his *Iconographic Researches*, when commenting on
such examples of the art of American nations as have
come under his observation, re-
marks on his selected Mexican illustrations : "All of them are characterized by the peculiar features
of the Central American group
of the Red man in the formation
of the skull, as well as by their
high cheek bones."[2]   But no such
conclusion is suggested by the
group of masks now referred to.
The cheek bones are moderately
developed, the nose is prominent
and generally sharp, and a small
mouth is accompanied in most

Fig. 36.—Mexican Clay Mask.

cases by a narrow, projecting chin.   The example
figured above (Fig. 36) illustrates the character of
those large clay masks, or modellings of the human
features, in which the ethnologist will look in vain for
the characteristic physiognomy of the Red Indian.   Nor
are the caricatures less interesting or useful in this re-

---

[1] In the inventory printed in the American Philosophical Society's Transactions, they are described as "eighteen masks of pottery, representing the
human face, of natural size, but very grotesque figures."   In reality, however, I counted twenty-eight specimens, of which the larger number are
valuable for their obviously truthful portraiture.

[2] *Indigenous Races of the Earth*, p. 183.

spect. When the English Wellington figured in the comic pages of the Paris *Charivari*, or the Emperor Napoleon III. receives the like honours from the caricaturists of the London *Punch*, the humour of the satiric pencil finds vent in the exaggeration of the familiar natural features ; and such is the tendency of all caricatures. But, as will be seen from the specimens figured here (Fig. 37), the ancient satirical modeller of

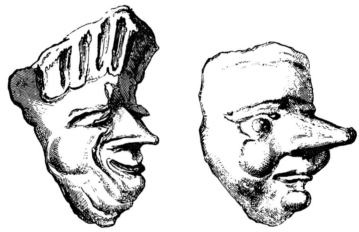

FIG. 37.—Comic Mexican Masks.

the New World sported with features in no degree corresponding to the familiar type of the North American Indian ; and indeed the illustrations which accompany the remarks already quoted from Mr. Francis Pulszky very imperfectly confirm the inferences deduced by him from the study of the originals, as to their proof of the prevalence of a uniform type of features throughout the American continent.

The forms of Mexican pottery are exceedingly varied, though more frequently exhibiting an ingenious fertility of invention, and an exuberant fancy, than much æsthetic refinement. Indeed I cannot imagine the large human masks in the collection of the American Philosophical

Society to be the work of the same people as the Mexican terra-cottas beside them, which correspond in style to the drawings on the Mexican hieroglyphic manuscripts, rendered familiar by Lord Kingsborough's great work. In this department of the subject, as in some others, it would require a special monograph of ample dimensions to illustrate all the varied details.

Alike in Mexico, Central America, and Peru, it is obvious that the native artists worked with the utmost ease in the plastic clay; and hence they employed it for a variety of purposes, one of the most singular of which was that of making musical instruments. Several earthenware flutes, flageolets, and other wind instruments are included in the Mexican collection of Philadelphia; and more curious specimens of the same novel class have recently been brought to light, along with a great variety of other interesting antiquities, in exploring the ancient graves of the province of Chiriqui, about fifty miles north of Panama. But between the Bay of Panama and the southern shores of the Gulf of Mexico lie the marvellous regions of Yucatan and Central America, rich with colossal statues, temples vast and gorgeous in their sculptured façades and their graven hieroglyphs as the ruins of the Nile Valley; and also with their characteristic ceramic art, highly important as an element of comparison with that which is found on other ancient sites, or perpetuated in the arts of modern tribes. Here also, as in other departments of our subject, we are as yet only on the threshold of disclosures which are destined to add many chapters to the detailed chronicles of aboriginal American history. But enough has been noted to prove how entirely we leave behind us the arts of the Red Indian when we proceed to explore the sepulchral and other depositories of Yucatan, Chiapas, or Central America. Not only is the pottery of finer material, but alike in

form and ornamentation it essentially differs from anything hitherto discovered to the north of the Rio Grande,
and reveals the style of thought which presents such remarkable and unique aspects in the forms into which it
has wrought itself on the mighty ruins throughout the
same regions. Among the illustrations of Mr. Stephens'
Travels in Central America, one of the plates is devoted
to the representation of specimens of pottery dug up by
him in a mound among the ruins of Guezaltenango, in
the ancient kingdom of Quiché. Of these the tripod
illustrates a form of vessel found under considerable
variations of detail, as far south as the Gulf of Panama,
while its ornamentation presents considerable resemblance
to patterns of constant occurrence on the more abundant
ornamental pottery of Peru. But a far higher interest
attaches to another vase, dug up amid the ruins of Ticul,
an aboriginal city of Yucatan. "The vase," says Mr.
Stephens, " is four and a half inches high, and five inches
in diameter. It is of admirable workmanship, and real-

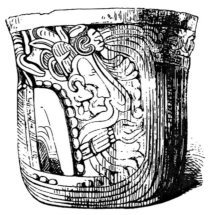

Fig. 38.—Ticul Hieroglyphic Vase.

izes the account given by Herrera of the markets at
the Mexican city of Tlascala. There were goldsmiths,
feathermen, barbers, baths, and as good earthenware as

in Spain." The chief device, it will be seen (Fig. 38), is a human bust, closely corresponding in features, attitude, and costume, to the sculptured and stuccoed figures observed at Palenque and elsewhere. But still more interesting, even than the reproduction of the sculptures of Palenque in the potter's clay, is a border of hiero-glyphics, running continuously with the feathered plumes of the human figure round the top of the vase, and there-by indubitably connecting it with the most advanced era of intellectual progress in the history of native American civilisation.

In Central America, and not in Mexico, lay the ancient seats of highest aboriginal civilisation on the northern continent ; and from thence the receding lines of its influence may be traced, with diminishing force, towards the northern borders of Mexico on the one hand, and the Isthmus of Panama on the other. In the latter region, recent discoveries, already referred to in de-scribing the remarkable gold relics found in the ancient cemeteries of Chiriqui, have largely added to our know-ledge of the arts of its ancient population. In a com-munication on the subject, made by Dr. J. King Merrit to the American Ethnological Society, and embodying the results of personal observation, he remarks that, while the golden ornaments were only met with occa-sionally, pottery was encountered more or less in every grave ; and he thus proceeds : "The specimens of pot-tery found associated with the gold figures are generally larger and of a finer quality than in the other huacals. To the antiquarian these possess a great interest, as they afford some idea of the domestic habits and the degree of civilisation attained by that ancient people, of whose history we as yet know nothing. The specimens which I have seen, and a few that I have brought from Chiriqui, exhibit a high degree of advancement in the most difficult art of pottery : forms as symmetrical and graceful as any of classic or modern dates. The glazing and painting of some are in a wonderful state of preservation, the colours being bright and distinct, and many are entirely unaffected by the lapse of time."[1] Specimens of the Chiriqui pottery in the cabinet of the Historical Society of New York, and in the private collection of Dr. E. H. Davis, furnish evidence of skill in the potter's art very far in advance of the work of the northern Indians, and exhibit forms and patterns essentially different. Many of the vessels are tripods, and these have frequently movable clay pellets inserted in the hollow legs. With them are also found sculptured stone tables, for grinding and baking corn. They are generally in the form of an animal, with the legs and tail minutely carved, and resting on a pedestal cut out of one block of stone ; and in the same graves occur curious musical instruments, wrought from the potter's clay in a variety of forms, but chiefly in those of birds and animals. A collection of these Chiriqui wind instruments, derived from various sources, has been reported on by a committee of the American Ethnological Society appointed for that purpose. They were nearly all whistles or flageolets, roundish, in the form of birds or beasts, from one and a half to four and a half inches in diameter. The most perfect instrument has three finger-holes to produce the notes A, G, F, E, downwards. A fourth finger-hole gives the semitones of these notes ; and by a particular process two or three lower notes are obtained. In one of the smaller instruments, a loose ball of baked clay within the air-chamber gives further variety to the notes. The most perfect of those are simple ; and, if they were the sole musical instruments possessed by their ingenious manufacturers,

---

[1] *Report on the Huacals of Chiriqui*, by J. King Merrit, M.D., p. 7.

they do not necessarily imply any great mastery of the science of music. They bear, however, no resemblance to the rude drums and medicine-rattles which furnish the only music for the favourite dances of the forest tribes; but, on the contrary, indicate in all respects a considerable advance beyond their highest attainments.

Fig. 39.—Chiriqui Musical Instrument.

The example here given (Fig. 39) is drawn from the original, in the possession of Dr. E. H. Davis, and furnishes a fair illustration of this ingenious yet primitive class of musical instruments. It is painted in red and black on a cream-coloured ground, and measures nearly five inches in length. Others, both of the Isthmus and of Mexico, are simpler in form, and with a greater number of notes; while some of those found in the Chiriqui graves are little more than whistles, and may possibly have been mere children's toys. This, however, we cannot fail to notice, that, alike in the prevailing forms of these musical instruments, as in the pottery and works in metal, the imitative tendency of the art of the southern isthmus reveals the same mental characteristics as are seen in so many diverse examples of native American art. The vases, and earthenware vessels of every kind, appear to have been modelled most frequently in imitation of the vegetables, fruits, and shells of the locality, and to have been decorated with devices

copied from the native fauna and other natural objects
most familiar to the ancient potters of Chiriqui. In
this respect their works disclose to us some of the same
mental characteristics which, in a peculiar manner, pervade all the phases of incipient civilisation in the New
World ; but are nowhere more strikingly manifested than
in that remarkable country, which still reveals so many
traces of its arrested civilisation among the terraced
steeps of the Cordilleras, where they look forth on the
Pacific Ocean within the tropics, and thence southward
to the 37th degree of latitude.

The want of any large public collection of native
American pottery and terra-cottas, or of any work ade-
quately illustrating its peculiar characteristics, has led
to an undue depreciation of the artistic skill of the
Peruvian potter. Mr. Joseph Marryat, in his tasteful and beautifully illustrated *History of Pottery and
Porcelain*, introduces a group from the British Museum,
which conveys a most inadequate idea of the better class
of Peruvian fictile ware, and abundantly accounts for
his depreciatory remarks. " The pottery of Peru, Chili,
and Columbia," he observes, " has a peculiar character,
which distinguishes it from any European, and approximates it to the Mexican, having the same clumsy and
uncouth shapes." Such, however, is far from being a
just estimate. The clearly defined differences which
distinguish Greek from Roman pottery are not more
strongly pronounced than those which mark the distinctions between the fictile ware of Mexico and Peru. No
one, indeed, who has had any adequate opportunities of
comparing them, can possibly confound the two. Yet
so little attention has hitherto been paid to the ingenious and singularly varied productions of the Peruvian
potter, that Prescott has omitted all reference to them in
his highly attractive introductory " View of the Civilisa-

tion of the Incas." Nevertheless, the historian of the Conquest has remarked, with acute discrimination, that " the character of the Peruvian mind led to imitation rather than invention, to delicacy and minuteness of finish rather than to boldness or beauty of design ;"[1] and it may be said as justly of his ceramic art, as of other products of his mechanical skill and artistic design, that they were frequently made on a whimsical pattern, evincing quite as much ingenuity as taste or inventive talent.

The intellectual characteristics which the peculiar phases of Peruvian art illustrate, originated fully as much in the social and political aspects of the national life, as in any original bent of the native artists. We discern in the architecture and sculpture, as well as in much else that pertained to ancient Egypt, the individual mental action controlled, in its formative expressions of thought, by the prescribed formulæ of the national creed and policy ; while Hellenic art and genius reflect the expansive freedom of the emancipated human mind. In the artistic design of the Peruvian, especially as applied to architecture and its attendant arts, we detect no less clearly the influences of its singular polity, and the unconscious restraints of national formulæ of thought; and we must give full value to such repressive elements before attempting to gauge the inventive originality of Peruvian genius. Contrasted with the repetition—unvarying as the nest-building instinct of birds,—of a few simple forms, in the pottery of the Indian tribes of North America, throughout all the generations which have come under European observation, the ceramic art of Peru illustrates mental characteristics of an essentially different kind. Some of the specimens of its pottery are purposely grotesque,

[1] Prescott's *Conquest of Peru*, B. I. ch. v.

and by no means devoid of true comic fancy ; while, in
the greater number, the endless variety of combinations
of animate and inanimate forms ingeniously rendered
subservient to the requirements of utility, exhibit a fertility of thought in the designer, and a lively perceptive
faculty in those for whom he wrought, which we look
for in vain among any other people of the New World,
not even excepting the ingenious pipe-sculptors of the
Mound-Builders. The vessels for common domestic use
were made in the simplest and most convenient forms,
and were so well executed, that Dr. Tschudi speaks of
many antique pitchers and large earthen jars still in
daily use, and generally preferred for their durability to
those of the modern potter.   But in the manufacture of
sacred vessels designed for religious or sepulchral rites,
or of those for the festive board, an unrestrained exuberance of fancy and curious ingenuity sport with the
pliant clay to an extent without a parallel in the arts of
any other people.   An ancient vessel brought from Peru
by Mr. Charles W. Farriss, and now in the collection of
the New York Historical Society, illustrates the form
and use of the common water-jar.   It represents an old
woman with a large jar at her back, and held by a
broad strap passing across her forehead, much in the
same manner as the old Edinburgh water-carriers were
wont to bear similar burdens, and as the Scottish fish-
wife still carries her " creel."   Many similar illustrations
are to be found among the multiform fictile ware of the
Peruvian potter, and evince the germs of an imitative
and even artistic faculty of no mean order.   The collection thus secured for the purposes of the historian
and the antiquary, includes nearly a hundred vessels of
different sizes and the greatest variety of forms.   Some
are double : in this respect repeating, with considerable
similarity, the *bijugué* or twin-bottle of the ancient

Egyptians ;[1] others have double spouts, which also constitute a characteristic feature of the water-pitcher called
the "monkey," still in universal use in Brazil.   A few
are of simple and graceful forms ; and others are modelled from melons, gourds, and other fruit, though

Fig. 40.—Peruvian Pottery.

generally with a grotesque animal-head added as the
mouth of the vessel.   The remainder include imitations
of the duck, parrot, pelican, turkey, land-turtle, monkey,
lynx, otter, llama, toad, cayman, shark, etc., arranged
with ingenious and endless diversity, to modify the form
of the bottle, jar, or pitcher which they decorate.   Others
are adorned with figures or ornamental patterns in relief;
in addition to which the painted pottery is also greatly
varied both in shape and ornamentation.[2]

The ingenuity of the Peruvian potter was further
employed in sundry curious and whimsical applications
of acoustics to the more complicated specimens of his

---

[1] *Vide* Marryat's *History of Pottery*, 2d edit. fig. 190, and also a Chinese
porcelain double-bottle, fig. 129.

[2] The following collections have afforded to the author opportunities of
studying several hundred specimens of the rarer forms of Peruvian pottery,
viz. :—The British Museum ; the Society of Antiquaries of Scotland ; the
Historical Society of New York ; the American Philosophical Society, Pennsylvania ; the Museums of Boston and New York ; the cabinets of J. H.
Blake, Esq., Boston, Dr. E. H. Davis, New York, and Joseph A. Clay, Esq.,
Philadelphia.   The tripod in the group Fig. 40, is from Panama ; all the
others are Peruvian.

skill. This has been minutely illustrated by Dr. Tschudi, from the abundant means within reach of an observer resident in the country. "All the moulded works of the ancient Peruvians," he observes, "have a peculiar character, which distinguishes them from those of the other American nations ; a character which, by those versed in antiquities, will be recognised at first sight." Having then referred to some of those accidental correspondences among vessels of simpler form which appear to reproduce Egyptian, Etruscan, or other antique types, he thus proceeds : "The greater part of the sacred vessels buried with the mallquis, and destined to receive the chicha of sacrifice on feast-days, have an enlarged neck, placed ordinarily near the handle, with a hole to pour out the liquid, and an opposite opening, for the air to escape when the vessel is filled. Many are double, and it seems that they made them thus from preference; others are quadruple or sextuple, or even octuple ; that is, the principal vessel is surrounded with regular appendages, which communicate among themselves and with the principal vessel. The double ones were made in such perfection, that when they were filled with a liquid, the air, escaping through the opening left for that purpose, produced sounds at times very musical : these sounds sometimes imitated the voice of the animal which was represented by the principal part of the vessel : as in a beautiful specimen we have seen, which represents a cat, and which, upon receiving water through the upper opening, produces a sound similar to the mewing of that animal. We have in our possession a vessel of black clay, which perfectly imitates the whistle of the thrush, the form of which is seen on the handle. We also preserve two circular vases, which, being filled with water through a hole in the bottom, on being turned over, lose not a single drop, the water coming out, when

it is wished, by simply inclining the upper part of
the vase."

Mr. Blake, whose personal observations, as well as his
valuable collections, have furnished interesting materials
for various chapters of this work, collected some curious
specimens of the ancient potters' art from the Peruvian graves explored by him. One example, measuring
twenty-two inches long, is in the form of a fish, with its
tail partially turned round, like a salmon in the act of
leaping ; and another in that of a deer's head carrying
a vase between its antlers. A third is modelled as a
bird, with long legs like a crane ; and when filled with
water, and moved gently backward and forward, it emits
sounds not unlike the notes of a bird, which most probably were designed to imitate the peculiar cry of the
one represented in the form of the vessel. Small spherical vessels are very common, and Mr. Blake, who
possesses several of them, conceives that they were probably designed for holding tea made from the leaves of
cocoa, or some other plant. Similar vessels, he informs
me, are now in use among the Indians ; and an infusion
of leaves of cocoa is frequently prescribed by their medical men. It is sipped from the cup through a small
tube of reed or silver, eight or nine inches long.

The apparent reproduction of Etruscan and other
antique forms in the Peruvian vases, has been referred
to, nor does the correspondence between such relics of the
arts of ancient nations of the Old and New Worlds stop
here. Mr. Joseph Marryat, while referring with undue
disparagement to the products of Peruvian art, consequent on his limited means for its study, remarks,
—" Though this pottery is generally very uncouth in
form and ornament, yet in some specimens the patterns,
carved or indented, represent those well known as the
' Vitruvian scroll' and ' Grecian fret.' It is curious that a

people so apparently rude should have chosen ornaments similar to those adopted in the earliest Grecian age, and found on the Lantern of Demosthenes at Athens, 336 B.C., but which, however, it appears the Greeks themselves borrowed from the Assyrians. The 'honeysuckle pattern' is found also upon the earliest known monuments of Buddhist art, and the Etruscan upon the earliest Chinese bronzes."[1] But while such coincidences have hitherto been turned to little account in the support of favourite theories of ancient migration, a much simpler ornament has supplied materials for endless speculation. An example of Peruvian black pottery, brought from Otusco, and now in the collection of the Historical Society of New York, measuring seven and a half inches high, is decorated with a row of well-defined Maltese crosses. The same "Cross of the Order of Malta" had already been noted with wonder among the sculptures at Mitla;[2] while the cross at Palenque, detached from numerous accessories which are no less indispensable parts of the elaborate sculptured Tablet, as figured by Catherwood, has been made the basis of the most extravagant deductions : from the assumed mission of the Apostle Thomas to Anahuac, which solved all difficulties for the elder Spanish priests, to the Phœnician Hercules, and the Astarte of the Sidonians, which the equally fanciful speculations of later times have substituted for the ecclesiastical legend.[3] If indeed we found any general correspondence in forms and details between the ceramic arts of Greece and Peru, or the elaborate symbolism of mediæval Christian art was reproduced even to a limited extent on the tablets of Mitla or Palenque, the idea of ancient relations to a common

---

[1] Marryat's *History of Pottery and Porcelain*, p. 398.
[2] Kingsborough's *Mexican Antiquities*, vol. vi. p. 481.
[3] Wilson's *Conquest of Mexico*, p. 158.

source would be inevitable. But while the Vitruvian scroll is discernible on pottery. in the Collection of the Historical Society of New York, brought from Huarmachuco and Otusco, and the classic fret may be traced alike on the pottery and the sculptures of Central America and Peru, they are associated with a variety of designs bearing no trace of foreign origin, or with cruciform ornaments as little referrible to a Christian source as the constellation of the Southern Cross.

Whilst, however, in their highest, no less than in their ruder stages, the arts of the New World are manifestly of native growth, and display in their ornamentation a style essentially peculiar and unique, there are not wanting specimens that challenge a comparison with some of the finer productions of classic art. They combine a grace and beauty of design which amply demonstrate the capacity of their executors for higher attainments, as is the case with two terra-cotta helmeted busts found at Oaxaca, and figured in the *Antiquités Mexicaines.* Of these Prescott remarks,—" They might well pass for Greek, both in the style of the heads and the casques that cover them."[1] The same might be said with nearly equal truth of the ancient vase of the Quichuas of Bolivia, figured in the group, Fig. 42, and also of a gracefully-modelled pendant vase, beautifully painted in patterns executed in red, yellow, and dark brown, which is engraved in D'Orbigny's *L'Homme Américain*, along with other curious and characteristic specimens of the ancient pottery of Bolivia and Peru.[2]

But the most interesting and valuable examples of the ceramic art of Southern America, are those which illustrate the physiognomy of its ancient civilized popu-

---

[1] *Antiquités Mexicaines,* tom. iii. ; *Exp.* ii. pl. 36 ; Prescott's *Mexico,* App. part i.

[2] *L'Homme Américain,* plates v. xiv.

lation. By means of cranial and other physiological
evidence, it has been maintained that the type of red
man of the New World, from the Arctic circle to the
Straits of Magellan, is so slightly varied, that, as Morton
and Agassiz unite in affirming, " All the Indians constitute but one race, from one end of the continent to the
other."[1] The crania of the ancient graves are full of
interest for us, and their revelations are considered in a
subsequent chapter. But here, meanwhile, by means of
the ingenious portraitures of the Peruvian potter's art,

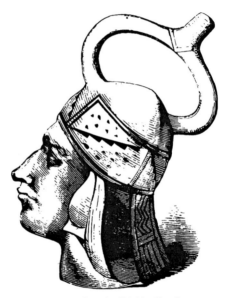

Fig. 41.—Peruvian Drinking Vessel.

we find in the sepulchre, along with the fleshless skull,
the sacred ùrn, which preserves for us the living features,
the costume, and the familiar habits of the dead ; and
these features are neither those of the forest Indian, nor
of the semi-civilized Mexican, but national features, as
replete with a character of their own, as the fictile ware

[1] *Indigenous Races of the Earth,* p. 14.

which supplies such valuable illustrations of the generations of an ancient and unknown past. One of those
Peruvian drinking-vessels, of unusual beauty, from the
Beckford Collection (Fig. 41), is placed by Mr. Marryat
alongside of a beautiful Greek vessel of similar design,
from the Museo Borbonico, Naples, without its greatly
suffering by the comparison. In this Peruvian vessel,
there is an individuality of character in the head at
once suggestive of portraiture ; and of the perfection to
which the imitative arts had been carried by the ancient
workmen, in the modelling perchance of some favourite
inca, prince, or noble. A selection of portrait-vases is
grouped together in Fig. 42, derived from various sources,

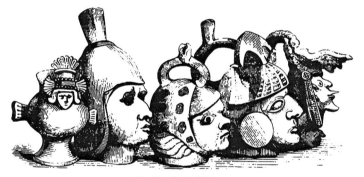

Fig. 42.—Portrait Vases.

but all illustrating a diversity of physiognomy in which
we look in vain for the familiar characteristics of the
Indian countenance, with its high cheek-bones, its peculiar form of mouth, and strongly-marked salient nose.
The group, ranging from left to right, includes a small
Mexican vase of unglazed red ware, in the collection of
the American Philosophical Society, at Philadelphia ; an
ancient portrait vase of the Quichuas of Bolivia, from
D'Orbigny's *L'Homme Américain ;* another of inferior
workmanship, in the cabinet of the Historical Society
of New York. This was brought from Berue, and re-

presents apparently a female with a close-fitting cap, and the hair gathered up under it behind. The next, from the collection of Dr. E. H. Davis, is a Peruvian drinking-vessel, with crested helmet or head-dress, and ear-pendants such as are frequently introduced in the small Mexican terra-cottas. The vase on the right hand, brought by Colonel Thorpe from Mexico, includes a group of comic masks designed with great spirit. Grotesque and humorous designs are by no means rare. One singular example figured by D'Orbigny, presents a grotesque pitcher, in which, though the face is human, the nether limbs appear rather to belong to the quadrumanous monkey; but the monkey is a frequent subject both of the American sculptors' and potters' art. At Copan, Stephens was first rewarded with a glimpse of architectural remains, which clearly told of extinct arts and an obliterated civilisation of native growth, and awoke in his mind an interest stronger than he had felt when wandering among the ruins of Egypt, or exploring the strange architecture of the long-lost Petra. Following his Indian guide with hope rather than expectation of finding remains of a higher character than the combined labours of the forest-tribes were capable of producing, he suddenly found himself arrested amid the dense forest by a squared stone-column about fourteen feet high, sculptured in bold relief on every side. " The front," he says, " was the figure of a man curiously and richly dressed; and the face, evidently a portrait, solemn, stern, and well fitted to excite terror." In this, as in all the other portrait-sculptures, carefully drawn by Catherwood in Central America and Yucatan, we look in vain for the Indian features, which, according to the deductions of the native school of American ethnologists, ought to be found as surely in such ancient portraits, as the universal type of American cranium was affirmed by Morton to be disclosed by every open grave. But by whatever race such ancient sculptures were wrought, they place certain truths of the past beyond doubt or cavil. " The sight of this unexpected monument put at rest at once and for ever, in our minds, all uncertainty in regard to the character of American antiquities ; and gave us the assurance that the objects we were in search of were interesting, not only as the remains of an unknown people, but as works of art, proving, like newly discovered historical records, that the people who once occupied the continent of America were not savages." Searching amid the forest-glades, other sculptured statues lay broken or half-buried in the luxurious vegetation ; and " one standing, with its altar before it, in a grove of trees, which grew around seemingly to shade and shroud it as a sacred thing. In the solemn stillness of the woods, it seemed a divinity mourning over a fallen people. The only sounds that disturbed the quiet of this buried city, were the noise of monkeys moving among the tops of the trees, and the cracking of dry branches broken by their weight. They moved over our heads in long and swift processions, forty or fifty at a time, some with little ones wound in their long arms, walking out to the end of boughs ; and, holding on with their hind-feet or a curl of the tail, sprang to a branch of the next tree, and, with a noise like a current of wind, passed on into the depths of the forest. It was the first time we had seen those mockeries of humanity, and, with the strange monuments around us, they seemed like wandering spirits of the departed race guarding the ruins of their former habitations."[1]

Such is a slight glimpse of the teachings embodied in the ancient ceramic art of the New World. It reveals a very striking diversity among the art-products of differ-

[1] Stephens' *Travels in Central America*, vol. i. ch. v.

ent localities and widely-separated areas; discloses to
us some of the customs, the personal characteristics,
and even the intellectual attributes of long-extinct
generations; and furnishes an important gauge of native American civilisation. We have known of Mexican
and Peruvian arts chiefly from the glowing pages of
Spanish chroniclers; and among these their pottery is
frequently described as equal to the best of Spanish
manufacture.[1] But the finest examples of Spanish fictile ware of the date of the Conquest were of Moorish
workmanship; and though the lost ceramic art of
Europe first reappeared in Spain under its Maho-
metan conquerors, it may be that the conquistadors
were chiefly familiar with the commoner pottery of an
inferior quality: even if we acquit them of all exaggeration in their descriptions of Mexican or Peruvian
manufactures. Whether among either people any approximation to the potter's wheel had been made is
generally questioned. The more elaborate and complicated designs rather indeed illustrate the modeller's than
the potter's dexterity and skill; and scarcely admitted
of the useful application of the lathe or wheel. But
their ingenious devices, and endless varieties of form,
were well calculated to impress the conquerors with the
evidence they afforded of native culture and inventive
power, while the quality of the ware would appear of
secondary significance. In examining broken specimens
of their pottery, it is seen that the more complicated
designs were formed in pieces and wrought in moulds.
In general it is imperfectly baked, and inferior in
strength either to the ancient or modern pottery of
Europe. A semi-barbarous element is also apparent in
the frequent sacrifice of convenience and utility to gro-
tesqueness of form, or ingenious trifling with the simplest

---

[1] *Relation Sig. de Cortez ap. Lorenzana,* c. 58.

laws of acoustics. Such characteristics confirm the doubts already suggested by other evidence as to the literal accuracy of early Spanish writers in their glowing pictures of native industrial and ornate arts. Nevertheless, the contrast between the rude pottery made by the Mandans of the North-west, or turned up on the sites of northern Indian villages, and that which is found in the ancient sepulchres of Mexico, Central America, and Peru, truly illustrates the wide difference between the nomades of the northern forest and those nations which partook of the influences of a native-born civilisation under Aztec and Inca rule, notwithstanding the partial development of that civilisation, which Cortes and Pizarro rudely trod out under the heels of conquerors more barbarous than the barbarians they dethroned.

CHAPTER XIX.

THE INTELLECTUAL INSTINCT: LETTERS.

In comparing the very diverse characters of Mexican and Peruvian civilisation, we are equally struck with the parallels and the contrasts which they illustrate in the progress of man from primeval darkness to intellectual life and light. But in one respect the civilisation of the southern continent, as illustrated by its *quipus*—with all the help of amautas, or chroniclers of history, annalists, and quipucamayus, or accountants and registrars, —must be regarded as immeasurably inferior to that hieroglyphic system which tantalizes the student of American antiquities by its suggestive mysteries, amid the sculptured ruins of the older civilisation of the north. Compared even to the picture-writing of the Aztecs, the Peruvian system of mnemonics exhibits a method of preserving and communicating information singularly devoid of the intellectual characteristics which pertain to every other device of civilisation for a nation's chronicles. It was essentially arbitrary; dependent entirely on the memory of those who employed and transmitted the ideas and images, which of itself it was incapable of embodying; and, above all, it had within itself no germ of higher development, like the picture-writing or sculpturing of the Egyptians, out of which grew, by natural progression, first ideography, and then the symbols of the phonetic analysis of speech: the rudi-

ments of all higher knowledge, and the indispensable
elements of intellectual progress.

It is consistent with the very nature of a highly
developed written language that the origin of its first
germs of uttered expression should be lost among the
vague shadows of primeval history, or preserved in
mythic embodiment in an ideal Thoth, Cadmus, or
Mercury. The discovery of letters approaches, indeed,
so near to the divine gift of speech that Plutarch tells us
in his *De Iside et Osiride*, when Thoth, the god of letters, first appeared on the earth, the inhabitants of Egypt
had no language, but only uttered the cries of animals.
They had, at least, no language with which to speak to
other generations ; and hence Bacon, passing in his reasoning beyond " that wherein man excelleth beasts " to
that immortality whereunto man's nature doth aspire,
exclaims :—" If the invention of the ship was thought so
noble, which carrieth riches and commodities from place
to place, and consociateth the most remote regions in
participation of their fruits : how much more are letters
to be magnified, which as ships pass through the vast
seas of time, and make ages so distant to participate of
the wisdom, illuminations, and inventions, the one of the
other ? " [1]   But it is not altogether to be ascribed to the
forgetfulness by later generations of the benefactor to
whom so great a gift as letters was due, that the origin
of writing is obscurely symbolized in mythic characters.
The Egyptian Thoth was in reality no deified mortal,
but the embodiment of an intellectual triumph slowly
achieved by the combined labours of many generations,
and the successive steps in the progress of which can
still be discerned. The origin of the hieroglyphics of
Egypt is clearly traceable to the simplest and rudest form
of picture-writing, the literal figuring of the objects de-

---

[1] *Advancement of Learning.*

signed to be expressed. Through a natural series of progressive stages this infantile art developed itself into a phonetic alphabet, the arbitrary symbols of the simple sounds of the human voice. The first process was that of abbreviation, whereby a part was made to stand for the whole ; a crown, for the Pharaoh, or king ; the head for the whole animal, etc. The next step was that of associated ideas, or symbolism employed to express abstract terms, as the sceptre for *power*, the flowing urn for *libation*, the ringed cross, or tau, by some peculiar association, for *life*, the serpent for *eternity*, and the two combined for immortality. By this means the crude picture-writing became a series of ideographic symbols capable of expressing abstract thought ; but in all probability it was not until the Egyptian was compelled to record on his monuments foreign names, with which he had no associated ideas, that he adopted the plan of phonetic signs, by assigning to the pictured object the value of its initial sound. Thus the tuft of a reed, *ake*, stood for A ; a goat or ram, *baampe* for B, etc. ; but while we find the name of Menes, the founder of Egyptian monarchy, written phonetically, the inscription on the Rosetta stone, graven in the reign of Ptolemy Epiphanes, combines with the purely alphabetic use of hieroglyphic signs, both picture and symbolical writing. The word *writing* or *letters* is literally figured by an ink-horn and reed, and the honorary title *ever-living* by the handled cross and serpent. Thus the primary picture-writing was never deliberately abandoned. It only passed, undesignedly, into the arbitrary representation of sounds by the process of writing on the papyrus leaves instead of engraving on granite or limestone, whereby the abbreviations of a current hand tended more and more to deviate from the original sculptured symbol. To these demotic characters we owe the letters of Cadmus, the

alphabets of Phœnicia, Greece, Rome, England : whereby
" have not the verses of Homer continued twenty-five
hundred years or more, without the loss of a syllable or
letter ; during which time infinite palaces, temples,
castles, cities, have been decayed and demolished ?" [1]
When we turn from the consideration of all the won
drous intellectual progress which is associated with the
letters of Cadmus, to that other hemisphere which no
solitary ray of Grecian intellect and culture helped to
illuminate, there is a charm of singular interest in the
discovery that there, too, the human mind had followed
on the very same path in its struggle to emerge from
darkness into the light of civilisation. Longfellow, in
his embodiment of the Algonquin legends, represents
Hiawatha mourning that all things fade and perish, even
the great traditions and achievements, from the memory
of the old men :—

> " Great men die and are forgotten,
> Wise men speak ; their words of wisdom
> Perish in the ears that hear them,
> Do not reach the generations
> That as yet unborn, are waiting
> In the great mysterious darkness
> Of the speechless days that shall be."

And so the Indian Cadmus, with his paints of diverse
colours, depicts, on the smooth birch-bark, such simple
figures and symbols, as are now to be found engraven on
hundreds of rocks throughout the North American continent ; and are in constant use by the forest Indian in
chronicling his own deeds on his buffalo robe, or recording those of the deceased chief on his grave-post. This
is a simple process of picture-writing, readily translatable, with nearly equal facility, into the language of every
tribe. His deeds of daring against Indians or white
men, are indicated in his primitive art by the most cha-

---

[1] Bacon's *Advancement of Learning.*

racteristic costumes and weapons of each. Headless figures are the symbols of the dead, scalps represent his own special victims ; and in like manner his feats against the buffalo, or grizzly bear, are recorded in graphic depictions, as intelligible to the Indians as any chronicle or monumental inscription of ancient or modern times. The totem of the tribe, and the name of each member of it, can in like manner be pictorially represented. An Indian signs his name in any written transaction with white men, by sketching his own adopted symbol, the eagle, bear, snake, or buffalo ; the pine-tree, pumpkin, arrow, etc., sometimes adding thereto the totem of his tribe. Mr. Schoolcraft has engraved a census of a band of Chippewa Indians in the Minnesota Territory, numbering in all one hundred and eight souls drawn up in an intelligible form, and rendered to the United States agent by Nagonabe, a Chippewa chief. Each family is denoted by a picture of the object expressive of their common or current name. Some of these are simple, such as a beaver-skin, an axe, a cat-fish ; but others require the Indian interpreter's aid. An oval, coloured brown, with a crescent line drawn through it, represents a valley, the name of the master of the wigwam ; a yellow circle, with eyes, and radiating lines, is the sun ; and a human bust, with the hair in loose locks, is described as "easily recognised as the chief possessing sacerdotal authority." Added to each symbol, are a series of units, simple as those on the Rosetta stone, indicating the number in the family ; and to the Indian agent, already familiar with the band and the names of its individual members, the whole formed a census-roll as intelligible as any regular return, in writing and Arabic numerals, could have been.[1] This system of writing includes well-recognised symbols for the Great

---

[1] *History of the Indian Tribes of the United States*, vol. ii. p. 222.

Spirit and many inferior objects of worship or superstitious reverence. The sun, the moon, lightning, rain, the earth, the sky, life and death, have all their appropriate renderings ; and thus the rude Indian has developed for himself the very same means of ideographic inscription as lie at the root of the whole hieroglyphic and demotic writing of Egypt, with its phonetic alphabet, and all the later triumphs of letters traceable to that source. Moreover, his whole mode of thought is carried out under a process of symbolism, readily translatable into picture-writing ; and when the Indians are gathered in the neighbourhood of white settlements or trading-posts, each of the white men speedily becomes known by an Indian name, sometimes more pointedly distinctive than flattering, *e.g.*, crooked-pine, pumpkin-belly, or lame duck. This mode of descriptive surnames is common to all primitive people, and indeed survives in a much later stage, as is seen in our Malcolm Canmore, William Rufus, and Edward Longshanks. It appeals to the same universal appreciation of associated ideas, out of which grow the family crests, rebuses, and canting heraldry of mediæval Europe.

The picture-writing of the Aztecs, though greatly improved in execution, and simplified by many abbreviations, was still the same in principle as the rude art of the northern Indians. When Cortes held his first interview with the emissaries of Montezuma, he observed one of the attendants of Teuhtlile, the chief Aztec noble, busily sketching on canvas the Spaniards, their peculiar costumes and arms, their horses and ships. The skill with which every object was delineated excited the admiration of the Spaniards ; and by such means a vivid report of all that pertained to the strange invaders of his dominions was transmitted to the Aztec sovereign. But however greatly superior the execution of this Aztec report might be, it was manifestly no advance on the principle of Indian picture-writing ; nor can we be in much doubt as to its style of execution, since Lord Kingsborough's elaborate work furnishes so many fac-similes of nearly contemporary Mexican drawings. In the majority of these, the totemic symbols, and the representations of individuals by means of their animal or other cognomens, are abundantly apparent. The figures are for the most part grotesque and monstrous, from the very necessity of giving predominance to the special feature in which the symbol is embodied. To the generation for which such were produced, the connexion between the sign and the person or thing signified would be abundantly manifest. Each nation and every age have their recognised symbols and abbreviations, which need for them no interpretation ; but a very brief interval suffices to render them unintelligible, and within less than a century after the Conquest, De Alva could not find more than two surviving Mexicans, both very aged, capable of interpreting this Aztec literature. It was, in truth, only a system of mnemonics, superior to the quipus of the Peruvians, but still mainly dependent on memory and an arbitrary association of ideas ; and thereby suggesting to the initiated what no literal interpretation could deduce from them. Such associated ideas when once lost are for the most part irrecoverable, and it does not seem probable that the art of deciphering the picture-writings of Mexico will ever be carried much further than it has been ; or indeed, that the majority of its records would be found to embody any new or important fact. Attempts have indeed been made to apply the Mexican language to its symbols in the same way that the Coptic has proved the key to the phonetic signs of the Egyptian writing. But the process is to a great extent one of self-deception. A writer in the *Foreign*

Quarterly Review, remarks : " The phonetic system of the Toltecans is intelligible at the first glance. The sounds intended to be conveyed by the symbols are conveyed symbolically and heraldically. The names common even to this day among the American aborigines, such as wolf, great bear, rattlesnake, etc., are represented by crests rudely fashioning the same animal form, which surmount the helmets of their warriors and the diadems of their kings. The head of a Toltecan king appears along with the others sculptured in the pyramidal tower of Palenque. Over it is the name inscribed, in an oblong phonetic rectangle, corresponding to the Egyptian cartouche. The name is Acatla-Potzin. It is composed of two words ; the first implies *reeds,* the other *hand.* The symbol of *reeds,* therefore, and the symbol of *a hand,* convey the sound of the name Acatla-Potzin."[1]

Supposing this reading to be correct, what does the reader conceive he has gained by it, in the absence of all known history of any Toltecan or Aztec king Acatla-Potzin, that would not be equally plain if he called him King Reed-hand ; as we have Red Jacket, Black Hawk, and other well-known Indian chiefs ? It is abundantly manifest that neither in the northern Indian, nor in the Aztec picture-writing, did the symbol or totem possess any phonetic value, strictly speaking. A painted *black hawk* was not the visual equivalent of the sound of the Indian words in the Sac or Pottawatomie dialect of Black Hawk's tribe, but of the chief known by that name, in any of its translations ; just as the picture brought by Montezuma's scout was meant as a representation of the Spanish leader, and not a phonetic symbol of the words Fernando Cortes. Whilst, therefore, the name of the fertile region of *Tlascala* or *Tlaxcallan,* "the place of bread," or of the Tezcucan chief

---

[1] *Foreign Quarterly Review,* No. xxxv. *Delafield,* p. 44.

Nezahualcoyotl, " the hungry fox," might be represented by objects, which, united together according to the Mexican vocabulary, constituted a rebus of the names : it is a confusion of terms to call such representations of familiar objects phonetic signs or symbols of sounds. As civilisation advanced, however, many signs were introduced as symbols of ideas ; and hence involved the germs of a word-alphabet, like the Chinese. Thus, *footprints* denoted migration, or travelling ; a *tongue,* speaking, or life ; and a *bloody heart,* sacrifice ; but in these the very tendency of such advancement was in an opposite direction from any phonetic system, such as the assumed interpretation of the Palenque sculpture points to. But if the Toltec and Aztec systems of writing bore any affinity to each other, it is quite as probable that the hieroglyphic first referred to was a date instead of a name. A *reed* was one of the four signs of the Aztec year, and a *bundle of reeds* the symbol of a cycle of fifty-two years, within which the calendar was rectified to true solar measurement by the addition of thirteen days. The latter symbol accordingly preceded each sign of a year relating to certain subdivisions of time in the calendar. Humboldt does indeed supply a reading somewhat similar to that suggested by the reviewer. After noting that in all Mexican paintings the objects tied to a head indicate the names of the persons drawn, he adds : " *Chimalpopoca* signifies a buckler that smokes ; *Acamapitzin,* a hand that holds reeds. Thus, to indicate the names of these two kings, predecessors of Montezuma, the Mexicans painted a buckler and a fist tied by a thread to two heads ornamented with a royal fillet." And he adds in illustration, that the native picture-writers indicated in like manner the name of the valiant Pedro Alvarado by drawing two keys, in allusion to the keys of St. Peter figured on his symbol.[1] But thus limited to names, which were themselves attributive or symbolic, such picture-writing was no more phonetic writing than the heraldic *padlock* and *heart* of the Lockharts, or the *doe* and *bell* of the Dobells.

It is in the figures employed in the chronology of the Aztecs that we find the highest development of their system of writing, and there the symbolic character of the signs is unmistakable. Their four symbols of the year, a *rabbit, reed, flint,* and *house,* were equivalent to the signs of the four elements : a correspondence to the system of symbols in use in the calendar of the Chinese, Japanese, and other Asiatic nations dwelt upon by Humboldt, as one of the many traces of the Asiatic origin of American civilisation apparent to him in the Aztec chronology. Again, there were twenty signs of the days, including a repetition of those of the year, in a manner that admitted of an ingenious indication of the subdivisions of months into weeks of five days, but which seems wholly incompatible with any idea of phonetic writing of the names of the days. The process was rather the reverse, the name of the sign being employed for the day, as in our own names for the days of the week.

The important evidence of the character and extent of the civilisation of the Aztecs, whether original or borrowed from their Toltec predecessors, which is furnished by their measurement of time, and the construction of their calendar, has been so largely dwelt upon by Humboldt as to render a mere reference to it sufficient. By the unaided results of native science, they had effected so accurate an adjustment of civil to solar time, that when the Europeans first landed in Mexico,

[1] Humboldt's *Researches,* Lond. 1814, vol. i. p. 141.

their reckoning, according to the unreformed Julian
calendar, was nearly eleven days in error, compared with
that of the barbarian nation whose civilisation they so
speedily extinguished. In the construction of their
calendar the four symbols of the year marked each
of the four subdivisions of the great cycle of fifty-two
years : the annual portions of which were expressed by
a series of dots, from one to thirteen, and beyond the
first subdivision, by a change of the symbol, and a
repetition of the dots associated with a second line of
these simple arithmetical signs. A bundle of reeds,
indicating a group of years, was the sign of the completed cycle, and in association with the year-sign,
marked the half-centuries in the calendar. By such
combinations a periodical series of conjunct signs admitted of the construction of the whole chronological
table with a very few symbols, and numerals, employed
in a manner that seems to involve the germ of that value
of position by which the modern European system of
arithmetic is specially distinguished.

The system of notation in the arithmetic of the Aztecs
may also properly come under notice along with their
writing. Like that of nearly all other nations, it was
essentially decimal, or more strictly, vigesimal. The
first twenty numbers were expressed by a corresponding
series of dots. There were separate names for the first
five, and for ten, fifteen, and twenty, the last of which
had its special sign of a *flag.* Intermediate numbers
were written like the Roman numerals, five and one
being six, five and two seven ; and in addition to those
signs and combinations, four hundred, the square of
twenty, was marked by a *plume,* and eight thousand,
the cube of twenty, by a *purse.* The latter signs, halved
or quartered, were sometimes used to indicate corresponding fractions of the sums ; and by this means,

imperfect as it may seem, the Mexicans were able to indicate any numerical quantity, and to work out arithmetical calculations with ease. We thus see that the very simplest of all arbitrary signs sufficed for the system of notation devised by the Aztecs, with only the addition of the flag, plume, and purse : symbols, and not phonetic signs ; though used in designation like our own term a *score*. They may suffice to remind us that in our more perfect system of notation we still employ a series of arbitrary signs· essentially unphonetic ; for whether the Roman or Arabic numerals are employed, they represent the idea of numbers only, and are translated with equal propriety into the equivalent sounds of every language in which they are employed.

But America has still, beyond this, a higher system of writing, more correctly styled hieroglyphics, to which reference has been already made, in alluding to the interpretation of the sculptures of Palenque. On the sculptural tablets of Copan, Quirigua, Chichenitza, and Palenque, as well as on the colossal statues at Copan and other ancient sites in Central America, groups of hieroglyphic devices occur, arranged in perpendicular or horizontal rows as regularly as the letters of any ancient or modern inscription. The analogies to Egyptian hieroglyphics are great, for all the figures embody more or less clearly defined representations of objects in nature or art. But the differences are no less essential, and leave no room to doubt that, in those columns of sculptured symbols we witness the highest development to which picture-writing attained, in the progress of that indigenous American civilisation so singularly illustrative of the intellectual unity which binds together the diverse races of man. A portion of the hieroglyphic inscription which accompanies the remarkable Palenque sculpture of a figure offering what has been assumed to represent an infant, before a cross, will best suffice to illustrate the characteristics of this form of writing. The sculpture is given by Dupaix, Lord Kingsborough, and Stephens, and has been made the subject of many extravagant and profitless theories and conjectures. Mr. Stephens vouches for the accuracy of Mr. Catherwood's drawings of the hieroglyphics both of Copan and Palenque; and he adds in describing those of the latter site : "There is one important fact to be noticed. The hieroglyphics are the same as were found at Copan and Quirigua. The intermediate country is now occupied by races of Indians speaking many different languages, and entirely unintelligible to each other ; but there is room for the belief that the whole of this country was once occupied by the same race, speaking the same language, or, at least, having the same written characters."[1] The impressions produced on the mind by the investigation of the few specimens yet recovered of those ancient and still unintelligible native chronicles, are of a singularly mixed kind. They furnish proofs of intellectual progress which cannot be gainsayed, while baffling us at the same time by a mystery which all our higher intellectual progress leaves still unsolved. It would be presumptuous indeed to deny the possibility of some future solution of the mystery ; but if such is ever found it will be by a totally different process from that which led Young and Champollion to the solution of the Egyptian riddle. In the specimen given here (Fig. 43), from the Palenque tablet, the inscription begins with a large initial symbol, extending over two lines in depth, like the illuminated initials of a mediæval manuscript. It is obviously not a simple figure, but compounded of various parts, so abbreviated that their original pictorial significance has as utterly disappeared,

---

[1] *Incidents of Travel in Central America*, vol. ii. ch. 20.

as the meaning of the primary monosyllables surviving in syllabic fragments in the vocabularies of living languages. The principal figure, which might be described as a shield, reappears in combination with a human profile, in the fifth line ; again, slightly modified, in another combination, at the end of the same line ; and twice, if not three times, in the line below. In carefully com-

Fig. 43.—Palenque Hieroglyphics.

paring all the examples of such hieroglyphic inscriptions hitherto published, the like recombinations of the several elements of detached figures are detected ; while, as seen in the last line of the example given above, occasional signs, closely corresponding to European alphabetic figures occur, in union with hieroglyphic groups. But, while the recurrence of the same signs, and the reconstruction of groups out of the detached members of others, clearly indicate a written language, and not a mere pictorial suggestion of associated ideas, like the Mexican picture-writing, it is not alphabetic writing. In the most complicated tablet of African hieroglyphics, each object is distinct, and its representative significance is rarely difficult to trace. But the majority of the hieroglyphics of Palenque or Copan appear as if constructed on the same polysynthetic principle which gives the peculiar and distinctive character to the languages of the New World. This is still more apparent when we turn to the highly elaborated inscriptions on the colossal figures of Copan, illustrated on a subsequent page. In these all ideas of simple phonetic signs utterly disappear. Like the *bunch-words,* as they have been called, of the American languages, they seem each to be compounded of a number of parts of the primary symbols used in picture-writing, while the pictorial origin of the whole becomes clearly apparent. In comparing these minutely elaborated characters with those on the tables, it is obvious that a system of abbreviation is employed in the latter; and thus each group appears with the greater probability to partake of that peculiar characteristic of the whole grammatical structure of American language, as shown in its word-sentences. The plan of thought of the American languages is concrete, while certain euphonic laws lead to the dropping of portions of the words compounded together, in a manner exceedingly puzzling to the grammarian. By the same compounding process, new words are formed, as in the Algonquin *shominaubo,* wine, *i.e., sho,* a grape, *min,* a berry, *aubo,* liquor; *ozhebiegunaubo,* ink, *i.e., ozheta,* a prefix signifying to prepare to do, or act; *nindozheta,* I prepare to do; *ozhebiegade,* a writer; whence *ozhebiegai,* he writes; and *aubo,* liquor. The latter, like all abstract terms, is only used in compound words, as *ishkodaiwaubo,* fire-liquid, or whisky. The specific word for water is *nebeesh*. So also *makuhdaw-ekoonuhya*, a priest, or clergyman, *i.e.*, *muhkuhda*, black; *ekoonuhya*, he is so dressed, the person who dresses in black, etc. An analogous process seems dimly discernible in the abbreviated compound characters of the Palenque inscription. But if the inference be correct, this of itself would serve to indicate that the Central American hieroglyphics are not used as phonetic, or pure alphabetic signs; and this idea receives more certain confirmation from the extreme rarity with which the same group recurs.

These inscriptions cannot, however, be confounded with the Mexican picture-writings, by any one who attempts an intelligent comparison of the two. In the latter, as in a picture, the eye searches for the most prominent features of the ideographic picturing, and interprets the various parts as independent members of one representation. But the Palenque inscriptions have all the characteristics of a written language in a matured state of development. They appear to be read in horizontal lines, and from left to right; for the groups on both the Palenque tablets begin with a large hieroglyphic on the left-hand corner; and the left-hand figure for several lines thereafter occupies a double space on the line, as though it were equivalent to the use of capitals in the beginning of the lines in verse. It is further noticeable that in the frequent occurrence of human and animal heads among the sculptured characters they invariably look towards the left; an indication, as it appears to me, not only of the lines being read horizontally from left to right, but also that they are the graven inscriptions of a lettered people, who were accustomed to write with the same characters on paper or skins. Indeed, the pictorial groups on the Copan statues seem to be the true hieroglyphic characters; while the Palenque inscriptions show the abbreviated hieratic writing. To the sculptor the direction of the characters was a matter of no moment; but if the scribe held his pen, or style, in his right hand, like the modern clerk, he would as naturally draw the left profile as we slope our current hand to the right.

The enterprising traveller, to whose researches we owe so much of all the knowledge yet acquired of those singularly interesting evidences of the intellectual progress of an ancient American people, dwells with fond favour on the idea he latterly adopted, that the ruins he explored were of no very remote date; because he felt that the nearer he could bring the builders of those cities to our own times, the greater is our chance of recovering the key to their language and the inscriptions in which their history now lies entombed. Palenque, it cannot be doubted, was a desolate ruin at the date of the Conquest. Backward behind the era of Europe's first knowledge of the New World, we have to grope our way to that age in which living men read its graven tablets, and spoke the language in which they are inscribed; yet other cities survive to share in the later desolation of the Conquest, and Stephens thus sanguinely records his latest cherished hopes: " Throughout the country the convents are rich in manuscripts and documents written by the early fathers, caciques, and Indians, who very soon acquired the knowledge of Spanish and the art of writing. These have never been examined with the slightest reference to this subject; and I cannot help thinking that some precious memorial is now mouldering in the library of a neighbouring convent, which would determine the history of some one of these ruined cities; moreover, I cannot help believing that the tablets of hieroglyphics will yet be read. No strong curiosity has hitherto been directed to them; vigour and acuteness of intellect, knowledge and learning, have never

been expended upon them. For centuries the hieroglyphics of Egypt were inscrutable, and though not perhaps
in our day, I feel persuaded that a key surer than that
of the Rosetta Stone, will be discovered. And if only
three centuries have elapsed since any one of those unknown cities was inhabited, the race of the inhabitants
is not extinct. Their descendants are still in the land,
scattered perhaps, and retired like our own Indians, into
wildernesses which have never yet been penetrated by a
white man, but not lost; living as their fathers did,
erecting the same buildings of lime and stone, with ornaments of sculpture and plaster, large courts and lofty
towers with high ranges of steps, and still carving on
tablets of stone the same mysterious hieroglyphics ; and
if, in consideration that I have not often indulged in
speculative conjecture, the reader will allow one flight :
I turn to that vast and unknown region, untraversed by
a single road, wherein fancy pictures that mysterious
city, seen from the topmost range of the Cordilleras, of
unconquered, unvisited, and unsought aboriginal inhabitants." It is indeed a fascinating dream, but lettered
nations do not dwell apart through long centuries, hidden
beyond the untravelled wilderness of so narrow a continent. It may indeed be that the tablets of Palenque
shall yet be read, but it will be by no mysterious
emergence of the lettered descendants of their sculp
tors from the shadows of that unexplored forest which
stretches between the Cordilleras and the Caribbean Sea.
Some of the simpler elements of the graven characters
appear, as we have seen, to admit of re-arrangement into
new groups, like the alphabetic elements of our written
or printed words. Others of the figures are also simple,
representing a human or animal profile, a shield or crescent ; but others are highly complicated, and defy any
attempt at intelligible interpretation of their represent-

ative or symbolic significance. They are no crude
abbreviations, like the symbols either of Indian or Aztec
picture-writing; but rather suggest the idea of a matured
system of ideography in its last transitional stage, before
becoming a word-alphabet like that of the Chinese at the
present day. Such I conceive it in a less simple condition actually to have been : a holophrastic or word-
sentence alphabet; and, as such, a uniformity of hieroglyphics may have been compatible with the existence
of diverse dialects throughout the extensive region in
which they were used. If, however, any single living
language is calculated to aid in the attempt to solve this
great riddle of the American sphinx, it is not to the
Mexican, but to the Maya language that the imagination
turns for expected aid : that language still believed to be
spoken by the Candones, or unbaptized Indians, of the
region of the mysterious city seen by the Cura of Quiché,
from the lofty summit of the Sierra.

The elaborately sculptured colossal figures already referred to, found on various sites, but chiefly at Copan,
are covered on the back, and in some cases also on the
sides, with rows of hieroglyphics executed with a minuteness of detail, compared with which those on the tablets
of Palenque appear as mere demotic characters. But
the elaborateness of their execution only increases the
mystery of their significance, and confirms the conviction
that so far from their having any phonetic value, either
of primary radical sounds, or of simple words, each
hieroglyphic embraces the abbreviated depiction or symbolism of a complete sentence. Fig. 44 represents the
back of one of the colossal idols at Copan, sculptured
with a succession of hieroglyphics in double columns.
Each compartment contains human figures, sometimes
curiously grouped together, and as grotesque and dis-
proportioned as those of the Mexican picture-writing.

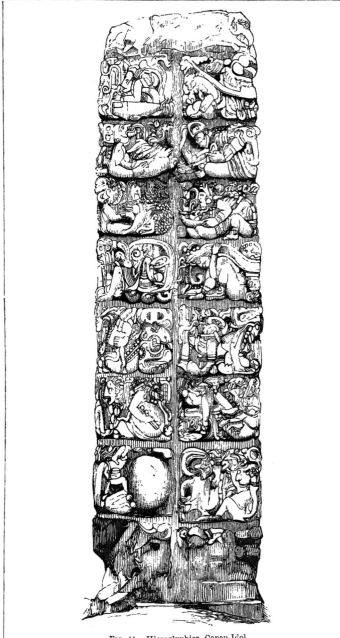

Fig. 44.—Hieroglyphics, Copan Idol.

They are marked also by great variety in dress and ornaments ; but the mythic significance only becomes the more obscure to us by the minuter details of its characters in this example. On the back of another of the Copan idols, the hieroglyphic characters, though more elaborate, closely resemble those of Palenque.

In tracing the natural progress of a native American system of writing through so many successive stages, from the primary and infantile condition of the rude Indian's birch-bark paintings to the most advanced stage of letters short of true alphabetic characters and phonetic signs, it is impossible to overlook the evidence thus afforded of the great lapse of time which is thereby implied. The Chinese, whose civilisation and arts present so many points of resemblance to those of the New World, had advanced little, if at all, beyond the same stage in their system of writing, with its two hundred and fourteen hieroglyphic characters, when they paused, and left to more favoured races the simpler vehicles of written thought. But by this arresting of their intellectual development at the stage of symbolized ideas instead of radical sounds, they possess a series of written characters which are employed with equal facility in Cochin-China, Japan, Loo-Choo, Corea, and in China itself, for expressing the words of languages mutually unintelligible. In this there is no analogy to the common use of the Roman alphabet among so many of the nations of Europe ; but in our simple Arabic, or even in the Roman numerals, we have an apt illustration of written characters representing ideas, entirely independent of specific words or sounds. Thus 20 equally signifies *viginti, venti, vingt,* or *twenty ;* and when we write Louis xiv., it may be read with equal correctness, Louis the fourteenth, or Louis quatorze. In reality, however, the analogy is greater when we compare the

symbolic writing of Egypt with the supposed graven signs
of word-sentences on the tablets of Palenque ; and the
interpretation of each doubtless depended for its precision on associated ideas, such as no mere philological
investigations could enable us to recover. A single
illustration of this will suffice. On the wall of the
temple of Philæ, at the first cataract of the Nile, the
ram-headed god Kneph is represented seated, and at
work on a potter's wheel, with a group of hieroglyphics
over his head, which have been thus translated. Mr.
George R. Gliddon, adopting the version of Dr. W. C.
Taylor, reads thus : " Knum the Creator, on his wheel,
moulds the divine members of Osiris (the type of
man) in the shining house of life, or the solar disk."[1]
Mr. Birch of the British Museum furnishes this very
different reading of the same hieroglyphic inscription :
" Phtah Totonem, the father of beginnings, is setting in
motion the egg of the sun and moon, director of the
gods of the upper world."[2] Without the pictorial symbol
of the divine ram-headed potter, significant to all eyes,
it may be doubted if the two readings would have even
presented such slight correspondence as they do. It is
not, therefore, without reason that Prescott, after commenting on the Palenque writing as exhibiting an advanced stage of the art, with little indications of anything
more than the common elements of such writing to
connect it with Egyptian hieroglyphics, adds : " That
its mysterious import will ever be deciphered is scarcely
to be expected. The language of the race who employed
it, the race itself, is unknown. And it is not likely that
another Rosetta Stone will be found with its trilingual
inscription to supply the means of comparison, and to
guide the American Champollion in the path of discovery."

---

[1] *Ancient Egypt*, 12th Edition, p. 28.
[2] Arundale and Bonomi's *Antiquities*, British Museum, p. 13.

Among the examples of ancient picture-writing illustrated in Lord Kingsborough's elaborate work on Mexican
antiquities, the most curious of all is the Dresden codex,
to which Prescott directs special attention as bearing
scarcely any traces of a common origin with the highly
coloured and fantastic picturings of the Aztec manuscripts. The figures of objects, though delicately drawn,
frequently consist of arbitrary or nondescript designs,
and as Prescott says, "are possibly phonetic. Their

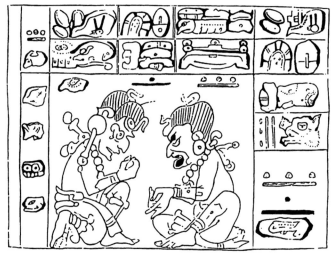

Fig. 45.—Hieroglyphic Writing.

regular arrangement is quite equal to the Egyptian.
The whole infers a much higher civilisation than the
Aztec, and offers abundant food for curious speculation."
Many of them are, indeed, pictorial representations accompanied by hieroglyphic characters arranged in lines,
as though constituting a written commentary or description accompanied with numerical notation, and certainly
suggest a resemblance to the Palenque hieroglyphics
which is totally wanting in the Mexican paintings. Nor
is there any improbability in the supposition that the

traces of a higher Toltec civilisation survived, and exercised its ameliorating influences on the fierce Aztec conquerors. In the accompanying illustration (Fig. 45), copied from Lord Kingsborough's version of the Dresden codex, it seems in no degree irreconcilable with the traces of a higher antiquity in the ruined cities of Central America, that we have here an example of the written characters which figure on the sculptured tablets of Palenque.

Compared with the hieroglyphic writing of ancient Central America, or even the ruder picture-writing of the Aztecs, the Peruvian science of the quipus was a most primitive and barbarous substitute. The word *quipu* signified a knot ; and the quipu in use for recording facts, or committing ideas to safe keeping for transmission to future generations, consisted of a cord of different-coloured strings, to which a number of other cords were attached, distinguished by their colours. With these specific ideas were associated. Thus *yellow* denoted gold and all the allied ideas ; *white*, silver or peace ; *red*, war or soldiers ; *green*, maize or agriculture, etc. ; and each quipu was in the care of its own *Quipu-camayoc* or keeper, by whom its records were interpreted in any doubtful case. Upon the cords the requisite number of knots were made, and when used for arithmetical purposes, they could be combined to represent any series of numbers, and were used in difficult computations with great facility. In their arithmetical system a single knot meant *ten ;* two single knots together, *twenty ;* a knot doubled and intertwined, *one hundred ;* tripled after the same fashion, *one thousand ;* and by the union of two or more of such, *two hundred, two thousand,* etc. The colour, the mode of intertwining the knots, the twist of the cord, the distance of the knot from the main cord, or of the several knots from each

other, had each a special significance, indispensable to
the proper interpretation of the quipu. By means of
such records, well-trained officials kept registers of the
census and military rolls, accounts of the revenues, and
much other important statistical information. Each
province had its own registrars, with varying details
suited to the specialities of their district, its form of
tribute, or the nature of its mineral, pastoral, or agricultural resources ; and the interpretation of the national
quipus required the aid of registrars from many remote
provinces. Annalists, chroniclers, genealogists, and poets
were all trained to transmit by oral tradition the chain
of facts or ideas associated with the arbitrary signs of
the quipus, and by the like means information of every
kind was perpetuated. Acosta mentions that he saw a
woman with a handful of knotted strings of diverse
colours, which she said contained a general confession
of her life. With the fall of Montezuma's empire, its
picture-writings were abandoned to the same fate as the
Arabic manuscripts of Granada, and only a few imperfect
fragments or chance copies have survived to reflect the
ingenuity and determine the progress of Aztec culture.
But the rude system of the Peruvian quipu perished with
its keepers ; and a fragment of pottery, or the masonry
of a ruined roadway station, is more eloquent for us
than all the many-coloured and knotted registers of the
Incas could be. But in another respect, the quipus of
the Peruvians have a singular interest for us, for it is
impossible to overlook the remarkable correspondence
between them and the wampum in use by the American
Indians for a similar purpose. Boturini, indeed, discovered a specimen of the quipu in Tlascala, which had
nearly fallen to pieces with age ; and both M'Culloch
and Prescott only reject his inference that the ancient
Mexicans were acquainted with the Peruvian mode of

recording events, by assuming the Tlascalan quipu to have been an Indian wampum belt. But altogether apart from this solitary specimen, the close correspondence between the Peruvian quipus and the Indian wampum belts, and their use in almost precisely the same way for the purpose of registering events, present coincidences too remarkable to be hastily assumed as mere accidental resemblances. Nor is our wonder diminished, when it is borne in remembrance that the wampum belt of the North American Indian seems to reproduce the arbitrary mnemonic system of Peru, alongside of a universally recognised and totally independent native system of picture-writing.

But before comparing the almost identical *memoria technica* of the southern Peruvians and northern Indians, it is important to ascertain precisely the actual acquirements and usages of the Peruvians in relation to painting or picture-writing. Prescott, indeed, assumes their total ignorance in this respect, and derives from it an additional proof of the entirely distinct origin of all the characteristic elements of Peruvian and Mexican civilisation.[1] But it is inconceivable that a people skilled in modelling in clay the copies of every familiar object in nature, and sporting with an exuberant fancy in endless grotesque and ingenious devices ; and who, moreover, painted their pottery and wove their parti-coloured dresses with considerable taste and great variety of pattern : should have made no attempt at drawing or painting on agave-paper or canvas. Humboldt, who notices the discovery of bundles, or books of picture-records among the Panoe Indians of South America to the east of the Andes,[2] puts this beyond question. " It has recently been doubted," he remarks in a supple-

---

[1] *Conquest of Peru*, B. I. ch. iv. p. 121.

[2] Humboldt's *Researches*, London, 1814, vol. i. p. 174.

mentary note, " whether the Peruvians were acquainted
with symbolic paintings in addition to their *quipus.* A
passage taken from the *Origen de los Indios del Nuevo
Mundo* (Valencia, 1610, p. 91), leaves no uncertainty
on this point. After speaking of the Mexican hieroglyphics, Father Garcia adds : ' At the beginning of the
Conquest, the Indians of Peru made their confessions by
paintings and characters, which indicated the Ten Com-
mandments, and the sins committed against these com-
mandments.' Hence we may conclude that the Peruvians
made use of symbolic paintings ; but that these were
more grotesque than the hieroglyphics of the Mexicans,
and that the people generally made use of knots or
quipus."[1] It was not, therefore, because of their ignorance of the rude picture-writing, equivalent, probably, to
all that was effected by the Aztec chronicler in the depiction of sensible objects with their associated ideas,
that the Peruvians adhered by preference to their quipus.
The rudest picture-writing is, indeed, far before the most
perfect system of quipus as a germ of possible development. But if we look, for example, at the " Lawsuit in
Hieroglyphical Writing," engraved by Humboldt, a docu-
ment prepared for pleading and evidence before a legal
tribunal, we find no series of word-symbols setting forth
the case, but a mere ground-plan accompanied by pictorial references to the parties, and some leading points in
the suit, which must have depended almost as entirely
on memory and the association of ideas for its practical
use as the parti-coloured and knotted quipus in the
hands of well-trained Peruvian amautas.

Bearing in remembrance, then, the perfection to which
the use of the quipu had been brought by a well system-
atized training and division of labour, and the faith
reposed in its accuracy in the most practical questions

---

[1] Humboldt's *Researches*, vol. ii. p. 221.

of Peruvian reckoning and statistics, let us now inquire
what the Indian wampum was in its most perfect form
and use. The germs of a possible native civilisation
among the Indian˙tribes of North America are naturally
to be sought for in that remarkable league of the Iroquois,
by which the conquests of France were so effectually
arrested to the south of the St. Lawrence ; and among
the members of that league we find the wampum belt in
use for all their most sacred and important records. By
means of the wampum the laws of the League were
recorded, and every contract or treaty was defined and
guaranteed.

Wampum consists of beads of different colours strung
together, and generally woven into a belt. Hubbard
describes it as "of two sorts, white and purple. The
white is worked, out of the inside of the great concho,
into the form of a bead, and perforated to string on leather.
The purple is worked out of the inside of the muscle
shell. They are woven as broad as one's hand, and about
two feet long. These they call belts, and give and receive at their treaties as the seals of their friendship."[1]
The colours of the wampum, however, and indeed its
whole material, varied at different periods and among
diverse tribes. One singularly interesting example of its
use as the evidence and sole title-deed of an extensive
transfer of land, was preserved in England, until very
recent years, by Mr. Granville John Penn, a descendant
of William Penn, and is now in the cabinet of the Historical Society of Philadelphia. It is the belt of wampum delivered by the Lenni-Lenape sachems to the
founder of Pennsylvania, at "the Great Treaty," under
the elm-tree at Shackamox in 1682. After having been
handed down for generations in the founder's family, it
was presented to the Historical Society of Philadelphia

[1] Hubbard's *Narrative, Indians in New England*, p. 40.

in 1857. It is composed of eighteen strings of wampum, formed of white and violet beads worked upon leather thongs ; and the whole is woven into a belt twenty-eight inches long, and two and a half inches broad. On this five patterns are worked in violet beads on a white ground, and in the centre Penn is represented taking the hand of the Indian sachem : the former being the larger figure of the two, and indicated by his European head-dress.[1]

In 1675 the famous war of the New England chief, Metacomet, the sachem of the Wampanoags, — better known as King Philip,—broke out, and threatened for a time the extermination of the colonists. Before its close, thirteen towns in Massachusetts, Plymouth, and Rhode Island had been destroyed, and scarcely a family in New England had escaped the loss of some of its members. When at length Philip had fallen, and the hostile tribes were almost exterminated, Annawon, an aged chief, one of the last surviving sachems of the Wampanoags, approached Captain Church, the leader of the colonists, and thus addressed him : "Great Captain, you have killed Philip, and conquered his country. I and my company are the last that war against the English. You have ended the war, and therefore these belong to you." He then handed to him two broad belts elaborately worked in wampum, "edged with red hair from the Mahog's country." One of them reached from the shoulders nearly to the ground. It was the Magna Charta of the New England tribes, who had now fought their last fight. They were pitilessly exterminated. Old Annawon himself was put to death, along with Tispaquin, the last of Philip's great sachems, and all the prisoners who had been active in the war. The remainder were sold as slaves, including a poor boy, the son of Philip, whose

---

[1] This wampum belt is accurately figured, the size of the original, in the *Memoirs of the Historical Society of Pennsylvania*, vol. vi.

only crime was his relationship to the great chief. After keen discussion as to his fate, in which Increase Mather pleaded against mercy, the boy's life was spared. The New England divine urged the case of Hadad, of the king's seed in Edom, spared as a little child, when Joab, the captain of the host, had smitten every male among the Edomites, who survived to rise up as the adversary of Solomon, when he heard in Egypt that David slept with his fathers, and Joab, the captain of the host, was dead. The son of the great Wampanoag sachem was finally sent as a slave to Bermuda, from whence he never returned to dispute the possession of his father's wampum, and the rights of which it was the symbol.

The original Wampum of the Iroquois, in which the laws of the League were recorded, is described by Mr. Lewis H. Morgan, in his history of the League, as made of spiral fresh-water shells, which were strung on deerskin strings or sinews, and the strands braided into belts, or simply united into strings. His narrative of the mode of using these northern *quipus* will best illustrate the close analogies they present to those of the southern continent. Describing the great councils of the League, he says : "The laws explained at different stages of the ceremonial were repeated from strings of wampum, into which *they had been talked* at the time of their enactment. In the Indian method of expressing the idea, the string or the belt can tell, by means of an interpreter, the exact law or transaction of which it was made, at the time, the sole evidence. It operates upon the principle of association, and thus seeks to give fidelity to the memory. These strings and belts were the only visible records of the Iroquois, and were of no use except by the aid of those special personages who could draw forth the secret records locked up in their remembrance." [1] There

---

[1] *League of the Iroquois*, p. 120.

was, accordingly, a sachem specially constituted as "Keeper of the Wampum;" and verbal promises, interchanged either among themselves or with foreign tribes, were regarded as of little moment if no strings or belts had been employed to ratify them and secure their remembrance. Sir William Johnston records, as the result of his experience : " They regard no message or invitation, be it of what consequence it will, unless attended or confirmed by strings or belts of wampum, which they look upon as we our letters, or rather bonds."[1] A belt of wampum was also used at their festivals, when a council of repentance preceded the rejoicings, and public confession of faults, with the pledge of amendment, was put on record by its means.

The resemblance between the two systems of the quipu and wampum, with their appointed keepers, and the perpetuation of the national chronicles and enactments by means of these as mnemonic guides, is so remarkable, as to appear highly suggestive of a common origin ; however remotely we may be compelled to seek for that dividing line on which the essentially distinct elements of picture-writing and recording by an arbitrary association of ideas met, as it were, and exchanged their diverse modes of giving form and perpetuity to fleeting words. The picture-writing is of indigenous growth among the northern tribes, the quipu seems no less essentially native to Peru ; but we are not without some faint indications of a source other than the northern forest Indian, from whence his mode of quipu-registering and ratification of contracts may have been derived ; or rather perhaps, from whence the Indian tribes of the northern continent may have borrowed this product of the immature civilisation of the Peruvian Cordilleras. In the great sepulchral mounds of the Mississippi Valley, the relics of art present

---

[1] *Documents relating to Colonial History of New York,* vol. ii. p. 624.

great uniformity of character; and among these, beads
of shell, bone, and other materials, have been found in
greater quantities than seems to be readily accounted for
as mere personal ornaments. In the Grave Creek Mound
the shell-beads, such as constituted the wampum of the
forest tribes, amounted to between three and four thousand; and it seems singularly consistent with the partial
civilisation of the ancient Mound-Builders that, in such
deposits of shell-beads, we have the relics of sepulchral
records which constituted the scroll of fame of the illustri-
ous dead, or copies of the national archives deposited with
the great sachem to whose wisdom or prowess the safety
of his people had been due. The wampum chronicle,
unstrung by Time's own decaying fingers, seems no un-
meet inscription for the nameless dead over whom the
great earth-pyramid was reared. The memories once
associated with its many strings have irrecoverably
passed away; yet not more so than the annals of the
civilized Incas; stored up in their many-coloured skeins
of knotted threads; or even, perhaps, than the sculptured
inscriptions of Copan or Palenque, which mock us with
their voiceless mysteries. The Peruvian quipu served,
as we know, like an abacus, for facilitating the most
elaborate computations of the census, revenues, and
official registers of the Incas; and in its northern form
of bead-wampum it may have equally sufficed for the
scale and mensuration of the great earthworks. But one
other striking element of parallelism in the civilisation of
the Mound-Builders and Peruvians is the apparent possession by both of the balance and recognised standards
of weight. The penannular copper rings, found alike in
the sepulchral mounds and on the mound-altars, prove
not only to correspond in size but in weight. In diameter they measure 2·9 inches; in thickness 0·4; and
when perfect weigh exactly four ounces each. Ten cop-

per rings thus uniform in weight and dimensions lay in two heaps of five each, on an altar under one of the sacrificial mounds in the Scioto Valley, tempting us to recognise in their numbers, weight, and measurements, not only evidences of a long-extinct civilisation, but the memorials of a decimal system of numeration.[1]

[1] *Ancient Monuments of the Mississippi Valley,* pp. 157, 204.

CHAPTER XX.

ANTE-COLUMBIAN TRACES: COLONIZATION.

THE year 1492 marks in many important respects the close of the Old World's ancient, the beginning of its modern history. But for the native of the Transatlantic hemisphere it is the dawn of all definite annals. It constitutes for America what the era of Julius Cæsar's landing is for Britain : the lifting of the veil behind which lay unrecorded centuries of national story, and the admission into the great family of nations of those who there, isolated and apart, had through unnumbered generations enacted the drama of history.

In previous chapters some attempt has been made to look upon that past, which, though relatively speaking so modern, is nevertheless remoter from all our preconceived ideas and sympathies than the old Roman world. The fifteenth century is, in fact, as ancient for America as the first century is for Britain, or B.C. 2000 for Egypt. No wonder, therefore, that every glimpse of a fancied memorial of ante-Columbian relations with the Old World should present a fascinating charm to the American archæologist; or that even a pardonable credulity should occasionally be exercised in the reception of any apparent evidence of such intrusive antiquities disclosing themselves among relics of aboriginal native arts. "He who calls what has vanished back into being enjoys a bliss like that of creating;" so says the great Niebuhr, himself foremost among those who have revelled in this bliss of resuscitating the long-buried past. But to the impulse which such a generous ambition awakens has been added the no less influential stimulus of national pride and emulation, both in the Old and the New World. To such combined motives we owe in an especial manner, not only the *Antiquitates Americanæ*, and the *Grönland's Historiske Mindesmærker* of the Danish antiquaries; but also a singular harvest reaped on American soil, from the novel impetus to which the former of these publications has given rise. The idea of ancient intercourse between America and Europe is not indeed of such recent growth. It mingles with the very earliest study of Mexican antiquities, and was indeed inseparable from that recognition of the American race, as in the strictest meaning of the term of one blood with the whole human family, which has only been seriously challenged within very recent years. One favourite idea, accordingly, long found acceptance, which traced the peopling of the American continent to the long-sought ten tribes of Israel; and discovered in the Indian languages Hebrew words and idioms, and in native customs relics of the ancient Jewish ceremonial rites. Still older traces have been sought in the lost Island of Atlantis; in the obscure allusions of Herodotus, Plato, Seneca, Pliny, and other classical writers, to mythic islands or continents in that Atlantic Ocean which swept away in undefined vastness beyond the western verge of their world; in the Ophir, to which the ships of Tyre, manned by servants of Hiram, "that had knowledge of the sea," sailed for gold and algum trees, for Solomon's great works; in the Antilla mentioned by Aristotle as a Carthaginian discovery; and in that other obscure island which Diodorus Siculus assigns to the same Carthaginian voyagers, as a secret reserved for their own behoof, should fate ever compel them to abandon their African homes.

Again, the probabilities of undesigned intrusion of early colonists on the New World, from the eastern shores of the Atlantic, find confirmation from various independent sources. According to Pliny, Hanno preceded Vasco de Gama by some two thousand years in the passage of the Cape, reaching the coast of Arabia through the Straits of Gibraltar. Again, in obedience to the commands of Pharaoh-Necho, cir. B.C. 600, Phœnician voyagers effected the circumnavigation of the African continent in the opposite direction : sailing from a port on the Red Sea, and reaching the Nile through the Pillars of Hercules. The account of the latter voyage is given by Herodotus with circumstantial minuteness ; and the cautious Humboldt has looked with sufficient favour on such narratives to induce him to credit the Phœnician and Carthaginian circumnavigations of Africa. This granted, it follows from such prolonged Atlantic voyages, not only that Madeira, the Canary, and Cape Verde Islands, but even the Azores, may have been among the Carthaginian discoveries referred to by Aristotle. Humboldt, indeed, assigns reasons entirely satisfactory to his own mind for believing that the Canary Islands at least were known, not only to the Phœnicians and Carthaginians, but also to the Greeks and Romans, and, as he adds, "perhaps even to the Etruscans." Northward to the Tin Islands of the English Channel, as well as southward beyond Cape Verde, across the stormy Bay of Biscay and the Gulf of Guinea, the ancient voyagers of Tyre and Carthage sailed into the wide waste of the Atlantic ; and from our knowledge of the winds and currents of that ocean, it is manifestly no inconceivable thing that some of those venturous voyagers should have been driven out of their course, and landed on more than one point of the American continent. To such an accidental landing America may be said to owe its name. Pedro Alvares de Cabral, sailing in command of a Portuguese fleet in the last year of the fifteenth century, on the eastern route just rediscovered by Vasco de Gama, was carried by the equatorial current so far to the west of his intended course that he found himself unexpectedly in sight of land, in 10° s. latitude, thereby discovering Brazil. The king of Portugal thereupon despatched the Florentine, Amerigo Vespucci, who explored the coast, prepared a map of it, and thereby achieved the honour, more justly due to Columbus, of giving his name to the new continent. So recently as 1833 the wreck of a Japanese junk on the coast of Oregon showed how, in like manner, across the wider waste of the Pacific, the natives of the Old World may have been borne to plant the germs of a new population, or to leave the memorials of Asiatic civilisation on American shores.

It is not, therefore, altogether without reason that the obscure and vague references of classic writers to lands lying beyond the Pillars of Hercules have had an exaggerated value assigned to them. The conviction of some ancient intercourse between the Old World and the New has furnished a fruitful theme for speculation, almost from the year in which the Genoese voyager achieved his long-cherished dream of discovery. It has only required the asserted recovery of Egyptian, Phœnician, or Punic traces of graphic or plastic art, to revive the faith in an American commonwealth old as that Atlantis which the Egyptian priesthood told of to Solon as even then among the things of an ancient past.

Such speculations have been discussed in all their changing forms, and investigated with loving enthusiasm, though ever proving intangible when pressed to any practical deduction. In Humboldt's *Researches* is engraved a fragment of a supposed inscription copied by Ranson Bueno, a Franciscan monk, from a block of granite which he discovered in a cavern in the mountain chain between the Orinoco and the Amazon. Unfortunately, Humboldt was unable to inspect it for himself. Possibly it would have proved only the natural markings on a block of graphic granite. He remarks of the copy furnished him by the monk : " Some resemblance to the Phœnician alphabet may be discovered in these characters, but I much doubt whether the good monk, who seemed to be but little interested about this pretended inscription, had copied it very carefully." Not much could be made out of "Phœnician" characters heralded in this fashion. But the appearance in 1837 of the *Antiquitates Americanæ, sive scriptores septentrionales rerum ante-Columbiarum in America,* issued by the Royal Society of Northern Antiquaries at Copenhagen, under the learned editorship of Professor Charles Christian Rafn, produced an entire revolution, alike in the form and the reception of illustrations of ante-Columbian American history. While the publication of that work gave a fresh interest to the vaguest intimations of a dubious past, it seemed to supersede them by tangible disclosures, which, though "but of yesterday" in comparison with such mythic antiquities as the Egyptian Atlantis, nevertheless added some five centuries to the history of the New World. From the appearance of the *Antiquitates Americanæ,* accordingly, may be dated the systematic resolve of American antiquaries and historians to find evidence of intercourse with the ancient world prior to that recent year of the fifteenth century in which the ocean revealed its great secret to Columbus.

From the literary memorials of the old Norsemen, thus brought to light, we glean sufficient evidence to place beyond doubt, not only the discovery and colonization of Greenland, by Eric the Red—apparently in the year 985,—but also the exploration of more southern lands, some of which, we can scarcely doubt, must have formed part of the American continent. Of the authenticity of the manuscripts from whence these narratives are derived there is not the slightest room for question; and the accounts which some of them furnish are so simple, natural, and devoid of anything extravagant or improbable, that the internal evidence of genuineness is worthy of great consideration. The exuberant fancy of the Northmen, which revels in their mythology and songs, would have constructed a very different tale had it been employed in the invention of a southern continent for the dreams of Icelandic and Greenland rovers. Some of the latter Sagas do, indeed, present so much resemblance in their tales of discovery to those of older date, as to look like a mere varied repetition of the original narrative with a change of actors, such as might result from different versions of an account transmitted for a time by oral tradition before being committed to writing. But, with all reasonable doubts as to the accuracy of details, there is the strongest probability in favour of the authenticity of the American Vinland of the Northmen.

About the year 1000—when Saint Olaf was introducing Christianity into the Norse fatherland,—Leif, a son of Eric, the founder of the first Greenland colony, is stated in the old Eric Saga to have sailed from Ericsfiord or other Greenland port, in quest of southern lands already reported as seen by Bjarni Herjulfson. Pursuing his voyage of discovery, Leif landed on a barren coast where no green was to be seen; but a great plain covered with flat stones stretched from the sea inward to a lofty range of ice-clad mountains. To this he gave the name of Helluland, from *hella*, a flat stone; and the modern

Danish editor conceives he finds in such characteristics sufficient evidence to identify it with Newfoundland. The next point touched presented a low shore of white sand ; and stretching away beyond this was a level country covered with forest, to which Leif gave the name of Markland, or Woodland. This, which, so far as the name or description can guide us, might be anywhere on the American coast, is supposed by the Danish editor of the *Antiquitates Americanæ* to have been Nova Scotia. After leaving Markland the voyagers were two days at sea before they again saw land, and of this the only characteristic noted was that the dew upon the grass tasted sweet. But this has been assumed as sufficient evidence that Nantucket, where honey-dew abounds, is the place referred to. Their further course shoreward, and up a river into the lake from which it flowed, is supposed to have been up the Pacasset River to Mount Hope Bay ; and there the voyagers passed the winter. After erecting temporary lodgings, Leif divided his followers into two parties, which alternately proceeded on exploring excursions. One of these, Tyrker, a southerner, *sudrmadr,*—or German, as he is supposed to have been,— having wandered, he reported on his return the discovery of vines and grapes such as he had been familiar with in his own Rhine-land. With these, accordingly, the vessel was laden, and Leif commemorated the discovery by giving to the locality the name of Vinland.

The same narrative reappears in Sagas of later date, with slight variations and some inconsistencies, but the local features described are equally vague ; and it depends much more on geographical probabilities than on any direct evidence furnished either in the account of Bjarni Herjulfson's voyage, or in the somewhat more definite story of Leif Ericson, if we concur in the

assumption of their modern editor that in these we have
the earliest records of the discovery of Newfoundland,
Nova Scotia, Massachusetts, Rhode Island, Long Island,
and Connecticut. In a subsequent brief *résumé* of the
subject, Professor Rafn remarks : " It is the total result
of the nautical, geographical, and astronomical evidences
in the original documents, which places the situation of
the countries discovered beyond all doubt. The number
of days' sail between the several newly-found lands, the
striking description of the coasts, especially the white
sand-banks of Nova Scotia, and the long beaches and
downs of a peculiar appearance on Cape Cod (the *Kia-
larnes* and *Furdustrandir* of the Northmen), are not to
be mistaken. In addition hereto we have the astronomical remark that the shortest day in Vinland was
nine hours long, which fixes the latitude of 41° 24' 10",
or just that of the promontories which limit the en-
trances to Mount Hope Bay, where Leif's booths were
built, and in the district around which the old Northmen had their head establishment, which was named by
them *Hóp.*" This nautical and astronomical evidence,
however, is far from being so precise as the geographical
deductions imply. Montgomery, in the notes to his
Greenland, observes : " Leif and his party wintered
there, and observed that on the shortest day the sun
rose about eight o'clock, which may correspond with the
forty-ninth degree of latitude, and denotes the situation
of Newfoundland, or the River St. Lawrence." The
data are the mere vague allusions of a traveller's tale;
and it is indeed the most unsatisfactory feature of those
Sagas that the later the voyagers, the more confused and
inconsistent their narratives become on all points of
detail. This is specially observable in reference to
Thorfinn Karlsefne's expedition to Vinland, in the beginning of the eleventh century, "when the folks in

Brattahlid began to urge greatly that Vinland the Good should be explored." He, too, visited Litla Helluland, or Newfoundland, and discovered Cape Sable Island, as is supposed ; giving to it the name of Bjarney, or Bear Island, from a bear (*björn*) killed by some of his party there. Pursuing their coasting voyage, he and his company visited the same points seen before by Leif; gathered grapes, and also corn in Vinland; settled there for a time, and—as we shall find by and by,—left their mark behind them.

That voyagers from the Old World may long before have gazed on the same shores which first delighted the watchers from the deck of the " Santa Maria," on the 12th of October 1492, is by no means an improbable thing. The rude undecked " Pinta" and " Niña," which, with the " Santa Maria," constituted the squadron of Columbus, were certainly not better fitted to dare the broad Atlantic than the ships which bore to Tyre and Carthage the mineral wealth of the Kassiterides. Much less can it excite any reasonable doubt that the hardy Norse voyagers who made permanent settlements on the coasts and islands of the Mediterranean, established themselves in the Orkneys and the Hebrides, and discovered and colonized Iceland and Greenland, should have extended their exploratory voyages southward from the latter to the coasts of Newfoundland or the New England shores. The voyage from Greenland, or even from Iceland, to the coast of Maine, was not more hazardous or difficult than from the native fiords of the vikings to the coasts and islands of the Mediterranean. The wonder rather seems that those whom the bleak northern ocean, and the dreary shores of Iceland, could not deter from discovery and permanent colonization ; and to whose hardy endurance the icebound coasts of Davis Straits presented an aspect begirt with such at-

tractions that they conferred on it the name of Greenland, should have failed, not only to discover, but
permanently to colonize the Atlantic shores of the New
World with the same indomitable adventurers who supplanted the Franks of Gaul, and conquered the Saxons
of England.

The question naturally suggests itself to the mind,
after dwelling on earlier or later glimpses of such ante-
Columbian explorers : Has no memorial of ancient
Phœnician or Carthaginian, Egyptian, Greek, or younger
Norse voyager, survived as a voice from the past, to tell
of such early intercourse between the Old World and
the New? The presence of the pagan and Christian
Norsemen is still attested in the British Isles by weapons,
implements, sepulchral memorials, and above all by inscriptions. Norse runic inscriptions have been found
even beneath the foundation of ancient London, mingling
with its Roman, Saxon, and mediæval heirlooms. They
have followed the Northmen to their Mediterranean
homes ; and Professor Rafn has recently undertaken the
interpretation of an inscription in the same northern
runes, on the marble lion of the Piræus, now at the
Arsenal of Venice, which, among other Varangians in
the service of the Greek Empire, commemorates, as he
believes, the same Harold Hardrada, who fell at the
battle of Stamford Bridge, A.D. 1066, to whom our
Saxon Harold offered " seven feet of ground, or, since
he was so tall, a few inches more !" Numerous similar
inscriptions in the native land of the Northmen, preserve the memorials of their wanderings. These Norse
adventurers are frequently designated *Englandsfari*, on
account of their expeditions to England ; one Icelander
is specially styled *Rafn Hlymreksfari*, owing to his
voyages to Iceland ; nor was King Sigurd of Norway
the only Norseman who won for himself the title of

Jórsalafari, or traveller to Jerusalem.[1] Northern inscriptions repeatedly refer to adventures in "the western parts," meaning, however, in general the British Isles, where corresponding evidence proves their presence. Seventeen runic inscriptions, more or less perfect, still remain in the Isle of Man, to attest the presence of Norse colonists there, six or seven centuries ago. On Holy Island, in the Firth of Clyde,—where King Haco's fleet lay for some days after his defeat at Largs in 1263, —is still legibly graven the runic memorial of Nicholas á Hæne, a Norwegian, probably of Haco's fleet. In Orkney, runic inscriptions, remarkable for their character and extent, have recently been discovered : preserving, as elsewhere, the literate memorials of the adventurous Northmen ; and precisely the same kind of evidence bears testimony to the existence of Norse colonies on the shores of Greenland, in the eleventh and twelfth centuries.

It is of importance to note the precision and simplicity of such memorials of ancient Scandinavian colonization ; for runic inscriptions are referred to by some assertors of their discovery in America, with about as definite a comprehension of what such really are, as that of the Mandan Indian, who seeing an English traveller busy reading a newspaper, pronounced it to be a medicine for sore eyes. They are spoken of as though runic inscriptions were mysterious hieroglyphics ; instead of being, as they are, records inscribed in a regular alphabet, and in a living language familiar to the student of Icelandic literature. The Greenland inscriptions, the work of contemporaries of Bjarni Herjulfson and Leif Ericson, are of this character ; and therefore show us what we have to look for, should any such records survive to

---

[1] *Mémoires de la Société Royale des Antiquaires du Nord,* 1845-49, p. 334.

attest the visits of Northmen in the tenth and eleventh centuries, to Vinland, or other early discovered locality of the American continent. To the modern Norwegian and Dane, such memorials of the hardihood and enterprise of their Norse ancestry are full of interest; nor can we fail to sympathize in the gratification with which the Danish antiquary has recovered from the ice-bound coasts of Greenland, evidence of the presence of his Norse fathers there long prior to the era of Columbus. The Scandinavian characteristics of the Greenland tablets are unmistakable; but their minute correspondence to the graven memorials of the Norsemen, alike in their native land and in the later scenes of their wanderings in Europe, has not sufficed to prevent an over-credulous zeal from persuading itself into the belief that rude Indian tracings, if not also the cracks and fissures of the natural rock, are graven inscriptions of such ante-Columbian voyagers.

The following is an accurate representation of the

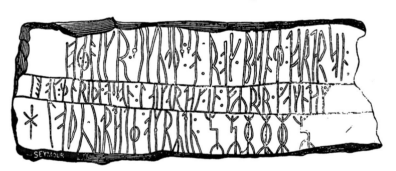

Fig. 46.—Kingiktórsoak Runic Inscription.

most remarkable among the Greenland inscriptions, and will suffice, better than any description, to convey a correct idea of a genuine Norse runic tablet. It was found in 1824, on the Island of Kingiktórsoak, in Baffin's Bay, 72° 55′ N. lat., 56° 5′ W. long.; and is now preserved in the Christiansborg Palace at Copenhagen. Of the genuine Norse characters and language of this inscription no doubt can exist. The only dubious points are the word *rydu*, variously rendered " cleared the ground," " explored," and " engraved ;" and the concluding group of figures which follow it at the right hand side of the lowest line, interpreted by Professor Rafn as the date 1135. Tied letters, or *binderuner*, are not less frequent in Runic than in Roman inscriptions. The only ones open to any difference of opinion here are at the commencement of the first and second lines. The first GV or GO, is of little moment as modifying the proper name *Guelligr*, supposed by Professor Rafn to stand for Erling. The puzzling compound rune with which the second line begins is possibly only the terminal *r* of the *Tortarsonr*, as in the previous *Sigvathsonr*, both familiar Icelandic proper names. The whole forms a record of discovery consistent with the spirit of the old Sagas.

> GOELLIGR SIGVATHSSONR OK BIANIE TORTARSON
> R OK ENRITHI OSSON LAVGARDAG IN FYRIR GAKNDAG
> HLOTHV VARDATE OK RYDV, MCXXXV.

i.e., *Elligr Sigvathson and Bjarni Tortarson, and Enrithi Odsson, on the seventh day before victory day, raised these stones and explored,* 1135.[1] The interpretation of the final date is disputed, and is certainly open to question. If the correspondence of the two first characters with the last be allowed to be sufficiently close to admit of their being regarded as repetitions of the same figure, it will be observed that the intermediate ones also agree. Rendered on this principle into Roman numerals, it would be vvxxxv, or 1035. Dr. Bryn-

---

[1] The day of victory (*Gagndag*, lit. gain-day), is stated by the Editor of the *Antiquitates Americanæ*, to be an ancient festival of the Northmen, which fell on the 25th of April.

julfson of Iceland, who concurs in the interpretation otherwise, regards the supposed numerals as merely an ornamental completion of the line. Still less room for any diversity of opinion exists in regard to an inscribed sepulchral slab graven in the same familiar runic characters, which was discovered by a Christianized Greenlander at Igalikko, about nine miles from the Danish colony of Julianeshaab, in 1829. The legend is inscribed without any alphabetic complexities or obscurities, on a thin slab of red sandstone; and reads with simple pathos as follows :—

FIG. 47.—Igalikko Runic Inscription.

VIGDIS M[AGNVS] D[OTTIR] HVILIR HER GLEDE GVTH SAL HENAR,

i.e., *Uigdis, Magnus' daughter, rests here ; may God gladden her soul.* The abbreviated proper name *Magnus*, is necessarily conjectural now ; though when the simple memorial of affection was reared, there was no need of more than the initial to preserve among the members of the little Greenland community the memory both of Norse father and child. This simple monument indicates the recognition of the Christian faith, and the presence of Christian worshippers in Greenland, certainly not later than the twelfth century. A still simpler memorial of the same kind is a wooden cross found in the cemetery of Herjulfsnes, with the single word MARIA graven in runic letters on one of its limbs. Such ancient evidences of Christian settlements on the shores of Greenland acquire an additional interest from the associations which gather around these dreary Arctic regions, with the zeal of the Moravian missionaries of a later era ; and the ruins of more than one early Christian church have been discovered, in confirmation of those proofs that Christianity was first transplanted to the New World by hardy Scandinavian voyagers from Norway and Iceland. One of these primitive ecclesiastical ruins,—memorials alike of the pious zeal and the architectural skill of the first Norse colonists,—is a plain but tastefully constructed church of squared hewn stone, which stands nearly entire, though unroofed, at Kakortok, in the same district of Brattahlid, and only a few miles distant from Igalikko, where the sepulchral tablet of Vigdis was discovered. Numerous objects of less importance, including iron implements, pottery, fragments of church bells, etc., have been found in the same locality ; throwing additional light on the civilisation of the ancient colonists of the inhospitable shores of Davis Straits, and indicating such traces as may be looked for in proof of their settlement further south on the American coasts. The latest in date of all the literate memorials of the ancient Arctic colony is probably a sepulchral slab found in 1831, at Ikigeit, lat. 60° N. It is in Roman characters, though in the old Norse tongue. The letters are ranged in two lines, on either side of a plain cross cut on a slab of granite, one end of which, with a fragment of the inscription, is broken off. It furnishes this simple memento of the long-forgotten dead :—

HER HVILIR HRO[ALD] R KOLGRIMSS[ON]

i.e., *Here rests Roald the son of Kolgrim.*

The Norse colonies of Greenland, after being occupied,

according to Norwegian and Danish tradition, from the tenth to the fifteenth century, were as entirely lost sight of as the mysterious Vinland of the ancient Sagas ; and when at length an interest in their history revived, much fruitless labour was expended in the search for an East Greenland colony on the coast lying directly west from Iceland. Of the fabled charms of the new Hesperian region discovered within the Arctic Circle, yet meriting by the luxuriant verdure of its fertile valleys its name of Greenland, many a Norse legend pictured the enviable delights ; and some of these, as well as the traditions of the lost Vinland, our English poet, James Montgomery, had embodied in the cantos of his *Greenland*, long before the *Antiquitates Americanœ* issued from the Copenhagen press.

Among older memorials of the colonies of Greenland and the mythic Vinland, it is recorded that towards the middle of the seventeenth century, an oar was drifted on the coast of Iceland bearing this inscription in runic characters : OFT VAR EK DASA DUR EK DRO THICK. *Oft was I weary when I drew thee.* To this the poet refers in his fourth canto when alluding to the then unrecovered traces of the old Greenland colonies, in following the later route of the Moravian Brethren in their generous exile :—

> " Here, while in peace the weary pilgrims rest,
> Turn we our voyage from the new-found west,
> Sail up the current of departed time,
> And seek along its banks that vanished clime,
> By ancient Scalds in Runic verse renowned,
> Now like old Babylon no longer found.
> ' *Oft was I weary when I toiled at thee ;*
> This on an oar abandoned to the sea
> Some hand had graven. From what foundered boat
> It fell ; how long on ocean's waves afloat ;
> Who marked it with that melancholy line :
> No record tells. Greenland, such fate was thine ;

> Whate'er thou wast, of thee remains no more
> Than a brief legend on a foundling oar ;
> And he whose song would now revive thy fame,
> Grasps but the shadow of a mighty name."

Since the poet penned these lines, other and more
definite evidences, as we have seen, have revealed contemporary records, telling of the ancient Greenland
Norsemen, the reputed discoverers of Vinland, and the
explorers of Rhode Island and Massachusetts. They are
also affirmed to have pursued their explorations far beyond such accessible points of the American continent,
and to have acquired a knowledge of lands alike in the
northern latitude of Wellington Channel, and on the
coast of Florida.[1] We have seen the characteristics of
their undoubted memorials on the Western shores of the
Atlantic, and know what to look for on other sites.
They were prone to leave such graphic records of their
presence, and have transmitted the habit to their collateral descendants. But the modern Englishman and
the Anglo-American are notorious for the furor which
finds its gratification in inscribing alike on the walls of
temple or ruined tower, and on the remotest and most
inaccessible cliffs, the memorials of their presence. The
pyramids, temples, and catacombs of the Nile Valley ;
the summits of the Alps, the Andes, and the Himalayas ;
cliffs of remotest Arctic and Antarctic regions ; and all
the more familiar and favourite haunts of modern travel,

---

[1] In the sketch of the discovery of America by the Northmen already
referred to, Professor C. C. Rafn adds :—"The Northmen were also acquainted
with American land still farther to the south, called by them *Hvitramanna-
land* (the land of the White Men), or *Irland it Mikla* (Great Ireland). The
exact situation of this country is not stated ; it was probably North and
South Carolina, Georgia, and Florida. In 1266, some priests at Gardar, in
Greenland, set on foot a voyage of discovery to the Arctic regions of America.
An astronomical observation proves that this took place through Lancaster
Sound and Barrow's Strait to the latitude of Wellington's Channel. The
last memorandum supplied by the old Icelandic records is a voyage from
Greenland to Markland in 1347."

will tell to other ages of the wanderings of the venturous
Briton and his sturdy American sons. But this craving
for such fame is acquired by neither as an Anglo-Saxon
heritage. Anglo-Saxon runes are of the rarest occurrence
in Britain, and nearly unknown beyond its limits; and
Englishmen doubtless inherit this, as well as the spirit of
maritime enterprise, and many other characteristic attributes of the modern stock, from their hardy Danelagh
ancestry. The Norseman was proud of his wanderings,
and delighted to record explorations of far-distant regions,
on his father's or his brother's *bautastene.* No wonder,
therefore, when the antiquaries of Copenhagen were on
the track of the long-lost Vinland, that they demanded
of their American correspondents the production of
monuments and inscriptions corroborative of the supposed ante-Columbian wanderings of Leif Ericson or
Thorfinn Karlsefne, similar to those produced by themselves from Greenland. Nor were our modern Vinlanders
less eager to respond; for the Rhode Island Historical
Society, replying through its learned secretary, did forthwith produce the required inscriptions and memorials:
even to the famous "Danish Round Tower" at Newport,
which the vulgar had been profane enough to reckon
nothing more than an old windmill!

But the most memorable, if not notorious of all the
so-called monuments of the Massachusetts Northmen is
the famous Assonet or Dighton Rock, on the east bank
of the Taunton river: a relic of considerable value in
relation to our present inquiries. It might be assumed
with great probability that investigations instituted fully
three centuries after the opening up of a regular intercourse between Europe and America should fail to discover, in the long-settled New England States, any memorials of older colonists; though such evidence may
have been in existence at a time when the Pilgrim

Fathers had other things to occupy their thoughts than the relics of imaginary predecessors. Anglo-Roman inscriptions, as we know, have been built into the masonry of ancient churches, mediæval strongholds, and even modern farm-houses. The · islanders, who were thus indifferent to the memorials of older British colonists, were not likely, when transplanted to the wilds of the New World, to give greater heed to graven rocks, or such rudely inscribed runic slabs as Leif Ericson or Thorfinn Karlsefne may have left behind them. Such seemed a reasonable argument; but happily for us, the Dighton Rock supplies an unanswerable reply to any such assumptions, though not precisely in the form which some of its modern interpreters have assigned to it.

The history of this inscription is scarcely surpassed in the interest it has excited, or the novel phases it has exhibited at successive epochs of theoretical speculation, by any Perusinian, Engubine, or Nilotic riddle. When the taste of American antiquaries inclined towards Phœnician relics, the Dighton inscription conformed to their opinions; and with changing tastes it has proved equally compliant. In 1783 the Rev. Ezra Stiles, D.D., President of Yale College, when preaching before the Governor and State of Connecticut, appealed to the Dighton Rock, graven, as he believed, in the old Punic or Phœnician character and language : in proof that the Indians were of the accursed seed of Canaan, and were to be displaced and rooted out by the European descendants of Japhet! " The Phœnicians," he affirms, " charged the Dighton and other rocks in Narraganset Bay with Punic inscriptions remaining to this day, which last I myself have repeatedly seen and taken off at large, as did Professor Sewell. He has lately transmitted a copy of this inscription to Mr. Gebelin of the Parisian Academy of Sciences, who, comparing them with the Punic palæography, judges them to be Punic, and has interpreted them as denoting that the ancient Carthaginians once visited these distant regions."[1] To this, accordingly, Humboldt refers, when he remarks : " The Anglo-American antiquaries have an inscription which they suppose to be Phœnician, and which is engraved on the Dighton rocks in Narraganset Bay, near the banks of Taunton River, twelve leagues south of Boston. From the end of the seventeenth century downward, drawings have been repeatedly made, but so dissimilar, that it is difficult to recognise them as copies of the same original. Count de Gebelin does not hesitate, with the learned Dr. Stiles, to regard these marks as a Carthaginian inscription. He says, with that enthusiasm which is natural to him, but which is highly mischievous in discussions of this kind, that this inscription has arrived most opportunely from the New World, to confirm his ideas on the origin of nations ; and that it is manifestly a Phœnician monument. A picture in the foreground represents an alliance between the American people and the foreign nation, who have arrived by the winds of the north from a rich and industrious country."[2] Here, then, we perceive the very materials we stand in need of. Change but this *Punic* into a *Runic* inscription, and the winds of the north will fit the Scandinavian Icelanders far better than voyagers from the Mediterranean Sea. Humboldt, indeed, throws out the hint in a subsequent paragraph, which was ultimately turned to good account. But meanwhile let us retrace the history of this famous inscription.

So early as 1680, Dr. Danforth executed what he characterized as " a faithful and accurate representation of the inscription" on Dighton Rock. In 1712, the celebrated Dr. Cotton Mather procured drawings of the same, and transmitted them to the Secretary of the

[1] *Archæologia*, vol. viii. p. 291.   [2] *Vues des Cordillères*, vol. i. p. 180.

Royal Society of London, with a description, printed in the *Philosophical Transactions* for 1714, in which it is described as an inscription in which are seven or eight lines, about seven or eight feet long, and about a foot wide, each of them engraven with unaccountable characters, *not like any known character.*" In 1730, Dr. Isaac Greenwood, Hollisian Professor at Cambridge, New England, took up the subject, and communicated to the Society of Antiquaries of London a drawing of the same inscription, accompanied with a description which proves the great care with which his copy was executed. In 1768, Mr. Stephen Sewell, Professor of Oriental Languages at Cambridge, New England, took a careful copy, the size of the original, and deposited it in the Museum of Harvard University ; and a transcript of this was forwarded to the Royal Society of London, six years later, by Mr. James Winthrope, Hollisian Professor of Mathematics. In 1786, the Rev. Michael Lort, D.D., one of the Vice-Presidents of the Society of Antiquaries of London, again brought the subject, with all its accumulated illustrations, before that learned society ;[1] and Colonel Vallency undertook to prove that the inscription was neither Phœnician nor Punic but Siberian.[2] Subsequently, Judge Winthrops executed another drawing in 1788 ; and again we have others by Dr. Baylies and Mr. Goodwin in 1790, by Mr. Kendall in 1807, by Mr. Job Gardner in 1812 ; and finally, in 1830, by a Commission appointed by the ·Rhode Island Historical Society, and communicated to the Antiquaries of Copenhagen with elaborate descriptions : which duly appear in their *Antiquitates Americanæ*, in proof of novel and very remarkable deductions.

Surely no inscription ancient or modern, not even the Behistun cuneatics, or the trilingual Rosetta Stone, ever

---

[1] *Archæologia*, vol. viii. p. 290. [2] *Ibid.* p. 302.

received more faithful study. After inspecting the rude
scrawls of which it chiefly consists, it is pleasant to
feel assured of this, at least : that when learned divines,
professors, and linguists have thus perseveringly questioned this New England sphinx for upwards of a century and a half, we have good proof that no more
valuable inscriptions have been allowed to perish unrecorded. But the most curious matter relating to this
written rock is that after being thus put to the question
by learned inquisitors for a hundred and fifty years, it
did at length yield a most surprising response. The
description given by Professor Greenwood of his own
process of copying, and by Professor Winthrope of the
method pursued by his colleague, Mr. Sewell,—as well
as the assiduity and zeal of other copyists,—would under
all ordinary circumstances have seemed to render any
further reference to the stone itself superfluous. But
no sooner do the Danish antiquaries write to their Rhode
Island correspondents, with a hint of Leif Ericson and
other old Norsemen's New England explorations, than
the Dighton Rock grows luminous; and the Rhode Island
Commission sends a new drawing to Copenhagen, duly
engraved, with all the others, in the *Antiquitates Americanæ*, from which the learned Danes, Finn Magnusen, and
Charles C. Rafn,—as indeed the most unlearned of English
or American readers may,—discern the name of Thorfinn,
with an exact, though by no means so manifest enumera-
tion of the associates who, according to the Saga, accompanied Karlsefne's expedition to Vinland, in A.D. 1007.

The annals of antiquarian exploration record many
marvellous disclosures, but few more surprising than
this. One could fancy the learned Dr. Danforth, or the
painful Dr. Cotton Mather, responding with the delighted
antiquary, when Lovel—like our Rhode Island Commissioners, having ascertained what to look for,—made out

on the lintel of Monkbarns' postern the mitre of the
venerable Abbot of Trotcosey, "*See what it is to have
younger eyes!*" The inscription, as has been said, is
readable by the most unlearned; for, notwithstanding
sundry efforts in the pages of the *Antiquitates Americanæ* to discover runic characters, the letters which had
so surprisingly come out on the oft-copied Dighton Rock,
read in tolerably plain Roman capitals : : O R F I N S.
At the meeting of the American Association for the
Advancement of Science, held at Albany in 1856, I had
an opportunity of inspecting a cast of the Dighton Rock.
No more confused and indistinct scrawl ever tried the
eyes of antiquarian seer. Mine proved wholly unable to
discern the invaluable holograph of the ancient Norse
Columbus. Indeed, the rough natural surface of the
weathered rock on which the figures have been sketched
with the imperfect tools of some Indian artist, and their
own indistinctness, account for the variations in the successive copies, as well as for the fanciful additions which
enthusiastic copyists have succeeded in tracing amid the
obscure lines.

Mr. Schoolcraft tested the origin and significance of
the Dighton Rock inscription, by submitting a copy of
it to Chingwauk, an intelligent Indian chief, familiar
with the native system of picture-writing. The result
was an interpretation of the whole as the record of an
Indian triumph over some rival native tribe; and the
conviction on Mr. Schoolcraft's part that the graven
rock is simply an example of Indian rock-writing, or
muzzinnabik, attributable to the Wabenakies of New
England.[1] In the engraving of 1790 an O R appears,
which expanded into Thorfinn, and his fifty-one followers, in 1830. These Chingwauk could make nothing
of, and hence Mr. Schoolcraft inferred that they were

[1] *History of the Indian Tribes,* vol. iv. p. 120, plate 14.

genuine additions, made by the Norsemen to an Indian record.   But subsequent inspection of the original satisfied him that the runic or Roman characters are imaginary, and that the whole is of Indian origin, an opinion which General Washington is said to have expressed at Cambridge so early as 1789.

Such is the conviction reluctantly forced on the mind of the most enthusiastic believer in the ante-Columbian discovery and colonization of New England by the Northmen, in reference to this famous Dighton Rock, after all the fascinating glimpses of an American prehistoric era which the learning of Danish antiquaries had conjured up for his behoof.   The runic records of the Dighton Rock, it may be presumed, have lost credit with every honest inquirer ; not so, however, the traditions of the Northmen, or the faith in the discovery of some more credible memorial of their presence.

One of the latest discoveries of these supposed records of the Northmen was produced before the Ethnological section at the Albany meeting of the American Association, in 1856, by Dr. A. E. Hamlin, of Bangor, and is described in the printed Transactions.[1]   The accompanying woodcut (Fig. 48) is copied from the cast, then

FIG. 48.—Monhegan Inscription.

exhibited, of this supposed runic inscription, which appears on a ledge of hornblende, on the Island of Monhegan, off the coast of Maine.   Dr. Hamlin suggests that the inscription is the work of " some illiterate Scandinavian, whose knowledge of the runic form was very imperfect ;" and he then proceeds to adduce reasons for assigning Monhegan, the Kennebec River, and Merry Meeting Bay, as the true localities of Leif's wintering place in Vinland, instead of the previously assumed Pacasset River and Mount Hope Bay. Dr. Hamlin, however, duly forwarded a copy of the inscription to Copenhagen, and a version of it appears in the *Séance Annuelle du* 14 *Mai* 1859, bearing a very remote resemblance to the accompanying engraving of it, and looking a great deal liker runes than the original can possibly do. The Danish antiquaries on this occasion, however, abandoned the attempt at interpretation ; though there is something amusing in the contrast between the New Englander's theory of an illiterate Norseman scrawling incomprehensible runic characters on the rock, and that of the Danish elucidator, who observes : " The Indians have, without doubt, profited in various ways by their intercourse with the Northmen, to whom they were probably indebted for much knowledge ; and it is apparently to their instruction, acquired in this manner, that we owe several of their sculptures on the rocks which are met with in these regions."[1] The Monhegan inscription, thus bandied about between illiterate Northmen and Indians, is in irregular lines about six inches long, and runs obliquely across the face of a rock, where the general lines of stratification are horizontal, and presented no impediment to its characters being placed in the usual upright position. It is just as truly a record in Scandinavian runes as that of the Dighton Rock. When properly classed, it will more probably take its place with the famous Swedish Runamo inscription, which, after its characters had been interpreted with wonderful minuteness, turned

---

[1] *Société Royale des Antiquaires du Nord,* 1859, p. 25.

out to be only the natural markings on a block of granite.

Of a very different character is another inscription to which we now turn. If the "Grave Creek Stone" could be relied upon as a genuine relic, it would constitute the most remarkable of all disclosures which the explorations of the ancient mounds and earthworks of the New World have brought to light. Mr. Schoolcraft has specially devoted himself to the elucidation of this marvellous inscription; and after corresponding on the subject with learned societies both in Europe and America, he has finally placed it in his class of Intrusive Antiquities. In the year 1838, soon after the publication of the *Antiquitates Americanæ*, the famous Grave Creek mound, on the banks of the Ohio River, was excavated by its proprietor, and converted into an exhibition. The mound, which is one of the largest on the continent, has already been described; and its genuine characteristics are such as stand in need of no adventitious aid to confer a legitimate interest. But along with the shell-beads, copper bracelets, and other relics common to such sepulchral mounds, which were recovered in the

Fig. 49.—Grave Creek Mound Inscription.

course of the excavations, an inscribed oval disk of white sandstone—engraved here the same size from a wax impression of the original,—was produced as having been found near one of the skeletons at the base of the mound. The stone measures three-fourths of an inch in thickness, and is engraved with three lines of unknown characters, as shown in the woodcut (Fig. 49). It is unique among American graven or sepulchral relics, and of its genuineness Mr. Schoolcraft does not express the slightest doubt ; nor can he be considered unreasonably mysterious as to the indications of its ancient source. After corresponding with Professor Rafn of Copenhagen, M. Jomard of Paris, and other foreign and native scholars, he communicated an elaborate analysis of the inscription to the American Ethnological Society.[1] In this he shows that the cosmopolitan little disk of sandstone contains twenty-two alphabetic characters, four of which correspond with the ancient Greek, four with the Etruscan, five with the old Northern runes, six with the ancient Gaelic, seven with the old Erse, ten with the Phœnician, fourteen with the Anglo-Saxon—or old British as it is somewhat oddly designated,—and sixteen with the Celtiberic ; besides which, he adds, " possibly equivalents for these characters may be found in the old Hebrew," a suggestion designed, no doubt, for those who may still have faith in the descent of the red men from the lost ten tribes. It thus appears that this ingenious little stone is even more accommodating than the Dighton Rock, in adapting itself to all conceivable theories of ante-Columbian colonization ; and in fact constitutes an epitome of the prehistoric literature of the New World. Had Sir Henry Rawlinson dug up such an olio of all languages at one of the corners of the tower of Babel it might have less surprised us, than as the product of the great Virginian sepulchral mound.

This curious analysis, so contrary to all previous philological experience, does not seem to have staggered

---

[1] *Transactions of the American Ethnological Society*, vol. i. p. 392.

the faith of its elucidator, in an inscription, which, if genuine, certainly merits all the attention it has received, as without exception the most remarkable among the antiquities hitherto recovered from the ancient mounds. That a series of simple linear alphabetic figures should be found to present certain analogies to runic and other alphabets, even including the cuneatic characters on the Assyrian marbles, will surprise no one who has made for himself the easy experiment of trying to invent a new series of combinations of lines and curves differing from such alphabets. But apart from internal evidence, the fact was notorious that Dr. James W Clemens communicated to Dr. Morton all the details of the exploration of the Grave Creek mound, which appear in the *Crania Americana*, without any reference to the discovery of the inscribed stone. Nor was it till the excavated vault had been fitted up by its proprietor for exhibition, to all who cared to pay for the privilege of admission, that the marvellous inscription opportunely came to light to add to the attractions of the show. Nevertheless, Mr. Schoolcraft retains his faith unchanged, and after raising the question of Phœnician, Iberian, Danish, or Celtic origin in his first paper on the subject, he thus sums up his later and more matured views in his *History of the Indian Tribes:*—" An inscription in apparently some form of the Celtic character came to light in the Ohio Valley in 1838. This relic occurred in one of the principal tumuli of Western Virginia (the ancient *Huitramannaland*). It purports to be of an apparently early period, viz., 1328. It is in the Celtiberic character, but has not been deciphered. Its archæology appears corroborative of the Cimbrian and the Tuscarora traditions, representing a white race in the ante-Columbian periods in this part of America."[1]   The

[1] *History of the Indian Tribes*, vol. iv. p. 118.

genius of archæology might well lavish her favours more
liberally on votaries who make so much out of her
smallest contributions. The parenthetical introduction
of Professor Rafn's *Huitramannaland* is a fine example
of rhetorical allusion. The unhesitating determination
of its inscription as in "*the* Celtiberic character" won-
derfully simplifies the previous alternatives ; and it
could never be surmised from his text, that the historian
of the Indian tribes assigns his precise date of 1328 on
no better authority than the statement of Mr. Tomlinson,
the proprietor of the mound, that the section of a large
white oak which stood on its summit disclosed about
five hundred annual rings ; which, supposing the oak
to have taken root the very year of the mound's completion, and the rings to have been exactly the product
of five centuries, would indicate the said date. Dr.
Clemens, however, a much more impartial and trustworthy witness, states the annual layers of the oak at
three hundred, and says nothing about the inscription.
But its alphabetic marvels were hailed with rapture by
the wondering *savans* to whom they were submitted.
The antiquaries of Copenhagen published a description
of this "Runic inscription found in America ;" hesitated
as to its authors between "tribes from the Pyrenean
Peninsula," and inhabitants of the British Isles ; but
apologized for qualifying with any possibility of doubt
the certainty as to its being "of European origin, and
of a date anterior to the close of the tenth century,"
because the European alphabets with which they had
compared it are themselves of a very ancient Asiatic
origin. They added, moreover, the somewhat dangerous
hope, "that the numerous amateurs of antiquity in
America may continue to exert themselves for the discovery of more monuments of such high value."[1]

[1] *Mémoires de la Société Royale des Antiquaires du Nord*, 1840-44, p. 127

Ancient European, then, the Virginian inscription is, unless it be still more ancient Asiatic. But Africa, too, has its champions. M. Jomard, President of the Geographical Society of Paris, pronounced the riddle to be Libyan ; and his opinion has since met with independent confirmation. Mr. William B. Hodgson, formerly American Consul at Tunis, in his *Notes on Northern Africa,*[1] after discussing the vestiges of the ancient Libyan languages, and noticing certain Numidian inscriptions found at the oasis of Ghraat and elsewhere : proceeds to comment on the Grave Creek Stone as " an inscription found in the United States, and containing characters very similar to the Libyan ;" and after detailing the discoveries in the mound, he thus exclaims : " Whence was the ivory brought ? Who was the gorgeous chieftain whose engraved signet was found by his side ? Did he come from the Canary Islands, where the Numidian language and characters prevailed ? or from the land of the Celto-Iberians, whose writing was somewhat similar ? Shall we recur to the lost Atlantis ? Could any of the Carthaginian or African vessels, which usually visited the Fortunate or Canary Islands, have been carried by accident to the New World ? The peopling of America is quite as likely to be due to Africa and Europe as to Asia." Without attempting to determine the true answer to his queries, Mr. Hodgson concludes that there is no apparent difficulty in supposing the inscribed stone to have been brought from Africa by accident or design. Dr. Wills de Hass, an American archæologist, has recently communicated to the American Ethnological Society an elaborate paper, which he intimates his intention of publishing, in proof of the authenticity of the Grave Creek Stone ; meanwhile we can only regret that

[1] *Notes on Northern Africa, the Sahara and Soudan, in relation to the Ethnography, Languages, etc., of those Countries,* p. 44.

a relic which, if genuine, is an object of such just interest, should have been given to the world under such equivocal circumstances, and elucidated with so much indiscreet zeal.

The Virginian inscription is not, however, the sole example of graven characters found on the American continent in connexion with native antiquities. In 1859, Dr. John C. Evans of Pemberton, New Jersey, communicated to the American Ethnological Society an account of a stone axe inscribed in unknown characters, which had been recently ploughed up on a neighbouring farm. The axe, which measures about six inches long by three and a half broad, is engraved here (Fig. 50) from a

FIG. 50.—Pemberton Inscribed Axe.

drawing furnished to me by Dr. Evans. When exhibited to the Ethnological Society, Mr. Thomas Ewbank remarked, that " it seemed strange that the characters, if intended to signify anything, should be placed where they would be most exposed to being worn away by the use of the instrument." Two of the characters are placed on one side, in the groove for the handle, the others apparently form a continuous line, running round both

sides of the axe-blade, as extended here (Fig. 51). This
is not, however, an altogether unique example of an engraved axe. The practice of decorating implements of

FIG. 51.—Pemberton Axe Inscription.

the simplest forms with graven and hieroglyphic characters has already been illustrated in a previous chapter, in
one of the Carib shell knives (Fig. 6) from Barbadoes.[1]
Such devices probably indicate the dedication of the
weapon or implement to some special and sacred purpose, such as the rites of Mexican sacrifice rendered so
common.

Humboldt figures, in his *Vues des Cordillères,* a
hatchet made of a compact feldspar passing into true
jade, obtained by him from the Professor of Mineralogy
in the School of Mines at Mexico, with its surface
covered with graven figures or characters. In commenting on this interesting relic, M. Humboldt adds : " Notwithstanding our long and frequent journeys in the
Cordilleras of the two Americas, we were never able to
discover the jade *in situ;* and this rock being so rare,
we are the more astonished at the great quantity of
hatchets of jade which are found on turning up the soil
in localities formerly inhabited, extending from the Ohio
to the mountains of Chili." [2]   Here also, therefore, we
have a glimpse of wide-spread ancient trade and barter
carried on throughout the American continent in ancient

[1] See vol. i. p. 209.   [2] *Vues des Cordillères,* vol. ii. p. 146, plate xxviii.

FIG. 52.—Engraved Aztec Hatchet.

times, and of a wider intercourse, embracing both North and South America, than the investigators of the traces of former civilisation have been willing to recognise. The accompanying woodcut (Fig. 52) represents the graven "Aztec Hatchet," as Humboldt designates it. It has a certain interest in illustrating a practice of which the Pemberton axe furnishes a new example. Dr. E. H. Davis, who has carefully examined the latter, informs me that though the graven characters have been retouched in the process of cleaning it, and apparently attempted to be deepened by the original discoverer, yet that their edges present an appearance of age perfectly consistent with the idea of their genuineness. Mr. S. R. Gaskell, by whom this axe was found on his own farm, is described as a highly respectable and trustworthy man ; and no attempt to turn the relic to account, either for notoriety or pecuniary gain, furnishes any tangible reason for questioning its authenticity. It may be worth while adding, that this discovery of an inscribed stone axe is not without a parallel among the antiquities of the old country. A writer in the *Londonderry Sentinel* of November 19, 1858, after noticing the exhumation of various ancient cinerary urns at Cumber and Kincull, County Derry, adds : "Some time ago a curious mallet, or hatchet of gigantic dimensions, composed of solid flint, and apparently covered with ancient characters, was dug up in the same district, but through the ignorance of the parties into whose hands it came, this invaluable relic was unfortunately destroyed. It weighed, we are informed, twelve or thirteen pounds, having been broken up to make *a ten-pound weight* for common uses ! Had this precious stone been preserved, it might have thrown light on a period of our national history which at present is involved in nearly total obscurity. The urns referred to are now in the valuable antiquarian collection of

William L. Browne, Esq., proprietor of the Cumber
estate."

The report is too vague to be of much value ; but no
relics are so fascinating in their promised disclosures of
the past, or so justly entitled to value, as those graven
with inscriptions, even in unknown characters ; if their
genuineness be only well attested and free from all suspicion. The Grave Creek Stone and the Pemberton
wedge inscriptions, if once authenticated, would altogether contradict the idea that "no trace of an alphabet
existed at the time of the conquest of the continent of
America."[1] The sole literate remains of Pelasgic Italy,
found at Ægylla in Southern Etruria, do not greatly
exceed in amount these supposed relics of America's forgotten tongues. Dennis gives a list of some thirty-six
or thirty-seven words as the extreme limits of our knowledge of the Etruscan language. Even the precise value
of its alphabet is undetermined ; and the solitary inscription on the Perusinian pillar has supplied the chief
materials for such linguistic inductions relative to the
ancient Rasena, as the Engubine tablets have done for
the Umbrian. The doubt and confusion introduced into
such ethnographic inquiries by a single forgery are so
mischievous, that the meekest conclave of scholars could
scarcely be trusted with the functions of the American
Judge Lynch against such an offender. Happily for
science, the knowledge of the culprit is generally on a
par with his morality.

Of another class of mound-disclosures, which gather
their chief marvels under the light of modern eyes, one
figured and described by Mr. Schoolcraft, in the *American Ethnological Transactions*, opens up, with the help
of its ingenious interpreter, glimpses of ante-Columbian
science, and of comprehensive significance in its graven

---

[1] *Types of Mankind*, p. 283.

devices, not less marvellous than the polyglot characters of the Grave Creek Stone. Having undertaken to treat, by an exhaustive process, " the Grave Creek Mound, the antique inscription discovered in its excavation, and the connected evidences of the occupancy of the Mississippi Valley during the Mound period, and prior to the discovery of America by Columbus," he introduces this subsidiary Mound relic as a "figured stone sphere, an antique globe, the most important discovery in the minor mounds in its bearing on the inscription." It is a spherical stone, with no other characteristic of a globe about it than pertains to any schoolboy's marble, but having sundry lines graven on one side within a circle. As shown in

the woodcut, these form a lozenge, triangle, etc., with no greater appearance of art or mystery to the uninitiated eye than an ordinary masonic mark. But here is what can be made of such markings, by one whose fancy has been stimulated to the degree requisite for interpreting their esoteric teach-

Fig. 53.—Graven Stone Sphere.

ings :—" The stone, which is a sphere, measures $4\frac{1}{10}$ inches in circumference. The inscription lines are enclosed in a circle of $\frac{8}{10}$ths ; they are accompanied by a single alphabetic sign. It is the Greek Delta, which is also the letter T or D in several of the ancient alphabets. This character is also the letter Tyr, in the Icelandic Runic, representing the god Tyr, or a bull. On the assumption that this inscription is geographical, it may be inquired whether it is a figure of the globe, denoting the divisions of land and water, or a minor portion of it. The ancients did not believe the world to have a spherical shape. Either the stone, therefore, is of an astronomical character, or is of a date subsequent to Copernicus ; or it evinces that he was anticipated in the theory of convexity by the ancient Americans."[1] This inscribed stone sphere has attracted little attention compared with the "Grave Creek Stone ;" but if the above alternatives logically exhaust the choice of inferential truths, it is surely the more marvellous relic of the two!

A like process is pursued with sundry other Mound relics. A stone ornamented with a simple pattern of alternate circles and squares, becomes a "heraldic record." "It may be regarded, perhaps, as astrological and genealogical, and as such a memorial or species of arms of a distinguished person or family." Again, several perforated cylinders of soft steatite, found in one of the mounds, included a tube twelve inches long. This forthwith becomes a "telescopic device." The bore, which is four-fifths of an inch in diameter, diminishes at one end abruptly to one-fifth. "By placing the eye at this diminished point, the extraneous light is shut from the pupil, and distant objects are more clearly discerned. The effect is telescopic, and is the same which is known to be produced by directing the sight to the heavens from the bottom of a well, an object which we now understand to have been secured by the Aztec and Maia races, in their astronomical observations, by constructing tubular chambers."[2]

One other and genuine graven tablet, from the mounds discovered within the limits of Cincinnati, has already been engraved in a previous chapter,[3] and a new hypothesis offered as to its original significance and object, which may perhaps appear little less extravagant and fanciful than any that have been noted with reference to the relics of the ancient mounds. But apart from the question of its precise original use, its proprietor, Mr.

---

[1] *American Ethnological Transactions*, vol. i. p. 405.
[2] *Ibid.* vol. i. p. 406. [3] Vol. i. p. 344, Fig. 16.

Guest, remarked, in his first account of it, with equal justice and sagacity:—"The best evidence of its genuineness is this, that a person in our times could scarcely
make so perfect an engraving as this, and not make it
more perfect. The engraving represents something, whatever it is, the two sides of which are intended to be
alike, and yet no two curves or lines are precisely alike;
nor is there the least evidence of the use of our instruments to be discovered in the work. So difficult is it to
imitate, with our cultivated hands and eyes, the peculiar
imperfection of this cutting, that some excellent judges
who at first doubted the genuineness of the relic, have
changed their opinion upon trying to imitate it." Its
graven device has been characterized as a hieroglyphic
inscription, and its graduated lines have been interpreted
to embody the record of a native calendar; while the
idea of its preserving a scale of measurement on which
the great geometrical earthworks of the Mississippi
Valley were constructed, is suggested on a previous page.
Mr. Squier appears to attach no special significance to
the peculiar arrangement of lines; although the manner
in which they are introduced, limited only to part of the
border, does not seem consistent with any idea of mere
ornament. As to the devices of the Cincinnati "Cartouche," he discovers in them more resemblance to the
stalk and flower of a plant, than to any astronomical or
chronological hieroglyphic; and accordingly supposes it
may have been a mere pattern cut in relief for stamping
cloth or prepared skins.[1] If so, it embodied the germ of
wood-engraving, type-printing, and the press itself. But
it is worthy of note, that a flower-pattern so extremely
conventional as this, is at variance with the minute and
accurate imitative faculty displayed in other artistic
works of the Mound-Builders. Possibly future discoveries

[1] *American Ethnological Transactions*, vol. ii. p. 199.

of objects of the same class may help to a more certain determination of its purpose and meaning.

Sober after-thought has led the historical antiquaries of Rhode Island so thoroughly to reject their older faith in the ante-Columbian relics of the district, attested by the Copenhagen authorities, that not only the Dighton Rock is in danger of being undervalued, but the famous Round Tower of Newport is unduly slighted, now that sceptics threaten to rob it of some six centuries of its reputed age. As a genuine American ruin of former generations, the old Tower forms an exceedingly attractive feature on Newport common, and the historical and poetical associations which have been ascribed to it by no means diminish its interest. When the Danish antiquaries were in search of relics of the long-lost Vinland, drawings of the Tower were despatched to them, and its authentication as an architectural monument of the Norse colonists of New England is thus unhesitatingly set forth in the supplement to the *Antiquitates Americanæ :* " There is no mistaking, in this instance, the style in which the more ancient stone edifices of the North were constructed. . . . From such characteristics as remain, we can scarcely form any other inference than one, in which I am persuaded that all who are familiar with old Northern architecture will concur, that this building was erected at a period decidedly not later than the twelfth century."[1] The poet Longfellow, accordingly, assuming its venerable origin, has associated it with another discovery of so-called Norse relics, and made it the scene of his ballad of *The Skeleton in Armour.* But the modern Skald is not the less satisfied, for all purposes of sober prose, with the date of 1678, furnished by the will of Governor Arnold for his " stone-built windmill in ye town of Newport."

[1] *Antiquitates Americanæ*, Supplement, p. 18.

In the able and well-digested review of *American Archæology*, prepared by Mr. Samuel F. Haven for the Smithsonian Institution, reference is made to the "Rutland Stone," an American counterpart to the famous Swedish Runamo Inscription, in its graphic freaks of natural crystallization.[1] It was described to the authors of the *Antiquitates Americanæ* as "a large stone, on which is a line of considerable length in unknown characters, regularly placed, and the strokes are filled up with a black composition nearly as hard as the rock itself." Ancient enough this inscription is for the most ambitious stickler for the antiquity of the New World; ancient, indeed, as the oldest of those interpreted by the author of *The Testimony of the Rocks*, and inscribed by the same hand that formed its rocky matrix. Other inscriptions, not much more available for historical purposes, are produced by the same author in his review of the spurious as well as the genuine *Antiquities of the United States.* Among these "The Alabama Stone" is an innocent piece of blundering, not without its significance. It was discovered near the Black Warrior river, upwards of thirty years ago, when no rumours of the old Northmen's visits to Vinland or Huitramannaland stimulated the dishonest zeal of relic-hunters; and its mysterious Roman uncials, and remote ante-Columbian date, were only wondered at as an inexplicable riddle. As copied by its original transcribers, this inscription of the thirteenth century ran thus :--

HISKNEHNDREV.

1232.

Had this Alabama stone turned up opportunely in 1830, when the antiquaries of New England were in possession of a roving commission on behoof of Finn Magnussen

---

[1] *The Archæology of the United States*, p. 134.

and other Danish heirs and assignees of old Ari Marson,
who knows what might have been made of so tempting
a morsel? From the *Annales Flateyenses*, we learn of
"Eric Grœnlandinga biskup," who, in A.D. 1121, went
to seek out Vinland ; and in the following century, the
Annales Holenses, recovered by Torfæus from the epis-
copal seat of Holum in Iceland, supply this tempting
glimpse : "*faunst nyja land*," *i.e.*, new land is found.
With such a hint, what might not learned ingenuity
have done to unriddle the mysteries of the New World
in the year of grace 1232 ? Unhappily, its fate has
been to fall into the hands of Mr. Samuel F. Haven
for literary editing, which he does in this unromantic
fashion : "We have before us the Alabama Stone found
some thirty years ago near the Black Warrior river. To
our eyes, it reads HISPAN · ET · IND REX as plainly as
the same inscription on a Spanish quarter of a dollar
somewhat worn. The figures may be as above represented, but of course they cannot be intended for a
date," unless indeed it be 1532. Earlier dates than that
exist in genuine inscribed memorials of the old Spanish
Hidalgos' presence in the New World, of which the Manlius Stone is perhaps the most interesting, on account
of the locality where it was discovered.

This inscribed stone was discovered about the year
1820, in the township of Manlius, Onondaga County,
New York, by a farmer, when gathering the stones out
of a field on first bringing it into culture. It is an
irregular spherical boulder about fourteen inches in
diameter, now deposited in the museum of the Albany
Institute. On one side, which is smooth and nearly
flat, is the inscription :

Leo . De | L . . 11
VI. 1520 | ×

with the device of a serpent twining round the branch

of a tree. Like most other American relics of this class, it has been tortured into interpretations not very easily discernible by ordinary processes of rendering such simple records. " By the figure of a serpent climbing a tree, a well known passage in the Pentateuch is clearly referred to. By the date, the sixth year of the reign of the Pontiff Leo x. has been thought to be denoted. This appears to be probable, less clearly from the inscriptive phrase *Leo de Lon* vi., than from the plain date 1520, being six years after the Pontiff took the chair."[1] Again, it is assumed to be a memorial of Juan Ponce de Leon, the discoverer of Florida, and to " tally exactly with the sixth year after his landing," which, however, it does not, as that took place on *Pasqua Florid,* or Palm Sunday, A.D. 1512. The attempt, indeed, to identify the name thus rudely graven on a stray boulder either with that of the sovereign Pontiff Leo x., or with Don Juan Ponce de Leon, is only less extravagant than the persistent deciphering of that of the Icelandic Thorfinn on the Dighton Rock. Apart, however, from any such special identification of the object of the memorial on the Manlius Stone, it is a relic of considerable interest. No reasonable grounds exist for questioning its genuineness ; and we are thus supplied with an inscription of a date within twenty-eight years of the first landing of Columbus on the mainland. A discovery of this nature, associated with the earliest known period of European exploration of the American continent, in a locality so far to the northward, and so remote from the sea-coast, when taken into consideration along with the authentic traces of older Norse settlements still discoverable in Greenland, is calculated to confirm the doubts of any Scandinavian colonization of Vinland in the ages

---

[1] Schoolcraft's *Notes on the Iroquois,* p. 326. But 1520 is not the sixth year of the pontificate of Leo x., who succeeded Julius ii. in 1513.

before Columbus. That the old Northmen visited some portions of the American coasts appears to be confirmed by most credible testimony ; but that their presence was transient, and that they left no enduring evidence of their visits, seems little less certain. To the Spanish pioneers of American discovery and civilisation, in the centuries subsequent to the era of Columbus, we must, therefore, look for the earliest memorials of European adventure in the New World.

Such is an attempted review of the evidence of intercourse between the Old and the New World prior to the voyage of Columbus in 1492, and of the monumental or graven relics which seem to furnish any traces of an ante-Columbian civilisation in America otherwise than of native growth. The early traces of European presence subsequent to that date are chiefly of value, as proving the probability of some corresponding evidence of still older colonization having been recovered, if such had ever existed. The results, however, appear only to restore to vague conjecture and the doctrine of probabilities all ancient colonization or discovery of the continent of America beyond the Arctic Circle, except in so far as the Sagas of the Northmen furnish trustworthy indications that the old colonists of Iceland and Greenland coasted the North American shores, and gathered the grapes of New England six hundred and twenty-six years before the Pilgrim Fathers effected their first settlement amid the primeval forests of the New World. But if so, the glimpses they obtained were sufficiently transient. The hardy Northmen who dictated terms to the heir of Charlemagne, planted their flourishing republic on the shores of Iceland, and colonized the wintry realms of Greenland, seemed equally fitted to secure for themselves the triumphs of Columbus, Cabot, and Cortes. And how would the whole course of the world's history

have been changed had Leif Ericson and Thorfinn proved
the Pilgrim Fathers of New England ?   But it was not
so to be ; and the fruitless search which has been so
zealously pursued in the hope of recovering some trace
of the presence of Scandinavian colonists on the site of
the mysterious Vinland ; or of still older Egyptian,
Phœnician, Greek, or Punic wanderers landed by choice
or chance along the American shores : has served only
to place beyond doubt that if any such did precede
Columbus in his great discovery, they turned their visit
to no permanent account, and have left no memorials of
their premature glimpse of the Western Hemisphere.

CHAPTER XXI.

THE AMERICAN CRANIAL TYPE.

THE unsuccessful search after traces of an ante-Columbian intercourse with the New World, suffices to confirm the belief that, for unnumbered centuries throughout that ancient era, the Western Hemisphere was the exclusive heritage of nations native to the soil. Its sacred and sepulchral rites, its usages and superstitions, its arts, letters, metallurgy, sculpture, and architecture, are all peculiarly its own ; and we must now direct our attention to the physical characteristics which mark the American type of man, and endeavour to ascertain what truths may be recoverable from that source, relative to the origin, mutual influences, or essential diversities, pertaining to the civilized nations and barbarous tribes and confederacies of the continent.

Among the various grounds on which Columbus founded his belief in the existence of a continent beyond the Atlantic, special importance was attached to the fact that the bodies of two dead men had been cast ashore on the island of Flores, differing essentially in features and physical characteristics from any known race. When at length the great discoverer of the Western World had set his foot on the islands first visited by him, the peculiarities which marked the gentle and friendly race of Guanahanè were noted with curious minuteness ; and their " tawny or copper hue," their straight, coarse, black hair, strange features, and well-developed forms, were all recorded as objects of interest by the Spaniards. On his return, the little caravel of Columbus was freighted not only with gold and other coveted products of the New World, but with nine of its natives, brought from the islands of San Salvador and Hispaniola : eight of whom survived to gaze on the strange civilisation of ancient Spain, and to be themselves objects of scarcely less astonishment than if they had come from another planet. Six of these representatives of the western continent, who accompanied Columbus to Barcelona, where the Spanish court then was, were baptized with the utmost state and ceremony, as the first-fruits offered to Heaven from the new-found world. Ferdinand and the enthusiastic and susceptible Isabella, with the Prince Juan, stood sponsors for them at the font ; and when, soon after, one of them, who had been retained in the prince's household, died, no doubt as to their common humanity marred the pious belief that he was the first of his nation to enter heaven.

Such was the earliest knowledge acquired by the Old World of the singular type of humanity generically designated the Red Indian ; and the attention which its peculiarities excited, when thus displayed in their fresh novelty, has not yet exhausted itself, after an interval of upwards of three centuries and a half. That certain special characteristics in complexion, hair, and features, do pertain to the whole race or races of the American Continent, is not to be disputed. Ulloa, who spent ten years in the provinces of Mexico, Colombia, and Peru, says,—" If we have seen one American, we may be said to have seen all, their colour and make are so nearly alike."[1] Remarks involving the same idea have been

---

[1] *Chronica del Peru,* parte i. c. 19.

recorded, both before and since the visit of Ulloa to the seats of ancient American civilisation, by Spanish and other writers ; and have been subsequently quoted, with a comprehensive application undreamt of when they were uttered. In the sense in which the remark of Ulloa was made, relative to the living tribes now occupying the tropical regions of the continent, of which alone he spoke from personal observation, there is nothing specially to challenge ; but that which was originally the mere loose generalization of a traveller, has been quoted as though it involved an unquestionable dogma of science. Various causes, moreover, have tended to encourage the development of scientific theory in this direction ; so that, with the exception of the Esquimaux, the universality of certain physical characteristics peculiar to the tribes and nations of America, has been assumed by American ethnologists as an absolute postulate for the strictest purposes of scientific induction ; and is reaffirmed dogmatically, in the words of Ulloa : "*He who has seen one tribe of Indians, has seen all.*"

An idea which embraces in a simple form the solution of many difficulties, is sure to meet with ready acceptance ; and this one, affirming the homogeneous physical characteristics of the whole Red race, has been adopted almost without inquiry ; so that opinions, resulting from its easy acceptance, have been quoted by later writers in confirmation of its truth. Authorities such as Robertson the historian, and Malte Brun, who advance mere generalizations founded on no personal observation, may be classed even below Spanish travellers and colonists in estimating the value of such opinions. " The Esquimaux," says the former, " are manifestly a race of men distinct from all the nations of the American continent, in language, in disposition, and in habits of life. But

among all the other inhabitants of America there is such
a striking similitude in the form of their bodies and the
qualities of their minds, that, notwithstanding the diversities occasioned by the influence of climate, or unequal
progress of improvement, we must pronounce them to
be descended from one source."[1] Malte Brun, with more
caution, simply affirms, as the result of a long course of
physiological observations, that "the Americans, whatever their origin may be, constitute at the present day
a race essentially different from the rest of mankind."[2]
But greater importance is due to the maturely defined
views of the scientific traveller, who combined the results
of varied knowledge and profound philosophical speculation with conclusions derived from his own personal
observations.   "There is no proof," says Humboldt, in
the Introduction to his *Researches*, "that the existence
of man is much more recent in America than in the
other hemisphere. . . . The nations of America, except
those which border on the polar circle, form a single
race, characterized by the formation of the skull, the
colour of the skin, the extreme thinness of the beard,
and straight glossy hair."   But this recognition of homogeneous characteristics of the American aborigines has
been quoted to maintain views which the accompanying
remarks of this scientific traveller entirely contradict;
for, as will be afterwards noted, in the very next sentence Humboldt dwells on the striking resemblance
which the American race bears to the Asiatic Mongols,
and refers to the transitional cranial characteristics which
constitute links between the two.

Very few and partial exceptions can be quoted to the
general unanimity of American writers—some of them
justly regarded as authorities in ethnology,—in reference
to this view of the nations of the whole American con-

---

[1] Robertson's *America*, B. IV.   [2] Malte Brun, *Geog.* lib. xxv.

tinent, north and south. With the solitary exception of the Esquimaux, they are affirmed to constitute one nearly homogeneous race, varying within very narrow limits from the prevailing type ; and agreeing in so many essentially distinctive features, as to prove them a well defined, distinct species of the genus *Homo*. Lawrence, Wiseman, Agassiz, Squier, Gliddon, Nott, and Meigs, might each be quoted in confirmation of this opinion, and especially of the prevailing uniformity of certain strongly-marked cranial characteristics ; but the source of all such opinions is the justly distinguished author of the *Crania Americana*, Dr. Morton, of Philadelphia. His views underwent considerable modification on some points relating to the singular conformation observable in certain skulls found in ancient American graves, especially in reference to the influence of artificial means in perpetuating changes of form essentially different from the normal type ; but the tendencies of his matured opinions all went to confirm his original idea of universal approximation to one type throughout the New World. In some of his latest recorded views he remarks, as the result of his examination of a greatly extended series of Peruvian crania : " I at first found it difficult to conceive that the original rounded skull of the Indian could be changed into this fantastic form, and was led to suppose that the latter was an artificial elongation of a head remarkable for its length and narrowness. I even supposed that the long-headed Peruvians were a more ancient people than the Inca tribes, and distinguished from them by their cranial configuration. In this opinion I was mistaken. Abundant means of observation and comparison have since convinced me that all these variously-formed heads were originally of the same rounded shape."

Such are the latest views of Dr. Morton, as set forth

in the posthumous paper on "The Physical Type of the American Indians," contributed by him to the second volume of Mr. Schoolcraft's *History of the Indian Tribes.* In that same final contribution to his favourite science, Dr. Morton's matured views on the cranial type of the American continent—based on the additional evidence accumulated by him, in the interval of twelve years which elapsed between the publication of the *Crania Americana* and the death of its author,—are thus defined : "The Indian skull is of a decidedly rounded form. The occipital portion is flattened in the upward direction, and the transverse diameter, as measured between the parietal bones, is remarkably wide, and *often exceeds the longitudinal line.*[1] The forehead is low and receding, and rarely arched, as in the other races,—a feature that is regarded by Humboldt, Lund, and other naturalists, as a characteristic of the American race, and serving to distinguish it from the Mongolian. The cheek-bones are high, but not much expanded ; the maxillary region is salient and ponderous, with teeth of a corresponding size, and singularly free from decay. The orbits are large and squared, the nasal orifice wide, and the bones that protect it arched and expanded. The lower jaw is massive, and wide between the condyles ; but, notwithstanding the prominent position of the face, the teeth are for the most part vertical."[2] The views thus set forth by him who has been justly designated

---

[1] In this statement Dr. Morton would seem to have had in view his theoretical type, rather than the results of his own careful observations, unless he accepted as evidence the artificially abbreviated and flattened skulls ; and even of these his *Crania Americana* furnishes only one exceptional example, from a mound on the Alabama river (plate liv.) "It is flattened on the occiput and os frontis in such manner as to give the whole head a sugar-loaf or conical form, *whence also its great lateral diameter, and its narrowness from back to front.*"

[2] "Physical Type of the American Indians," Schoolcraft's *History of the Indian Tribes,* vol. ii. p. 316.

"the founder of the American School of Ethnology,"[1] have been maintained and strengthened by his successors; and scarcely any point in relation to ethnographic types has been more generally accepted as a recognised postulate, than the approximative homogeneous cranial characteristics of the whole American race.

The comprehensive generalization of the American cranial type, thus set forth on such high authority, has exercised an important influence on all subsequent investigations relative to the aborigines of the New World. It has, indeed, been accepted with such ready faith as a scientific postulate, that Agassiz, Nott, Meigs, and other distinguished physiologists and naturalists, adopted it without question; and have reasoned from it as one of the few well-determined data of ethnological science. It has no less effectually controlled the deductions of observant travellers. Mr. Stephens having submitted to Dr. Morton the bones rescued by him from an ancient grave among the ruins of Ticul, "so crumbled and broken, that in a court of law their ancient proprietor would not be able to identify them," he succeeded in piecing together, out of the broken fragments, the posterior and lateral portions of the skull; and from these imperfect data pronounced it to be that of a female, presenting "the same physical conformation which has been bestowed with amazing uniformity upon all the tribes on the continent, from Canada to Patagonia, and from the Atlantic to the Pacific Ocean."[2] Some of Mr. Stephens' own personal observations pointed, as we have seen, to a very different conclusion; but he resigned his judgment to this scientific dogma, and accepted it as conclusive proof that the ancient ruins he had been exploring are the work of elder generations of the same Indians who

---

[1] *Types of Mankind*, p. 87.
[2] Stephens' *Travels in Yucatan*, vol. i. p. 284.

now, miserable and degraded, cling around their long-deserted sites.

Apart from its bearing on the question of the indigenous origin of the American race, as an essentially distinct species in the genus *Homo*, this idea of a nearly absolute homogeneity pervading the tribes and nations of the Western Hemisphere, through every variety of climate and country, from the Arctic to the Antarctic circle, is so entirely opposed to the ethnic phenomena witnessed in other quarters of the globe, that it is deserving of the minutest investigation. It is, indeed, admitted by Morton that the agreement is not absolute throughout all the American tribes ; and a distinction is drawn by him, and to some extent recognised and adopted by his successors, between the " barbarous or American," and the " civilized or Toltecan," tribes. Accordingly, one of the three propositions with which Dr. Morton sums up the results deduced from the mass of evidence set forth in his *Crania Americana* is, " That the American nations, excepting the polar tribes, are of one race and one species, but of two great families, which resemble each other in physical, but differ in intellectual character." [1] But the distinction, when thus defined, is manifestly not an ethnological one at all, but a mere accompaniment of civilisation with its wonted intellectual development. An essential difference in physical type is recognised as separating the Esquimaux, or polar tribes, from the true American autochthones, while any physical difference between the remaining two great families into which the American nations are divided is expressly denied. Such a distinction is, for ethnological purposes at least, arbitrary, indefinite, and valueless.

Other differences, or varieties, recognised among the tribes of North and South America, have been acknow-

[1] *Crania Americana*, p. 260.

ledged, but only in such a manner as to harmonize with Morton's postulate of one American physical type of man ; and to confirm the assumption of his indigenous origin among the fauna peculiar to the Western Hemisphere. Agassiz, when alluding to the conflicting opinions maintained by zoologists as to the number of species into which the genus *Cebus* is divisible, remarks : " Here we have, with reference to one genus of monkeys, the same diversity of opinion as exists among naturalists respecting the races of man. But in this case the question assumes a peculiar interest, from the circumstance that the genus Cebus is exclusively American ; for that discloses the same indefinite limitation between its species which we observe also among the tribes of Indians, or the same tendency to splitting into minor groups, running really one into the other, notwithstanding some few marked differences : in the same manner as Morton has shown that *all the Indians constitute but one race,* from one end of the continent to the other. This differentiation of our animals into an almost indefinite number of varieties, in species which have, as a whole, a wide geographical distribution, is a feature which prevails very extensively upon the two continents of America. It may be observed among our squirrels, our rabbits and hares, our turtles, and even among our fishes ; while, in the Old World, notwithstanding the recurrence of similar phenomena, the range of variation of species seems less extensive, and the range of their geographical distribution more limited. In accordance with this general character of the animal kingdom, we find likewise that, among men, with the exception of the Arctic Esquimaux, there is only one single race of men extending over the whole range of North and South America, but dividing into innumerable tribes ; whilst, in the Old World, there are a great many well-defined and easily distinguished races, which are circumscribed within comparatively much narrower boundaries."[1] Such is the line of argument by which one distinguished American naturalist seeks to harmonize the theory of Morton with seemingly irreconcilable facts ; and thereby to confirm his idea of a complete correspondence between the circumscribed areas of the animal world and the natural range of distinct types of man. The difficulties arising from admitted physical differences in the one American race, are solved by other writers who hold to this indigenous unity, by such gratuitous hypotheses or assumptions as that advanced by Mr. Gliddon, that "in reality these races originated in *nations,* and not in a single pair ; thus forming proximate, but not identical species."[2] In spite of such theories, however, the irreconcilable variations from any assumed normal type could not be altogether ignored ; and the difficulty is repeatedly glanced at, though it is not fairly grappled with by any of the writers of "the American School of Ethnology." The closest approximation to a recognition of the legitimate deduction from such contrasting cranial characteristics, is made by Dr. Morton himself, where he remarks, in reference to the larger cerebral capacity of the Indian in his savage state, than of the semi-civilized Peruvian or ancient Mexican,—" Something may be attributed to a primitive difference of stock, but more, perhaps, to the contrasted activity of the two races."

Whilst, however, this supposed unity in physical form is so strongly asserted throughout the writings of Dr. Morton, and has been accepted and made the basis of many comprehensive arguments dependent on its truth, its originator was not unaware that it was subject to

---

[1] *Indigenous Races of the Earth,* p. xiv.
[2] *Types of Mankind,* p. 276.

variations of a very marked kind, although he did not allow their just weight to these when determining the conclusions which seemed legitimately to result from his carefully accumulated data. He thus remarks, in his *Crania Americana*, on certain unmistakable diversities of form into which the assumed American cranial type may be subdivided, when classing the so-called *barbarous nations :*—" After examining a great number of skulls, I find that the nations east of the Alleghany Mountains, together with the cognate tribes, have the head more elongated than any other Americans. This remark applies especially to the great Lenapé stock, the Iroquois and the Cherokees. To the west of the Mississippi we again meet with the elongated head in the Mandans, Ricaras, Assinaboins, and some other tribes."[1] The Minetaries, Crows, Blackfeet, and Ottoes, are named along with these, in his latest reference to the subject, thereby transferring the Ottoes from the brachycephalic to the dolichocephalic class, in which he had previously placed them ; for, to his earlier statement, Dr. Morton superadds the further remark :—" Yet even in these instances the characteristic truncature of the occiput is more or less obvious, while many nations east of the Rocky Mountains have the rounded head so characteristic of the race, as the Osages, Ottoes, Missouris, Dacotas, and numerous others. The same conformation is common in Florida ; but some of these nations are evidently of the Toltecan family, as both their characteristics and traditions testify. The heads of the Caribs, as well of the Antilles as of *terra firma*, are also naturally rounded ; and we trace this character, as far as we have had opportunity for examination, through the nations east of the Andes, the Patagonians and the tribes of

---

[1] *Crania Americana,* p. 65 ; *Physical Type of the American Indians ; History of Indian Tribes,* vol. ii. p. 317.

Chili. In fact, the flatness of the occipital portion of the cranium will probably be found to characterize a greater or less number of individuals in every existing tribe from Terra del Fuego to the Canadas. If their skulls be viewed from behind, we observe the occipital outline to be moderately curved outward, wide at the occipital protuberances, and full from those points to the opening of the ear. From the parietal protuberances there is a slightly curved slope to the vertex, producing a conical, or rather a wedge-shaped outline." These opinions are still more strongly advanced in Dr. Morton's most matured views, where he affirms the American race to be essentially separate and peculiar, and with no obvious links, such as he could discern, between them and the people of the Old World, but a race distinct from all others.

Following in the footsteps of the distinguished Blumenbach, Dr. Morton has the rare merit of having laboured with patient zeal and untiring energy, to accumulate and publish to the world the accurately observed data which constitute the only true basis of science. His *Crania Americana* is a noble monument of well-directed industry in the cause of science ; and the high estimation in which it is justly held, as an accurate and well-digested embodiment of facts, has naturally tended to give additional weight to his deductions. But it is obvious that his mind dwelt too exclusively on one or two of the leading characteristics, more or less common, amid many equally important variations in American crania ; and the tendency of his views, as based on the results of his extended observations, was to regard the most marked distinctions in American crania as mere variations within narrow limits, embraced by the common and peculiar type, which he recognised as characteristic of the whole continent, both north and south. In this opinion his successors have not only concurred, but they even attach less importance to the variations noted by his careful eye. Dr. Nott, for example, remarks on the peculiarities of the very remarkable brachycephalic skull taken from a mound in the Scioto Valley, and figured the natural size in Messrs. Squier and Davis's *Ancient Monuments of the Mississippi Valley:* "Identical characters pervade all the American race, ancient and modern, over the whole continent. We have compared many heads of living tribes, Cherokees, Choctaws, Mexicans, etc., as well as crania from mounds of all ages, and the same general organism characterizes each one."[1]

Şince the death of Dr. Morton, his greatly augmented collection, now numbering upwards of eleven hundred skulls, has been deposited in the Cabinet of the Academy of Natural Sciences of Philadelphia, and his catalogue has been carefully edited and extended under the care of Dr. J. Aitken Meigs. The rearrangement and classification has not led to any change in the inferences deduced from this valuable accumulation of evidence ; and, in a later publication, Dr. Meigs remarks : "Through the *Crania Americana,* it has long been known to the scientific world that a remarkable sameness of osteological character pervades all the American tribes, from Hudson's Bay to Terra del Fuego."[2]

Such, then, is the opinion arrived at by Dr. Morton, as the result of extensive study and observation, accepted and confirmed by his successors, and now made the starting-point from whence to advance to still more comprehensive and far-reaching conclusions. It is not necessary, therefore, to prove the recognition of this well-known ethnological postulate by further references

---

[1] *Types of Mankind,* p. 291.
[2] *Cranial Characteristics of the Races of Men ; Indigenous Races,* p. 332.

to recent authorities. Its influence is sufficiently apparent, from its adoption by one of the very foremost among American men of science in support of the peculiar views already referred to, of the indigenous and local origin of distinct types of man, as well as of the inferior animals. But while some of the conclusions of American ethnologists have been combated with the most earnest zeal, it has not occurred to their opponents to challenge this physiological postulate, which lies at the basis of the whole.

When my attention was first directed to the investigation of the cranial conformation of ancient races, it was with a view to the illustration of the physical characteristics of the primitive occupants of the British Islands. Nothing had then been attempted with this purpose in view, so far as Scotland was concerned, and the contribution then offered as a beginning towards the accumulation of the requisite data, has since been followed up by the observations of efficient labourers in this new field of research. At that time I had little anticipation of devoting attention to the physical conformation of the ancient or modern races of the New World, with the facilities arising from long residence on the American continent. Nevertheless, the special characteristics ascribed to the American race had already been noted, and certain points of correspondence traced between them and such as pertain to the crania of ancient British tumuli, when producing a table of comparative measurements of Scottish crania, in the *Prehistoric Annals of Scotland.* It is there remarked : " There is no primitive race known to us which seems so fit to be selected as a type or standard of comparison, in relation to cranial development, as the Aztecs or Ancient Mexicans. They were the last dominant race among numerous native tribes, who, progressing from the rudimentary stone-

period, were excluded from influences such as those which
in Europe superseded the ages of stone and bronze by
the more perfect arts of civilisation." Accordingly, two
of the most characteristic crania of the Mexican brachycephalic type, were selected from the *Crania Americana*,
in order to afford a comparative estimate of the cranial,
and thereby of the cerebral capacity of the primitive
races of the Scottish tumuli. When in more recent years
I found myself among living primitive races, and enjoying opportunities of judging for myself of the physical
characteristics of the aboriginal occupants of the American forests and prairies, I availed myself of these in
the full anticipation of meeting with such evidences of
a general approximation to the assigned normal American cranial type, as would confirm the deductions of
previous observers. My chief aim, when first exploring some of the Indian cemeteries in Canada, was to
acquire specimens of skulls approximating to the peculiar brachycephalic type found in one important class of
early British graves. It was, accordingly, simply with a
sense of disappointment, that I observed the results of
repeated explorations in different localities furnish crania,
which, though undoubtedly Indian, exhibited little or no
traces of the rounded form with short longitudinal diameter, so strikingly apparent in certain ancient Mexican
and Peruvian skulls, as well as in the rare examples
hitherto recovered from the mounds of the Mississippi
Valley. Slowly, however, the conviction forced itself
upon me, that to whatever extent this assigned typical
skull may be found in other parts of the continent, those
most frequently met with along the north shores of the
great lakes, are deficient in some of its most essential
elements. Similar conclusions have been recorded by
different observers. They are indicated by Dr. Latham,
when comparing the Esquimaux and American Indian

forms of skull, as determined by Dr. Morton;[1] and no less strongly affirmed by Dr. Retzius, who states that it is scarcely possible to find a more distinct separation into dolichocephalic and brachycephalic races than in America;[2] while Dr. Knox, in his *Races of Men*, not only expresses his doubt of "the asserted identity of the Red Indian throughout the entire range of continental America," but he ridicules the matured opinion of Dr. Morton that the difference between the extreme forms of Peruvian and other American skulls is the result of artificial compression differently applied to the same primary cranial form.[3] It is indeed necessary to determine what must be regarded as the essential requisites of Dr. Morton's American typical cranium; for neither he nor his successors have overlooked the fact of some deviation from this supposed normal type, not only occurring occasionally, but existing as a permanent characteristic of certain tribes. As has been already shown, Dr. Morton recognised a more elongated head as pertaining to certain tribes, but this he speaks of as a mere slight variation from the more perfect form of the normal skull; and he adds: "Even in these instances the characteristic truncation of the occiput is more or less obvious."[4] So also Dr. Nott, after defining the typical characteristics of the American cranium, remarks: "Such are more universal in the Toltecan than the barbarous tribes. Among the Iroquois, for instance, the heads were often of a somewhat more elongated form; but the Cherokees and Choctaws, who, of all barbarous tribes, display greater aptitude for civilisation, present the genuine type in a remarkable degree. My birth and long residence in

---

[1] *Natural History of the Varieties of Man*, p. 453.

[2] *Arch. des Sciences Naturelles*, Geneva, 1860.

[3] *Races of Men*, pp. 127, 276.

[4] *Crania Americana*, p. 69; *History of Indian Tribes*, vol. ii. p. 317.

Southern States have permitted the study of many of these living tribes, and they exhibit this conformation almost without exception. I have also scrutinized many Mexicans, besides Catawbas of South Carolina, and tribes on the Canada Lakes, and can bear witness that the living tribes everywhere confirm Morton's type."[1]

In selecting a skull, which seemed to Dr. Morton in all respects to fulfil the theoretical requirements of his typical cranium, we are guided, under his directions, to that ancient people who, in centuries long prior to the advent of Europeans, originated some remarkable traits of a native civilisation in the valleys of the eastern tributaries of the Mississippi. It will, therefore, coincide with his choice of an example of the true American head, if, starting from that ancient race, we pursue our comparisons downward to the nations and tribes familiar to Europeans by direct intercourse and personal observation.

The ingenious and learned author of *Iconographic Researches on Human Races and their Art*, deduces, as we have already seen, from one of the portrait pipe-sculptures of the ancient Mounds,—or rather from the engraving of it furnished in the first volume of the *Smithsonian Contributions to Knowledge*,—the comprehensive conclusions ; that the Mound-Builders were American Indians in type, and were probably acquainted with no other men but themselves ; to which he adds, "in every way confirming the views of the author of *Crania Americana.*" Mr. Schoolcraft goes still further ; and, ignoring not only the unquestionable proofs of the lapse of many centuries since the construction of the great earthworks in the Ohio Valley, but also all the evidences of geometrical skill, a definite means of determining angles, a fixed standard of measurement, and the capacity, as

[1] *Types of Mankind*, p. 441.

well as the practice of repeating geometrically constructed earthworks of large and uniform dimensions; he thus sums up his account of the Alleghans, the oldest known occupants of the Ohio Valley: " The tribes lived in fixed towns, cultivated extensive fields of the zea-maize, and also, as denoted by recent discoveries, of some species of beans, vines, and esculents. They were in truth the Mound-Builders."[1]

Reference has been made in a previous chapter to the discovery of the " Scioto Mound cranium," the best au-

Fig. 54.—Scioto Mound Skull.

thenticated and most characteristic of the crania of the Mound-Builders. It lay embedded in a compact mass of carbonaceous matter, intermingled with a few detached bones of the skeleton and some fresh-water shells. Over this had been heaped a mound of rough stones, on the top of which, incovered by the outer layer of clay, lay a large plate of mica, that favourite material of the ancient Mound-Builders. This is the skull which, according to the description of Dr. Morton, furnishes the best example of the true typical American head. It is produced as such by Dr. Nott, in the *Types of Mankind,*

[1] *History of Indian Tribes,* vol. v. p. 135.

and as described in the words of Dr. Morton, in Dr. Meigs' "Catalogue of Human Crania in the Collection of the Academy of Natural Sciences of Philadelphia," it supplies a definition of the features deemed essential to this assigned normal type. It is designated "an aboriginal American; a very remarkable head. This is, perhaps, the most admirably-formed head of the American race hitherto discovered. It possesses the national characteristics in perfection, as seen in the elevated vertex, flattened occiput, great interparietal diameter, ponderous bony structure, salient nose, large jaws and broad face.

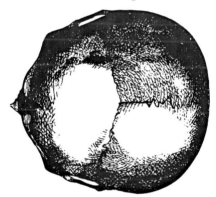

Fig. 55.—Scioto Mound Skull.

It is the perfect type of Indian conformation, to which the skulls of all the tribes from Cape Horn to Canada more or less approximate."

Of this skull the measurements which involve the most essential typical elements, and so furnish precise materials for comparison, are :—

Longitudinal diameter,	.	.	.	6·5	inches.
Parietal „	.	.	.	6·	„
Vertical „	.	.	.	6·2	„
Inter-mastoid arch,	.	.	.	16·	„
Horizontal circumference,	.	.	19·8	„

So that, in fact, the cranium very closely corresponds in its measurements, in length, breadth, and height. Still

further it may be noted, on examining the skull, as
figured here from the full-sized view in the *Ancient
Monuments of the Mississippi Valley*, that the singular
longitudinal abbreviation of this skull is nearly all pos-
teriorly. A line drawn through the meatus auditorius
externus in profile, parallel to the elevated forehead,
divides it into two unequal parts, of which the anterior
and posterior parts are nearly in the ratio of three to
two. If, however, we turn from the definition as recorded in relation to this particular skull, and reduce it
to the general formulæ derived by its originator from the
examination of numerous examples, it amounts to this :
A small receding forehead, somewhat broad at the base,
but with a greatly depressed frontal bone ;[1] a flattened
or nearly vertical occiput ; viewed from behind, an occipital outline which curves moderately outwards, wide at
the occipital protuberances, and full from these points
to the opening of the ear; from the parietal protuberances a slightly curved slope to the vertex, producing a
wedge-shaped outline ; a great vertical diameter; and
the predominant relative interparietal diameter of the
brachycephalic cranium. If to these are added the large
quadrangular orbits, the cheek-bones high and massive,
the maxillary region salient and ponderous, and the nose
prominent, we have, nearly in Dr. Morton's own words,
the characteristic features of that American cranium
which prevails among both the ancient and modern
tribes of the brachycephalic type, and has been assumed
by him as universal.

It is with great diffidence that I venture to challenge
conclusions, adopted after mature consideration by the
distinguished author of the *Crania Americana*. But in

---

[1] "There is no race on the globe in which the frontal bone is so much
pressed backwards, and in which the forehead is so small."—*Humboldt.* "All
possess alike the low receding forehead."—*Morton.*

proceeding to apply the evidence of physical conformation as a means of comparison between the ancient and
the modern races of the New World, a revision alike of
the evidence and the deductions therefrom becomes indispensable. Tried by his own definitions and illustrations, the Scioto Valley skull essentially differs from the
American typical cranium in some of its most characteristic features. Instead of the low, receding, unarched
forehead, assigned independently by Humboldt and
Morton, we have here a finely arched frontal bone, with
corresponding breadth of forehead. The conical or
wedge-shaped vertex is, in like manner, replaced by a
well-rounded arch, curving equally throughout ; and the
cranium is altogether a well and uniformly proportioned
example of an extreme brachycephalic skull. It has been
selected, in the *Types of Mankind*,[1] for the purpose of
instituting a comparison with the well-developed and
characteristic head of a modern Indian, a Cherokee chief,
who died, while a prisoner at Mobile, in 1837, and the
two crania are there engraved side by side, with other
examples : " to show through faithful copies, that the
type attributed to the American races is found among
tribes the most scattered ; among the semi-civilized and
the barbarous ; among living as well as among extinct
races ; and that no foreign race has intruded itself into
their midst, even in the smallest appreciable degree." [2]
But, judging merely by the reduced profile drawings,
placed in juxtaposition, without reference to precise
measurements, the points of agreement are very partial.
The vertical occiput of the ancient skull rounds some-

---

[1] *Types of Mankind*, p. 442.

[2] Dr. Nott's definition is as follows : "The most striking anatomical characters of the American crania are, small size ; low, receding forehead ; short
antero-posterior diameter ; great inter-parietal diameter ; flattened occiput ;
prominent vertex ; high cheek-bones ; ponderous, and somewhat prominent
jaws."—*Types of Mankind*, p. 441.

what abruptly into a flat horizontal vertex, and with the well-developed forehead, and short longitudinal diameter, gives a peculiarly square form to it, in profile. In the modern skull, on the contrary, the occipital flattening is not so much that of the occiput proper, as of the posterior part of the parietal, together with the upper angle of the occipital bone; thereby uniting with the receding forehead of the latter, to produce a conoid outline, in striking contrast to the square form of the other. Still further, a vertical line drawn through the meatus auditorius, shows a remarkable preponderance of posterior cerebral development in the ancient skull, constituting indeed its most striking peculiarity. But a comparison of the measurements of the two skulls, serves no less effectually to refute the supposed correspondence, adduced in proof of a typical unity traceable throughout tribes and nations of the Western Hemisphere the most widely separated alike by time and space.[1]

	Ancient.	Modern.
Longitudinal diameter, . . .	6·5	6·9
Parietal, ...	6·0	5·7
Vertical, ...	6·2	5·4
Frontal, ...	4·5	4·6
Inter-mastoid arch, ...	16·0	15·5
Inter-mastoid line, ...	4·5	4·75
Occipito-frontal arch, . . .	13·8	14·4
Horizontal circumference, . . ·	19·8	20·4

It is not to be supposed that any single skull can be selected as the embodiment of all the essential typical characteristics either of the ancient or the modern cranial conformation; nor can we deduce general conclusions

---

[1] The measurements of the modern skull are given, as above, in the *Proceedings of the Boston Natural History Society*, vol. v. p. 77. I owe it to the frank liberality of Dr. Nott, that I was able to identify this as the skull referred to. My own measurements, taken in 1860, give a still greater longitudinal diameter. It will be seen by comparing the two columns, that the modern skull is in excess in longitudinal diameter, while both in breadth and height it is decidedly less.

as to the physical characteristics of the ancient Mound-Builders from the remarkable example above referred to. We lack, indeed, sufficient data as yet for any absolute determination of the cranial type of the mounds ; but the Scioto Valley skull cannot with propriety be designated as "the only skull incontestably belonging to an individual of that race." The Grave Creek Mound cranium, figured by Dr. Morton, belongs no less indisputably to the same race, and presents in its arched forehead, prominent superciliary ridges, and compact, uniformly rounded profile, a general correspondence to the previous example.[1] In 1853, Dr. J. C. Warren exhibited to the Boston Natural History Society the cast of a second and more perfect skull from the same mound,[2] which I have since examined and measured in the collection of Dr. J. Mason Warren. It is also worthy of note that several inferior maxillary bones of the mound skeletons have been recovered nearly entire. They are remarkable for their massiveness, and are described as less projecting than those pertaining to the skeletons of a later date.[3] Another skull given by Dr. Morton, from a mound on the Upper Mississippi, was obtained from an elevated site bearing considerable resemblance to that where the Scioto Valley cranium was found ; but the evidence is insufficient to remove the doubts which its proportions suggest, that in this, as in so many other cases, we have only one of those later interments habitually made by the modern Indians in the superficial soil of the mounds. It is better meanwhile to reject all doubtful evidence than to incur the risk of cumbering such future well-authenticated evidence as we may confidently anticipate, with uncertainty

---

[1] *Crania Americana*, pl. liii. p. 223.
[2] *Proceedings of Boston Nat. Hist. Soc.*, vol. iv. p. 331.
[3] *Ancient Monuments of the Mississippi Valley*, p. 290.

and confusion. The following table includes a series of measurements of mound and ancient cave crania, mostly taken by myself from the originals in the Collection of the Academy of Natural Sciences at Philadelphia and elsewhere :—

TABLE I.—MOUND AND CAVE CRANIA.

	LOCALITY.	L. D.	P. D.	F. D.	V. D.	I. A.	I. L.	O. F. A.	H. C.
1	Scioto Mound, .	6·5	6·0	4·5	6·2	16·0	4·5	13·8	19·8
2	Grave Creek Mound,	6·6 ?	6·0	...	5·0	...	...	14·2 ?	...
3	,, ,,	6·6	6·0	4·0	5·4	15·6	4·3	...	20·2
4	Tennessee ,,	6·6	5·6	4·1	5·6	15·2	4·4	14·0	19·5
5	Huron River, Ohio,	6·7	5·7	4·0	...	14·8	4·4	14·?	19·8
6	,, (Fem.)	6·7	5·4	4·0	5·4	14·0	4·2	13·7	19·9
7	Ohio Mound, (Fem.)	6·4	5·3	4·0	5·0	14·2 ?	4·?	...	19·0
8	Alabama Mound, .	6·2	5·4	4·3	4·9	14·6	3·8	13·3	18·5
9	Golconda Cave, .	6·7	5·4	4·3	5·5	14·5	4·1	14·0	19·3
10	Steubenville Cave, .	7·0	6·1	4·6	5·6	15·5	4·3	14·0	20·5
11	,, .	6·8	5·9	4·4	5·7	15·5	4·5	14·4	20·5
12	,, .	6·3	5·9	4·9	5·7	15·8	5·0	14·1	20·0
13	,, .	6·6	6·0	4·6	5·1	14·6	4·2	13·3	20·0
14	,, F.	6·6	5·4	4·3	5·1	14·?	4·3	13·9	19·0
15	,, .	7·0	5·8	4·5	5·5	14·9	4·5	14·4	20·3
16	,, .	6·7	6·0	4·5	5·7	15·4	4·7	14·1	20·3
17	,, F.	6·2	6·1	4·5	4·9	15·?	4·?	13·3	19·4
18	,, .	7·1	5·7	4·6	5·0	15·0	4·4	14·2	20·2
19	,, .	6·2	6·0	4·5	5·5	14·8	4·0	13·2	19·4
20	Kentucky Cave, .	6·1	5·4	4·4	5·6	14·5	4·4	13·6	18·4
21	,, .	6·7	5·5	4·5	6·2	13·5	5·0	...	19·7
	Mound Crania Mean,	6·54	5·67	4·13	5·36	14·91	4·23	13·83	19·53
	Cave Crania Mean,	6·62	5·78	4·51	5·47	14·85	4·42	13·87	19·77
	Total Mean,	6·58	5·74	4·37	5·43	14·87	4·35	13·86	19·68

Nos. 1. Scioto Mound Cranium.
   2. *Cran. Amer.*, pl. liii.
   3. Cast, Dr. J. M. Warren's Collection.
   4. *Cran. Amer.*, pl. lv.
 5, 6. A. N. S. Philadelphia, Cat. Nos. 5, 6 (1271, 1272).
   7. Dr. J. M. Warren's Collection.
   8. *Cran. Amer.*, pl. liv.
   9. *Cran. Amer.*, pl. lxii.
10-19. A. N. S. Philadelphia, vide *Cran. Amer.*, pl. lxiii.
  20. Mr. C. S. Fowler's Collection, N.Y.
  21. Mummy from Mammoth Cave, Kentucky, Mus. Amer. Antiq.
     Soc., Worcester.

Of the series embraced in this table, though all are ancient, only the first four can be relied upon as undoubted examples of the crania of the Mounds. In comparing them with others, there are indications of a peculiar cranial type partially approximating to the brachycephalic Peruvian cranium ; but this assumed correspondence has been exaggerated, and some important differences have been slighted or ignored, in the zeal to establish the affinities which such an agreement would seem to imply. In vertical elevation the Peruvian cranium is decidedly inferior ; and another point of distinction borne out by the few well-authenticated Mound crania, is the great prominence of the superciliary ridges in the latter. These were overlooked by Dr. J. C. Warren, who pronounced the Mound and Peruvian crania to be identical. A greater correspondence seems to me to be traceable between the most ancient crania of the Mexican valley and those of the mounds. But, tempting as are the conclusions which such analogies suggest, any final decision on the subject must be reserved until further discoveries place within our reach a sufficient number of skulls of the ancient Mound-Builders as well authenticated as those of the Scioto Valley and Grave Creek Mounds. This, there is little hope of achieving, until a systematic exploration is instituted under the direction of a carefully constituted scientific Commission, the organization of which would reflect credit on the Government of the United States. The cave crania, Nos. 9-21, are a remarkable series of undoubted antiquity, and present a nearer approximation to those of the mounds than any other class. Their most notable divergence from the mound type, in the parietal diameter, disappears if the doubtful examples of the latter, Nos. 5-8, are excluded, as in Table xv.

Turning from this review of the meagre data hitherto recovered from the ancient sepulchral mounds, let us next consider the two great civilized nations of the New World, the Peruvians and Mexicans. Their civilisation had an independent origin and growth. The scenes of its development were distinct; and each exhibited special characteristics of intellectual progress. Nevertheless, they had so much in common, that the determination of the physical type peculiar to each, will be best secured by ascertaining what is common to both.

When Dr. Morton first undertook the investigation of the cranial characteristics of the American races, he admitted the force of the evidence presented to him in the examination of a number of ancient Peruvian skulls; and has recorded in his *Crania Americana* a distinct recognition of the traces of well-defined brachycephalic and dolichocephalic races among the ancient Peruvians.[1] But the seductive charms of his comprehensive theory of an American ethnic unity ultimately prevailed over the earlier opinion; which, even in the *Crania Americana,* was stated as the legitimate deduction from the evidence in question, without being incorporated into the author's concluding propositions. Accordingly, in his latest recorded opinions, when commenting on the artificial modifications of the Peruvian skull, Dr. Morton remarks: "I at first found it difficult to conceive that the original rounded skull of the Indian could be changed into this fantastic form; and was led to suppose that the latter was an artificial elongation of a head remarkable for its natural length and narrowness. I even supposed that the long-headed Peruvians were a more ancient people than the Inca tribes, and distinguished from them by their cranial configuration. In this opinion I was

[1] *Crania Americana,* p. 98.

mistaken. Abundant means of observation and comparison have since convinced me that all these variously
formed heads were originally of the same rounded shape,
which is characteristic of the aboriginal race, from Cape
Horn to Canada, and that art alone has caused the
diversities among them."[1]

A revision of the evidence in relation to this important physical characteristic of the Ancient Peruvians
appears to suggest conclusions at variance with this idea
of a universally prevalent rounded, or brachycephalic
Peruvian head. On a recent visit to Boston, I had an
opportunity of minutely examining and measuring an
interesting collection of crania and mummied bodies in
the possession of John H. Blake, Esq., which were
brought by him from ancient Peruvian Cemeteries, on
the shore of the Bay of Chacota, near Arica, in latitude
18° 30' s.; and since then I have been favoured with
his own carefully elaborated notes on the subject. The
desert of Atacama, between the eighteenth and twenty-
fifth degrees of south latitude, has been the site of sepulture for ancient Peruvian races through a period of
unknown duration, and numerous cemeteries have been
opened and despoiled. The mode of sepulture, and the
articles deposited with the dead, present so uniform a
resemblance, that, excepting in one point, Mr. Blake
observes, a description of one may suffice for the whole.
The difference noted arises from the varying soil. The
greater number are interred in the dry sand, which
generally covers the surface to a sufficient depth; but
in some instances the excavations have been made in a
soft rock (gypsum) which here and there approaches the
surface. In this arid district, such is the nature of the
soil and climate, that articles which speedily perish in a
damp soil and a humid atmosphere, are found in perfect

[1] *Physical Type of the American Indians*, p. 326.

preservation after the lapse of centuries. Added to the facilities which nature has thus provided for perpetuating the buried traces of the ancient Peruvians, they themselves practised the art of embalming their dead. One of the largest cemeteries referred to is situated on a plain at the base of a range of low hills in lat. 18° 30′ s. and long. 70° 13′ w. It is on the shore of the Bay of Chacota, a little southward of Arica, and about 185 leagues south-east of Lima. This plain is formed of silicious sand and marl, slightly impregnated with common salt, and nitrate and sulphate of soda. It is exceedingly light, fine, and dry; and such is its preservative nature, that even bodies interred in it without any previous preparation have not entirely lost the fleshy covering from their remains. In the cemeteries of this vast arid plain, the objects which, in all probability, were most highly prized by their owners, were deposited beside them, and every article required in preparing the body for interment appears to have been preserved with it. Thus the needles used for sewing the garments and wrappings of the dead, the comb employed in dressing the hair, and even the loose hair removed in this last process of the toilet, are all found deposited in the grave.

The following is Mr. Blake's description of the cemeteries explored by him on the Bay of Chacota :—" The tombs or graves are near to each other, and cover a large extent of ground in two places distant the one from the other about an eighth of a mile. A few of them are marked by circles of stones, while others are readily discovered by slight concavities in the soil above them. They are all circular, from three to five feet in diameter, and from four to five feet deep. Some of them are walled with stone, and all are lined with a coarse matting of flags. The bodies in them are always found in a sitting posture, with the knees elevated toward the chin, and the arms crossed upon the breast. They are generally seated upon flat stones, under which are the articles of food, and part of the implements found with them. They are closely wrapped in woollen garments, which are sewed about them ; and the needles of thorn used for this purpose are found thrust into the outer covering, often with thread remaining in them. These garments are of various degrees of fineness, colour, and pattern of figures in which they are woven. Many are of a uniform brown colour, while in others the colours are diversified, and have retained in a remarkable manner their brightness : particularly the red and scarlet, showing that the art of dyeing was well understood. Some of the bodies have been carefully embalmed, the flesh being saturated with a gum resin ; others appear to have been subjected to careful desiccation without the employment of any preservative ; while those of which scarce any parts but the skeletons remain were probably subjected to no process for their preservation. There is no record or tradition concerning this and similar cemeteries, of the period when they were made use of ; and it is by no means certain that they contain the remains of the ancestry of the Indians who now occupy the country."

The collection of Peruvian antiquities formed by Mr. Blake, and now in his possession, includes curious specimens of native pottery, implements wrought in stone, bronze, and wood, and numerous interesting sepulchral relics illustrative of native arts and customs. But the most valuable department of his collection embraces the entire contents of a Peruvian tomb, including the mummies of a man and woman, and the partially desiccated remains of a child. Some of the contents of this grave have already been referred to in illustration of Peruvian

civilisation in a previous chapter; but a minute notice
of the human remains, with the special accompaniments
of their interment, will furnish information on various
obscure points in the social history of this remarkable
people. It was obviously a family tomb. The male
mummy is that of a man in the maturity of life, in the
usual sitting position with the knees drawn up to the
chin. With the exception of a part of the integuments of
the lower jaw, the body is in a good state of preservation.
On its transference to the humid atmosphere of New England, the flesh became somewhat softened, but it exhibits
no symptoms of decay. It is dark brown, and possesses
a peculiar penetrating odour, somewhat similar to that of
an Egyptian mummy. The head is of the common
rounded Peruvian form, with retreating forehead, high
cheek bones, and prominent nose; but some of the other
measurements are worthy of note :—

Length of ulna,	.	.	10·0	inches.
,, tibia,	.	.	16·5	,,
,, hand,		.	7·5	,,
,, middle-finger,			4·5	,,
Breadth of hand,	.	.	2·5	,,

The breadth of hand, as noted here, is measured across
the extremity of the metacarpal bones; and, with every
allowance for the contraction produced in the process of
mummification, it is remarkably small. The hair has
undergone little or no change, and differs essentially
from that most characteristic feature of the Indian of the
northern continent. It is brown in colour, and as fine
in texture as the most delicate Anglo-Saxon's hair. It
is neatly braided and arranged, the front locks being
formed each into a roll on the side of the head, while the
hair behind is plaited into a triangular knot of six braids.
The garments and wrappings of this mummy were of
fine texture, woven in woollen materials of diverse

colours ; and the head-dress was first an oblong hood with parti-coloured stripes, and over this a cap formed of woollen threads of various colours, ingeniously woven, and surmounted by feathers and an ornament formed of the quills of the condor. A quiver made of the skin of a fox contained five arrows, the shaft of each consisting of two pieces of reed, tipped with sharp-pointed and barbed flint-heads, regularly formed, and attached by a tough green cement. Also suspended to one side, by a hair cord passing over the shoulder, was a woollen bag, finely woven in stripes of black, white, and brown, and curiously sewed at the sides with threads of various colours. This contained leaves of the coca, and a thin silver disk or medal, surrounded by a series of one hundred small indentations near the edge, and in the centre a space of three-fourths of an inch countersunk and perforated with a small round hole. To this a hair cord of about two feet in length is secured, probably to suspend it round the neck. When the hood was removed from the head there was found deposited under the chin a small earthen vessel, with rounded base, measuring about two inches in greatest diameter. The top had been covered by a membrane, part of which remains attached to the rim by the cord with which it was originally secured.

The body of the female from the same tomb presents in general similar characteristics. The hair is shorter, and somewhat coarser, but fine when compared with that of the northern Indians. It is of a light brown colour, smooth, and neatly braided across the upper part of the forehead, then carried backward and secured on each side of the head. The flesh of the legs, from the ankles to the knees, is covered with red paint, and marks of the same pigment are also traceable on the hair and on the outer woollen wrappings, presenting the impress of a hand.

Such marks are of common occurrence on the Peruvian mummies, and, taken into consideration along with the small size of the hand already noticed, they forcibly recall the prints of the red hand which Stephens observed amid the ruins of Uxmall : the impress of a living hand, but so small that it was completely hid under that of the traveller or his companion. It afterwards stared them in the face, as he says, on all the ruined buildings of the country; and on visiting a nameless ruin, beyond Sabachtsché, in Yucatan, Mr. Stephens remarks : " On the walls of the desolate edifice were prints of the *mano colorado,* or red hand. Often as I saw this print it never failed to interest me. It was the stamp of the living hand. It always brought me nearer to the builders of these cities ; and at times, amid stillness, desolation, and ruin, it seemed as if from behind the curtain that concealed them from view was extended the hand of greeting. The Indians said it was the hand of the master of the building." Such indications of any community of customs or usage between the Peruvians and the ancient builders of Yucatan or Central America are full of interest, however slight ; nor does it detract from their value that the same practice pertains to the northern tribes, and is curiously interwoven with their symbolic decorations.

The symbol of the expanded hand appears among the devices on the engraved Aztec Hatchet, Fig. 52 ; and constantly occurs in painted or graven ideography. One example figured here, copied by Lieut. J. H. Simpson, U.S.A., from a remarkable series of ancient native hieroglyphics and European inscriptions, on the Moro Rock, in the valley of the Rio de Zuñi, exhibits the open hand in a group of Indian characters, or devices, alongside of which is a Spanish inscription of the seventeenth century. Another example, apparently of early Spanish

origin, on the same Moro Rock, shows the open hand,
with the singular addition of a double thumb, enclosed
in one cartouche alongside of the sacred monogram I. H. S.,

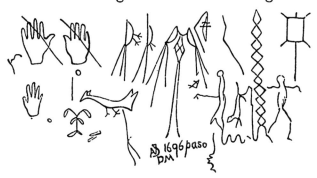

Fig. 56.—Moro Rock Inscription.

as though it were the recognised native counterpart of
the Christian symbol.   On the same subject Mr. School-

Fig. 57.—Moro Monogram.

craft observes : " The figure of the
human hand is used by the North
American Indians to denote supplication to the Deity or Great Spirit ;
and it stands in the system of picture-
writing as the symbol for strength,
power, or mastery thus derived."   It admits, however, of
comprehensive application, with varying significance.

Irving remarks in his *Astoria :* "The Arickaree warriors were painted in the most savage style.   Some had
the stamp of a red hand across their mouths, a sign that
they had drunk the life-blood of a foe."   Catlin found
the same symbol in use for decoration, and as the actual
sign-manual among the Omahaws and the Mandans ; and
I have repeatedly observed the red hand impressed in a
similar manner both on the buffalo robe and on the
naked breast of the Chippewas of Lake Superior.

The following are the principal measurements of the
female Peruvian mummy, on which the impress of the

red hand occurs. The flesh is soft, and the joints are slightly flexible :—

Length of humerus,	. .	9·0 inches.
„ ulna,	. . .	8·0 „
„ hand,	. . .	5·5 „
Greatest breadth of hand,	.	2·0 „
Length of middle-finger,	. .	3·5 „
„ femur,	. . .	13·0 „
„ tibia,	. .	12·0 „
„ foot,	. . .	7·7 „
Greatest breadth of foot,	. .	2·5 „

Upon removing the outer wrapper of this mummy, a wooden comb, a pair of painted sandals of undressed skin, a package of rutile, or oxide of titanium, and other articles, were found beneath. In addition to these, the tomb contained many other objects, such as ears of maize, leaves of coca, a roll of cotton cord, etc., enclosed in bags of fine texture, ingeniously woven of woollen threads, in patterns and devices of various colours, and evidently such as had been in use by their owner. The contents of one of these have a double significance for us. Woven of a peculiar pattern differing from all the others, and of an unusually fine texture : it was found, on being opened, to contain a small bead of malachite, the only one discovered in the tomb, and locks of human hair, each secured by a string tied with a peculiar knot. All the hair is of fine texture, of various shades, from fine light brown to black, and to all appearance has undergone no change. The colour and texture of the hair are facts of great importance to the ethnologist, as indicating essential differences from the modern Indians in one important respect ; and therefore confirming the probability of equally important ethnic differences, suggested by other evidence. But the discovery has also another aspect of interest. In this family tomb, in which lay the parents with their infant child, we may assume with little hesitation that we have the locks of hair of the surviving relatives : in all probability of elder members of the same family as the infant interred here in its mother's grave. It is a touch of genuine human tenderness and feeling such as " makes the whole world kin," and gives a life to that long-forgotten past to which the kindliest sympathies of our common nature respond. Alongside the female there also lay an unfinished piece of weaving stretched upon its frame, and with its yarn of various colours still bright. The needle of thorn was in it, and beside it several balls of yarn. There can be little doubt that it was the work of the deceased, and the last labour that had engaged her hands ; nor need we assume that it was laid beside her under the belief that she would resume the task in another life. It appears rather another of those traits of a gentle loving nature of which the voices from this ancient Peruvian grave seem to speak, and which derive further illustration from other contents of the Atacama cemeteries.

In the same grave lay the remains of the young infant, carefully wrapt in a soft black woollen cloth, and then enclosed in the skin of a penguin with the feathered side inward. Fastened to the woollen wrapper was a pair of little sandals, two and a half inches long. The head was partially covered with a loose cap lined with a wadding of human hair, and cotton stained with a red pigment. Within the cap was a large lock of hair resembling that of the female, which, as already described, had been cut short, probably as a sign of mourning, as is still practised by the women of many Indian tribes. Beside it there also lay, in a cloth envelope, secured with elaborate care, a brown cord with seven knots, and at the end what is believed to be the umbilicus. This is, no doubt, the quipu, or sepulchral record, which to the eye of the bereaved mother recalled every fondly cherished incident

in her loved child's brief career. Around its neck was a
green cord attached to a small shell; and within the
wrappings were several others of the same *Littora Peru-
viana*, already referred to, and also small rolls of hair of
the vicuna, and of cotton, the former enclosing leaves of
coca. Similar little rolls were found wrapped in like
manner in the winding shrouds of other infants, and suggested to their explorer a correspondence with the *charms*
described by Catlin, among the toys suspended to the
cradles of the Sioux papooses. "They were very willing
to sell them," Catlin says, "but in every instance they
cut them open, and removed from within a bunch of
cotton or moss, the little sacred medicine, which to part
with would be to endanger the health of the child."

The process of embalming does not seem to have been
applied to the bodies of young children. In the example
described above little more than the skeleton remains,
excepting the scalp, which is thickly covered with very
fine dark brown hair. Yet it is obvious that all the care
which the fondest tenderness of unavailing sorrow could
bestow, had been expended on the little lost one, which
lay cradled in its last resting-place, like a young bird in
its downy nest under its mother's wing. In another
Peruvian cemetery, several hundred miles to the south
of the Bay of Chacota, Mr. Blake noted the discovery of
many bodies of infants, found each enclosed in an oval
sarcophagus cut out of a single block of wood. But
another singular feature in the Peruvian cemeteries is
the frequent discovery of the fœtus in all stages of development, and deposited in the grave with the same
elaborate evidences of care as was expended on the deceased infant. The practice is remarkable, if not indeed
unique.

Such are some of the illustrations of ancient customs
and sepulchral rites, as disclosed by explorations in the

cemeteries of Peru, along with evidence of characteristics
which go far to disprove the assumed unity of physical
type throughout the Western Hemisphere. No feature
of the modern Indian is more universal, or yields more
slowly even to the effacing influences of hybridity, than
the long, coarse black hair, which so strikingly contrasts
with the short woolly covering of the Negro's head. I
have repeatedly obtained specimens from Indian graves,
as from the Huron graves near Lake Simcoe, the most
modern of which cannot be later than the middle of the
seventeenth century. In all these the hair retains its
black colour and coarse texture, unchanged alike by time
and inhumation; and in this respect corresponds with
that of the Modern Indians of South America, and also
of the Chinese and other true Mongols of Asia. The
Peruvians, Dr. Morton observes, "differ little in person
from the Indians around them, being of the middle
stature, well limbed, and with small feet and hands.
Their faces are round, their eyes small, black, and rather
distant from each other; their noses are small, the mouth
somewhat large, and the teeth remarkably fine. Their
complexion is a dark brown, and their hair long, black,
and rather coarse. In this respect, therefore, the disclosures of the ancient Peruvian cemeteries of Atacama reveal important variations from one of the most persistent
and universal characteristics of the modern American
races; nor is their evidence less conclusive as to the essential diversity in cranial conformation. On this latter
point the collections of Mr. Blake throw great light; and
the conclusions forced on him by much more extended
observations carried on during his residence in Peru led
him to the conviction that two distinct forms of skull are
found in the ancient cemeteries of that country, "the
one rounded or globular, the other elongated." Those
of the bodies found in the tomb described above are of

the former, or brachycephalic type ; but the collection of
crania formed by Mr. Blake was selected by him from a
very large number, as fair average specimens of each of
the two distinct types which presented themselves to his
observation during his exploration of the ancient cemeteries of the desert of Atacama ; and, with those described by Dr. Morton, and others which I have had
opportunities of examining in various collections, furnish
materials from whence the following conclusions are
derived. The skulls are generally small : a characteristic
in part, at least, probably ascribable to the average sta-

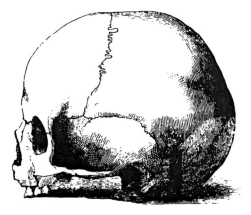

FIG. 58.—Peruvian Brachycephalic Skull.

ture of the people. Of the brachycephalic type, Mr.
Blake has noted : " The occipital bone is flat, and the
forehead retreating, but elevated and broad when compared with the elongated skull. The temporal fossa is
not remarkably large. When the eye is directed downward upon these skulls, the occiput being towards the
observer, the zygomatic arch is nearly in most, and entirely in some of them hidden from the sight. Viewed
in the same position, the face is completely hidden by
the upper and front part of the cranium. The orbits are
deep, and their margins quadrangular. The bones of the

nose are prominent, and the orifices large. The cheek-bones are high. The alveolar edges of the jaws are obtusely arched in front, and the chin projects on a line with the teeth. Compared with the elongated skulls, the face is small, and its outlines more rounded. The cheek-bones descend in nearly a straight line from the external angular process of the frontal bone." Figure 58 illustrates the characteristics of this form of the ancient Peruvian head, as seen in one of the examples brought from the cemeteries of Atacama ; and the following table of measurements includes those of four selected by Mr. Blake, from a large number, as fair average specimens of the prevailing type (Nos. 1-4) :—

TABLE II.—PERUVIAN BRACHYCEPHALIC CRANIA.

	LOCALITY.	L. D.	P. D.	F. D.	V. D.	I. A.	I. L.	O. F. A.	H. C.
1	Atacama,	6·0	5·2	3·5	5·2	...	...	...	...
2	,,	6·3	5·0	3·5	5·3	...	...	...	...
3	,,	6·6	5·3	3·4	5·3	...	...	...	...
4	,,	6·7	5·6	3·6	5·4	...	...	...	...
5	S. of Arica,	6·1	5·6	3·4	5·1	14·6	4·1	...	18·4
6	,,	6·4	5·1	3·2	5·1	14·5	4·1	...	19·0
7	Peru,	6·2	5·8	3·7	5·6	15·1	4·2	...	19·1
8	Lima,	6·3	5·8	3·6	5·4	15·6	4·2	...	19·7
9	Titicaca,	6·3	5·9	4·0	5·3	16·0	4·1	...	19·2
10	,, (145).	6·2	5·9	3·4	5·0	14·7	4·3	...	20·1
11	,, (146).	6·5	5·9	4·0	5·3	15·5	4·9	...	19·5
12	Arica,	6·5	5·2	4·3	5·1	14·5	4·0	13·8	18·5
13	Temple of Sun, F.	5·8	5·7	4·4	5·1	14·5	4·1	12·7	18·4
14	,,	6·1	6·0	4·7	5·5	16·0	4·5	14·1	19·5
15	Pachacamac,	6·7	6·0	4·5	5·6	16·2	4·5	14·5	20·2
16	,,	6·3	5·8	4·5	5·3	15·0	4·0	13·2	19·0
17	Santa,	6·2	5·4	4·3	4·9	14·6	3·8	13·3	18·5
18	Rimac,	6·5	5·6	4·5	5·0	14·7	3·8	13·2	19·2
19	Pachacamac, F.	6·6	6·0	4·6·	5·1	15·5	4·1	13·5	19·8
20	,,	6·6	5·7	4·2	5·2	15·5	4·4	13·0	19·4
21	,, F.	6·3	5·5	4·2	5·0	14·5	3·7	13·2	18·5
22	,,	6·3	5·3	4·4	4·6	14·0	3·9	13·0	18·7
23	,,	6·4	5·5	4·3	5·2	14·8	4·0	13·2	19·0
24	,, F.	6·2	5·5	4·4	5·0	13·6	3·8	12·6	18·7
25	,, F.	6·1	5·9	4·6	5·2	15·2	4·1	13·2	19·2
26	,,	6·2	5·8	4·3	4·9	14·5	4·1	12·6	18·7
	Mean,	6·32	5·62	4·06	5·18	14·96	4·12	13·27	19·10

Nos. 5, 6 are also in Mr. Blake's collection, and Nos.
7-9 in that of Dr. J. Mason Warren, of Boston. Nos.
10, 11 belong to the Boston Natural History Society,
and the remainder are examples collected by Dr. Morton, including those figured in the *Crania Americana*,
plates iii. viii. ix. xi. xi. A, xi. B, lvi. lviii.

In his earlier observations, as has already been seen,
Dr. Morton was led to believe "that the long-headed
Peruvians were a more ancient people than the Inca
tribes, and distinguished from them by their cranial
configuration." This opinion, however, he subsequently
abandoned, and set forth as his final belief that the elongated Peruvian head was artificially produced. But the
materials upon which this later opinion was founded are
still accessible to the inquirer, along with additional
evidence ; and the comprehensive conclusions which
have been based upon the theory of a homogeneous
cranial type, of which this is one of the most essential
foundations, justify a reconsideration of the proofs. Few
who have had extensive opportunities of minutely examining and comparing normal and artificially formed
crania, will, I think, be prepared to dispute the fact that
the latter are rarely if ever symmetrical. The application of pressure on the head of the living child can easily
be made to change its natural contour, but it cannot
give to its artificial proportions that harmonious repetition of corresponding developments on the opposite sides
of the head which is the normal condition of the unmodified cranium. But in so extreme a case as the
conversion of a brachycephalic head, averaging about
6·3 in longitudinal diameter, by 5·3 in parietal diameter,
into a dolichocephalic head of 7·3 by 4·9 in diameter, the
retention of anything like the normal symmetrical proportions is impossible. Yet the dolichocephalic Peruvian
crania present no such abnormal irregularities as could

give countenance to the theory of their form being an
artificial one; while peculiarities in the facial proportions confirm the idea that they are of ethnic origin,
and not the product of deformation. Mr. Blake derived
his opinions from observations made upon numerous
examples brought under his notice among the extensive
cemeteries of the great Peruvian desert of Atacama;
and having enjoyed the advantage of his co-operation
in comparing the selected examples brought home by
him, with others included in the extensive collection
formed by the late Dr. J. C. Warren of Boston, I have
the more confidence in stating the following conclusions
arrived at by such means.

The dolichocephalic Peruvian skull is small, narrow,
and greatly elongated. In several which were measured,
the average distance from a vertical line drawn from the
meatus auditorius externus to the most prominent part
of the frontal bone was only 2·7 inches, while from the
same line to the most prominent part of the occipital
bone it was 4·3 inches. Fully two-thirds of the cavity
occupied by the brain lies behind the occipital foramen,
and the skull, when supported on the condyles, falls
backward. Compared with brachycephalic skulls, the
forehead is low and retreating; the temporal ridges
approach near each other at the top of the head: a
much larger space being occupied by the temporal
muscles, between which the skull seems to be compressed. The zygoma is larger, stronger, and more
capacious, and the whole bones of the face are more
developed. The superior maxillary bone is prolonged
in front, and the incisor teeth are in an oblique position.
The bones of the nose are prominent, the orifices larger,
and the cribriform lamella more extensive. The bony
substance of the skull is thicker, and the weight greater.
Some of those characteristics would require to be deter-

mined from the minute comparison of a much larger
number of skulls before they could be accepted as generic characteristics ; but a sufficient number of them recur
on all observed examples to place beyond question that
the elements of difference between the Peruvian brachycephalic and dolichocephalic skulls amount to something
greatly more radical than could be effected by any artificial change in the form of the calvarium. The woodcut,
Fig. 59, illustrates the characteristics of the elongated

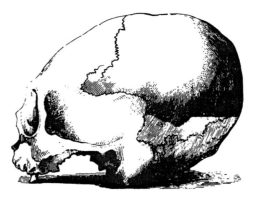

Fig. 59.—Peruvian Dolichocephalic Skull.

Peruvian skull, as exhibited in one of those brought by
Mr. Blake from an ancient cemetery on the Bay of
Chacota ; and the following table of measurements includes three crania, selected by him from a very large
number, as fair average specimens of this type of skull
It is not at all necessary for the confirmation of the
opinion, reasserted here, that there are two essentially
distinct types of Peruvian crania, to affirm that the form
of the elongated skull never owes any of its peculiarities
to artificial compression.   Both forms of cranium are
frequently found bearing unmistakable evidence of having been more or less distorted by this process.   The
depressed frontal bone has, in many cases, been produced
or exaggerated by such means ; and wherever this has

been carried to a great extent, it is accompanied not
only by a corresponding enlargement of the posterior
portion of the cranium, but also by a lateral expansion
of the parietal bones, which almost invariably exhibit
considerable inequality and unsymmetrical variation between the two sides. But of several hundred skulls of
the elongated type examined by Mr. Blake, a large proportion exhibited no certain signs of distortion ; while
an examination of brachycephalic Peruvian crania, with
artificially depressed frontal bones,—of which I have had
opportunities of studying a considerable number in different collections,—has disclosed no indication of their
being thereby converted into those of the normal brachycephalic form.

Among the numerous interesting illustrations of Peruvian characteristics obtained by Mr. Blake from ancient
cemeteries on the Pacific coast, the most valuable for the
purpose now in view, are the skulls of two children,
both of the dolichocephalic or elongated type ; but the
one evidently in a normal condition, while the other
betrays manifest traces of artificial deformation. It is
impossible to examine the former without feeling convinced that it illustrates a type of head entirely distinct
from the more common brachycephalic crania, while
the latter shows the changes wrought by compression.
Figures 60, 61, exhibit the unaltered skull. It is that
of a child, which, judging chiefly from the state of the
dentition, may be pronounced to have been about seven
years of age. It is an exceedingly well-proportioned
symmetrical skull, unaltered by any artificial appliances,
and will be observed to present the most striking typical
contrast, if compared with an unaltered juvenile skull
of the brachycephalic type from the Peruvian cemetery of Santa, engraved in the *Crania Americana*,
Plate VII.

The other elongated skull, exhibited in Figures 62, 63, is of the same type as the previous one, but considerably altered by compression. The forehead is depressed, and the frontal suture remains open. It is that of a child

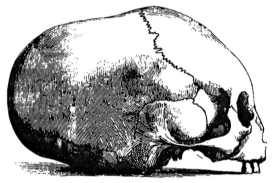

FIG. 60.—Peruvian Child's Skull, Normal.

of about five years of age, and is proportionally less; but as all the process of cranial compression is completed in infancy, those two juvenile skulls illustrate the

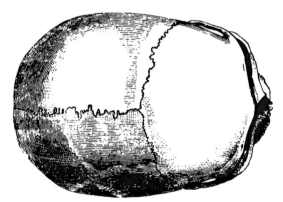

FIG. 61.—Peruvian Child's Skull, Normal.

changes wrought by its means even more effectually than adult crania. The comparative measurements are as follows. The first column exhibits the relative proportions of the normal dolichocephalic Peruvian child's

skull, Fig. 60 ; the smaller measurements in the second
column indicate those of the compressed skull, Fig. 62;
and the third column presents those of another skull
of a child, also about five years old, and of the same

FIG. 62.—Peruvian Child's Skull, Abnormal.

type, procured from that part of the sandy tract of
Atacama which is nearest Arica, and therefore from
the same locality explored by Mr. Blake. It is en-

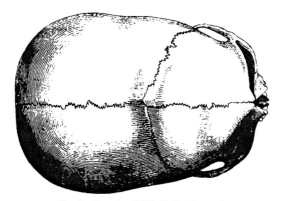

FIG. 63.—Peruvian Child's Skull, Abnormal.

graved in the *Crania Americana*, Plate II. It contrasts
strikingly with the Santa juvenile cranium already referred to, the measurements of which occupy the fourth
column :—

Longitudinal diameter,	.	.	6·6	6·1	6·9	5·4
Parietal diameter, .		.	4·6	4·4	4·5	5·4
Frontal diameter, .	.	.	3·3	3·1	3·7	4·
Vertical diameter, .		.	4·8 ?	4·3 ?	4·3	4·6
Inter-mastoid arch,	.	.	12·6	11·6		
Inter-mastoid line,	.	.	3·4	3·1		
Horizontal circumference,		.	18·2	17·3		

From observations carried on in the cemeteries of
Peru, Mr. Blake was led to the conclusion that the distinguishing traits, thus far noted, between two classes of
the ancient Peruvians, are not limited to the crania, but
may be discerned in other traces of their physical organization. In describing those of the rounded or brachycephalic type of cranium, he adds : " The bones of the
latter struck me as larger, heavier, and less rounded than
those of the former (the elongated crania), and in the
larger size of the hands and feet they also present a
noticeable difference. The remarkable narrowness and
delicacy of the hands, and the long and regularly-formed
finger-nails of the former, are strong evidence that they
were unaccustomed to severe manual labour, such as
must have been required for the construction of the
great works of which the ruins remain. In all the
cemeteries examined, where skulls of the rounded form
have been found, those which are elongated have also
been obtained." Remembering, however, that the sepulchral rites of the royal and noble Inca race were
commonly accompanied by the same human sacrifices
traceable among so many semi-civilized as well as barbarous nations, it is in no degree surprising that the
crania of the two distinct classes, noble and serf, should
be found deposited together in the same grave. After
a minute comparison of all the brachycephalic Peruvian
crania in the Morton collection, I have found that these
also admit of subdivision into two classes distinguished
by marked physiognomical diversity. The bones of the

face in the one are small and delicate, while the other exhibits the characteristic Mongol maxillary development and prominent cheek-bones. In the following table, Nos. 1-4 are the carefully selected examples procured by Mr. Blake during his journey in Peru ; Nos. 5, 6, are also in Mr. Blake's collection ; Nos. 7, 8, in the collection of Dr. J. Mason Warren of Boston ; and Nos. 9-13, in the cabinet of the Academy of Sciences of Philadelphia, including the examples figured by Dr. Morton, plates IV. V.

TABLE III.—PERUVIAN DOLICHOCEPHALIC CRANIA.

	LOCALITY.	L. D.	P. D.	F. D.	V. D.	I. A.	I. L.	O. F. A.	H. C.
1	Atacama,	7·2	5·2	3·6	5·1	...	...	...	...
2	„	7·3	4·9	3·3	4·9	...	...	...	...
3	„	7·0	4·7	3·2	5·1	...	...	...	...
4	„	7·1	5·2	3·2	5·0	14·1	4·0	15·0	20·0
5	S. of Arica,	6·9	5·3	3·6	5·2	14·6	4·1	...	19·8
6	Peru,	7·2	5·3	3·5	5·6	14·6	4·0	...	20·0
7	„	7·0	4·9	3·0	5·3	14·0	4·1	...	19·0
8	„ F.	7·2	5·1	3·5	5·2	13·9	4·0	...	20·0
9	Arica,	7·3	5·3	4·3	5·3	14·0	4·3	15·0	19·8
10	Atacama,	7·2	5·5	5·1	5·1	14·8	4·1	13·7	20·2
11	Titicaca,	6·8	5·4	4·8	5·3	14·8	4·2	...	19·4
12	Royal Tombs, F.	6·8	5·2	3·8	5·3	14·1	4·0	...	19·4
13	Pàchacamac,	6·8	5·4	4·5	5·3	14·7	4·2	14·1	19·5
	Mean,	7·06	5·18	3·80	5·21	14·36	4·10	14·45	19·71

In some rare cases not only are crania of diverse forms found in the same grave, but the head appears to have been embalmed, and deposited separately in the tomb alongside of bodies interred in the more usual way. In plate I. of the *Crania Americana*, Dr. Morton has introduced a view of an embalmed head from the Peruvian cemetery at the Bay of Chocota, but without giving any detailed description of it, though in several respects it is very remarkable. It was brought by Mr. Blake from the same locality as the crania already described, and is

now in his collection at Boston ; for the investigations
of this intelligent traveller were made altogether prior
to the publication of Dr. Morton's great work, and his
conclusions were adopted from earlier and independent
observations. The head was found detached, and carefully preserved without the body. It appears to have
been prepared by desiccation, without the use of resins
or other antiseptics, and was enveloped in a thick cotton
bag. From the manner in which the neck is drawn
together, the preservative process to which it was subjected must have been applied very soon after death. It
is unique, so far as the observations of its finder extend,
and presents some striking points of dissimilarity to any
of the crania already described. It is remarkable for its
great height compared with its diameter. Measured
from the most prominent part of the os frontis to the
extreme projection of the occiput, it is 6·4 inches ; from
the most prominent protuberances of the parietal bones
the diameter is 5·8 inches, and vertically, from a horizontal line drawn across the orifice of the ear to the
highest part of the head, is 5·2 inches. The forehead is
broad and high, the nose prominent, the cheek-bones
strongly developed, the alveolar edges of the jaws obtusely arched in front, and the incisor teeth stand in a
vertical position. The hair, which is brown, and slightly
grey, is remarkably fine, waved in short undulations,
with a tendency to curl. It has been neatly braided,
and several of the plaited braids are passed across the
forehead, for which purpose they have been lengthened
by the addition of false hair, so ingeniously joined as
nearly to escape detection. The orifices of the ears are
filled with tufts of cotton, and the same are passed
through slits in the lobuli. Mr. Blake suggests that
this may have been the head of some noted curaca or
chief of a hostile country taken in battle, and preserved

as a trophy ; but Dr. Morton refers to the practice of
the natives at Port Mulgrave on the north-west coast,
as well as those of other tribes, of decapitating their dead
chiefs, and preserving their heads apart. The same
singular custom prevails in the Ladrone and Society
Islands, as well as in others of the South Sea Islands,
from which it may be inferred that it was not the head
of an enemy, but of a person of distinction. The form
of the head has probably been modified by artificial
means. The abrupt prominence of the superciliary
ridges indicates the effect produced by compression on
the forehead, which has depressed the os frontis, and
given greater lateral width to the head.

The teeth in this head, and in all the adult Peruvian
skulls examined, are much worn. The incisors are ground
down from their cutting edge to a broad flat surface, and
the cuspidati have assumed a similar appearance. It is
a condition very common in the crania of primitive races
where simple diet preserves the teeth, subjecting them
to attrition without exposing them to decay. A nearly
similar appearance is presented in the crania found in
ancient British barrows and cromlechs ; though variations in the character of the food are sometimes traceable
by means of corresponding changes on the teeth. The
Walla-walla Indians on the Columbia river occupy a
barren waste, where they suffer greatly from the drifting
sand. They subsist almost entirely upon salmon, which
is dried in the sun. During this process, it becomes filled
with sand to such an extent that it wears away the teeth
with great rapidity. It is rare, indeed, to meet with a
Walla-walla Indian much beyond maturity whose teeth
are not worn down to the gums. The attrition of the
Peruvians' teeth Mr. Blake ascribes to a habit, still prevalent among the Indians, of chewing the leaf of the
coca, mixed with a substance they call *llute*, made by

compounding the wild potato with calcined shells and
ashes obtained from plants rich in alkali.

Such are the prevailing characteristics of Peruvian
crania, apart from the artificial conformation which many
of them exhibit, in common with others both of ancient
and modern times. Both the brachycephalic and the
dolichocephalic crania have been subjected to compression, and moulded by its means into a variety of fantastic
and distorted forms ; but there is no trace of the transformation by such means of the one form into the other.
They remain essentially distinct, whether in their normal
condition, or under all the variations begotten by
the strange custom of flattening and compressing the
skull in early infancy ; and furnish data altogether irreconcilable with the theory of one uniform and undeviating cranial type, shared by the Peruvians in common
with all other tribes and nations of the New World.

In an inquiry into the physical characteristics of the
Peruvian nation, we are by no means limited to the
cranial or the mere osteological remains recoverable from
its ancient cemeteries. Like the Egyptians, the Peruvians employed their ingenious skill in rendering the
bodies of their dead invulnerable to the assaults of
"decay's effacing fingers ;" and like the inhabitants of
the Nile Valley, they were able to do so under peculiarly
favourable circumstances of soil and climate. The
colours on Egyptian paintings, and the texture of their
finer handiwork, which have shown no trace of decay
through all the centuries during which they have lain
entombed in their native soil or catacombs, fade and
perish almost in a single generation when transferred to
the humid climates of Paris or London. The natural
impediments to decay probably contributed, alike in
Egypt and Peru, to the origination of the practice of
embalming. The cemeteries already referred to are

situated in a region where rain seldom or never falls ; and the dryness alike of the soil and atmosphere, when added to the natural impregnation of the sand with nitrous salts, almost precludes the decay of animal or vegetable matter, and preserves to us the finest woollen and cotton textures, with their brilliant dyes undimmed by time. By the same means we are enabled to judge of the colour and texture of the hair, the proportions and delicacy of the hands and feet, and the comparative physical development of two seemingly different races at various stages, from infancy to mature age. When we pass from the southern continent of America to the seats of ancient native civilisation lying to the north of the Isthmus, a different class of evidence, in like manner, enlarges our range of observation. The artistic ingenuity of the ancient Peruvian potter has left for us valuable memorials of native portraiture, and the Mexican picture-writing, with the sculptures and terra-cottas, the products of Toltec and Aztec ceramic art, in like manner contribute important evidence illustrative of the physiognomy and physical characteristics of the ancient races of Anahuac. Still more, the elaborate sculptures and stuccoed bas-reliefs of Central America, perpetuate in unmistakable characters the records of an ancient race, differing essentially from the modern Indian ; and the study of their cranial characteristics serves to confirm the deductions derived from those other independent sources.

The traditions of the Mexican plateau pointed to the comparatively recent intrusion of the fierce Mexican on older and more civilized races ; and various independent observers have at different times been tempted to trace associations between the ancient Mound-Builders of the Ohio, the elder civilized race of Mexico, and the Peruvians whose peculiar remains are recovered from the tombs around Lake Titicaca. That the predominant

Mexican race, at the era of the Conquest, belonged to
one of the great stocks of the Red Indian tribes of the
northern continent, appears to be demonstrable by various lines of independent proof, some of which have
been already glanced at ; but by none more so than the
portraiture in the Mexican paintings: The features there
are thoroughly Indian, with the single exception of the
remarkable Dresden Codex, where, on the contrary, the
striking correspondence has already been noted between

its portraiture and the bas-
reliefs of Palenque ; and a
comparison between the terra-
cotta figured here, from the
original in the collection of
the Society of Antiquaries of
Scotland, and others already
produced in previous chapters,
from various localities, will illustrate the same ethnic diversity. This example was found
in a tumulus on the Bay of
Honduras, and as strikingly
corresponds to some of the
Mexican paintings as the ma-

Fig. 64.—Terra-Cotta, Bay of Honduras.

jority of the Mexican terra-cottas differ from them. The
seats of ancient civilisation, both in Asia and Europe,
were confined, through all their earliest historic ages, to
the fertile and genial climates and warm latitudes of the
south. The north contributed the hardy barbarians to
whom, in their degeneracy, they became a spoil and a
prey. It is only in very modern times that Transalpine
Europe has given birth to a native northern civilisation,
while in Asia its northern latitudes still remain in the
occupation of wandering hordes descended from the
spoilers who ravaged the elder empires of Asia, and

shared with the barbarians of Europe in the dismemberment of decaying Rome. It is not from a mere accidental coincidence that we are able to recover traces of a nearly similar succession of events in the New World. Civilisation took root for a time in the Mississippi Valley, whether self-originated, or as an offshoot from the more favoured scenes of its mature development; but the great plateaus of Mexico and Peru were like well provisioned and garrisoned palaces and strongholds, where the spontaneous fertility of tropical climates relieved the wanderers who settled there from the all-absorbing struggle which elsewhere constitutes the battle with nature for life ; and the physical character of the country protected them alike from the temptations to wander, and the instability of settled communities in a nomade country. Yet they could not escape the vicissitudes which have befallen every nation, whose wealth and luxury have so far surpassed the acquisitions of its neighbours as to tempt the cupidity of the barbarian spoiler ; and the beautiful valleys of Mexico, the ancient Anahuac, appear to have experienced successive revolutions akin to those which render the ethnology of Italy's equally smiling soil and delightful climate so complicated and difficult. There are vague traditions of Olmecs, Miztecas, and Zapotecs, all highly-civilized precursors of the ancient Toltecs, whose entry on the plateau has been dated by most authorities about A.D. 600, and whose independent rule is supposed to have endured for nearly four and a half centuries. Then came the migration from the mythic Aztalan of the north, and the founding of the Aztec monarchy. The details of such traditions, with their dates and whole chronology, are valueless. But the general fact of the successive intrusion of conquering nations, and the consequent admixture of tribes and races, cannot be doubted. The civilized countries beyond the southern isthmus may have contributed some of them, and the dispersed Mound-Builders of Ohio may have been the intruders of other centuries; while the regions immediately surrounding the high valleys more frequently furnished the invading spoilers. But one result is to throw considerable uncertainty on any inferences drawn from cranial observations, unless deduced from numerous instances, accompanied with accurate data as to the circumstances and probable age of the exhumed remains. Of the crania obtained by Dr. Morton, only eight were of older date than the Conquest; and the names of Toltec, Aztec, and other national distinctions are frequently attached to such on no satisfactory grounds. A general uniformity is traceable in a considerable number of Mexican crania, but not without such notable exceptions as to admit of their division also into distinct dolichocephalic and brachycephalic groups, as in the following tables :—

TABLE IV.—MEXICAN DOLICHOCEPHALIC CRANIA.

	LOCALITY.	L. D.	P. D.	F. D.	V. D.	I. A.	I. L.	O. F. A.	·H. C.
1	Mexico, .	7·1	5·0	3·8	5·5	...	4·2	...	19·8
2	Otumba, . . .	7·1	5·6	4·6	5·5	15·5	4·1	15·0	20·2
3	Cerro de Quesilas, .	7·1	5·7	4·4	5·2	15·9	4·0	14·0	20·5
4	Acapacingo, F.	6·9	5·2	4·2	5·4	14·5	4·1	14·0	19·2
5	Tacuba, . .	7·1	5·6	4·5	5·4	15·2	4·3	14·2	20·0
6	,, . .	7·0	5·3	4·3	5·3	14·5	4·1	14·0	20·0
7	Mexico,	7·0	5·4	4·3	5·3	15·0	4·1	14·0	19·8
8	,, . .	7·1	5·5	4·4	5·2	15·8	4·1	14·0	20·4
	Mean, .	7·05	5·41	4·31	5·35	15·20	4·12	14·17	19·99

Of Table IV., No. 1 is in the collection of Dr. J. Mason Warren, of Boston, where it is simply marked "Mexican, ancient." No. 2, from an ancient tomb at Otumba, in Mexico, is noted by Dr. Morton (plate LXI.) as "approaching nearer to the Caucasian model, both in proportions and in facial angle." No. 3, on the same

authority, is characterized as "a relic of the genuine
Toltecan stock, having been exhumed from an ancient
cemetery at Cerro de Quesilas, near the city of Mexico."
No. 4 is also from an ancient tomb near that city, where
it was exhumed along with some of the remarkable terra-
cottas, pottery, masks, etc., now preserved with it in
the collection of the American Philosophical Society at
Philadelphia.　The remainder are in the collection of
the Academy of Natural Sciences.

TABLE V.—MEXICAN BRACHYCEPHALIC CRANIA.

	LOCALITY.	L. D.	P. D.	F. D.	V. D.	I. A.	I. L.	O. F. A.	H. C.
1	Mexico, .	6·6	5·8	3·9	5·9	14·7	4·3	...	20·0
2	,, .	6·6	5·7	4·0	...	15·0	...	14·5	20·0
3	Otumba, .	6·3	5·3	4·4	5·4	14·3	4·2	13·5	19·2
4	,, .	6·6	5·3	4·4	5·4	14·0	4·0	14·0	19·3
5	Tacuba, . .	6·8	5·5	4·6	6·0	15·6	4·4	14·6	19·9
6	San Lorenzo,	6·4	5·7	4·5	5·4	14·6	4·5	13·5	20·2
7	Mexico, Modern,	6·6	5·3	4·3	5·2	14·6	4·1	13·6	19·0
	Mean,	6·56	5·51	4·30	5·55	14·69	4·25	13·95	19·66

Of the brachycephalic group (Table v.), Nos. 1, 2,
are in the collection of the Natural History Society of
Boston.　No. 2 is characterized as an Aztec skull, but
is referred to in the Proceedings of the Society (vol. iii.
p. 272), on the authority of Dr. Kneeland, as belonging
to the Toltecan family.　Nos. 3, 4, are from ancient
tombs of Otumba; and Dr. Morton remarks, in reference
to No. 3, that its striking resemblance to Peruvian skulls
cannot be overlooked ; while of No. 5, with its remarkable vertical diameter, he notes its no less striking pre-
sentation of "all the prominent characteristics of the
American race."　No. 6 is figured by Morton, pl. xvii.
No. 7 is a pure breed native Mexican of the modern
race.　A comparison of those tables, along with the
incidental comments of Dr. Morton on some of the more
remarkable crania, suffices to show how little dependence

can be placed on any theory of homogeneous cranial characteristics pertaining to the races of Anahuac. From such evidences of the diversity of cranial type, which are found alike within the Mexican and Peruvian limits, we may admit, with the less hesitation, that a certain conformity may be traced between some of the ancient Mexican and Peruvian skulls and those of northern barbarous tribes. Notwithstanding the greater apparent proximity of Mexico than Peru, much more accurate cranial data have hitherto been obtained from the latter than the former country ; and while the great collection of the Academy of Natural Sciences of Philadelphia is furnished with ample materials for the study of Peruvian craniology, and has been largely augmented in this department since Dr. Morton's death ; it is still very imperfectly supplied with illustrations of the more complicated ethnic characteristics of the Mexican plateau, and has no materials derived from the ancient cemeteries of Central America. Until intelligent native Mexican observers shall carry on extensive observations on the spot, and classify the ancient crania, by means of archæological and other trustworthy evidence, so as to furnish some means of determining what is the typical Olmec, Toltec, and Aztec cranium, no satisfactory comparisons can be drawn between ancient Mexican crania and the corresponding types of the barbarous northern tribes. Unfortunately the Spanish-American colonists of Mexico, Yucatan, and Central America, have hitherto, with a few honourable exceptions, rather impeded than cooperated in any investigations calculated to throw light on the history and ethnology of those remarkable seats of a native American civilisation.

The Peruvians and Mexicans, with the ancient populations of Central America and Yucatan, constitute the Toltecan family of the two great divisions into which Dr.

Morton divided his one American " race or species." The nations lying to the north of those seats of a native civilisation, were all classed by him into one family of the barbarous tribes, resembling the other in physical, but differing from it in intellectual characteristics. Yet, as we have seen, even Dr. Morton recognised some differences among them ; and Professor Agassiz speaks of their tendency to split into minor groups, though running really one into the other. The following tables, however, will show that the differences are of a far more

TABLE VI.—AMERICAN DOLICHOCEPHALIC CRANIA.

	TRIBE	L. D.	P. D.	F. D.	V. D.	I. A.	I. L.	O. F. A.	H. C.
1	Seminole,	7·1	5·6	4·7	5·5	15·0	4·1	14·8	20·3
2	,,	7.3	5·9	4·6	5·8	15·9	4·4	15·3	20·7
3	,,	7·0	5·6	4·7	5·4	15·0	4·1	14·7	20·2
4	,,	7·3	5·6	4·2	5·6	15·2	4·7	15·0	20·4
5	,,	7·0	5·9	4·5	5·8	14·7	4·6	14·2	20·5
6	Cherokee, F.	7·2	5·2	4·2	5·5	14·5	4·0	14·6	20·2
7	,, F.	7·0	5·3	4·1	5·4	14·5	4·0	14·0	19·5
8	,,	7·2	5·3	4·3	5·3	14·1	4·5	14·0	19·1
9	Choctaw,	7·2	5·0	4·2	5·5	14·6	3·9	14·7	19·2
10	Sauk, F.	7·4	5·9	4·6	5·5	15·3	4·7	14·2	20·2
11	Ottigamie,	7·0	5·9	4·7	5·5	15·0	4·2	14·2	20·9
12	Chippewa,	7·3	5·8	4·8	5·5	15·1	4·6	14·2	20·9
13	,,	7·2	5·5	4·3	5·5	14·8	4·1	14·6	20·2
14	Pottowatomie,	7·8	5·7	4·4	5·3	16·0	4·0	15·8	22·1
15	Mississaga,	7·0	5·2	4·3	5·2	13·8	4·1	14·2	19·5
16	Delaware,	7·8	5·4	4·6	5·1	14·4	4·2	14·5	20·0
17	,,	7·0	5·5	4·4	6·2	15·6	4·3	16·0	21·5
18	Miami,	7·6	5·3	4·3	5·5	15·0	4·1	15·5	20·5
19	,,	7·3	5·5	4·3	5·5	14·6	4·6	14·9	21·0
20	Naumkeag,	7·4	5·5	4·4	5·9	15·0	4·3	14·0	...
21	,,	6·9	5·0	4·2	5·3	14·3	3·9	14·4	19·8
22	Assinaboine,	7·6	5·8	4·6	5·1	14·9	4·3	14·9	21·2
23	,,	7·5	5·7	4·4	5·2	14·7	4·6	14·7	20·8
24	Mandan, F.	7·1	5·4	4·3	5·1	14·2	3·8	14·6	20·0
25	,, F.	7·0	5·3	4·1	5·3	13·9	4·2	14·1	19·8
26	Ricara,	7·0	5·2	4·1	5·1	13·5	4·0	14·0	19·5
27	Mingo,	7·1	5·5	4·5	5·2	14·7	4·1	14·5	20·2
28	Menominee,	7·1	5·8	4·1	5·5	14·7	4·0	...	20·3
29	,,	7·1	5·4	3·9	5·2	13·3	4·4	...	19·3
30	,,	7·5	5·4	4·0	5·5	14·5	4·2	...	20·6
31	Minetari, F.	7·3	4·4	4·4	5·1	14·1	4·1	14·7	20·2
	Mean,	7·24	5·47	4·36	5·42	14·67	4·23	14·62	20·29

clearly defined nature, and in reality embrace the two
well-marked classes of brachycephalic and dolichocephalic
forms ; while of these, the latter seems decidedly the most
predominant. The examples are chiefly derived from the
Philadelphia collection, though with additional illustrations from the Boston cabinets already referred to, as
well as from Canadian collections. This table, which
illustrates the form of head most widely diverging in
proportions from the theoretical type, shows in reality
the prevailing characteristics of the north-eastern tribes,
and could easily be greatly extended. The opposite
or brachycephalic cranial formation is illustrated in
Table VII.

TABLE VII.—AMERICAN BRACHYCEPHALIC CRANIA.

	TRIBE.	L. D.	P. D.	F. D.	V. D.	I. A.	I. L.	O. F. A.	H. C.
1	Muskogee,	6·8	5·8	4·2	5·6	15·4	4·3	15·0	20·0
2	,,	6·6	5·7	4·5	5·3	15·3	4·5	14·0	20·4
3	Uchee,	6·8	5·4	4·3	5·5	15·0	4·4	14·3	20·1
4	Minsi,	6·7	5·0	4·2	5·3	14·0	4·1	13·8	19·3
5	Natick,	6·7	5·2	4·1	5·7	14·5	4·1	14·3	19·0
6	,,	6·7	5·2	4·3	5·3	14·2	3·9	14·1	19·1
7	Dacota,	6·7	5·7	4·2	5·4	14·7	4·4	13·5	19·8
8	,,	6·8	5·7	4·3	5·5	15·1	4·4	14·4	20·1
9	Pawnee, F.	6·6	5·4	4·4	4·9	13·7	4·3	13·0	19·1
10	,,	6·6	5·5	4·1	5·4	15·0	4·4	14·0	19·5
11	,,	6·5	5·5	4·0	5·4	14·8	4·4	14·1	19·3
12	,,	6·7	5·6	4·3	5·5	15·1	4·4	14·2	19·6
13	Chetimachee,	6·5	5·7	4·3	5·9	15·5	4·1	14·0	19·1
14	Chimuyan,	6·5	5·4	4·2	5·2	14·3	3·8	13·4	18·8
15	Osage,	6·6	5·7	4·3	5·2	14·8	4·7	13·8	19·5
16	,,	6·5	5·9	4·6	5·3	15·1	4·1	13·4	19·5
17	Creek,	6·9	5·7	4·6	5·4	15·5	4·7	14·4	20·4
18	Choctaw,	6·5	5·1	4·0	4·7	12·5	4·1	13·0	18·7
19	,,	6·4	5·1	4·0	5·1	14·0	4·0	...	19·7
20	"Ohio Mound," F.	6·4	5·3	3·9	5·0	14·2	4·0	...	19·0
21	Goajiro,	6·7	5·3	...	5·2	...	...	13·4	19·3
22	,,	6·5	5·1	...	4·9	...	...	13·0	18·5
	Mean,	6·62	5·45	4·24	5·30	14·63	4·25	13·85	19·44

But I now turn to the region around the northern
lakes, where opportunities of personal observation first
suggested to me the obvious discrepancies between the

actual evidence disclosed by exhumation on the sites of
native sepulture, and the theory of a typical unity manifested in the physical and peculiar cranial characteristics
of the most widely-separated tribes and nations of the
American continent. The Scioto Mound skull, characterized by Dr. Morton as " the perfect type of Indian
conformation to which the skulls of all the tribes from
Cape Horn to Canada more or less approximate," presents the remarkable anterior development of a cranium
whereof two-thirds of the cerebral mass was in front of
the meatus auditorius externus ; whereas in the elon
gated Peruvian skull, unaltered by artificial means, this
is almost exactly reversed, showing by the proportions
of the cerebral cavity that fully two-thirds of the brain
lay behind the meatus auditorius. These may be considered as representing the two extremes ; but both of
the two great stocks between whom the northern region
around the great lakes has been chiefly divided since
the first intrusion of Europeans, belong to the dolichocephalic division. These are the Algonquins and the
Iroquois, including in the latter the Hurons, who, with
the Petuns, Neuters, and Eries, all belonged to the same
stock, though involved in deadly enmity with each
other. In the supposed typical Scioto Mound skull the
longitudinal, parietal, and vertical diameters vary very
slightly ; and as the Mexican and Peruvian crania
chiefly attracted Dr. Morton's attention, and are illustrated minutely, as a series, in his great work, it only
required the further theory, which referred all the elongated skulls to an artificially modified class, to confirm
in his mind that idea of a peculiarly formed cranium
pertaining uniformly and exclusively to the New World.
To the theoretical type of a head very nearly corresponding in length and breadth, though not in height, the
most numerous class of Peruvian and Mexican brachy-

cephalic crania unquestionably approximate. Of one of the former, from the Temple of the Sun (Plate xi.), Dr. Morton remarks : " A strikingly characteristic Peruvian head. As is common in this series of skulls, the parietal and longitudinal diameter is nearly the same," viz., longitudinal, 6·1 ; parietal, 6·0 ; and, tested by this standard, he was even more justified in recognising marked points of correspondence between the Mound skulls, and what he calls " the Toltecan branch of the American race," than might seem reasonable from the miscellaneous character of the crania referred to by him as " Mound skulls." But the moment we test by actual measurement, and not by the eye, a very wide difference is apparent between the brachycephalic crania of the class referred to, and the prevailing form of the head in many of the northern tribes, as among the Algonquins, Hurons, and Iroquois. The Algonquin stock are represented by Ottawas, Mississagas, Chippewas, and other tribes, within the area of Upper Canada and along the shores of Lake Superior. Of Indians belonging to Iroquois and Algonquin tribes I have examined, and compared by the eye, many at widely-scattered places : on the Thames and Grand Rivers, Rice Lake, Lake Simcoe and the Georgian Bay ; at Mackinaw in Lake Huron, and at Sault Ste. Marie ; at Ontonagon, La Point, the Apostle Islands, and the St. Louis River, on Lake Superior ; and on the Saguenay, St. Charles, St. Maurice, and Ottawa rivers, in Lower Canada ; as well as on such chance opportunities as occur in the neighbourhood of our Canadian towns and villages. Physiognomically they present the large and prominent mouth, high cheek-bones, and broad face, so universally characteristic of the American Indian ; but they by no means possess in a remarkable degree the wide and massive lower jaw, which has been noted as of universal occurrence among the Red Indians. Still more noticeable is the absence of the aquiline nose, so characteristic generally of the true Indian in contradistinction to the Esquimaux. The eye may be fully depended on for physiognomical characteristics ; though of little service in testing minuter variations of cranial proportions, especially when dependent on observations made on the living head, covered with the thickly-matted and long coarse hair of the Indian. Nor are actual measurements very readily obtained ; for other obstacles—even more difficult to surmount than such natural impediments to observation,—interfere, and enlist both the superstitions and the fears of the Indian in antagonism to the inquisitions of science. I have been baffled repeatedly in attempts to induce an Indian to submit his head to the dreaded appliance of the callipers ; and have found him not only resist every attempt that could be ventured on, backed by arguments of the most practical kind, but on the solicitation being pressed too urgently, have seen him tremble, and manifest the strongest signs of fear, not unaccompanied with anger, such as made retreat prudent. In other cases where the Indian has been induced to submit his head to examination, his squaw has interfered and vehemently protested against the dangerous operation. The chief object of dread seems to be lest thereby the secrets of the owner should be revealed to the manipulator ; but this rather marks the more definite form of apprehension in the mind of the Christianized Indian. With others it is simply a vague dread of power being thereby acquired over them, such as Mr. Paul Kane informs me frequently interfered to prevent his taking portraits of the Indians of the North-west, unless by stealth.

The following Table (VIII.) embodies the results of examinations of twelve living representatives of Algon-

quin tribes, including six Chippewas at the Indian reserve on Lake Couchiching, three Ottawas from Lake
Huron, and three Abenakis from the St. Maurice.

TABLE VIII.—ALGONQUIN INDIANS.

	NAME.	L. D.	P. D.	F. D.	I. M. A.	H. C.
1	Kobsequan,	7·4	6·0	5·0	14·8	22·3
2	Nowkeisegwab,	7·1	6·0	5·4	15·4	22·1
3	Pahtahsega,	7·3	5·8	5·4	15·0	22·6
4	Shilling, Joseph,	7·5	6·1	5·6	14·4	22·9
5	Shilling, Jacob,	6·9	6·0	5·1	14·7	22·0
6	Snake, William,	7·1	6·0	5·5	15·1	22·0
7	Kahgosega,	7·4	5·8	5·0	15·2	21·6
8	Ganahwahbi,	7·2	5·9	4·8	14·9	21·8
9	Assikinack,	7·2	6·0	4·7	14·2	22·4
10	Nanahmahbiquan,	7·3	5·9	5·1	14·3	22·0
11	Nowgosedah,	7·2	6·0	5·4	15·0	22·3
12	Mosunhkirhine,	7·4	6·6	5·0	14·2	22·4
	Mean,	7·25	6·00	5·17	14·77	22·20

Some of the measurements in the living head are
necessarily affected by the hair, always coarse and abundant with the Indian. Others again, such as the vertical diameter, cannot be taken ; but the mastoid processes
are sufficiently prominent to leave little room for error
in the measurement of the inter-mastoid arch ; and this
suffices to show the very exceptional approximation of
the modern Algonquin head to the ancient type, in the
proportional elevation of the vertex : in so far, at least,
as it is illustrated by these examples. In the horizontal
circumference some deduction must be made for the hair,
to bring it to the true cranial measurement in all the
six living examples.

From the above measurements, along with other observations, the Abenakis and Chippewas appear to indicate a less marked deviation from some of the assumed
characteristics of the American cranial type, in this
widely-spread branch of the Indian stock, than is observable in other northern races ; and especially than

is apparent on an examination of skulls belonging to the original Huron occupants of the greater part of the country around Lakes Simcoe and.Couchiching, where the Chippewas more especially referred to are now settled. The proportions thus given as characteristic of the widely-diffused Algonquin stock, indicate that they pertain to the dolichocephalic division, of which Tables XI., XII., XIII. furnish evidence suggestive of a generally prevailing divergence from the more common Peruvian and the supposed Mound type among the northern tribes. The extent of this divergence will be no less clearly shown by referring to some of the most characteristic examples furnished in the *Crania Americana.* The radical variation from the assumed typical proportions is obvious, for example, in the Miami cranium : the head of a celebrated chief, eloquent, of great bravery, and uncompromising hostility to the whites ; and is equally apparent in those of the Potowatomies, the Blackfeet, Menominees, and the Delawares. In most of those of which measurements are given by Dr. Morton, the longitudinal diameter is nearly, and in some more than two inches in excess both of the parietal and vertical diameters ; and in other respects they differ little less widely from the characteristics of the brachycephalic crania.

Such are indications of data—derived from a source altogether unexceptionable in the present argument,— which seem to render it impossible to uphold the views so repeatedly affirmed, of the physiognomical, physiological, and, above all, the cranial unity characterizing the whole ancient and modern aborigines of the New World. But the Algonquins, Iroquois, and Hurons of the St. Lawrence valley and the Lake regions, which have been recognised by many writers as specially typical of the predominant characteristics of the northern Red Indian, furnish evidence equally confirmatory of the diversified physical characteristics of American nations. Of them Dr. Latham remarks : " The Iroquois and Algonquins exhibit in the most typical form the characteristics of the North American Indians, as exhibited in the earliest descriptions, and are the two families upon which the current notions respecting the physiognomy, habits, and moral and intellectual powers of the so-called Red race are chiefly founded."[1] In many respects, however, they presented a striking contrast. The Algonquin stock, chiefly represented by the modern Chippewas, is only known to us as embracing rude hunter tribes; or where found under the protection of the government of the province, and settled on the Indian reserves of Upper Canada, they illustrate in a remarkable manner the unstable condition of savage life prior to the introduction of any foreign disturbing elements : for they are, with very partial exceptions, more recent intruders within the Canadian clearings than the Europeans; and the extirpation of the aboriginal occupants of Canada is wholly ascribable to native wars. In the brief interval between Cartier's first discovery of Canada, and its exploration and settlement by Champlain, the whole country between the Ottawa and Lake Simcoe appears to have been depopulated ; and the Wyandots and allied tribes, driven westward by their implacable Iroquois foes, were settled in palisaded villages in the country around Lake Simcoe and the Georgian Bay. The Huron nation embraced four tribes among whom agriculture was systematically pursued : probably with all the more assiduity that the restriction of their hunting-grounds by the encroachments of the Iroquois must have made them more dependent on its resources. To the south-west of this

---

[1] *Varieties of Man,* p. 333.

country, in the high ground between the Georgian Bay
and Lake Erie, the allied nation of the Tiontonones was
settled. The Niagara district was in like manner filled
up by the Attiwendaronks or Neuters, of the same stock;
and all along the river banks and smaller lake shores, traces
of Indian villages and cemeteries prove that at an earlier
date the whole country was filled up with a corresponding native population. The Wyandots, as they styled
themselves, only became known to Europeans in their
decline, and immediately before their extirpation. They
were then in alliance with the Adirondacks against their
common Iroquois foe, and probably a certain portion of
the skulls found in Upper Canadian cemeteries belongs
to the latter. But the Algonquin cranium, though less
markedly dolichocephalic than the Huron or Iroquois
skulls, belongs to the same class ; and to one or other of
these nearly all the Canadian crania may with little hesitation be assigned.

Of Indian skulls chiefly dug up within the district
once pertaining to the Huron or Wyandot branch of the
Iroquois stock, I had observed and cursorily examined a
considerable number, before my attention was especially
drawn to the peculiar characteristics now under consideration, owing to repeated rejection of those which
turned up, as failing to furnish specimens of the assigned
typical American head. Since then I have carefully
examined and measured seventy-one Indian skulls belonging, as I believe, to the Wyandot or the Algonquin
stock, with the following results :—

1. Only five exhibit such an agreement with the assigned American type, as, judged by the eye, to justify
their classification as true brachycephalic crania. One of
these (Table IX. No. 23), a very remarkable and massive
skull, was turned up at Barrie, on Lake Simcoe, with, it
is said, upwards of two hundred others. It differs from

all the others in exhibiting the vertical occiput so very
strikingly, that when resting on it, it stands more firmly
than in any other position. This is, without doubt, the
result of artificial compression; and in so far as fashion
regulated the varying forms thus superinduced on the
natural cranial conformation, it is suggestive of an intruder from the country lying towards the mouth of the
Mississippi, where the ancient graves of the Natchez
tribes disclose many skulls moulded into this singular
form. No note has been preserved of the general character of the crania discovered at the same time; but
this one no doubt owed its selection to its peculiar form.
The whole subject of occipital and varied cranial compression is deserving of minuter consideration than is
admissible in reference to the Huron crania, which exhibit in general no traces of an abnormal formation.
Nor is Dr. Morton's assignment of the vertical occiput
as one of the most characteristic features of the true
American cranium borne out by an examination of those
found in Canadian cemeteries. On the contrary, I have
been struck with the evidence afforded by the majority
of skulls examined by me, that such was certainly no
prevailing characteristic of the Huron or other tribes, by
whom Upper Canada was occupied prior to its European
settlement. Many of them, indeed, exhibit a total absence of any approximation to the flattened occiput.
Twenty of the crania referred to show a more or less
decided posterior projection of the occiput: eighteen of
these being markedly so, and ten of them presenting
such a prolongation of it, as constituted one of the most
striking features in one class of ancient Scottish crania,
which chiefly led to the suggestion of the term Kumbecephalic, as a distinctive term for them. But since my
observations on this subject were first published,[1] the

---

[1] "Supposed prevalence of one Cranial Type throughout the American

special question of the prevailing form of the occiput has
been taken up in a valuable monograph contributed by
Dr. J. Aitken Meigs to the Transactions of the Academy
of Natural Sciences of Philadelphia.[1]　The conclusions
he arrives at are : that the form of the human occiput is
not constant, but varies even among individuals of the
same race or tribe.　He divides the different forms into
three primary classes: 1st, The protuberant occiput, which
is exhibited among the nations of the New World by the
Esquimaux, Chippewas, Hurons, and more or less among
thirty-six different American tribes or nations.　2d, The
vertically flattened occiput he assigns as more or less
prevalent among sixteen tribes, and characteristic of the
majority of the Mound-Builders.　3d, The full and
rounded or globular occiput characterizes nine American
nations or tribes, and occurs occasionally in a greater
number.　But the final summary of Dr. Meigs goes even
further than this ; and, treating as it does, not solely of
the American, but of the human occipital formation, it
very effectually deals with all theories of radical diversities of human varieties or distinct species, in so far
as this important subdivision of osteological evidence
is concerned, by affirming, as the result of observations
made on eleven hundred and twenty-five human crania,
" that there is a marked tendency of these forms to graduate into each other, more or less insensibly.　None of
these forms can be said to belong exclusively to any race
or tribe.　None of them, therefore, can be regarded as
strictly typical : for a character or form to be typical
should be exclusive and constant."　In his elaborate
observations, Dr. Meigs has still left untouched the pecu-

Aborigines."—*Canadian Journal*, November 1857 ; *Edinburgh New Philosophical Journal*, January 1858.
[1] *Observations upon the Form of the Occiput in the Various Races of Men*,
by J. Aitken Meigs, M.D.　Philadelphia, 1860.

liarities which distinguish the female occiput. One elongated protuberant form appears to me to be found only in the female head ; but a comparative estimate of the occipital variations in the two sexes, as exhibited in the different races, is necessary to complete this interesting inquiry.

2. The tendency to the pyramidal form, occasioned by the angular junction of the parietal bones, is apparent in the majority of the skulls examined. I have noted its occurrence as a prominent characteristic in twenty-three Canadian crania, of which ten exhibit a strongly marked pyramidal form, extending to the frontal bone. Nevertheless, it is by no means constant. Both in the Morton Collection, and in the examples specially noted here, it is only slightly indicated in some, while in others it is entirely wanting.

3. I am further struck with the frequency of the very partial projection, and in some examples with the total absence of the superciliary ridge : a characteristic which, so far as I am aware, has not been noted by other observers. In some the prominent ridge stretches entirely across the brow, forming a deep hollow at the junction of the os frontis and the bones of the nose ; and this appears to be the case in the best authenticated Mound skulls. In the Scioto Valley cranium it is markedly so, and it is little less apparent in the Grave Creek Mound, Tennessee, and Mississippi skulls. In this respect they differ from the majority of the Peruvian crania, with which in other respects they have been supposed so nearly to agree, that, overlooking this prominent physiognomical feature, the lost Mound-Builders have been thought to reappear as the ancient architects of Peru. In the great majority of the crania figured by Morton, the very slight development, and in some, the total absence of a projecting superciliary ridge, is very notice-

able. In thirteen of the Canadian skulls carefully noted
by me, the same feature is particularly manifest. In
the majority of these the os frontis slopes without
any indentation to the edges of the orbits ; and when
taken into consideration along with the pyramidal
vertex and predominant longitudinal diameter, suggests
affinities, hitherto overlooked, with the Esquimaux form
of skull.

4. It is also worthy of note that, whereas Dr. Morton
states, as the result of his experience, that the most distant points of the parietal bones are for the most part
the parietal protuberances, out of fifty-one Canadian
skulls, I have only found such to be the case in three,
all of which were female. The widest parietal measurement is generally a little above the squamous suture,
and in some examples a still wider diameter is given
between the temporal bones. Somewhat minute observations, accompanied in part with measurements, of
numerous examples in the unrivalled collection of the
Academy of Sciences of Philadelphia, incline me to
believe that this is a common characteristic of American
crania.

The following tables (Tables IX., XI.) exhibit the relative proportions of the crania found in Upper Canada,
in so far as they can be shown by such a series of
measurements. Embracing, as they do, the indices of
the comparative length, breadth, height, and circumference of seventy skulls, procured without any special
selection from Indian cemeteries lying, with only four
exceptions, to the north of Lakes Erie and Ontario, they
supply a series derived from a sufficient number to indicate some constant proportions, and to mark certain
elements of contrast instead of comparison, when placed
alongside of the corresponding relative proportions in
the tables of brachycephalic crania.

TABLE IX.—WESTERN CANADA : HURONS.

	LOCALITY.	L. D.	P. D.	F. D.	V. D.	I. A.	I. L.	O. F. A.	H. C.
1	Orillia, . . .	7·5	5·7	4·5	5·6	15·6	4·2	15·0	21·1
2	,, . . .	7·4	5·5	4·4	5·4	14·7	4·5	...	20·6
3	,, . . .	7·3	5·7	4·2	5·7	15·3	4·3	14·1	20·5
4	,, . . .	7·5	5·6	4·2	5·4	14·7	4·3	14·6	21·1
5	,, . . .	7·2	5·3	4·3	5·3	14·5	4·3	14·3	20·3
6	,, F. .	7·3	5·5	4·3	5·1	13·7	4·2	14·3	20·5
7	Owen Sound, . .	7·0	5·5	4·2	5·0	13·8	4·0	14·0	19·8
8	,, . .	7·3	5·3	4·3	5·3	14·4	4·2	14·2	20·4
9	,, . .	7·2	5·4	3·8	5·2	14·5	3·9	14·2	19·9
10	,, . .	7·7	5·4	4·7	5·6	14·6	4·2	15·0	21·4
11	,, . .	7·5	5·9	5·1	5·5	15·0	4·3	15·6	21·8
12	,, . .	7·6	5·5	4·5	5·4	14·6	4·5	14·9	21·3
13	Georgian Bay, .	7·6	5·6	4·2	5·4	14·6	4·7	15·0	21·1
14	,, F. .	6·8	5·2	4·0	5·2	13·3	3·8	13·7	19·0
15	,, F. .	7·4	4·9	4·2	5·3	13·3	...	14·1	20·0
16	Oro, . . .	7·5	5·6	4·4	5·5	15·6	4·3	15·2	21·4
17	,, . . .	7·4	5·4	...	4·3	15·2	4·0	14·9	20·4
18	Medonte, . .	7·6	5·2	3·9	5·6	14·8	4·5	15·2	20·5
19	,, . . .	7·2	5·5	4·4	5·8	15·2	4·5	14·5	20·2
20	,, . . .	7·6	5·6	4·5	5·6	15·4	4·2	15·0	21·4
21	,, . . .	7·3	5·3	4·2	5·4	14·2	4·1	14·4	20·4
22	Penetanguishene, .	7·8	5·6	4·6	5·9	15·5	4·5	15·6	21·3
23	Barrie, . . .	6·6	6·4	5·2	5·3	16·0	4·6	14·4	20·7
24	,, . . .	6·9	5·5	4·1	5·1	14·0	4·1	...	19·7
25	,, . . .	7·4	5·4	4·2	5·2	14·5	4·4	...	20·7
26	,, . . .	7·3	5·3	4·2	5·4	14·6	4·1	14·4	20·5
27	Tecumseth, . .	7·3	5·6	4·4	5·5	14·5	4·9	14·4	20·2
28	,, F. .	7·2	5·2	3·9	5·0	14·1	3·6	14·2	19·7
29	,, . .	7·9	6·0	4·6	5·7	16·0	3·4	16·1	20·0
30	,, F. .	7·6	5·3	4·3	5·6	14·0	4·1	14·3	20·2
31	,, F. .	7·5	5·2	4·1	5·1	13·4	4·2	14·8	20·5
32	,, . .	7·4	5·6	4·6	5·5	15·0	4·4	15·0	20·9
33	,, . .	7·6	5·4	4·2	5·7	15·1	4·4	15·3	20·9
34	Whitchurch, . .	7·5	5·3	4·2	5·7	15·1	4·2	14·6	20·4
35	Newmarket, . .	7·2	5·6	4·6	6·7	15·7	4·2	15·0	20·3
36	,, F. .	7·6	5·2	4·1	5·3	14·7	4·0	14·1	19·5
37	Oakridges, . .	7·6	5·5	4·7	6·0	15·7	4·6	15·0	21·2
38	,, F. . .	6·8	4·8	4·2	5·0	13·6	4·0	13·2	18·9
	Mean, . .	7·37	5·46	4·34	5·43	14·70	4·23	14·65	20·50

Of the Crania in Table IX., Nos. 3, 13-16, 18, 37, 38, are in the Museum of the University of Toronto ; Nos. 4-10, in the Museum of Trinity College, Toronto ; Nos. 22, 23, in the Museum of the Canadian Institute ; Nos. 11, 12, 24-26, 35, 36, in the Collection of Professor Bovell, M.D., Toronto; No. 17, Rev. J. Gray, Orillia; Nos. 19, 20, Mr. B. W. Gossage, C.E. ; Nos. 27-33, Dr. Hodder; No. 34, Mr. Cawthra, Toronto ; and Nos. 1, 2, 21, in the Author's possession.

The measurements in Table IX. are derived from thirty-eight crania obtained from Indian graves in the localities to the north of the water-shed, between Georgian Bay and Lakes Erie and Ontario; and the greater number of them from ossuaries opened within the area lying between Lake Simcoe and Lake Huron. The graves, therefore, were situated in the ancient country of the Hurons, and may be assigned without hesitation to the tribes found in occupation of that country when first visited by the French Jesuit missionaries in the seventeenth century. The materials thus obtained embrace a sufficient number of examples to illustrate the average proportions and relative measurements of the Huron cranium, and to furnish satisfactory data for comparison with those of other Indian nations. Belonging as the Hurons did, to the same ethnic group as the Indians of the Iroquois League, though at deadly enmity with them, their skulls exhibit the same remarkable deviation from the assumed typical American head, in the great preponderance of the longitudinal diameter. In this respect, indeed, they exceed the relative proportions of the Algonquin crania, though these also decidedly belong to the dolichocephalic class.

Table X. which follows, rests on a very different authority from the preceding one. No. 1 supplies the proportions of the skull of the celebrated Mohawk chief, Joseph Brant (Tyendanaga), from a cast taken on the opening of his grave, at the interment of his son, John Brant, in 1852. Nos. 2-7 are from the *Crania Americana*, and include all the Iroquois and Huron examples given there. Nos. 8-10 are ancient skulls from the Island of Montreal, now in the Museum of M'Gill College, and correspond closely to the other crania of the Iroquois stock. As a whole it will be seen that these results agree in the main with those arrived at by my own independent observations ; while a comparison of the tables will be satisfactory to those who may still hesitate to adopt conclusions adverse to opinions reaffirmed under various forms by Dr. Morton, and adopted and made the basis of such comprehensive inductions by his successors.

TABLE X.—IROQUOIS CRANIA.

	TRIBE.	L. D.	P. D.	F. D.	V. D.	I. A.	I. L.	O. F. A.	R. C.
1	Mohawk, Brant, ·	7·8	6·0	5·0	...	15·6 ?	...	...	22·0
2	Oneida, 33, · ·	7·5	5·6	4·1	5·8	14·4	4·3	14·9	20·8
3	Cayuga, 417, · ·	7·8	5·1	4·2	5·4	14·2	4·5	15·5	20·8
4	Huron, 607, F. ·	6·7	5·6	4·1	5·2	14·5	3·9	14·0	19·2
5	,, 15, ·	7·2	5·3	4·3	5·5	15·0	4·4	14·2	19·8
6	Iroquois, 16, ·	7·5	5·5	4·5	5·7	15·2	4·5	15·1	20·8
7	,, A.N.S. ·	7·1	5·4	4·2	5·3	14·3	4·0	14·1	20·0
8	Iroquet, F. ·	6·8	5·2	4·0	5·3	...	...	13·7	19·3
9	,, · ·	7·5	5·8	4·0	5·5	13·5	...	14·4	21·0
10	,, · ·	7·0	5·5	4·7	5·5	13·5	...	14·5	20·7
	Mean, ·	7·29	5·50	4·41	5·47	14·47	4·27	14·49	20·44

The intimate relations in language, manners, and the traditions of a common descent, between those northern and southern branches of the Iroquois stock, render these two tables, in so far as they present concurrent results, applicable as a common test of the supposed homogeneous cranial characteristics of the aboriginal American, in relation to the area of the great lakes. Thirty-eight skulls, such as the first table supplies, the larger number of which belong without doubt to the Huron stock, or forty-eight as the result of both, may, perhaps, appear too small a number on which to base conclusions adverse to those promulgated by an observer so distinguished and so persevering as Dr. Morton, and accepted by writers no less worthy of esteem and deference. But, in addition to the fact that the measurements now supplied, are only the more carefully noted data which have tended to confirm conclusions suggested by previous examinations, in a less detailed manner, of a much larger number of examples, in addition to minute observations of the living representatives of the Indian tribes : an investigation of the materials which supplied the elements of earlier inductions, will show that only in the case of the ancient "Toltecan" tribes did Dr. Morton examine nearly so many examples ; while, in relation to what he designated the "Barbarous Race," to which the northern tribes belong, even in Dr. Meigs' greatly enlarged cata- logue of the Morton Collection, as augmented since his death, the Seminole crania present the greatest number belonging to one tribe, and these only amount to sixteen.

In the following Table XI., the measurements of thirty- two Canadian skulls are given, the whole of which have been obtained from graves lying to the south and east of the true Huron country, towards the shores of Lakes Erie and Ontario, or on the north bank of the St. Law- rence. Some portions of Western Canada, including localities referred to, were occupied in the early part of the seventeenth century by tribes allied to the Hurons ; but on their deserted areas the Algonquin tribes from the north and west have everywhere preceded the Eng- lish settlers, and the greater number of the crania intro- duced in this Table may be assigned without hesitation to Algonquin tribes. No. 24 is designated by Dr. Morton a Mississaga skull, and probably most, if not all, of those numbered consecutively from 16 to 28 belong to the same tribe. Nos. 29 to 32 are from Abenakis graves on the St. Maurice. As a whole, the examples thus grouped together present a sufficient number to furnish some adequate approximation to the prevailing typical specialities of the Algonquin head. They exhibit, it will be observed, a greater preponderance in the char- acteristic excess of longitudinal diameter than is shown in the cognate Chippewa heads in Table VIII., though all alike pertain to the same dolichocephalic class, and essentially contrast with the familiar brachycephalic type of Peru, and of the Mississippi Valley mounds.

TABLE XI.—CANADA: ALGONQUINS.

	LOCALITY.	L. D.	P. D.	F. D.	V. D.	I. A.	I. L.	O F. A.	H. C.
1	Windsor, . .	7·0	5·7	4·7	5·7	15·2	4·3	14·5	20·1
2	,, . . .	7·0	5·7	4·5	5·7	16·1	4·0	14·4	20·1
3	,, . . .	7·4	6·1	4·9	5·7	...	4·5	15·5	21·4
4	,, . . .	6·6	5·3	4·2	5·5	14·5	4·2	13·5	19·0
5	Burford, . .	6·5	5·2	4·1	5·0	13·4	4·0	13·0	18·4
6	Grand River, . .	6·7	5·4	4·2	5·2	14·3	4·0	13·5	19·3
7	,, . .	7·5	5·6	4·4	5·4	15·0	4·1	15·2	21·0
8	Burlington Bay, .	7·0	5·3	4·4	5·3	14·0	4·0	13·6	19·5
9	,, .	7·6	5·6	4·4	5·4	15·2	4·2	14·9	20·9
10	Nelson, F. . .	7·5	5·2	4·2	5·5	14·0	4·6	15·0	20·4
11	,, . . .	8·2	5·5	4·3	5·5	14·9	4·3	15·5	21·0
12	,, . . .	7·7	5·9	5·3	5·4	15·0	4·7	15·3	21·5
13	,, F. . .	7·3	5·5	4·1	5·1	14·0	4·3	14·7	20·5
14	,, F. . .	7·3	5·4	4·0	5·2	14·4	4·3	14·4	20·5
15	,, F. . .	7·2	5·4	3·7	5·3	14·3	4·0	14·3	19·8
16	River Humber, .	7·6	5·9	5·7	5·5	15·4	4·7	14·2	21·1
17	,, .	6·8	5·6	4·5	5·1	14·1	4·5	13·9	19·9
18	,, .	7·5	5·5	4·2	5·3	14·5	4·2	14·3	20·3
19	Burwick, .	7·5	5·7	4·2	5·6	15·3	4·5	14·9	21·0
20	,, .	7·2	5·1	4·4	5·6	14·3	4·3	14·7	21·0
21	Peterboro', . .	7·7	5·5	4·9	5·3	15·4	4·6	15·0	21·1
22	,, .	7·4	5·3	4·2	5·3	13·8	4·2	14·1	20·6
23	,, .	6·5	5·2	3·9	4·9	13·3	3·8	13·7	19·2
24	,, .	7·0	5·2	4·3	5·2	13·8	4·1	14·2	19·3
25	Rice Lake, . .	7·1	6·5	3·9	6·3	14·5	4·3	14·2	20·0
26	Bay of Quinte, .	7·9	5·8	4·5	5·3	14·3	4·9	14·8	21·7
27	,, .	7·0	5·5	4·2	5·0	14·0	4·6	13·9	20·5
28	,, .	7·4	6·0	4·8	5·3	14·6	4·7	14·5	20·9
29	St. Maurice, . .	7·0	5·3	4·1	5·3	13·0	4.4	14·0	20·5
30	,, .	7·5	5·7	5·0	5·5	14·2	5·0	14·4	21·0
31	,, .	7·0	5·5	4·7	5·5	14·0	4·2	14·5	20·7
32	Three Rivers, . .	7·4	6·5	5·0	5·1	14·2	4·6	15·0	21·9
	Mean, . .	7·25	5·58	4·43	5·37	14·42	4·35	14·42	20·44

Of the Crania referred to in Table XI., Nos. 1-4, 8, 9, 16-18, are in the Museum of the University of Toronto; Nos. 22, 23, 25, in the Museum of Trinity College, Toronto; No. 20, Knox's College, Toronto; No. 24, Morton Collection (27); Nos. 6, 10-15, 19, Professor Bovell, M.D.; Nos. 26-28, Mr. T. C. Wallbridge, Toronto; and Nos. 5, 7, 29-32, in the Author's possession.

But the term Algonquin, though apparently specially employed originally in reference to Canadian tribes, is now used as a generic appellation of a very comprehensive kind, and embraces ancient and modern tribes extending from the Labrador and New England coasts to far beyond the head of Lake Superior. In this comprehensive use of the term, its application is chiefly based on philological evidence; and it points thereby to affinities of language connecting numerous and widely-severed nations throughout the whole area lying between the Rocky Mountains and the Atlantic.

The following Table XII. includes the measurements of twenty crania of New England tribes, partly derived from data furnished in the *Crania Americana,* and the remainder obtained directly from observations made on the original skulls preserved in American collections. At Providence, Rhode Island, where, from the zeal manifested by the Historical Society of that State, I had hoped to obtain access to valuable materials in this and other departments of American ethnography and archæology, I was informed that a considerable collection of aboriginal crania, formerly preserved there, had been recently sent to Paris. There they will doubtless be appreciated as links in a comprehensive craniological series; but it is difficult to conceive of their possessing so great a value as on the locality where they constituted interesting memorials of an extinct nation and a nearly obliterated history. I examined and measured the specimens preserved in the collections of the Natural History Society, and of Dr. J. Mason Warren, at Boston; but when at Philadelphia, my attention was chiefly occupied with the mound and cave skulls, and those of Mexico, Central and Southern America, so that I unfortunately neglected to secure measurements of the examples of Narraganset and Natick Indians preserved there, amounting to ten of the former, and five of the latter tribe. In the following Table, the measurements

of the skulls of Natick Indians of Nantucket are given
from Dr. Morton's Table, but none of them appear to
correspond with those now in the Collection of Philadelphia ; and no record is preserved of the sex. From
their smaller proportions it is probable that several of
them may be female skulls, and thereby render the general results below the fair average of the Natick cranium.
The mean proportions of the ten skulls are added to the
Table, along with the total mean :—

TABLE XII.—NEW ENGLAND CRANIA.

	LOCALITY.	L. D.	P. D.	F. D.	V. D.	I. A.	I. L.	O. F. A.	B. C.
1	Massachusetts,	7·0	5·55	4·0	5·3	15·1	3·8	...	20·4
2	Salem, Mass., .	6·9	5·0	4·2	5·3	14·3	3·9	14·4	19·8
3	,, . .	7·4	5·5	4·4	5·9	15·0	4·3	14·0	18·7
4	Milton, Mass., .	7·1	5·4	3·7	5·2	13·3	4·4	...	19·3
5	Nahant, . .	7·1	5·8	3·9	5·5	14·7	4·0	...	20·3
6	Nantucket, . .	6·7	5·2	4·1	5·7	14·5	4·1	14·3	19·0
7	,, .	6·9	5·4	4·3	5·3	14·3	4·1	13·9	19·9
8	,, . .	6·9	5·1	4·1	5·1	13·1	4·1	14·0	19·2
9	,, . .	6·7	5·2	4·3	5·3	14·2	3·9	14·1	19·1
10	,, .	7·0	5·1	4·1	5·2	13·3	4·1	13·9	19·5
11	,, . .	6·7	5·3	4·5	5·3	14·0	4·0	14·4	19·5
12	,, .	7·4	5·7	4·4	5·7	15·0	5·0	15·0	21·5
13	,, .	6·9	5·2	4·2	5·5	13·3	4·1	13·7	19·5
14	,, . .	7·0	5·1	4·3	5·1	13·5	4·1	14·2	19·0
15	,, .	6·9	5·1	4·0	5·2	13·9	4·1	14·1	20·2
16	East Haven, Con.,	7·0	5·7	4·7	5·3	15·1	4·1	14·1	20·2
17	Maine, . . .	6·8	5·1	4·2	5·6	14·5	4·0	14·4	19·0
18	Cumberland, R. I.,	7·4	6·1	4·9	4·8	14·3	4·2	...	21·3
19	,, .	7·5	5·6	3·7	5·9	15·3	4·2	...	20·7
20	,,	7·2	5·3	4·6	5·2	14·5	4·1	...	19·7
	Natick Mean, .	6·91	5·24	4·23	5·34	13·91	4·16	14·16	19·64
	Total Mean, .	7·02	5·37	4·23	5·37	14·26	4·13	14·18	19·79

Of the Crania referred to in Table XII., Nos. 1, 18, 19, 20 are in
the collection of the Boston Nat. Hist. Soc. ; Nos. 4, 5, in that of
Dr. J. M. Warren, Boston ; and Nos. 2, 3, 6-17, are from the Tables
of the Morton Collection.

The New England tribes are described as having all
presented a very uniform correspondence in their predominant characteristics. Dwight, in his *Travels in*

New England, says of them, " They were tall, straight, of a red complexion, with black eyes, and of a vacant look when unimpassioned ;" but he ascribes to them a good natural understanding, and considerable sagacity and wit. They are not, even now, entirely extinct, but, like others of the Eastern tribes that have been long in contact with the whites, it is difficult to find a pure-breed Indian among the remnants that still linger on some of their ancient sites. Judging, however, from the examples I have seen, it is probable that the red complexion, which Dwight assigns to the New England tribes, may have much more accurately justified the application of the term Red Indian to the aborigines first seen by European voyagers along the northern shores of the American continent, than is now apparent when observing the olive-complexioned Chippewas, Crees, and other tribes of the West. Gallatin has grouped the New England Indians along with the Delawares, the Powhattans, the Pamlicoes, and other tribes of the Atlantic sea-board, extending as far south as North Carolina, under the comprehensive title of Algonquin-Lenapé. There is no doubt that important philological relations serve to indicate affinities running through the whole, and to connect them with the great Algonquin stock ; while the essentially diverse Iroquois and Huron nations were interposed between them.

Under the double title of Algonquin-Lenapé have been included all the Indian nations originally occupying the vast tract of the North American continent, extending from beyond the Gulf of the St. Lawrence to the area of the Florida tribes, and claiming the whole territory between the Mississippi and the sea ; excepting where the Hurons and the aggressive Iroquois held the country around the lower lakes, and the Five Nations were already extending their hunting-grounds at the cost of Algonquin and Lenapé tribes. But however valuable comprehensive groupings may prove to the philologist, the physical characteristics of the tribes are best studied in smaller groups; and by this means we are able to trace the prevalence of dialects of a common language among tribes widely scattered, and frequently marked by important diversities of physical character. For this reason the New England Indians have been grouped apart; while another table of cranial measurements is added here, chiefly derived from the observations recorded by Dr. Morton, and including examples of various tribes embraced by the comprehensive classification of Algonquin-Lenapés, but omitting the tribes both of Canada and New England, which have already been given in the previous tables. Such a grouping of allied tribes is not without its value, as a means for comparing general results; though much greater confidence is felt in dealing with those results where the essentially distinctive features of each tribe or nation are made to appear, as in the case of the Hurons. I have accordingly added, in the following table, the mean results of the Menominee crania, nine in number, in addition to those of the whole. The Menominees originally occupied the country around Green Bay, on Lake Michigan, where they early attracted the attention of the Jesuit missionaries, from whom they received the appellation of *Folles Avoines*, from their hoarding up the wild rice for their winter's store. The unusual fairness of the Menominee complexion has been repeatedly commented on by travellers, and presents so remarkable a contrast to the colour of other Indian tribes in their vicinity, that Keating, after noting, in his *Expedition to the St. Peter's River*, the resemblance of the Menominee Indians he met with to the white mulattoes of the United States, adds,—"They are naturally so much fairer than the neighbouring tribes, that they are sometimes called the White Indians." How far this is a purely aboriginal trait, may be subject to doubt. Great variety unquestionably exists in the shades of colour of the American Indian tribes ; but besides this, the presence of the white man among them very early began to affect the race, and changes have been wrought by such intercourse on tribes, entirely beyond the most remote clearings of western settlement.

TABLE XIII.—ALGONQUIN-LENAPE CRANIA.

	TRIBE.	L. D.	P. D.	F. D.	V. D.	I. A.	I. L.	O. F. A.	H. C.
1	Sauk, . . .	7·4	5·9	4·6	5·5	15·3	4·3	15·0	21·0
2	Fox, . . .	7·0	5·9	4·7	5·5	15·3	4·7	14·2	20·9
3	,, . . .	6·9	5·9	4·7	5·5	15·0	4·2	14·2	20·2
4	Potowatomie, .	7·8	5·7	4·4	5·3	16·0	4·0	15·8	22·1
5	Chippewa, . .	7·3	5·8	4·8	5·5	15·1	4·6	14·2	20·9
6	,, .	7·2	5·5	4·3	5·5	14·8	4·1	14·6	20·2
7	Delaware, F. .	7·0	5·5	4·6	5·1	14·4	4·2	14·5	20·0
8	,, . .	7·8	5·4	4·4	6·2	15·6	4·3	16·0	21·5
9	Minsi, . . .	6·7	5·0	4·2	5·3	14·0	4·1	13·8	19·3
10	Manta, . . .	7·0	5·1	3·9	5·3	14·6	3·9	14·0	19·5
11	Miami, . . .	6·9	5·5	4·3	5·5	14·5	4·1	14·0	19·8
12	,, . . .	7·3	5·5	4·3	5·5	14·6	4·6	14·9	20·1
13	,, . . .	7·0	5·1	4·2	5·6	14·5	4·2	14·1	19·5
14	,, . . .	7·6	5·3	4·3	5·5	15·0	4·1	15·5	20·5
15	Menominee, F. .	6·7	5·6	4·2	5·1	14·3	4·4	13·5	19·5
16	,, F. .	6·8	5·4	4·3	5·5	14·0	3·2	14·0	19·7
17	,,. . .	7·3	5·7	4·5	5·3	14·2	4·5	14·2	21·0
18	,, . .	6·8	5·6	4·2	5·5	14·7	4·1	14·1	19·9
19	,, . .	7·1	5·8	4·5	5·4	14·9	4·6	14·1	20·6
20	,, F. .	6·9	5·7	4·5	5·3	15·3	4·5	14·0	20·4
21	,, . .	7·1	5·6	4·4	5·4	14·8	4·3	15·0	20·5
22	,, .	6·6	5·4	4·2	4·9	14·2	3·9	13·6	19·3
23	,, . .	7·5	5·4	4·0	5·5.	14·5	4·2	...	20·6
	Menominee mean,	6·98	5·58	4·31	5·32	14·54	4·19	14·06	20·17
	Total mean, . .	7·12	5·53	4·37	5·42	14·77	4·22	14·42	20·30

Nos. 15-22 are in the Morton Collection, No. 23 is in that of Dr. J. Mason Warren of Boston.

But this subject will be treated of more in detail in a subsequent chapter. No traces of physical degeneracy, however, are noted by the latest observers of the Menominees. Though reduced to a small remnant, they still maintain their ancient character for bravery and foresight; and appear to have possessed characteristics peculiarly fitting them for acquiring the elements of civilisation, had they been originally subjected to its influences under favourable circumstances. "Their language," Gallatin remarks, "though of the Algonquin stock, is less similar to that of the Chippewas, their immediate neighbours, than almost any dialect of the same stock." Excepting in the parietal diameter, the Menominee mean falls below the total mean; but this may be partly accounted for by the proportion of small female skulls to the whole. Nine is, under any circumstances, too small a number for anything but a very partial approximation to the average proportions of tribal or national crania. So far, however, as an opinion can be formed on such data, the relative parietal expansion of the Menominee cranium is remarkably in excess of that observed in any other of the Algonquin or Algonquin-Lenapé tribes.

In contrast to the form of head of the true American race, Dr. Morton appends to his *Crania Americana* drawings and measurements of four Esquimaux skulls, familiar to me, if I mistake not, in the collection of the Edinburgh Phrenological Society. In commenting on the views and measurements of these, he remarks: "The great and uniform differences between these heads and those of the American Indians will be obvious to every one accustomed to make comparisons of this kind, and serve as corroborative evidence of the opinion that the Esquimaux are the only people possessing Asiatic characteristics on the American continent." In some respects this is undoubtedly true; the prognathous form of the superior maxilla, and the very small development of the nasal bones, especially contrast with well-known characteristics of the American aborigines. But having had some familiarity in making comparisons of this kind, it appears to me, notwithstanding these distinctive points, that an impartial observer might be quite as likely to assign even some of the examples of Iroquois and other northern tribes figured in the *Crania Americana*, to an Esquimaux, as to a Peruvian, Mexican, or Mound-Builder type. Compare, for example, the vertical and occipital diagrams, furnished by Dr. Morton, of the Esquimaux crania (p. 248) with those of the Iroquois and Hurons (pp. 192-194). Both are elongated, pyramidal, and with a tendency towards a conoid rather than a flattened or vertical occipital form ; and when placed alongside of the most markedly typical Mexican or Peruvian heads, the one differs little less widely from these than the other. The elements of contrast between the Hurons and Esquimaux are mainly traceable in the bones of the face : physiognomical, but not cerebral. In all the arguments based on the assumed predominance of one uniform cranial type throughout the whole Western Hemisphere, the Arctic American, or Esquimaux, has invariably been excluded ; and he has been regarded either as the exceptional example of an Asiatic intruder on the American continent, or as the hyperborean autochthones of the Arctic realm, as essentially indigenous there as the rein-deer or the polar bear. An examination of Arctic crania, and a comparison of them with those of the North American Indians in the Morton Collection, has by no means tended to confirm my faith in the existence of any such uniform and strongly marked line of difference as Dr. Morton was led to assume from the small number of examples which came under his observation.

TABLE XIV.—ESQUIMAUX CRANIA.

	LOCALITY.	L. D.	P. D.	F. D.	V. D.	I. M. A.[1]	I. A.	I. L.	O. F. A.	H. C.
1	Baffin's Bay, . . .	7·2	5·1	4·2	5·3	...	13·8	4·3	14·3	20·2
2	Disco Island, . .	7·4	5·1	4·3	5·7	...	15·1	3·7	15·7	20·5
3	"In the Snow," Captain } Parry, . . . }	7·2	5·4	4·4	5·3	...	14·4	4·3	14·5	20·6
4	Sabine Island, . .	7·5	5·2	4·3	5·6	...	14·7	4·2	15·5	21·1
5	Hopedale, Labrador,	8·0	5·4	4·6	5·7	...	15·2	4·3	16·1	22·2
6	Icy Cape, Behring St.,	6·7	5·1	4·4	5·1	...	14·4	3·8	13·1	19·1
7	Cast, . . .	7·2	4·8	4·3	5·3	...	14·0	4·0	15·3	20·2
8	Lat. 69° 21′ 19″ N., } Long. 81° 31′ W., }	7·6	5·7	4·6	5·6	...	15·3	4·3	15·6	21·8
9	Cast, . . .	7·1	4·8	4·0	5·2	...	13·7	4·2	15·2	19·5
10	„ . . .	7·4	5·3	4·5	5·5	...	15·2	4·2	16·1	20·7
11	„ . . .	7·4	5·2	4·3	5·5	...	14·6	4·1	15·4	20·7
12	„ . . .	7·3	5·3	4·3	5·5	...	14·6	4·2	14·9	20·7
13	Hare Island, .	6·9	4·9	4·0	5·3	...	13·3	4·0	14·0	19·4
14	By M. Schwartz, Stockholm	7·7	5·6	4·6	5·7	...	15·1	4·3	15·4	21·7
15	„ „	7·4	5·1	4·2	5·2	...	14·3	4·1	14·6	20·5
16	„ „	7·4	5·4	4·5	5·4	...	14·6	4·2	15·1	21·3
17	„ „	7·4	5·1	4·5	5·4	...	14·3	4·1	14·6	20·7
18	„ „	7·2	5·0	4·2	5·5	...	14·4	4·0	14·5	20·0
19	„ „	7·2	5·2	4·4	5·5	...	14·6	4·0	14·7	20·4
20	Davis Straits, . .	7·5	5·4	4·6	5·4	...	14·3	4·1	15·2	20·4
21	„ . .	7·3	5·4	4·4	5·3	...	14·2	4·2	14·6	20·3
22	Greenland (167), .	7·1	5·5	...	5·6	...	...	...	14·8	20·0
23	Disco Island (168), .	7·0	4·9	...	5·6	...	...	...	14·9	19·8
24	Eskimo (166), .	7·1	5·5	...	5·6	...	...	...	14·8	20·6
25	Disco Island, .	7·8	4·6	4·3	5·8	12·7		4·2	15·8	21·4
26	„ . .	6·9	4·8	4·2	5·2	12·0		4·3	14·3	19·4
27	„ .	7·2	4·6	4·0	5·6	12·8		4·3	14·6	...
28	„ . .	7·5	4·8	4·4	5·5	13·0		4·1	14·9	21·0
29	„ . .	7·5	4·4	4·4	5·7	12·7		4·5	14·9	20·8
30	„ . .	6·9	4·1	3·8	5·3	11·8		4·3	13·6	19·0
31	„ . .	7·4	4·9	4·3	5·7	12·3		4·2	14·8	20·5
32	Greenland, Dr. Kane,	7·6	4·6	4·4	5·7	12·7		4·5	15·2	21·4
33	„ „	7·2	4·5	4·3	5·5	12·3		4·3	14·3	20·3
34	„ „	7·1	4·8	3·7	5·3	11·8		4·4	14·3	19·4
35	„ „	7·1	4·8	4·2	5·1	12·0		4·0	14·0	19·8
36	„ „	7·1	4·7	4·0	5·3	12·3	...	4·3	14·2	19·6
37	Upernavick, . .	7·0	5·3	4·9	5·5	12·9	...	4·3	14·6	20·4
38	„ . .	7·3	5·0	4·3	5·3	12·4	...	4·1	14·8	20·0
	Mean, . .	7·28	5·03	4·31	5·46	12·41	14·48	4·18	14·82	20·42

[1] An additional column, I. M. A., the *intermeatoid arch*, is added in this Table, measured from the meati, instead of the mastoid processes, owing to the defective condition of the latter in some of the crania. Nos. 1-19 are in the Collection of the Edinburgh Phrenological Society. No. 20, measurements by Mr. Geo. Combe. No. 21, Mr. P. S. Fowler, New York. Nos. 22-24, Professor Van Der Hoeven's Catalogue. Nos. 25-37, Collection of the Acad. Nat. Sciences, Philadelphia. No. 38, Private Collection, Philadelphia. The measurements of 25-38 were taken for the author by Dr. J. Aitken

In Table XIV. the measurements of thirty-eight well authenticated Arctic crania are given, furnishing the means for instituting comparisons between the Indian and Esquimaux cranium ; and also supplying additional data for testing the characteristics of the Esquimaux skull. This Dr. Meigs describes as " large, long, narrow, pyramidal ; greatest breadth near the base ; sagittal suture prominent and keel-like, in consequence of the junction of the parietal and two halves of the frontal bones ; proportion between length of head and height of face as seven to five ; . . . forehead flat and receding; occiput full and salient ; face broad and lozenge-shaped, the greatest breadth being just below the orbits ; malar bones broad, high, and prominent, zygomatic arches massive and widely separated ; nasal bones flat, narrow, and united at an obtuse angle, sometimes lying in the same place as the naso-maxillary processes."[1] The remarks of Mr. J. Barnard Davis on the last-named peculiarities, are worthy of note. In the Esquimaux of the eastern shores of Baffin's Bay, he observes, the nasal bones are scarcely broader, though frequently longer than in some Chinese skulls, where they are so narrow as to be reduced to two short linear bones. " In those of the opposite, or American shores of Baffin's Bay, they are very different, presenting a length, breadth, and angle of position, almost equal to those of European races, having aquiline noses."[2] This slight yet striking anatomical difference seems to supply a link of considerable value as indicative of a trait of physiognomical character in the more southern Esquimaux, tending, if confirmed by further observation, like other physical characteristics

Meigs, and in these the parietal diameter is at the parietal protuberances ; in the others, it indicates the extreme parietal diameter, generally nearer the squamous suture. This reduces the apparent mean parietal diameter, which if taken from the first twenty-four crania rises to 5·22.

[1] *Catalogue of Human Crania,* A.N.S., 1857, p. 50.

[2] *Crania Britannica,* p. 30.

already noticed, to modify the abrupt transition assumed heretofore as clearly defining the line of separation between the contrasting Arctic and Red Indian races of the New World.

From the relative measurements of the Esquimaux crania, the great length and narrowness of the skull are apparent, though in estimating the value of the parietal diameter in instituting comparisons with the other tables, it must be borne in remembrance that the parietal diameter in fourteen of the examples (21-34) is measured from the parietal protuberances, which are not necessarily the points of greatest diameter. In the Esquimaux, as in the Huron, and generally in the Indian skull, the greatest diameter appears to be towards the squamous suture. The elevation of the vertex is also in no degree remarkably divergent from the proportions of northern Indian crania, and, with the other points of correspondence or approximation, tends to confirm the idea that the supposed uniformity traceable throughout the continent, is no more than might fairly be looked for among nations placed to so great an extent under the operation of similar conditions of social life, and affected by so many corresponding extraneous influences.

Dr. Latham, after commenting on the manifest distinctions which separate the Esquimaux of the Atlantic from the tribes of the American aborigines lying to the south and west of them, as elements of contrast which have not failed to receive full justice, adds : " It is not so with the Eskimos of Russian America, and the parts that look upon the Pacific. These are so far from being separated by any broad and trenchant line of demarcation from the proper Indians or the so-called Red Race, that they pass gradually into it ; and that in respect to their habits, manner, and appearance, equally. So far is this the case that he would be a bold man who should venture, in speaking of the southern tribes of Russian America, to say : *here the Eskimo area ends, and here a different area begins.*[1] The difference thus pointed out may be accounted for, to a considerable extent, by the diverse geographical conformation of the continent, on its eastern and western sides, which admits in the latter of such frequent and intimate intercourse as is not unlikely to lead to an intermixture of blood, and a blending of the races, however primarily distinct and diverse. The evidence presented here, however, refers to tribes having no such intercourse with the Esquimaux, and distinguished from them by important characteristics, in manners, social habits, and external physiognomy. Nevertheless if the conclusions submitted here, deduced from an examination of several hundred Indian crania, are borne out by the premises, this much at least may be affirmed : that a marked difference distinguishes the Northern tribes, now or formerly occupying the country around the great lakes, and ranging through the ancient hunting-grounds between the Mississippi and the Atlantic seaboard, from some of those to the westward of the Rocky Mountains as well as in the southern valley of the Mississippi ; while, notwithstanding the prognathous maxillary development of the Esquimaux, intermediate forms supply nearly all the links of a graduated approximation, from the extreme brachycephalic skull with vertical occiput, to that of the dolichocephalic Esquimaux, with protuberant occiput, inclining in its upper part obliquely towards the vertex. This is best illustrated, in so far as cranial measurements are available for the purpose of comparison, by the following Table (xv.), where the eye will catch at a glance the distinctive elements of approximation or contrast which pertain to the different groups.

[1] *Varieties of Man,* p. 291.

The Peruvian crania of both classes are small, indicating a people of inferior size and stature, and presenting essential differences, even in the brachycephalic class, from those of the mounds. Their small vertical diameter is specially noticeable. In this, as well as in other respects, the greater correspondence between the Mexican brachycephali and the mound crania is suggestive, and calculated to increase our desire for the acquisition of a sufficient number of examples of both, whereby to test the evidence of physical correspondence between the elder races of Anahuac and the people who have left such remarkable evidences of a partially developed civilisation in the Mississippi Valley. The two extremes are the Peruvian brachycephali and the Esquimaux :—

	Length.	Breadth.	Height.	O. F. Arch.
Peruvian, . .	6·32	5·62	5·18	13·27
Esquimaux, . .	7·28	5·22	5·46	14·82

But between these the range of variations sufficiently illustrates the fallacy of the supposed uniform cranial type affirmed to prevail throughout the whole Western Hemisphere, from the Arctic Circle to Cape Horn.

TABLE XV.—COMPARATIVE MEAN CRANIAL MEASUREMENTS.

		L. D.	P. D.	F. D.	V. D.	I. A.	I. L.	O. F. A.	H. C.
1	Mound Crania, .	6·57	5·90	4·20	5·55	15·60	4·40	14·00	19·83
2	Cave Crania, .	6·62	5·78	4·51	5·47	14·85	4·42	13·87	19·77
3	Peruvian B. C., .	6·32	5·62	4·06	5·18	14·96	4·12	13·27	19·10
4	Peruvian D. C., .	7·06	5·18	3·80	5·21	14·36	4·10	14·45	19·71
5	Mexican B. C., .	6·56	5·51	4·30	5·55	14·69	4·25	13·95	19·66
6	Mexican D. C., .	7·05	5·41	4·31	5·35	15·20	4·12	14·17	19·99
7	American B. C., .	6·62	5·45	4·24	5·30	14·63	4·25	13·85	19·44
8	American D. C., .	7·24	5·47	4·36	5·42	14·67	4·23	14·62	20·29
9	Iroquois, . .	7·35	5·47	4·35	5·44	14·65	4·24	14·62	20·49
10	Algonquin, . .	7·25	5·58	4·43	5·37	14·42	4·35	14·42	20·44
11	Algonquin-Lenapé, .	7·12	5·53	4·37	5·42	14·77	4·22	14·42	20·30
12	Esquimaux, . .	7·28	5·22	4·31	5·46	14·48	4·18	14·82	20·42

No. 1 is the mean of the four undoubted Mound Crania, and No. 9 is that of the combined Tables IX., X., both of which pertain to the common Iroquois stock. In No. 12, the parietal diameter is the mean of the extreme parietal, as indicated in the note, Table XIV.

If the data thus selected as examples of the different groups, furnish any approximation to their relative cranial measurements, it seems scarcely possible to evade the conclusion that the ideal American typical head has no existence in nature ; and that if a line of separation between the Peruvian, or so-called Toltecan head, and other American forms is to be drawn, it cannot be introduced as heretofore to cut off the Esquimaux, and rank the remainder under varieties of one type ; but must rather group the hyperborean American cranium in the same class with others derived from widely separated regions, extending into the Tropics and beyond the Equator. In reality, however, the results of such attempts at a comparative analysis of the cranial characteristics of the American races go far beyond this, and prove that the form of the human skull is just as little constant among the different tribes or races of the New World as of the Old; and that, so far from any simple subdivision into two or three groups sufficing for American craniology, there are abundant traces of a tendency of development into the extremes of brachycephalic and dolichocephalic or kumbecephalic forms, and again of the intermediate gradations by which the one passes into the other. The measurements of two hundred and eighty-nine crania are given in the previous tables. A much larger number would be required to illustrate all the intermediate forms, but sufficient data have been furnished to point in no unmistakable manner to the conclusion indicated above. If crania measuring upwards of two inches in excess in the longitudinal over the parietal and vertical diameters, or nearly approximating to such relative measurements— without further reference here to other variations of occipital conformation,—may be affirmed, without challenge, to be of the same type as others where the longitudinal, parietal, and vertical diameters vary only by minute fractional differences, then the distinction between the brachycephalic and the dolichocephalic type of head is, for all purposes of science, at an end ; and the labours of Blumenbach, Retzius, Nilsson, and all who have trod in their footsteps have been wasted in pursuit of an idle fancy. If differences of cranial conformation of so strongly defined a character, as are thus shown to exist between various ancient and modern people of America, amount to no more than variations within the normal range of the common type, then all the important distinctions between the crania of ancient European barrows and those of living races amount to little ; and the more delicate details, such as those, for example, which have been supposed to distinguish the Celtic from the Germanic cranium ; the ancient Roman from the Etruscan or Greek ; the Slave from the Magyar or Turk ; or the Gothic Spaniard from the Basque or Morisco, must be utterly valueless. But the legitimate deduction from such a recognition, alike of extreme diversities of cranial form, and of many intermediate gradations, characterizing the nations of the New World, as well as of the Old, is not that cranial formation has no ethnic value ; but that the truths embodied in such physiological data are as little to be eliminated by ignoring or slighting all diversities from the predominant form, and assigning it as the sole normal type, as by neglecting the many intermediate gradations, and dwelling exclusively on the examples of extreme divergence from any prevailing type. Humboldt has been quoted as favouring the idea of American ethnic unity. It must be borne in remembrance that his observations were limited to tropical America ; and that it is therefore no presumption to assume that personal observation in reference to the northern tribes would have modified views thus expressed : " The nations of America, except those which border on the polar circle,

form a single race, characterized by the formation of the
skull, the colour of the skin, the extreme thinness of
the beard, and straight glossy hair." The formation of
the skull has been abundantly discussed here ; as to the
colour of the skin, extended observation tends in like
manner to disclose considerable variations, from the fair
Menominees, and olive-complexioned Chippewas, to the
dark Pawnees, and the Kaws of Kansas almost as black
as negroes. My own earlier observations led me to
assume that the name of *Red* Indian had been applied to
the cinnamon-coloured natives of the New World, in consequence of their free application of red pigments, such
as are in constant use among the Indians on Lake Superior ; until I fell in with an encampment of Micmacs, in
their birch-bark wigwams, on the Lower St. Lawrence,
and then saw for the first time a complexion to which
the name of red or reddish-brown may very fitly apply.
Again, as to the hair, the evidence of the ancient Peruvian graves furnishes some proof of hair differing essentially both in colour and texture from that of the modern
Indian ; and Mexican terra-cottas and sculptures of Central America indicate that the beard was not universally
absent. But it is not necessary thus to discuss in detail
a detached remark of Humboldt, in order to prevent his
observation from bearing out the inferences it has been
produced to support ; for he has himself furnished the
most conclusive evidence of the totally different inferences
drawn by him from those recognised characteristics of
the American race. Dr. Nott, when commenting on the
Esquimaux skulls engraved in the *Crania Americana,*
remarks : " Nothing can be more obvious than the contrast between these Esquimaux heads and those of all
other tribes of this continent. They are the only people
in America who present the characteristics of an Asiatic
race ; and being bounded closely on the south by genuine

aborigines, they seem placed here as if to give a practical illustration of the irrefragable distinctness of races."[1] Dr. Pickering, as we have seen, with no prejudice against the theory of an " irrefragable distinctness of races," nevertheless came to the conclusion that the Asiatic and American nations of the Mongolian type are one race ; and Humboldt, who enjoyed such preeminent opportunities of studying the Mongolian characteristics on the Asiatic continent, remarks in his introduction to his *American Researches :* " The American race bears a very striking resemblance to that of the Mongol nations, which include the descendants of the Hiong-Nie, known heretofore by the name of Huns, the Kalkas, the Kalmuks, and the Burats. It has been ascertained by late observations, that not only the inhabitants of Unalashka, but several tribes of South America, indicate by the osteological characters of the head a passage from the American to the Mongol race. When we shall have more completely studied the brown men of Africa, and that swarm of nations who inhabit the interior and north-east of Asia, and who are vaguely described by systematic travellers under the name of Tartars and Tschoudes : the Caucasian, Mongol, American, Malay, and Negro races, will appear less insulated, and we shall acknowledge in this great family of the human race one single organic type, modified by circumstances which perhaps will ever remain unknown." It is indeed an important and highly suggestive fact, in the present stage of ethnological research, that authorities the most diverse in their general views and favourite theories as to the unity or multiplicity of human species, can nevertheless be quoted in confirmation of opinions which trace to one ethnic centre, the Fin and Esquimaux, the Chinese, the European Turk and Magyar, and the American Indian.

[1] *Comparative Anatomy of Races, Types of Mankind,* p. 447.

CHAPTER XXII.

ARTIFICIAL CRANIAL DISTORTION.

THE evidences of an assumed cranial and physical unity pervading the aborigines of the American continent disappear upon a careful scrutiny, and the like results follow when the same critical investigation is applied to other proofs adduced in support of this attractive but insubstantial theory. Dr. Morton, after completing his elaborate and valuable illustrations of American craniology, introduces an engraving of a mummy of a Muysca Indian of New Granada, and adds : "As an additional evidence of the unity of race and species in the American nations, 1 shall now adduce the singular fact, that from Patagonia to Canada, and from ocean to ocean, and equally in the civilized and uncivilized tribes, a peculiar mode of placing the body in sepulture has been practised from immemorial time. This peculiarity consists in the sitting posture."[1] The author accordingly proceeds to marshal his evidence in proof of the practice of such a mode of interment among many separate and independent tribes ; nor is it difficult to do so, for it was a usage of greatly more extended recognition than his theory of "unity of race and species" implies. It was a prevailing, though by no means universal mode of sepulture among the tribes of the New World, as it was among many of those of the

[1] *Crania Americana*, p. 244.

Old, recorded by the pen of Herodotus, and proved by
sepulchral disclosures pertaining to still older eras. The
British cromlechs show that the very same custom was
followed by their builders in primitive times. The
ancient barrows of Scandinavia reveal the like fact,
and abundant evidence proves the existence of such
sepulchral rites, in ancient or modern times, in every
quarter of the globe ; so that if the prevalence of a
peculiar mode of interment of the dead may be adduced
as evidence of the unity of race and species, it can only
operate by reuniting the lost links which restore to the
red man his common share in the genealogy of the sons
of Adam. But ancient and modern discoveries also
prove considerable diversity in the sepulchral rites of
all nations. The skeleton has been found in a sitting
posture in British cromlechs, barrows, and graves, of
dates to all appearance long prior to the era of Roman
invasion, and of others unquestionably subsequent to
that of Saxon immigration ; but evidences are found of
cremation and urn-burial, in equally ancient times, of
the recumbent skeleton under the cairn, the barrow, in
the stone cist, and in the rude sarcophagus hewn out
of the solid trunk of the oak ; and in this, as in so many
other respects, the British microcosm is but an epitome
of the great world. Norway, Denmark, Germany, and
France all supply the same evidences of varying rites ;
and ancient and modern customs of Asia and Africa
confirm the universality of the same. In the Tonga
and other islands of the Pacific, as well as in the newer
world of Australia, the custom of burying the dead in
a sitting posture has been repeatedly noted ; but it is
not universal even among them ; nor was it so in
America, though affirmed by Dr. Morton to be traceable
throughout the northern and southern continents, and
by its universality, to afford " collateral evidence of the

affiliation of all the American nations." So far is this from being the case, that nearly every ancient and modern sepulchral rite has had its counterpart in the New World. Mummification, cremation, urn-burial, and inhumation, were all in use among different tribes and nations of South America, and have left their traces no less unmistakably on the northern continent. Figure 65

Fɪɢ. 65.—Chippewa Grave.

illustrates a common form of bier, sketched from a Chippewa grave on the Saskatchewan. The body is deposited on the surface, protected by wood or stones, and covered over with birch-bark. In the neighbourhood of the clearings, as at Red River, the grave is generally surrounded by a high fence. Among the Algonquins, the Hurons, the Mandans, the Sioux, and other tribes, the body was, and with the survivors still is, most frequently laid out at full length on an elevated bier or scaffold, or otherwise disposed above ground, where it was left to decay; and then after a time the bones of the dead, with all the offerings deposited beside them, were consigned to one common grave. Ossuaries of great extent, forming the general receptacle of large communities, have been repeatedly brought to light both in Canada and the northern states. Creuxius quotes from Le Jeune an account of one of the great general burials of the Hurons which he witnessed. A grand celebration was solemnly convoked. Not only the remains of those whose bodies had been scaffolded, but of all who had died on a journey or on the war-path, and been temporarily buried, were now gathered together and interred in one common sepulchre with special marks of regard. The pit was lined with furs ; all the relics and offerings to the dead were deposited beside the bones, and the whole were covered with furs before the earth was thrown over them. When the Mandans buried the remains of their scaffolded dead, they left the skull uninterred ; and Catlin describes their skulls as lying on the prairies arranged in circles of a hundred or more, with their faces towards the centre, where a little mound is erected, surmounted by a male and female buffalo skull.

When we pass to the westward of the Rocky Mountains, new modifications vary the Indian sepulchral rites. Along the Cowlitz and Columbia rivers, and among various north-west tribes on the Pacific, the canoe of the deceased is converted into his bier. In this he is laid at full length, adorned in his gayest attire, and surrounded with his weapons and favourite property, as well as with the offerings of his friends ; and after being towed in solemn funeral procession to the burial-place of the tribe, the canoe is elevated on poles, and protected by a covering of birch bark. Among the Chimpseyan or Babeen Indians the female dead are scaffolded, but the male are invariably burned ; and numerous evidences of the practice of cremation and urn-burial have been found in Georgia and South Carolina, as well as in the Brazils and other parts of the southern continent. Again, the Mammoth Cave of Kentucky, and the caves at Golconda, Steubenville, and other localities, filled with the bones and desiccated remains of the dead, or with their carefully preserved mummies, illustrate other and varying customs which have their counterpart in the practices of the Old World ; while the Ohio and Scioto mounds furnish unmistakable evidence that both cremation and incumbent mound sepulture were practised by the race whose works preserve to us so many traces of ancient arts and long extinct rites.

It is obvious, from such references, that there is little more proof of the universal prevalence of any single mode of sepulture among the American aborigines than can be traced in the practices of primitive nations of

Fig. 66.—Canoe Bier.

the Old World ; while the custom of interring the dead in a sitting posture, in so far as it prevails among them, is rather suggestive of borrowed Asiatic, or primitive European rites, than of anything peculiar to the western hemisphere. Of the latter, indeed, the exposure of the

corpse on its scaffolding, or elevated in its canoe-bier
(Fig. 66), constitutes a far more characteristic peculiarity
in the rites and customs of the New World ; and if universal, might have seemed to justify the inference which
Dr. Morton has attempted to maintain by assuming not
only the universality of a different practice, but also its
restriction to the continent of America.

But there is another remarkable characteristic of many
American tribes and nations that is much more suggestive of widely diffused affinities throughout the Western
Hemisphere, as well as of an aboriginal isolation, than
anything else disclosed by prevalent customs or peculiar
rites of sepulture.   Much attention has naturally been
attracted to the evidences of the singular practice of
moulding the human head into artificial forms, which
have been brought to light, alike in the cemeteries of
ancient Peruvian seats of civilisation, and in those of
the hunter tribes of the north.   But this also, though
unusually prevalent in the New World, proves to be no
exclusive American characteristic, but one which had its
counterpart among the customs of the ancient world,
and so is rather suggestive of a borrowed usage, and of
affinities with the nations of the eastern hemisphere.   It
seems, the further it is investigated, to suggest an Asiatic
origin for this as for so much else which the European
regarded with strange wonder when first noted by him
among the peculiarities of that New World, unless indeed it be an ancient gift from America to Asia.   References to the singular cranial conformation of certain
tribes, and to the strange practice of artificially moulding the human head, were familiar to Europe not only
prior to the first voyage of Columbus, but centuries
before the Christian era.   The earliest notice occurs in
the writings of Hippocrates, who, in his treatise *De
Aëris, Aquis, et Locis*, gives an account of a people in-

habiting the shores of the Euxine, whose cranial conformation bore no resemblance to that of any other
nation. He further states, that they considered those
most noble who had the longest heads, and ascribes this
peculiar form to an artificial elongation of the head by
compression during infancy. To this people, accordingly, he gave the name of the Macrocephali, and both
he and subsequent writers ascribe certain peculiar mental
endowments to this long-headed race. Strabo, Pliny,
and Pomponius Mela all allude to the subject at later
dates, though assigning different localities to the nations
or tribes they refer to, and also indicating diversities
of form in their peculiar cranial characteristics. This
tends still further to suggest that the name of Macrocephali does not properly belong to a distinct race or
single tribe on the shores of the Euxine Sea ; but that,
like the term Flatheads, as used at the present day
among the Indian tribes of the North-west, it was applied to all who practised the barbarous art of cranial
distortion. Strabo, in the eleventh book of his geography, describes the western portion of Asia, of which
alone he appears to have had any accurate ideas ; and
it is there that the remarkable passage occurs in which
he speaks of an Asiatic tribe as having anxiously striven
to give themselves a long-headed appearance, and to
have foreheads projecting over their beards. Pomponius Mela also describes the Macrocephali he refers
to as less hideous than other tribes in the same vicinity,
among whom it may be inferred that cranial deformation was carried to a greater extent, as among the
modern Chinook Indians, who depress the forehead
until the skull assumes the form of that of a brute.
The skulls of various ancient and modern American
tribes can be discriminated by means of the peculiar
form of head most in fashion with the tribe ; and all

the allusions of classical writers confirm the probability, that from the time of Hippocrates till long after the Christian era, the unknown regions eastward of the Euxine Sea were occupied by nations among whom the practice of artificial compression of the skull prevailed to a remarkable extent; though modified in part, probably, by the differing cranial proportions natural to certain tribes around Mount Caucasus, and also by the influence of taste and fashion on the strange hereditary custom. Stephanus Byzantinus is quoted by Retzius, as speaking in his *Geographica* of macrocephalic Scythians among the inhabitants of Colchis, the modern Mingrelia, on the east coast of the Euxine Sea. The Macrocephali of Pliny were in the vicinity of Ceresus in Natolia, and those of Pomponius Mela on the Bosporus; but from Strabo we learn of them in diverse localities both in Asia and Europe. His references, accordingly, greatly extend the area of this singular custom, and point to it as an ancient practice common among the migratory tribes of western Asia. He refers to a people in the region about Mount Caucasus towards the Caspian Sea, as well as to another in the valley of the Danube at the river Taler, both of whom modified the natural form of the head.

It thus appears that this barbarous practice is neither of modern origin nor peculiar to the New World; and since attention has been drawn to the subject in recent years, various examples of compressed and distorted crania have been discovered in ancient European cemeteries, amply confirming the notices of the Macrocephali in the pages of classical writers. Captain Jesse, in his *Notes of a Half-Pay Officer*, describes in his travels in Circassia and the Crimea an ancient example of an artificially compressed cranium which he saw in the Museum at Kertch. This was said to have been found in the

neighbourhood of the Don ; and he remarks in reference
to it : "According to the opinions of Hippocrates, Pomponius Mela, Pliny, and others, the Macrocephali appear
to have inhabited that part of the shores of the Euxine,
between the Phasis and Trapesus,—the modern Trebi-
zonde." The Russian occupation of the Crimea dates
only from a late period in the eighteenth century, but
since then an intelligent attention has been paid to the
traces of its ancient occupants. Some of the finest works
of art recovered on the sites of Hellenic colonization have
been transported to St. Petersburg, but others are preserved in the vicinity of the localities where they have
been found ; and for this purpose a museum was established at the town of Kertch, in which were preserved
many historical antiquities of the Crimean Bosporus ;
and especially sepulchral relics recovered from the tumuli which abound on the site of the ancient Milesian
colony.

It chanced, as is now well known, that, in the fortunes
of war, the town of Kertch fell into the hands of the
Anglo-French invaders ; and some few of its ancient
treasures were preserved and transmitted to the British
Museum. By far the greater portion of the Museum
collections, however, were barbarously spoiled by the
rude soldiery ; and among the rest doubtless perished
the little-heeded relic of the Macrocephali of the Crimea,
first described by Hippocrates, five centuries before our
era. Blumenbach has figured in his first Decade, an
imperfect compressed skull, received by him from Russia,
which he designates as that of an Asiatic Macrocephalus ;
and in 1843, Rathke communicated to Müller's *Archiv
für Anatomie,* the figure of another artificially compressed skull, also very imperfect, but specially marked
by the same depression of the frontal bone. This example is described as procured from an ancient burial-

place near Kertch in the Crimea; and no doubt other illustrations of the peculiar physical characteristics of the ancient Macrocephali of the Bosporus will reward future explorers, when the attention of those engaged in such researches, or even in ordinary agricultural labours on the site, is specially directed to the interest now attaching to them.

More recent discoveries of artificially compressed crania have chiefly been made on European sites, though generally under circumstances which tend to justify their reference to Asiatic tribes. One of the first examples which attracted the attention of scientific observers, subsequent to the publication of Blumenbach's somewhat imperfect engraving, was a skull found, in the year 1820, at Fuersbrunn, near Grafenegg, in Austria. Count August von Breuner, the proprietor of the land, acquired possession of the interesting relic, and at once assigned it to the Avarian Huns, who occupied that region from the middle of the sixth until the eighth century. Of this artificially compressed Avar skull, Professor Retzius gave a description in the proceedings of the Royal Academy of Sciences of Stockholm, in 1844, which has since been transferred to various scientific journals. In this he shows that the skull, which had been regarded as remarkable for its great elongation, is in reality a true brachycephalic skull, such as the Mongol affinities of the Avars would suggest, but that by artificial compression it had been elongated vertically, or rather obliquely. At this stage of the inquiry, however, attention was diverted from the true elements of interest pertaining to the inquiry, by Dr. Tschudi communicating to Müller's *Archiv für Anatomie* a memoir, in which he instituted a careful comparison between the Grafenegg skull and the artificially compressed crania of ancient Peruvian cemeteries, from whence he deduced the conclusion that the scientific men of Europe had been deceived in ascribing to an Avar or other Asiatic or European source, a skull which must have been originally derived from Peru. In confirmation of this the Peruvian traveller reminds them that widely as Austria and Peru are severed, in the seventeenth century the Emperor Charles v. embraced both within his wide dominion ; and he accordingly conceives it no improbable conjecture that the compressed skull was brought at that period, as an object of curiosity, from America, and being afterwards thrown aside, it was mistakenly assumed to pertain to native sepulture, when recovered at Grafenegg in 1820.

The testimony thus undesignedly rendered to the remarkable correspondence between the artificially formed crania of the Old and the New World, is full of interest for us now that further discoveries have placed beyond doubt the genuine native origin of the Grafenegg cranium. It is preserved in the Imperial Anatomical Museum at Vienna, along with another of precisely the same character subsequently dug up at Atzgerrsdorf, in the immediate vicinity of Vienna. Others have been found at the village of St. Romain, in Savoy, and in the valley of the Doubs, near Mandeuse ; and Dr. Fitzinger asserts that a close resemblance is traceable between these and the Crimean macrocephalic crania described by Rathke and Meyer. They are further illustrated by evidence of a curious and independent character.

Dr. Fitzinger, who has published his views on this subject, in the Transactions of the Imperial Academy of Vienna, has placed beyond all doubt the authenticity of the discoveries of macrocephalic skulls in Austria, in genuine sepulchral deposits, one of which was dug up in the presence of Dr. Müller, the resident physician of Atzgerrsdorf. He has investigated the whole subject with minute research and accurate scholarship ; and after tracing ancient Macrocephali, by means of the allusions of classic writers, to the Scythian region in the vicinity of the Mœtian moor, to the Caucasus, and the further regions extending towards the Caspian Sea, and to their various sites around the Euxine, and on the Bosporus, he mentions an interesting independent illustration of the subject. An ancient medal struck, apparently to commemorate the destruction of the town of Aquileia, by Attila the Hun, in 452, came under his notice. On one side is represented the ruined city, and on the other the bust of the Hunnish leader in profile, with the same form of head as that shown in the supposed Avar skulls. Professor Retzius subsequently confirmed this opinion from an examination of the same medal in gold, in the Royal Cabinet at Stockholm. Attention having now been called to the subject, confirmatory illustrations multiply. M. F. Troyon, of Bel-Air, near Lausanne, who has carried on an elaborate series of explorations in the ancient cemeteries of that locality, has recovered what we may style a Hun or Avar skull, precisely corresponding to those found in Austria, from a tomb of considerable depth; and has noted the discovery of several others at the village of St. Romain, in Savoy, though they were so fragile that they fell in pieces soon after their exposure to the air. One of the same class, however, recovered in an imperfect condition has been preserved sufficiently to exhibit the calvarium in profile with the singular vertical elongation which appears to have constituted the ideal type of masculine beauty among the Asiatic followers of Attila, as among the Natchez, the Peruvians, and other tribes and nations of the New World. It was found by M. Hippolyte Gosse, at Villy, near Reignier, in Savoy, and has been engraved by Professor Retzius, from a drawing furnished to him by the discoverer.

The hideous aspect ascribed by ancient chroniclers to the Hunnish invaders no doubt derived its justification, in part at least, from the strange distortions which custom thus assigned with the same imperative obligation of fashion which still perpetuates the deformity of the Mongol Chinese, in their barbarous efforts at the attainment of other prescribed proportions of an ideal female grace. Thierry, in his *Attila*, refers to the artificial means used by the Huns for giving Mongolian physiognomy to their children. The followers of Attila were a miscellaneous horde, dependent for their success on the influence of his personal character. The true wandering hordes of Scythian nomades, who constituted the Chunni, were of Ugrian race, and kindred to the Hungarians from Mount Ural; but the Huns partook more of the Kalmuk blood, while the Magyars appear to have intermingled that of the true Turk, against whose European aggressions they ultimately presented so impenetrable a bulwark. Attila, however, was in reality as much a leader of Goths as Huns; though the black Huns from the dreary Siberian steppes constituted the aristocracy of his wild followers, whose Mongolian physiognomy formed the ideal of ethnic beauty, at which the Gothic mother aimed, by bandaging the nose, compressing the cheekbones, and giving an artificial form to the cranium of her infant. The ravages of such a furious horde of nomadic invaders spread universal terror throughout the enervated and tottering Roman empire, and fear added fresh horrors to the wild visages of the Hunnish devastators. "Briefly and dolefully," says Palgrave, "do the chroniclers of France, Germany, and Italy describe and lament the vast fury of the Hungarian ravages. Tradition and poetry impart life and colour to these meagre narratives. The German boor still points at the haunted cairn as covering the uneasy bed or the troubled grave of the

restless Huns, whose swords are heard to clash beneath
the soil. Throughout fair France the grinning, boar-
tusked, ensanguined, child-devouring ogres appalled the
doubtingly incredulous delighted tremblers round the
blazing hearth." They are indeed described by the ter-
rified survivors of their desolating inroads as the most
hideous race of monsters the world ever saw; and the
old monk Jornandes says that their horrible bestial deformity gained for them more battles than their arms.
After the discomfited Huns retreated under Irnac, the
youngest son of Attila, to the Volga, and conquered
nearly the whole Tauric Chersonese, they were subdued
in their turn by the Avars under Zaber-Chan, in the
latter half of the sixth century, and thereafter they are
called indiscriminately Avars or Huns by all the European chroniclers of the time of Charlemagne. Thus
intermingled, they constituted once more a powerful
aggressive nation, who during the seventh and eighth
centuries kept Europe in continual dread. Their military capital was in Pannonia; but they extended their
ravages wherever the spoils of more civilized nations
tempted their cupidity, and doubtless the bones of many
a fierce Avar lie mouldering in the soil that once trem-
bled under their savage tread. Their name became a
synonym for inhuman monster, under its various forms of
German *Hune*, Russian *Obri*, French *Bulgar* or *Bougre*,
and English *Ogre*. Such were the people whose macrocephalic, or rather obliquely depressed skulls, are believed
to have been recovered in recent years, in Switzerland,
Germany, and on the shores of the Euxine, presenting
strange abnormal proportions, so singularly corresponding to those of the New World, that the experienced
traveller and physician, Dr. Tschudi, has claimed one
of the most characteristic of them as no true European discovery, but a lost relic from some ancient Peru-

vian tomb. Not to Europe, however, do they really belong, but seemingly to the nomade Mongols and Ugrians of the great steppes of Northern Asia, in the vast wilds of which we lose them as they spread away eastward towards the Okhotsk Sea, the Aleutian Islands, and Behring Straits.

A curious and unexpected confirmation of the Asiatic source of the compressed crania of Europe is furnished by a discovery made at Jerusalem in 1856, by Mr. J. Judson Barclay, an American traveller. The circumstances are sufficiently remarkable to merit detail. Mr. Barclay having received information of an extensive cave near the Damascus Gate, entirely unknown to Franks, he resolved to explore it in conjunction with his father and brother. The requisite permission was obtained without difficulty from the Nazir Effendi, and they repaired to the cave, the mouth of which is situated directly below the city wall and the houses on Bezetha. Through a narrow, serpentine passage which traverses it, they gained an entrance into the cavern, the roof of which is supported by numerous regular pillars hewn out of the solid limestone rock. Many crosses on the wall indicated that the devout pilgrim or crusader had been there ; and a few Arabic and Hebrew inscriptions, too much effaced to be deciphered, proved that the place was not unknown to the Jew and the Saracen. About one hundred feet from the entrance a deep and precipitous pit was discovered containing a human skeleton. The bones were of unusually large proportions, and gave evidence from their decayed state, of having long remained in their strange sepulchre. But the skull, though imperfect, was in good preservation, and this the explorers brought to America, and presented to the Academy of Natural Sciences of Philadelphia, where it attracted the attention of Dr. J. Aitken Meigs, and was made the subject of an elaborate communication, printed in the Academy's Transactions.[1]

Placed in the same cabinet with the American crania collected by Dr. Morton, this skull, recovered from beneath the rocky foundations of Jerusalem, presents some of the most striking characteristics of the artificially modified crania of the New World. Seen by Dr. Morton, without any clue to the circumstances of its discovery, it would have been pronounced, in all probability, a Natchez skull; shown to Dr. Tschudi, even in a European collection, it would be assigned unhesitatingly as the spoil of a Peruvian grave; but the widely-extended empire of the grandson of Ferdinand and Isabella fails to account for the discovery of such a skull, with all the remains of the skeleton, in an ancient quarry-cavern of Jerusalem. The most remarkable feature is that the occipital bone rises vertically from the posterior margin of the foramen magnum to meet the parietal bones, which bend abruptly downward between their lateral protuberances. After minutely describing the appearance which the several bones present, Dr. Meigs expresses his conviction that the head has been artificially deformed by pressure applied to the occipital region during early youth; and thus recognises in it an indisputable proof of the practice in ancient Asia of the same custom of distorting the human head which was long regarded as peculiar to America.

The arguments by which he aims at assigning to this skull its true ethnical relations rest on less certain foundations. After marshalling all the probable claimants, and assigning reasons for rejecting each, Dr. Meigs shows

---

[1] "Description of a Deformed Fragmentary Skull found in an ancient quarry-cave at Jerusalem; with an attempt to determine, by its configuration alone, the ethnical type to which it belongs." By J. Aitken Meigs, M.D. 1859.

that it unites some of the most characteristic elements
of the Mongolian and the Slavonian head, while differing
in some respects from both ; and he finally concludes
that it may be referred—not as a positive and indisputable conclusion, but as an approximation to the truth,
—to the people and the region about Lake Baikal.
Through the Slaves and Burats of that region the
short-headed races of Eastern Europe graduate apparently into the Kalmucks and Mongols proper of Asia ;
and here probably is a remarkable example of an artificially modified cranium of that transitional people of
Lake Baikal.   If these deductions are hereafter confirmed, we are thus guided by a process of purely
scientific induction far beyond the limits assigned by
Hippocrates, Strabo, Pliny, or Mela, to the Asiatic Macrocephali ; and recover traces of the strange practice
of the American Flatheads far to the north-east of the
Altai chain, in the valleys that skirt the Yablonoi mountains, as they trend eastward towards the Okhotsk Sea.
There it is, in the vast unknown regions of Asiatic
Russia, that we may hope to recover evidence which
shall confirm the Asiatic relations of the American race.

But as attention is directed to the proofs of artificial
modifications of the form of the human head practised
by diverse tribes and nations of the Old World, new and
unexpected disclosures tend still further to enlarge the
areas of such operations.   Dr. Foville, a distinguished
French physician, at the head of the Asylum for the
Insane in the department Seine-Inférieure and Charenton
has brought to light the remarkable fact that the practice of distorting the skull in infancy still prevails in
France, by means of a peculiar head-dress and bandages ·
and in his large work on the Anatomy of the Nervous
System, he has engraved examples of such compressed
heads, one of which might be mistaken for a Peruvian

sepulchral relic. The practice is probably one inherited
from times of remote antiquity, and is found chiefly
to characterize certain districts. Normandy, Gascony,
Limousin, and Brittany are specially noted for its prevalence, with some local variations as to its method and
results. Like other ancient customs, it is probably pursued with the unreasoning adherence to time-immemorial
usage by which many equally useless practices have been
perpetuated, and with no definite aim at changing the
form of the head.

In a section devoted to Distortions of the Skull, in the
Crania Britannica, two remarkable examples are engraved, derived from Anglo-Saxon graves, and others
are referred to, found in British barrows ; but those, Dr.
Thurnam and Mr. Davis concur in ascribing to causes
operating subsequently to interment. The influence to
which such posthumous change of cranial form is chiefly
ascribed, is the pressure of the superincumbent earth upon
the skulls of bodies interred in barrows, unprotected by
coffins, and exposed to an unusual amount of moisture.

The geologist has long been familiar with the occurrence of skulls distorted, or completely flattened, and
even with solid bones, and with shells, which have
undergone remarkable transformations, by compression
or distension operating on their rocky matrix before it
assumed its final consolidation. In some of those cases,
however, the palæontologist looks in reality only on the
cast of the ancient bone or shell, compressed along with
its once plastic matrix, probably at a date long subsequent to its original deposition. But the distortion by
which the human skulls referred to have acquired their
abnormal shape, must have taken place while the animal
matter still remained in sufficient abundance to preserve
the original flexibility of the bones. In an interesting
paper " On Aboriginal Antiquities recently discovered in

the Island of Montreal," communicated by Dr. Dawson
to the *Canadian Naturalist,* he has given a description
of one female and two male skulls, found, along with
many other human bones, at the base of the Montreal
mountain, on a site which he identifies with much probability as that of the ancient Hochelaga, an Indian
village visited by Cartier in 1535. Since the publication
of that paper, I have examined two other skulls recovered from the same cemetery, both of which are now
in the Museum of M'Gill College, Montreal. They are
those of a man and woman, whose remains were found
together, as they had been buried, in the sitting or
crouching position common in Indian sepulture, in the
fine sand which overlies the clay on the site referred to,
in a bed varying from about two to six feet in depth.
The female skull has the superciliary ridge very prominent, with a groove above it, while a prolongation of the
occiput, frequently seen in the female cranium, gives
a peculiarly marked predominance to the longitudinal
diameter. From this the male skull essentially differs.
It is that of a man about forty years of age, approximating to the common proportions of the Algonquin
cranium, but presenting unmistakable indications of
having undergone alteration in shape subsequent to
interment. It is marked by great but unequal depression of the frontal bone, with considerable lateral distortion, accompanied with bulging out on the right side,
and an abnormal configuration of the occiput, suggestive
at first sight of the effects of the familiar native processes
of artificial malformation during infancy. Such an idea,
however, disappears on minute inspection, and it seems
impossible to doubt that, in this Indian skull, we have a
very striking example of posthumous distortion. The
right side of the forehead is depressed, and recedes so far
behind the left, that the right external angular process

of the frontal bone is nearly an inch behind that of the left side. The skull recedes proportionally on the same side throughout, with considerable lateral development at the parietal protuberance, and a projection behind on the right side of the occiput ; which is further marked by the occurrence of an irregular group of wormian bones. The right superior maxillary and malar bones have become detached from the calvarium, but the nasal bones, and part of the left maxillary, still adhere to it, exhibiting in the former the evidence of the well-developed and prominent nose, characteristic of Indian physiognomy. The bones of the calvarium have retained

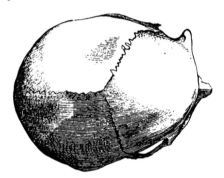

FIG. 67.—Hochelaga Skull.

their coherence, notwithstanding the great distortion which has taken place, although the sutures remain entirely unossified, and must have given way under any unequal pressure. The only exceptions to this are in the left temporal bone, which is so far displaced as to detach the upper edge of the squamous suture, and in the basilar portion of the occipital bone, part of which is wanting. On examining the base of this skull, the posthumous origin of its distortion is most readily perceived ; and this is proved beyond doubt on replacing the condyles of the lower jaw in apposition with the glenoid cavities, when it is seen that instead of the first teeth meeting the corresponding ones of the upper jaw, the lower front right and left incisors both impinge on the first right canine tooth of the upper maxillary, and the remaining teeth are thereby so placed as to preclude the possibility of their use in mastication, had such been the relative position of the jaws during life. The same distortion which has thus displaced the glenoid cavities, has produced a corresponding change on the position of the mastoid processes, which are twisted obliquely, so that the left one is more than an inch in advance of the right.

The circumstances under which the Hochelaga skull was found, tend to throw some light on the probable causes which may effect such posthumous malformation. It was covered by little more than two feet of soil, the pressure of which was in itself insufficient to have occasioned the change of form. The internal cavity, moreover, was entirely filled with the same fine sand in which the skull was imbedded. If, therefore, we conceive of the body lying interred under this slight covering of soil until all the tissues and the brain had disappeared, and the infiltration of the fine sand had filled the hollow brain-case ; and then, while the bones were still replete with animal matter, and softened by being imbedded in moist sand, and filled with the same, if some considerable additional pressure, such as the erection of a heavy structure, or the sudden accumulation of any weighty mass, took place over the grave, the internal sand would present sufficient resistance to the superincumbent weight, applied with nearly equal pressure on all sides, to prevent the crushing of the skull, or the displacement of the bones, while they would readily yield conformably to the general compression of the mass. The skull would thus be subjected to a process closely analogous to that by which the abnormal developments of the Flathead crania are effected during infancy, accompanied by great relative displacement of the cerebral mass, but by little or no diminution of the internal capacity.

In the remarkable example in Dr. Thurnam's collection, of a distorted Anglo-Saxon skull, from Stone, in Buckinghamshire,[1] there are indications, especially in the detached and gaping sutures on the base, that it has been subjected to an extraordinary amount of oblique posthumous compression. Among primitive nations, the dead are almost invariably committed to the earth entirely unprotected by any covering of stone or wood; and the more recent practice of inhumation in a coffin of wood subject to rapid decay, presents a protecting medium of little more avail against the distorting compression of the moist soil; yet of the many crania that I have examined, both in the Old World and the New, the traces of distortion have been in no degree more noticeable than a close observer will perceive to be common on the living head, when his attention is directed to its prevalence within certain limitations; while my opportunities of observation have been sufficient to satisfy me that crania recovered from British stone cists, entirely protected from any contact with the soil, frequently exhibit considerable irregularity of form, arising from accidental deformation during life, of which corresponding modern examples are less rare than is supposed. The normal skull may be assumed to present a perfect correspondence on its two sides, but very few examples fully realize the requirements of such a standard. Not only is inequality in the two sides of frequent occurrence, though not to the extent of deformity exhibited in the skull from Stone, in Buckinghamshire, or that of the Indian cemetery of Hochelaga; but a perfectly symmetrical skull is the exception rather than the rule. The

---

[1] *Crania Britannica,* chap. iv. p. 38.

plastic character of the bones of the head during infancy, which so readily admits of purposed deviation from its natural form, also renders it liable to many undesigned changes; nor has this been overlooked by Morton and other American cranioscopists, who concur in assigning the predominant vertical occiput to the form of the Indian cradle acting upon a naturally brachycephalic head. Dr. Morton remarks of the Peruvian skulls examined by him, " These neads are remarkable not only for their smallness, but also for their irregularity, for, in the whole series in my possession, there is but one that can be called symmetrical. This irregularity chiefly consists in the greater projection of the occiput to one side than the other, showing, in some instances, a surprising degree of deformity. As this condition is as often observed on one side as the other, it is not to be attributed to the intentional application of mechanical force ; on the contrary, it is to a certain degree common to the whole American race, and is sometimes no doubt increased by the manner in which the child is placed in the cradle. I am in fact convinced, that among the collection of Peruvian skulls alluded to, there is not one that has been designedly moulded by art."[1]

Without concurring in the latter untenable opinion, my attention has been repeatedly drawn to examples of unsymmetrical heads, the forms of which must be ascribed to the operation of external causes undesignedly modifying them during infancy. Here, for example, are notes taken from personal observation :— An Englishwoman : head markedly unsymmetrical. This she accounted for by the fact that her mother was only able to suckle at one breast. All her brothers and sisters, six in number, were characterized by the same irregular conformation of the head, except the youngest, a girl. This tendency

[1] *Crania Americana*, p. 115.

having attracted attention in the elder members of the
family, was at length traced to its true cause, and was prevented by watchful care in the youngest child. Another
case is that of the child of a Scottish woman, the wife of
a farmer at Scarborough, in Upper Canada. The boy
was about five years old at the time these observations
were made. His head is flat on the one side, and greatly
convex on the other. He was a very sickly child; his
teeth early decayed; and, as he was upwards of two
years old before he could walk, he was subjected to an
unusually protracted nursing. His mother was, in like
manner, only able to suckle at one breast, and to this she
ascribes the peculiar form of the head of her son, who is
now a healthy boy. This subject is further illustrated
by a series of paper shapes of the horizontal outlines of
heads, furnished to me by a hatter, which exhibit some
very odd and remarkable deviations from the normal
symmetry of the human cranium. Examples of both
classes of illustration of this subject of inquiry must be
accessible to many, and are well worthy of further attention. It is obvious that the skull during infancy is in
such a pliant condition as renders it peculiarly susceptible of abnormal changes of form, which may be carried
to a great extent without materially affecting the functions of the brain. Moreover, it is apparent, from the
illustrations already furnished, that many undesigned
changes may be effected on the form of the head during
infancy, by specialties pertaining to modes of nursing, or
the prevailing treatment to which children are subjected.
The cranial form designated by M. Foville the *Tête
annulaire*, may have predominated for many centuries
through certain rural districts of France, solely from the
unreasoning conformity with which the rustic nurse adhered to traditional and prescriptive usages, such as all
experience assures us are among the most likely customs

to survive the shock of revolutions. The mode of nursing and carrying the infant, as among certain African tribes, where it is borne on the back, and suckled over the shoulder; or with the American Indians, where it is almost invariably strapped tightly on a cradle-board : must have had some effect on the form of the skull, and even, in the former, may have affected the bones of the face; whilst the opposite practice of suckling the child at the breast, and laying it to sleep from earliest infancy on its side, especially if accompanied with a persistent adherence to one side, must tend to modify the cranial form in an inverse direction.

Dr. Morton recognised this element, as one tending to exaggerate, though not, as he believed, wholly to produce the flattened occiput, which he assigned as one of the most characteristic cranial features of the American aborigines. Nor did he fail to note the frequent irregularities observable in the class of skulls to which his attention was specially devoted. Of the Scioto Valley cranium, he remarks, in reference to its peculiarly characteristic vertical occiput : " Similar forms are common in the Peruvian tombs, and have the occiput, as in this instance, so flattened and vertical, as to give the idea of artificial compression ; yet this is only an exaggeration of the natural form caused by the pressure of the cradle-board in common use among the American nations." When commenting on this, in discussing the supposed prevalence of one cranial type throughout the American aborigines, I expressed a belief that further investigation would tend to the conclusion that the vertical or flattened occiput, instead of being a typical characteristic, pertains to the class of artificial modifications of the natural cranium familiar to the American ethnologist, alike in the disclosures of ancient graves, and in the customs of widely-separated living tribes. Vesalius is quoted, in the *Crania Britannica*, as affirming that the Germans of his day, the middle of the sixteenth century, had a broad head with compressed occiput, which he attributed to the custom of binding infants in cradles upon their backs. In commenting on the assumption that unsymmetrical conformation is characteristic of American crania, I remarked, in a paper already referred to, published in 1857,[1] " I have repeatedly noted the like unsymmetrical characteristics in the brachycephalic crania of the Scottish barrows ; and it has occurred to my mind on more than one occasion, whether such may not furnish an indication of some partial compression, dependent, it may be, on the mode of nurture in infancy having tended, in their case also,. if not to produce, to exaggerate the short longitudinal diameter, which constitutes one of their most remarkable characteristics." To this idea Mr. J. Barnard Davis has since given the weight of his concurrent testimony, and adds, " The bones of the head are very pliant in infancy, and are easily moulded to an artificial form. Among the Kanakas of the Sandwich Islands, the mother's habit of supporting the head of her nursling in the palm of her left hand, is considered to produce the flatness in the occipital region so commonly observed in Kanaka. Here, again, natural conformation affords the basis of that brachycephalic form which is increased by art."[2] But, according to Dr. Pickering, the flattened occiput is found among the islanders of the Southern Ocean, directly traceable to artificial pressure. Mr. Davis states that, in a large series of skulls of the Kanakas of the Sandwich Islands, procured for him by Mr. W. L. Green, and by General W. Miller, British Consul-general at Honolulu, the flatness in the occipital region is often remarkably

---

[1] *Canadian Journal,* vol. ii. p. 406.
[2] *Crania Britannica,* Decade iii.

expressed. In commenting on the characteristics of the Malay race, Dr. Pickering remarks : "A more marked peculiarity, and one very generally observable, is the elevated occiput, and its slight projection beyond the line of the neck. The face, in consequence, when seen in front, appears broader than among Europeans, as is the case with the Mongolian, though for a different reason. In the Mongolian the front is depressed, or the cranium inclines backwards, while in the Malay it is elevated or brought forwards. The Mongolian traits are heightened artificially by the Chinooks ; but it is less generally known that a slight pressure is often applied to the occiput by the Polynesians, in conformity with the Malay standard."[1]

Professor Retzius, after commenting on the unnatural deformations which mediæval chroniclers particularly describe as the characteristics of the Huns, adds : "Thus we see more and more traces showing that this absurd custom formerly has been common in the ancient world, and, after the authority of Thierry, we may suppose that it principally, and perhaps originally, belonged to the Mongols."[2] But it is among these very Mongols that Dr. Pickering classes the Chinook-Flatheads, and all the Indians of the American continent ; and thus, by the help of ancient historians and geographers, and the recent discoveries and observations of scientific men, we recover traces of this strange custom of artificial distortion of the skull in ancient European cemeteries among the valleys of the Alps, on the banks of the Danube and the Don, and on the shores of the Euxine Sea. Beyond this we trace the same practice, in ancient times, to the valleys of the Caucasus and the shores of

[1] Pickering's *Races of Man* (Bohn), p. 45.
[2] " On Artificially-formed Skulls from the Ancient World," *Proceed. Acad. Nat. Sciences, Philadelphia*, vol. vii. p. 405.

the Caspian Sea ; and as we follow back the track of the
Huns and Avars, by whom it seems to have been introduced into Europe, we lose the traces of it among the
unfamiliar Siberian steppes of Northern Asia ; and only
recover them once more after crossing Behring Strait,
and investigating the strange customs which pertain to
the American tribes on the Pacific Coast, and in the
regions which lie to the west of the Rocky Mountains.

The artificial forms given to the human head by the
various tribes among whom the custom has been practised in ancient and modern times, though divided by
Dr. Gosse of Geneva into sixteen classes, range between
two extremes.   One of these is a combined occipital and
frontal compression, reducing the head as nearly as possible to a disk, having its mere edge laterally, as in the
very remarkable Natchez skull, engraved in the *Crania
Americana* (plates xx. xxi.), or in the portrait of Caw-
wachan, a woman of the Cowlitz tribe of the Flathead
Indians, taken from the life by Mr. Paul Kane, during
his wanderings among the tribes on the Cowlitz river.
She is painted in profile, with her head tapering wedge-
like, from the forehead and occiput to a blunt point at
the vertex, and she holds in her arms her child strapped
to the cradle-board, with its head padded and bandaged
under the process of flattening ;[1] as shown in the frontispiece to this volume.   The other form, which is more
common among the flathead tribes on the Columbia
river and its tributaries, depresses the forehead, and
throws back the whole skull, so as to give it a near
approximation to that of a dog.   Under such a process
the brain must be subjected to great compression ; and
in a skull of the latter type, brought from a Flathead
cemetery on the Columbia river, I observe distinct traces
of hyperostosis at the sutures, evidently a result of

[1] *Wanderings of an Artist among the Indians of North America,* p. 205.

the process of compression. Accurate Flathead statistics would probably show an increased mortality in infancy resulting from this barbarous process ; although even this is denied by competent observers ; and the process having been completed during the first year, all further effects appear to be limited to the external conformation of the head, without affecting either the health or the intellect. Fashion regulates to some extent the special form given to the head among various tribes, but this is modified by individual caprice, and a considerable

Fig. 68.—Newatee Chief.

variety is observable in the strange shapes which it is frequently forced to assume. The Newatees, an exceedingly warlike tribe on the north end of Vancouver's Island, give a conical shape to the head by means of a cord of deer's-skin padded with the inner bark of the cedar-tree, frayed until it assumes the consistency of very soft tow. This forms a cord about the thickness of a man's thumb, which is wound round the infant's head, compressing it gradually into a uniformly tapering cone.

The process seems neither to affect the intellect nor the
courage of this people, who are remarkable for their
cunning as well as their fierce daring, and are the terror
of all the surrounding tribes. The effect of this singular
form of head is still further increased by the fashion of
gathering the hair into a knot on the crown of the head,
as shown in the accompanying portrait of a Newatee
chief (Fig. 68), from a sketch taken by Mr. Paul Kane
during his visit to Vancouver's Island.

The Flatheads extend over a wide range of country
from 130 miles up the Columbia river to its mouth, and
along the Pacific coast and the Straits of De Fuca,
Puget's Sound, and Canal Diaro to near the mouth of
Fraser's river; as well as on Vancouver's Island. They
include fully twenty different tribes, among which are
the Cowlitz Indians on the river of that name; the
Chinooks, Klatsaps, Klickatats, and Kalponets on the
Columbia river; the Chastays south of the Columbia,
near the River Umqua; the Klackamuss on the river of
the same name in Oregon; the Nasquallies, Sinahomas,
and Cumsenahos on Puget's Sound; the Songas and
Eusāniches on the southern shores of the Straits of De
Fuca; the Towanachuns on Whitby's Island; the Cowit-
chins on the Gulf of Georgia; and the Clalams and
Newatees on Vancouver's Island. Greatly varying dialects are spoken among these Flathead tribes, and as the
lingua Franca of Oregon is the usual means of communication between them and the whites, the little knowledge of their languages hitherto obtained has been too
vague to be of much value. During Mr. Paul Kane's
travels among those tribes he saw hundreds of children
undergoing the process of flattening the head, and thus
describes the mode of procedure. The infant is strapped
to the cradle-board, which is carefully covered with moss
of finely frayed fibres of cedar-bark, and is fitted with a

head-board which projects beyond the face, so as to protect it from injury ; as shown in the frontispiece to this
volume. In order to flatten the head, a pad, made of a
piece of skin stuffed with soft cedar-bark, is laid on the
infant's forehead, and on the top of this a slab of hard
bark with the smooth side under. This is covered with
a piece of pliant deer-skin, and is bound tightly by
means of a leathern band passing through holes in the
cradle-board, while the head is supported and kept in an
immovable position by a pillow of grass or frayed cedar-
bark placed under the back of the neck. This process
commences immediately after the birth of the child, and
is continued for a period of from eight to twelve months,
by which time the head has permanently assumed the
flattened or wedge-shaped form, which constitutes the
ideal of Chinook or Cowlitz grace. Another process is by
means of a square piece of leather with thongs attached
to the four corners, placed over a pad on the forehead,
and secured tightly to the board. Other pads are placed
under the head, and at its sides, according to the special
form which it is desired to give it. Mr. Kane remarks :
" It might be supposed, from the extent to which this is
carried, that the operation would be attended with great
suffering, but I have never heard the infants crying or
moaning, although I have seen the eyes seemingly starting out of the sockets from the great pressure. But, on
the contrary, when the thongs were loosened, and the
pads removed, I have noticed them cry until they were
replaced. From the apparent dulness of the children
whilst under the pressure, I should imagine that a state
of torpor or insensibility is induced, and that the return
to consciousness occasioned by its removal, must be
naturally followed by the sense of pain." The woodcut,
Fig. 69, is from a careful sketch of a Chinook child, made
at Fort Astoria on the Columbia river, and illustrates

the extraordinary appearance of the Flatheads at an early age. The brain in its process towards maturity seems partially to recover a less abnormal form, especially where the pressure has been applied so as to produce the elevated wedge shape, with the breadth of the whole mass presented in front and rear, as in the accompanying example. In this the head seemed to be reduced almost to a disk, exhibiting the results of the barbarous practice to an extent that is rarely if ever observed in adults who have undergone the same process in infancy.

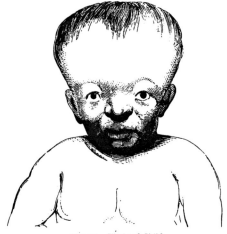

Fig. 69.—Flathead Child.

Mr. Kane was led to the conclusion that this violent process in no degree injures the health, as from inquiries made by him it did not appear that the mortality among the Flathead children is greater than amongst other Indian tribes. The evidence that it leaves the intellect unimpaired rests on more absolute proof. The Flathead tribes are in the constant habit of making slaves of the neighbouring roundheaded Indians, whom they treat with great barbarity ; and though living among them, these are not allowed to flatten or modify the form of their infants' heads, that being a distinguished mark of freedom, and the badge of aristocratic descent. They look with contempt on the whites as a people who bear in the shape of their heads the hereditary mark of slaves. They are, moreover, acute and intelligent, have singular powers of mimicry, and have been noted for very retentive memories : being capable of repeating passages of some length, with considerable accuracy, when recited in their hearing. It would, indeed, appear, that alike in the time of Hippocrates and in our own day, an idea has prevailed among those who practised the strange barbarian usage of remodelling the human head, that they thereby not only conferred and added grace to its form, but that they contributed no less to the mental superiority of those among whom this has ever been the peculiar symbol of aristocracy, and the mark of the dominant race. If it did, in reality, produce an opposite effect, and tend either to mental inferiority or absolute insanity, it would lead to speedy and inevitable revolutions among those tribes where the helots are rigorously excluded from the practice. But neither among the Peruvians, nor the ancient or modern North American tribes, is there any evidence of the normal cranium having thus practically demonstrated its superiority over the deformed or flattened skull.

It is an important fact that, excepting on the Gulf of Florida, where the north-west tribes, as they extended southward, overlapped the mountain range which divides the Pacific from the Atlantic regions of the New World, and there only to the west of the Mississippi, the traces of artificial moulding of the head are slight and quite exceptional ; whilst along the regions that border on the Pacific they reach beyond the most southern limits of ancient Peru. Dr. Morton quotes various early Spanish travellers and historians who generally concur in describing the Peruvian flattening or moulding of the skull as

having been effected by means of boards strapped on the
head, and thereafter by means of ligatures. Garcilasso de
la Vega produces proof to show that the custom is more
ancient than the Inca dynasty ; and it was so universally favoured, that a decree of the Ecclesiastical Court of
Lima, published in 1585, threatens with severe penalties
all parents who are found to persist in the practice. But
perhaps the most interesting passage is one from the
writings of Torquemada, where, referring to the Peruvians, he remarks : "As to the custom of appearing
fierce in war, it was in some provinces ordered that the
mothers or their attendants should make the faces of
their children long and rough, and the foreheads broad,
as Hippocrates and Galen relate of the Macrocephali,
who had them moulded by art into the elevated and
conical form. This custom is more prevalent in the
province of Chicuito, than in any other part of Peru."
In spite of ecclesiastical censures and penalties, the custom is not extinct even now in Peru ; and as our knowledge of the tribes of Northern Asia, and minuter observations on those of the Polynesian Islands, are extended,
further traces may be found of the same practice which
seems to furnish another curious link between the races
of the Old World and the New, and to confirm the idea
of a common origin for nations now separated by the
broad waters of the Pacific Ocean.

Some years since I instituted a series of observations
on two different classes of the labouring population in
Edinburgh and its vicinity, whose avocations subject
them to a process specially calculated to test the sus-
ceptibility of the adult cranium to compression and
change of form. Owing to the peculiar arrangement of
the middle-class dwellings in Edinburgh, in flats, approached by flights of stairs leading to their various
elevations, a special class of coal-porters is licensed by

the city authorities, chiefly for conveying fuel to its
elevated depositories. This they do by means of an
osier creel, supported by a broad leathern strap passed
over the head. On first proceeding to examine the
heads of those porters, I was struck with the general
prevalence of poorly developed, and even remarkably
low foreheads; but more careful observation showed
that the leathern band of the creel is placed by them,
not across the forehead, but directly over the coronal
suture; and here I could detect no prevailing indications of depression, although some of those examined
had been subjected for periods extending over more
than a quarter of a century to the almost daily pressure of the broad leathern strap supporting a heavy load
of coals, and this generally carried up steep flights of
stairs, where the weight would be less equally divided
between the back and the head. As to the poor frontal
development, it may be ascribed with little hesitation to
the fact that, as a general rule, only those whose capacity unfitted them for anything but the coarsest manual
toil, were likely to resort to what constitutes one of the
least attractive and most poorly remunerated branches
of unskilled labour. It is otherwise, however, with the
well-known class of Scottish fishwives. The introduction of railways has somewhat modified the habits of
this, as of so many other classes of the labouring population; but until recent years, the fisherwomen of
Newhaven, Fisherrow, Musselburgh, and Prestonpans
were in the habit of daily bringing to the Edinburgh
market a heavy load of fish, in an osier creel, supported,
like that of the coal-porters, by a leathern strap over
the head. This they carried a distance of from two to
five or six miles; and although by their stooping gait
the back is made to bear a considerable share of the
burden, nevertheless the pressure on the head must be

great. One of its results is that the fisherwomen acquire
a peculiar walk, consequent on the position they have
to assume in order to regulate the centre of gravity,
when carrying their load to market. Unlike the coal-
porters, they are a sagacious, intelligent class of women,
accustomed to look upon their husbands' sphere of labour
as limited to the sea ; and to consider the whole charge
of the household, and the sale of the produce of the
fishing expedition, as well as the judicious expenditure
of the proceeds, to devolve upon them. No question as
to women's rights troubles the amphibious communities
of the Scottish fishing-villages ; where the labours of
the men are limited on land to the repair of their
fishing-boats, and the getting ready again for sea ; and
the fisherman in the city market would be as much
out of his element as one of his own finny prey. Here,
therefore, we have a test of the intellectual influences
wrought by continuous external pressure on the cranium,
and the result of my own observations was to satisfy
me that the form of the head was as little affected by
it. In this I am confirmed by other observers of long
experience. Dr. Scott of Musselburgh thus writes :
" With the co-operation of a professional friend, who has
devoted much attention to phrenology, I made an extensive survey of the heads of our fisherwomen. I have
been unable to detect any marked change in the shape
of the skulls from carrying the creel. The leather band
of the creel is placed, not across the forehead, but
directly over the coronal suture ; and though in one or
two instances there seemed to be a slight depression in
that region, in all the others, including several instances
where the women had carried fish to Edinburgh for
upwards of forty years, there was no trace of change
of form in the skull." The fishing-village here referred
to is distant upwards of five miles from Edinburgh,

and consequently presents examples of heads subjected
to the most protracted operation of a pressure which,
if applied in infancy, would have completely distorted
the skull. The populous fishing-village of Newhaven
lies little more than two and a half miles distant from
the city market, and there my own investigations were
chiefly pursued. To these a medical friend adds the
following results of his own independent observations,
derived from long residence and professional practice
among them. " I have not observed any peculiar conformation of the cranium in the fishermen and fisherwomen of this neighbourhood. In point of shape I
think it very much resembles that of other classes of
the community. The pressure of the creel-band, of
course, does not affect the males, as they devolve the
duty of carrying it entirely on the females, and even in
their case the head is fully formed before they go regularly to market. In size the crania of the Newhaveners
are certainly below the average. This cannot fail to
strike you in the village church, if you sit on the south
side in front of the pews occupied by the fishers. There
are some exceptions ; indeed, there are families in the
village characterized by good heads, and among whom
this and other qualities appear to be hereditary ; but,
generally speaking, I believe actual measurement would
show that the size of the cranium among the fishing
population is under the average." How far actual
measurements would bear out the latter assertion, my
removal from Scotland prevented me from testing ; but
the testimony otherwise concurs with my own observations, and indicates that the head of the adult—beginning with the fisherwoman at sixteen or seventeen years
of age,—may be subjected to a considerable pressure,
applied daily on the same region, for hours together,
through a long series of years, without affecting the

shape. The infant, on the contrary, may at the period
of birth be subjected to a pressure by the obstetric
forceps, or by other causes operating in parturition,
which completely alters the form of the skull; and
during the first year its head may be moulded into the
most fantastic forms that the inherited customs of savage
tribes can dictate, without interfering with the healthful functions of the brain. Even by many apparently
trifling causes, consequent on nursing usages, the form
of the head is modified, so that the national cranial type
may be the unconscious product of hereditary customs.
But at a very early date the skull appears to acquire its
permanent form, and thereafter resists all external pressure, less than that which suffices to crush its bony arch;
nor does it seem consistent with those facts that the
adult skull should be found readily susceptible of posthumous distortion by the ordinary pressure of the superincumbent earth, which, in the great majority of cases,
is not found even to modify or displace the delicate
nasal bones generally exposed to its direct action.

CHAPTER XXIII.

THE RED BLOOD OF THE WEST.

THE theory of an aboriginal unity pervading one indigenous American race from the Arctic Circle to Terra-del-Fuego has been shown to be liable to challenge on indisputable evidence. Moreover, the proof that the American man is in any sense separated by essential physical differences from all other nations or races of the human family, in like manner fails on minute examination. The typical white, red, and black man, placed side by side, do indeed present very strikingly contrasting characteristics ; and the author still recalls with vivid force the question forced on his mind when, seated for the first time at a large public table in a southern American city, he found himself surrounded by the proscribed pariah race of Africa. A servile people, isolated from all community of interests, and from all share in the wondrous triumphs of the dominant race, presented itself there under aspects scarcely conceivable to the European, who sees a stranger of African blood mingle occasionally, like any other foreigner, in public assemblies or social circles, without being tempted to ask : Can he be indeed of one blood, and descended of the same primeval parent stock with ourselves ? But the isolation of the red man is even greater, for it is voluntary and self-imposed. No prejudice of caste precludes him from a perfect equality of intercourse with the white supplanter. Intermarriage of

the races carries with it no sense of degradation, and
intermingling of blood involves no forfeiture of rights or
privileges. Yet with all the advantages from which the
African race is utterly excluded, he yields his ground
even more rapidly than the encroachments of the intrusive supplanters demand ; and disappears scarcely less
swiftly under the guardianship of friendly superintendents and missionary civilizers, than when exposed to
the exterminating violence of Spanish cupidity.

Upwards of three centuries and a half have elapsed
since the landing of the Spanish discoverers on the first-
seen island of the Western Hemisphere ; and it may be
doubted if a single year has passed since that memorable
event, in which some historical memorial has not perished, without the preservation of any note of its records.
But the most valuable and irrecoverable of all those records are the nations that have died and left no sign.
The native races of the islands of the American archipelago have been exterminated ; and of many of them
scarcely a relic of their language, or a memorial of their
arts, their social habits, or religious rites, survives. So,
in like manner, throughout the older American States, in
Canada, and over the vast area which spreads westward
from the Atlantic seaboard to the Rocky Mountains,
whole tribes and nations have disappeared, without even
a memorial-mound or pictured grave-post to tell where
the last of the race is returning to the earth from whence
he sprung. But such being the case, it is impossible,
while regarding the claims of the American as a strictly
indigenous race, to overlook the significant fact, that the
negro, a foreign race, the most diverse of all from the
aborigines of the New World, was introduced there solely
because of his capacity of endurance and perpetuity,
which is wanting in the children of the soil. This
capacity of endurance experience has proved him to

possess; and the fact is singularly at variance with the supposed application of the same laws to the races of man which control the circumscription of the natural provinces of the animal kingdom. The aborigines of America are indeed a people by themselves. For unknown ages they have developed all the results of physical influences, habits of life, and whatever peculiarities pertained to their geographical position, or their primeval American ancestry. Yet when we go beyond that continent which has isolated them through all the unmeasured centuries of their independent existence, it is on the neighbouring one of Eastern Asia that we find an ethnic type so nearly resembling them, that Dr. Charles Pickering, the ethnologist of the American Exploring Expedition, groups the American with the Asiatic Mongolian, as presenting the most characteristic physical traits common to both. And as the American thus presents a striking ethnical affinity to the Asiatic Mongol ; so also the same physical diversities have been noted among the different tribes and nations of the New World, by which the other great ethnographic groups are broken up into minor subdivisions, and so gradually converge from opposite points towards the ideal type of a common humanity. But while those who maintain the existence of essential primary distinctions among a plurality of human species, explain such convergence towards one common type by the further theory of remote, allied, and proximate species, they accompany this with the idea that even the commingling of proximate species is opposed to natural laws, and involves the ultimate destruction of all ; while the rapid extinction of the inferior types of man when " remote species," such as the European and the Red Indian, are brought into contact and commingle, is produced in evidence of the essential and primary distinction in their origin. " Sixteen millions of aborigines in North America," exclaims Dr. J. C. Nott, " have dwindled down to two millions since the ' Mayflower' discharged on Plymouth Rock; and their congeners, the Caribs, have long been extinct in the West Indian Islands. The mortal destiny of the whole American group is already perceived to be running out, like the sand in Time's hour-glass."[1] By whatsoever means we may attempt to account for this, the fact is undoubted. Nor is this displacement and extinction of races of the New World, thus prominently brought under our notice as in part the result of our own responsible acts, by any means an isolated fact in the history of nations. The revelations of geology disclose to us displacement and replacement as the economy of organic life through all the vast periods which its records embrace ; and among the many difficult problems which the thoughtful observer has to encounter, in an attempt to harmonize the actual with his ideal of the world as the great theatre of the human family, none is more intricate and perplexing than the displacement and extinction of races, such as has been witnessed on the American continent since first the European gained a footing on its shores. But the very existence of a science of ethnology results from the recognition of essential physical and moral differences characteristic of the subdivisions of the human family. To some these resolve themselves into the radical distinctions of diverse species ; to others the well-ascertained development of varieties, within single recognised groups of a common descent, sufficiently accounts for the most marked diversities from a normal type of the one human species ; and the New World presents all the requisites for such a development of variation from the primary type of man.

---

[1] " Hybridity of Animals, viewed in connexion with the Natural History of Mankind."—*Types of Mankind*, p. 409.

The whole history of civilisation limits its Asiatic origin to the shores of the Indian Ocean and the Mediterranean Sea, and to the great plain watered by the Tigris and the Euphrates. From thence its path has been undeviatingly westward, and the New World has been reached by the daring enterprise that made of the ocean a highway to the West which lay beyond it. But it is in the great steppes of Northern Asia, where civilisation has never dawned, that the eastern Mongol presents the unmistakable approximation to the American type of man. Through all the centuries during which the historic nations have figured in the drama of the world's history, since Asshur and Nimrod founded the first Asiatic kingdoms, the unhistoric nations have also played their unheeded parts. Westward, in the path of the sun, went the ruling nations, shaping out the world's destinies in the northern hemisphere ; but eastward, meanwhile, wandered the nomade tribes, filled up the great Asiatic steppes, occupied the unclaimed wastes along the Arctic circle, and found an easy passage by their eastern route to the Western Hemisphere. That this is not the only, nor probably the earliest route from Asia to America, will be seen hereafter ; but it suffices for the present argument that access was thus possible. There settled, they took possession of a continent as different in every physical characteristic from that of Europe as it is possible for countries within the same parallels of latitude to be. In vain we search through all the world's ancient and mediæval history for a definite trace of intercourse between the two hemispheres ; and when at length, in 1492, Columbus opened for us the gates of the West, it was the meeting of those who, by opposite courses, had fled from each other until the race engirdled the globe. Assuming their descent from a common protoplast : if climate, social habits, civilisation, and the perpetuation of special peculiarities, uninterruptedly in a single direction, are capable of producing a permanent variety, the continent of America, and its human occupants, presented all the requisites for the development of a peculiar type, without the assumption of any primary distinction of species.

But the circumstances in which man was placed on the American continent were not the most favourable for his ethnic and intellectual maturity. In single families, a great diversity of physical and intellectual capacity is apparent; and among the family of nations the Asiatic Mongol, who presents the closest affinity to the American Indian, occupies a very inferior place. Brought from his wild steppes, directly in contact with the advanced civilisation of Europe, he is utterly incapable of standing his ground; yet when placed under favourable circumstances of training and pupilage, as seen in the older Hun, the Magyar, and the Turk, he is fully able to assert the claims of a common humanity. But no such opportunities were accorded to the American Mongol. We see him in the fifteenth and subsequent centuries brought into contact and collision with the most civilized nations of the world, in periods of their matured energy. It was the meeting of the two extremes : of the most highly favoured among the nations triumphing in their onward progress not less by constitutional superiority than by acquired civilisation; and of the savage, or the semi-civilized barbarian, in the stages of national infancy and childhood. Their fate was inevitable. It does not diminish our difficulty in dealing with the complex problem, to know that such had been the fate of many races and even of great nations before them. But if we are troubled with the perplexities of this dark riddle, whereby the colonists of the New World only advance by the retrogression of its aborigines, and in their western progress ever tread on the graves of nations, the consideration of some of the phenomena attendant on this same process of displacement and extinction, accompanying the human race from the very dawn of its history, may help to lessen the mystery.

One, and only one record supplies any credible statement on a subject concerning which the mythologies of all nations have professed to furnish some information. The Book of Genesis, or the Beginning, is divided into two separate and perfectly distinct histories : the first, an account of the Creation, and the general history of mankind till the dispersion, extending over a period of considerably more than two thousand years, and contained in the first ten chapters, and nine verses of the eleventh ; while the remaining chapters, and indeed nearly the whole of the historical Books of the Old Testament, are exclusively devoted to the one selected race, that of Abraham and his descendants.

Looking then to the first of those, and to its narrative in relation to the immediate descendants of Noah, the recognised protoplasts of the primary subdivisions of the human family, we perceive that certain very marked and permanent differences are assigned to each. Ham, the father of Canaan, is left without a blessing, while Canaan is marked as the progenitor of a race destined to degradation as the servant of servants. The blessing of Shem is peculiar, as if it were designed chiefly to refer to the one branch of his descendants, " to whom pertained the adoption, and the glory, and the covenants, and the giving of the law, and the service of God ;" but to his various descendants a special rank is assigned in the world's future : special, predominant in relation to some branches of the human family ; but yet inferior and of temporary duration when compared with the destinies of the Japhetic nations, who, enlarging their

bounds, and encroaching on the birthright of the elder
races, are destined to " dwell in the tents of Shem," and
Canaan shall serve them.

Thus we perceive that one important subdivision of
the human family is stamped, *ab initio*, with the marks
of degradation; while another, the Shemitic, though pri-
vileged to be the first partaker of the blessing, to be the
originator of the world's civilisation, and to furnish the
chosen custodiers of its most valued inheritance, through
the centuries which anticipated the fulness of time : yet
the nations of this stock are destined to displacement,
for " Japhet shall be enlarged, and shall dwell in the
tents of Shem."

Thus, also, from the very first we perceive a strongly
marked and clearly defined distinction between diverse
branches of the human family ; and this, coupled with
the apportionment of the several regions of the earth to
distinct types of man, distinguished from each other not
less definitely than are the varied *faunæ* of these regions,
seems to express very clearly the subdivision of the
genus *Homo* into diverse varieties, with a certain relation to their primary geographical distribution.

There have been ingenious attempts made to assign to
each generation of the Noachic family its national descendants ; but the majority of such results commend
themselves to our acceptance at best as only clever
guesses at truth.   Of the most remarkable of the
Hamitic descent, however, we can be at no loss as to
their geographical areas.   The Canaanites occupied the
important region of Syria and Palestine ; and Nimrod,
the son of Cush, moving to the eastward, settled his
descendants on the banks of the Euphrates ; so that of
the distinctly recognisable generations of Ham, it is in
Asia, and not in Africa, that we must look for them,
for centuries after the dispersion of the family of Noah ;

while among those, whom, on such an assumption of
descent, we may reckon with the offspring of the same
father of nations, are the Mongol wanderers on the great
steppes of Asia, eastward towards the passage to the
New World of the West.

But the Shemitic races were also to share the Eastern
Continent before they enlarged their area, and asserted
their right to the inheritance of the descendants of Ham.
By Nimrod, the grandson of Ham, the settlements along
the valley of the Euphrates were founded, "and the
beginning of his kingdom was Babel, and Erech, and
Accad, and Calneh, in the land of Shinar," all sites of
ancient cities which recent exploration and discovery
seem to indicate as still traceable amid the graves of the
East's mighty empires.   But the eponymus of the rival
kingdom on the banks of the Tigris was Asshur, the son
of Shem ; and in that region also it would appear that
we must look for the locality of others of the generations
of the more favoured Shem ; while nearly the whole
habitable regions between their western borders and the
Red Sea, were occupied from this very dawn of history,
by the numerous Shemitic descendants of Joktan, of
whom descended Mohammed and the Shemitic propa-
gators of the monotheistic creed of the Koran ; as came
the Hebrews, according to Jewish belief, and through
them, the great prophet of our faith, from Eber, the
assumed eponymus of those whom we must look upon,
on many accounts, as important above all other Shemitic
nations.

Deriving our authority still from the sacred record,
we ascertain as the result of the multiplication and dispersion of one minutely detailed generation of the sons
of Ham, through Canaan, that for eight hundred years
thereafter they increased and multiplied in the favoured
lands watered by the Jordan, and stretching to the shores

of the Levant ; they founded mighty cities, accumulated
great wealth, subdivided their goodly inheritance among
distinct nations and kingdoms of a common descent ;
and upwards of eleven hundred years afterwards, when
the intruded tribe of Dan raised up the promised judge
of his people, the descendants of Ham still triumphed
in the destined heritage of the seed of Eber. At length,
however, the Hebrew accomplished his destiny. The
promised land became his possession, and the remnant of
the degraded Canaanite his bond-servants. For another
period of more than eleven hundred years, the Shemitic
Israelites made the land their own. The triumphs of
David, the glory and the wisdom of Solomon, and the
vicissitudes of the divided nationalities of Judah and
Israel, protracted until the accomplishment of the great
destiny of the princes of Judah, constitute the epos of
those who supplanted the settlers in the historic lands
lying between the mountains of Syria and the sea, when
first "the Most High divided to the nations their inheritance, when he separated the sons of Adam, and set
the bounds of the people." Then came another displacement. The Hebrews were driven forth from the land ;
and for eighteen hundred years, Roman and Saracen,
Frank, Turk, and Arab, have disputed the possession of
the ancient heritage of the Canaanite.

For very special and obvious reasons the isolation of
the Hebrew race, and the purity of the stock, were most
carefully guarded by the enactments of their great lawgiver, preparatory to their taking possession of the land
of Canaan ; yet the exclusive nationality and the strictly
defined purity of race admitted of striking exceptional deviations. While the Ammonite and the Moabite are cut
off from all permissive alliance, and the offspring of a
union between the Hebrew and these forbidden races is
not to be naturalized even in the tenth generation : the

Edomite, the descendant of Jacob's brother, and the Egyptian, are not to be abhorred, but the children that are begotten of them are to be admitted to the full privileges of the favoured seed of Jacob in the third generation.

This exception in favour of the Egyptian is a remarkable one. The ostensible reason, viz., that the Israelites had been strangers in the land of Egypt, appears inadequate fully to account for it, when the nature of that sojourn and the incidents of the Exodus are borne in mind; and would tempt us to look beyond it to the many traces of Shemitic character which the language, arts, and civilisation of Egypt disclose. But its monuments reveal the traces of many intruders; and beyond it, throughout the northern regions of the same continent, Phœnician and Greek, Berber, Roman, Arab, and Frank have mingled the blood of the ancient world. Around the shores of that expressively designated *Mediterranean* Sea how striking are the varied memorials of the past. A little area may be marked off on the map, environing its eastern shores, and constituting a mere spot on the surface of the globe; yet its history is the whole ancient history of civilisation, and a record of · its ethnological changes would constitute an epitome of the natural history of man. All the great empires of the Old World clustered around that centre, and as Dr. Johnson remarked: "All our religion, almost all our law, almost all our arts, almost all that sets us above savages, has come to us from the shores of the Mediterranean." There race has succeeded race; the sceptre has passed from nation to nation, through the historical representatives of all the great primary subdivisions of the human family, and "their decay has dried up realms to deserts." It is worthy of consideration, however, in reference to our present inquiries, how far the political displacement of nations in that primeval historic area was accompanied by a corresponding ethnological displacement and extinction.

It is in this respect that the sacred narrative, in its bearings on the primitive subdivisions of the human family, and their appointed destinies, seems specially calculated to supply the initiatory steps in relation to some conclusions of general application. However mysterious it be to read of the curse of Canaan on the very same page which records the blessings of Noah and his sons, and the first covenant of mercy to the human race, yet the record of both rests on the same authority. Still more, the curse was what may strictly be termed an ethnological one. Whether we regard it as a punitive visitation on Ham in one of the lines of generation of his descendants, or simply as a prophetic foretelling of the destiny of a branch of the human family, we see the Canaanite separated at the very first from all the other generations of Noachic descent as a race doomed to degradation and slavery. Nevertheless, to all appearance, many generations passed away, in the abundant enjoyment, by the offspring of Canaan, of all the material blessings of the "green undeluged earth," while they accomplished, as fully as any other descendants of Noah, the appointed repeopling, and were fruitful and increased, and brought forth abundantly in the earth, and multiplied therein, even as did the most favoured among the sons of Shem or Japhet. When, some five centuries after the Canaanite had entered on his strangely burdened heritage, the progenitor of its later and more favoured inheritors was guaranteed, by a divinely-executed covenant, the gift to his seed of that whole land, from the river of Egypt to the great river, the river Euphrates, the covenant was not even then to take place until the fourth generation. When that appointed period had elapsed, and only the narrow waters of the Jordan lay between the sons of Israel and the land of the Canaanites, their leader and lawgiver, who had guided them to the very threshold of that inheritance on which only his eyes were permitted to rest, foretold them in his final blessing : "The eternal God shall thrust out the enemy from before thee, and shall destroy, and Israel shall dwell in safety alone." No commandment can be more explicit than that which required of the Israelites the utter extirpation of the elder occupants of their inheritance : "When the Lord thy God shall bring thee into the land, and hath cast out before thee seven nations greater and mightier than thou, thou shalt smite them and utterly destroy them ; thou shalt make no covenant with them, nor shew mercy unto them." Nevertheless we find that the Israelites put the Canaanites to tribute, and did not drive them out ; that the children of Benjamin did not drive out the Jebusites ; but according to the author of the book of Judges, they still dwelt there in his day ; and so with various others of the aboriginal tribes. The Gibeonites obtained by craft a league of amity with Israel, and they also remained : bondmen, hewers of wood, and drawers of water, yet so guarded by the sacredness of the oath they had extorted from their disinheritors, that at a long subsequent date we find seven of the race of their supplanters, the sons and grandsons of the first Israelitish king, sacrificed to their demand for vengeance on him who had attempted their extirpation.

Even more remarkably significant than all those evidences of a large remnant of the ancient Hamitic population surviving in the midst of the later Shemitic inheritors of Canaan, and intermingling with them, is the appearance of the names of Rahab, the harlot of Jericho, and Ruth the Moabitess, in the genealogy of

Joseph, as recorded by Matthew. The purity of descent of the promised seed of Abraham and David was most sacredly guarded through all the generations of their race, yet even in that line these remarkable exceptions are admitted ; and the son of Ham, and the seed of Canaan, have also their links in the genealogy of the Messiah.

From all this it would seem to be justly inferred that ethnological displacement and extinction must be regarded in many, probably in the majority of cases, not as amounting to a literal extirpation, but only as equivalent to absorption. Such doubtless it has been to a great extent with the ancient European Celtæ, notwithstanding the distinct historical evidence we possess of the utter extermination of whole tribes both of the Britons and Gauls by the merciless sword of the intruding Roman ; and such also is being the case to some extent with the aboriginal Red Indians of the New World. It is impossible to travel in the far west of the American continent, on the borders of the Indian territories, or to visit the reserves where the remnants of Indian tribes, displaced by us in Canada and the States, linger on in passive process of extinction, without perceiving that they are disappearing as a race, in part at least, by the same process by which the German, the Swede, the Irish, or the Frenchman, on emigrating to the Anglo Saxonized States of America, becomes in a generation or two amalgamated with the general stock.

This idea of the absorption of the Indian into the Anglo-American race will not, I am aware, meet with a ready acceptance, even from those who dwell where its traces are most perceptible ; but, fully to appreciate its extent, we must endeavour to follow down the course of events by which the continent has been transferred to the descendants of its European colonists. At every fresh stage of colonization or of pioneering into the wild

West, the work has necessarily been accomplished by the hardy youths, or the hunters and trappers of the clearing. Rarely indeed did they carry with them wives or daughters; but where they found a home amid savage-haunted wilds, they took to themselves wives of the daughters of the soil. To this mingling of blood, in its least favourable aspects, the prejudices of the Indian presented little obstacle. Henry, in his narrative of travel among the Cristineaux on Lake Winipegon, in 1760, after describing the dress and allurements of the female Cristineaux, adds :—" One of the chiefs assured me that the children borne by their women to Europeans were bolder warriors and better hunters than themselves." [1]   This idea frequently recurs in various forms. The patient hardihood of the half-breed lumberers and trappers is recognised equally in Canada and the Hudson's Bay Territory, and experience seems to have suggested the same idea relative to the Esquimaux. Dr. Kane remarks that " the half-breeds of the coast rival the Esquimaux in their powers of endurance." [2]   But whatever be the characteristic of the Indian half-breed, the fact is unquestionable that all along the widening outskirts of the newer clearings, and wherever an outlying trading or hunting-post is established, we find a fringe of half-breed population marking the transitional border-land which is passing away from its aboriginal claimants. I was particularly struck with this during a brief residence at the Sault Ste. Marie, and in the immediate vicinity of one of the Hudson's Bay forts, in the summer of 1855. When on my way to Lake Superior I had passed on the River Ste. Marie a large body of Christianized Indians, assem-

[1] Henry's *Travels and Adventures in Canada and the Indian Territories,* 1760-1776 ; p. 249.
[2] Kane's *Arctic Explorations,* 1853-55, vol. i. p. 246.

bling from various points both of the American and
the Hudson's Bay territories, on one of the large islands
in the River Ste. Marie ; and while waiting at the Sault
a considerable body of them returned, passing up in
their canoes. Having entered into conversation with
an intelligent American Methodist missionary, who accompanied them, I questioned him as to the amount of
intermarriage or intercourse that took place between
the Indians and the whites, and its probable effects in
producing a permanent new type resulting from the
mixture of the two very dissimilar races. His reply
was : "Look about you at this moment ; comparatively
few of these onlookers have not Indian blood in their
veins ;" and such I discovered to be the case, as my eye
grew more familiar with the traces of Indian blood. At
all the white settlements near those of the Indians, the
evidence of admixture was abundant, from the pure
half-breed to the slightly marked remoter descendant
of Indian maternity, discoverable only by the straight
black hair, and a singular watery glaze in the eye, not
unlike that of the English gipsy. There they were to
be seen, not only as fishers, trappers, and lumberers,
but engaged on equal terms with the whites in the trade
and business of the place. In this condition the population of all the frontier settlements exists ; and while,
as new settlers come in, and the uncivilized Indians re-
tire into the forest, the mixed element disappears, it
does so purely by absorption. The traces of Indian
maternity are gradually effaced by the numerical preponderance of the European; but nevertheless the native
element is there, even when the faint traces of its
physical manifestations elude all but the observant and
well-practised eye.

Nor are such traces confined to the frontier settlements. I have recognised the semi-Indian features in

the gay assemblies at a Canadian Governor-General's receptions, in the halls of the Legislature, among the undergraduates of Canadian universities, and mingling in the selectest social circles. And this is what has been going on in every new American settlement for upwards of three centuries, under every diversity of circumstance. In New England, for example, after the desolating war of 1637, which resulted in the extinction of the Pequot tribe, Winthrop thus summarily records the policy of the victors : " We sent the male children to Bermuda, by Mr. William Pierce, and the women and maid children are dispersed about in the towns." Two diverse processes are apparent in such intermixture. Where the half-breed children remain with their Indian mother, they grow up in the habits of the aborigines, and, intermingling with the pure-blood Indians, are re-absorbed into the native stock, where the tribe survives. But when, on the contrary, they win the regard of their white father, the opposite is the case ; and this occurs more frequently with the Spanish and French than with British colonists. In Lower Canada, half-breeds, and men and women of partial Indian blood, are constantly met with in all ranks of life ; and the traces of Indian blood may be detected, in the hair, the eye, the high cheek-bone, and the peculiar mouth, as well as in certain traits of Indian character, where the physical indications are too slight to be discerned by a casual observer. Dr. Tschudi, after describing the minute classification of half-castes in Peru, adds : " The white Creole women of Lima have a peculiar quickness in detecting a person of half-caste at the very first glance, and to the less practised observer they communicate their discoveries in this way with an air of triumph ; for they have the very pardonable weakness of priding themselves on the purity of their European descent."

There, however, as well as in Mexico, the pride of caste
interferes in no degree with the equality of the civilized
half-breed ; and while many of the varieties of mixed
blood are regarded as inferior to their progenitors, the
Mestizo, or offspring of a white father and Indian
mother, is believed to inherit many of the best qualities
of both. Like the Canadian half-breed, however, he is
mild and irresolute, capable of considerable endurance,
but little adapted for an independent course of action.
Nevertheless, among Canadian half-breeds there are men
at the bar and in the legislature; in the Church ; in
the medical profession ; holding rank in the army;
and engaged in active trade and commerce. No distinctive traits separate them, to the ordinary observer,
from the general community of which they form a
part ; and they will disappear after a generation or
two, simply by the numerical superiority of those of
European descent.

With the civilized and Christianized Indians it is
otherwise. Kept apart on their Indian reserves, and
guarded, in a state of pupilage, from the cupidity as
well as the stimulating competition of the white settler,
the benevolent intentions of their guardians are defeated
by the very process designed for their protection. The
Indian, under such a system, can only step forth to an
equality with the White by forfeiting his claims to the
Indian reserves, which he may till, but cannot sell; and
it is unquestionable that, congregated together in such
settlements, under the most careful superintendence, the
Indian, robbed of the wild virtues of the savage hunter,
acquires only the vices and the diseases of the white
man ; and as Sir Francis Bond Head remarks, in one of
the strangest official documents ever penned by a colonial
governor : " As regards their women, it is impossible for
any accurate observer to refrain from remarking that

civilisation, in spite of the pure, honest, and unremitting
zeal of our missionaries, by some accursed process, has
blanched their babies' faces." [1]

The following statistics, from an " Occasional Paper
on the Columbia Mission," issued, under the authority
of the Bishop of British Columbia, in 1860, sufficiently
illustrate the circumstances under which a modern
British colony frequently originates. The Indians in
Vancouver's Island and British Columbia are stated to
amount to 75,000, and the missionary at Port-Douglas
makes the following return of settlers in his district :—

Citizens of United States,	73
Chinese,	37
British subjects,	35
Mexicans and Spaniards,	29
French and Italians,	16
Coloured men,	8
Central Europe,	4
Northern Europe,	4
	206

Of these, the sexes are thus :—

Males,	204
Females,	2

The admixture of blood with the native population,
consequent on such a disproportion of the sexes, is inevitable ; and yet, long before the colony of Columbia
is as old as New England, the descendants of this varied
admixture of nationalities will doubtless talk as freely
of " Anglo-Saxon" rights and duties as any of the older
Anglo-American settlements.

Such is the process that has been going on, from
generation to generation, since ever the European colonist began his encroachments on the territory of the

---

[1] "Memorandum on the Aborigines of North America," addressed by
Sir F. B. Head to Lord Glenelg, 20th Nov. 1836.

American aborigines. Intermarriage and intermixture were inevitable in a community where the males so largely predominated among the intruding whites, and hardy bands of pioneer adventurers, or the solitary hunter and trapper, wandered forth to brave the dangers of the savage-haunted forests. Of the mixed offspring, a considerable portion grew up under the care of the Indian mother, aspired to the honours of the tribe, and were involved in its fate. But also a portion adhered to the fortunes of the white father, shared with him the vicissitudes of border life, and partook of the advantages which gradually gathered round the settled community. As the border land slowly receded into the farther west, Time wrought the while his gradual change; and long ere the little cluster of primitive log-huts had grown up into the city and capital of a state, the traces of Indian blood had been lost sight of. The intermixture, however, had taken place; a certain percentage of Indian blood was there, and that in sufficient amount to have exercised some influence in the development of characteristics which already distinguish the native Anglo-American from the old insular stock. But nowhere is the remarkable process of intermixture, absorption, and repulsion seen on so great a scale as at the Red River settlement, on the river of that name, which flows into Lake Winnipeg, along with that more recently formed on the Assinaboine river. The former settlement is situated along the banks of the river for about fifty miles, and extends back from the water, according to the terms of the original grant ceded by the Indians, as far as a man can be distinguished from a horse on a clear day. Begun in 1811, under the auspices of Lord Selkirk, and afterwards taken under the protection of the Hudson's Bay Company, the Red River settlement now numbers about two thousand whites, chiefly occupied in farming or in the service of the Company. The original settlers were from the Orkney Islands, but they have been subsequently increased by English, Scotch, and French Canadians. There, however, as well as at the remoter forts and trading-posts of the Hudson's Bay Company, the white immigration has consisted chiefly of young men. In 1849, there were 137 more males than females, including those of mixed blood, in the settlements ; and the result has been, not only the growth of a half-breed population greatly outnumbering the whites, but the formation of a tribe of Half-breeds, a race who keep themselves distinct in manners, habits, and allegiance, alike from the Indians and the Whites.

This rise of an independent half-breed tribe is one of the most remarkable phenomena connected with the grand ethnological experiment which has been in progress on the North American continent for the last three centuries. The number of the settled population, either half-breed, or more or less of Indian blood, in Red River and the surrounding settlements, is now, according to returns I have obtained,[1] about 7200, of whom 6500 are in the Red River settlement. A noticeable difference is observable according to their white paternity. The French half-breeds are more lively and frank in their bearing, but also less prone to settle down to the drudgery of farming, or other routine duties of civilized life, than those chiefly of Scottish descent. But in a border settlement, where the principal trade is still in peltries, the hunter life presents many attractions even for the white colonist ; and the half-breeds are exposed to temptations unknown in older settlements. They are a large and robust race, with greater powers of en-

---

[1] Returns in reply to printed queries about the Indian and half-breed population, circulated by the author in Red River settlement and elsewhere. Appendix A.

durance than any of the native tribes exhibit. With the reserved and unimpressible manner of the Indian, they are nevertheless capable of displaying much vivacity when interested or excited. They retain the coarse, straight black hair, and the full mouth, as the most persistent features derived from their Indian maternity ; but, even in the first generation, the dark eye has a soft and pleasing aspect compared with that of the pure Indian. As a general rule, the families descended from such mixed parentage are larger than those of white parents ; but the results of this are in some degree counteracted by the prevalence of consumption among them. In 1855, it was my good fortune to see an interesting example of the different types of the pure and hybrid Indian. At La Point, near the head of Lake Superior, we met with Buffalo, the chief of the Chippewas already referred to, a grand old specimen of the wild pagan Indian, seamed with the lines of age and the scars of many a forest adventure. He boasted of the scalps he had taken, showed the collar of claws of the grizzly bear and other trophies won by him in the chase ; and spoke, with the unimpressible indifference of a true Indian, of the civilisation of the European intruders, as a thing good enough for the white man, but in which neither he nor his people had any interest. He was accompanied by his son, a debased, dissipated-looking Indian, wrapped in a dirty blanket; and betraying only the degradation of the savage when robbed of the wild virtues of the forest-hunter, without replacing them by anything but the vices of civilisation. The group was completed by a grandson of the old chief, an intelligent, civilized half-breed, who spoke both French and English with fluency, and acted as interpreter during the interview. In this case, however, the grandson was smaller, and altogether inferior in physical characteristics to the aged forest-bred chief, who was a noble specimen of the Indian, untainted by intercourse with Europeans.

In the Red River settlements where the intermarriage has been invariably between a white husband and an Indian wife, the Indians are chiefly Plain Crees. Some have also belonged to the Swampies, another branch of the Crees, and also to the Blackfeet and Chippewas. But on the Manitoulin Islands, in Lake Huron, a few cases of marriage between an Indian husband and white wife have occurred. In every case the advantage to the Indian husband has been very marked. The children of such marriages are invariably superior to other half-breeds, but this may be traceable to the moral, quite as much as to the physical difference in their favour.[1] The greater number of the half-breeds on Lakes Huron and Superior are of French paternity, while their Indian mothers are chiefly Chippewa or Ottawa ; and the few examples of the Indian paternity belong to the same tribes.

But the civilized half-breed population of the Red River settlements occupy a peculiar position, and must not be confounded either with the remarkable tribe of Half-breeds, or with the Indians of mixed blood in the villages on the Canadian reserves. Remote as that settlement has hitherto been from all other centres of colonization, and, from its peculiar circumstances, tending rather to attract the Canadian voyageur, or the young adventurer, than the married settler, the inevitable tendency has been towards intermarriage, and the growth of a mixed population. Much property is now accordingly possessed by men of mixed blood. Their young men have, in some cases, been sent to the Colleges of Canada, and, after creditably distinguishing

[1] Answers to Queries, by Rev. Dr. O'Meara, long resident missionary among the Indians of the Manitoulin Islands.

themselves among their Canadian competitors, have returned to bear their part in advancing the progress of
the settlement. The result of this is already apparent
in an increasing refinement, and a growing desire for
the removal of every trace of their relation to the wild
Indian tribes, or the half-breeds who rival them in the
arts of savage life. Professor Hind accordingly remarks,
in his " Report on the Exploration of the Country between Lake Superior and the Red River settlement,"—
" The term *native*, distinguishing the half-breeds from
the European and Canadian element, on the one hand,
and the Indian on the other, appears to be desired by
many of the better class, who naturally look upon the
term half-breed, as applied to a race of Christian men,
scarcely appropriate." [1]

The venerable Archdeacon Hunter, of Red River, in
the replies to queries, with which he has favoured me,
says,—in answer to the inquiry, " In what respects do
the half-breed Indians differ from the pure Indians as to
habits of life, courage, strength, increase of numbers,
etc. ?"—" They are superior in every respect, both men-
tally and physically." Again, when my inquiries were
thus defined : " State any facts tending to prove or
disprove that the offspring descended from mixed white
and Indian blood fails in a few generations," Archdeacon Hunter gives this decided reply, as the result of
experience acquired by long residence and intimate intercourse among them as a clergyman of the Roman
Catholic Church :—" It does not fail, but, generally
speaking, by intermarriages it becomes very difficult to
determine whether they are pure whites or half-breeds."
Mr. S. J. Dawson, of the Red River Exploring Expedition, also describes the half-breeds as a hardy and vigorous race of men, and frequently with large and healthy

[1] *Report*, 1848, p. 305.

families. " I know," he writes, " from my own observation, that the French half-breeds at Red River are a gigantic race as compared with the French Canadians of Lower Canada."

The tribe of half-breed buffalo-hunters is not to be regarded as at all approximating to the nomade Indians. They belong to the settlement, possess land, and cultivate farms, though their agricultural operations are only such as might be expected, where the inducements to a wandering life are nearly as great as among the pure-breed Indians, who abandon such work to their squaws or slaves. They are, however, distinct from the half-breed members of the settled community, who have shared in all the domestic training and culture of their white fathers, and have entirely adopted European habits. The hunters are now divided into two distinct bands, known by their separate hunting-grounds. Of these, the White Horse Plain Half-breeds furnished the following returns, according to a census taken in 1849, near the Strayenne River, Dacotah territory :— " Six hundred and three carts, seven hundred half-breeds, two hundred Indians, six hundred horses, two hundred oxen, four hundred dogs, and one cat." According to Mr. Paul Kane, who joined their buffalo-hunt in the summer of 1845, the half-breed hunters of Red River then numbered 6000.

Few subjects of greater interest to the ethnologist can be conceived of than this remarkable origination of a numerous and independent tribe of half-breeds, partaking of characteristics derived alike from their white fathers and their Indian mothers. They are a hardy race of men, capable of enduring the greatest hardships. They all adhere to the Roman Catholic faith ; and occasionally a priest accompanies them on their hunting expeditions, in which case mass is celebrated on the prairie. They are at open feud with the Sioux and other Indian tribes, and carry on their warfare much after the fashion of the Indian tribes that have acquired fire-arms and horses; but they give proof of their "Christian" civilisation by taking no scalp-trophies from the battle-field. From about the 15th of June to the end of August, they are abroad on the prairie engaged in their summer hunt. A subsequent autumnal buffalo-hunt engages a smaller portion of their number; and then such as do not depend on winter-hunting, and the profits of trapping the fur-bearing animals, return to the settlement. It is complained that they make poor farmers, neglecting their land for the exciting pleasures of the chase. But this is inevitable, where the produce of their buffalo-hunts supplies the chief means of carrying on a profitable trade with the Hudson's Bay Company's agents and the American traders from St. Paul's. The distant hunt not only consumes the time required for agricultural labour, but it begets habits altogether incompatible with settled industry; and would produce the very same results on any body of white settlers as on this remarkable native population of Red River. But in the field, whether preparing for hunting or war, the superiority of the Half-breeds is strikingly manifested. They then display a discipline, courage, and self-control, of which the wild tribes of Sioux or Blackfeet are altogether incapable; and they accordingly look with undisguised contempt on their Indian foes. The organization displayed in their hunting expeditions shows a remarkable aptitude for self-government. When fairly started on the hunt, a general council is held, which proceeds to elect a president or leader. A number of captains are then nominated jointly by the leader and council, and each of these appoints a certain number of constables or deputy-

officers, whose duty it is to see that the laws of the
hunt are carried out, and that the nightly encampment
is made with strict attention to the general safety.
Guides are also chosen by popular election, who carry
flags as their badges of office, and control all arrangements for the camping.   The hunt being thus organized,
all who have joined it are under military law.   No
hunter can return home without permission ; no gun
may be fired when the buffalo country is reached, until
the leader has given the word, which lets loose the wild
array of hunters on the bewildered herd.   The captains
and their deputies also superintend the nightly arrangement of the carts in a circle, within which the horses
and cattle are picketed ; and, in case of any property
being missing, they can prohibit any member of the
hunt from stirring till it is found.   Every breach of
camp-laws is atoned for by fines.   A man who passes
the camp-guide of the day, while on duty, subjects himself to a fine of five shillings ; and he who ventures to
run a buffalo, before the leader has given the signal for
the hunt to begin, has to forfeit a penalty of twenty
shillings.

Such are the most noticeable characteristics of this
singularly interesting race, called into being by the contact of the European with the native tribes of the prairie
and forest.   With so much of the civilisation which no
pure Indian tribe has derived from intercourse with
white men, and such admirable organization and prompt
recognition of the obligations of law and order, there
seems good reason for believing in their capacity for all
the higher duties of a settled, industrious community.
They already know the use and value of money ; nor are
they unused to the labours of agriculture, though hitherto
this has offered no profits to tempt them to grain or
stock-farming on any adequate scale.   In the present

condition of the Red River settlement, with its unhealthful element of fur-trading posts, buffalo prairies, and remote and nearly inaccessible markets for farming produce, the Half-breeds are retained in that dangerous transitional stage from which all attempts at civilisation among the Indian tribes have derived the sources of failure. But they have within themselves elements of resistance to the destructive influences attendant on the transition from the hunter state to the settled life of the farmer and trader, and no race has ever offered stronger claims on the attention of the philanthropist or the statesman. But, under any circumstances, the Half-breeds of the Red River cannot permanently remain as a distinct race. Already the settlers of mixed blood intermarry freely with the white population, and share with perfect equality in all the rights and privileges of the community. As emigration increases the same results will follow there, as have already happened in all the older settlements, from the New England shores, or the St. Lawrence Gulf, westward to the remotest clearings of young civilisation. The last traces of the red blood will disappear, not by the extinction of the Indian tribes, but by the absorption of the half-breed minority into the new generations of the predominant race ; yet, along with all the changes wrought by climate, institutions, and habits, on the new people thus formed to be the inheritors and occupants of the deserted Indian hunting-grounds in the Western Hemisphere, this element will exercise some influence, and help to make them diverse from their European ancestry. On this account, therefore, as well as on others, we want some such term as Euroamerican to indicate the new race.[1]

But there is another aspect in the history of the American Indian tribes, in which their extinction is seen to

---

[1] *Vide* Appendix B.

be wrought out by means which we can look back upon
with very different feelings from those with which we
witness their extermination by the mere process of contact with the white settler, or their extirpation by the
combined influence of his violence and criminal cupidity.
The condition of the American tribes and nations to the
north of the Mexican centre of a native civilisation, may
be described at the period of European discovery as one
of unstable equilibrium. We trace the influence of one
or two dominant tribes from the St. Lawrence to the
Gulf of Mexico ; and the rival nations were exposed to
such constant and aimless exterminating warfare, that
it is more than doubtful if the natural increase of population was then equal to the waste of war. We are
accustomed to regard the Western Hemisphere as the
natural habitat of its aboriginal children ; wherein, as in
a world apart, they grew and multiplied, in the enjoyment of all that their simple natures were capable of,
until the intrusion of the white man brought misery and
desolation into their midst, and that exterminating process was begun which threatens, ere many more generations shall have passed away, to leave only their grave-
mounds to tell of the past existence of the red man
in the New World. A brief glance at some of the incidents in the history of extinct tribes, will tend to modify
this opinion.

The early notices of the first explorers, and the traditions since gathered from surviving nations, tell of many
that have utterly passed away, without the malign inter-
vention of European influence. " But language adheres
to the soil when the lips which spoke it are resolved into
dust. Mountains repeat, and rivers murmur the voices of
nations denationalized or extirpated in their own land."[1]
By such vestiges extinct nations assert their claims to an

---

[1] Palgrave's *Normandy*, vol. i. p. 700.

inheritance of the past, throughout all the ancient world ; and the same evidence tells of former occupants of the New World. The great mountain chain of the Alleghanies, constitutes in this manner the enduring monument of the Alleghans, the oldest tribe of the United States of which there is a distinct tradition. The beautiful Valley of the Ohio, with the tributary streams of that great river, once teemed with the warriors, and were enlivened by the numerous towns and villages of this ancient people. The traditions of the Delawares told that the Alleghans were a strong and mighty nation, reaching to the eastern shores of the Mississippi, when in remote times they came into the Great Valley from the west. But the Iroquois, who had established themselves on the head waters of the chief rivers which have their rise immediately to the south of the great lakes, combined with the Delawares or Lenapé nation to crush the power of that ancient people of the valley ; and the surviving remnant of the decimated Alleghans was driven down the Mississippi, and their name blotted out from the roll of nations. The very name of the Ohio is of Iroquois origin, and given to the river of the Alleghans by their ruthless conquerors. The Susquehannocks, who are believed to have been of the same ancient lineage, excited the ire of the dominant nation, and were in like manner extirpated ; at a later date the Delawares fell under their ban, and the remnant of that proud nation quitting for ever the shores of the noble river which perpetuates their name, retraced their steps into the unknown West. So, in like manner, the Shawnees, Nanticokes, Unamis, Minsi, and Illinois, were vanquished, reduced to the condition of dependent nations, or driven out and exterminated. Settlements of the conquerors were frequently established in the conquered lands ; and the only redeeming feature in this savage warfare was their system of absorption, by which they repaired the losses in battle by adopting prisoners rescued from death, and admitting them into the tribes of the conquering nation. All this was the work of the Indian. As the curtain rises on the aboriginal nations of the forest and the prairie, we find them engaged in this exterminating warfare ; and a glance on the map of successive centuries, or a reconstruction of the traditionary history of the oldest tribes, tells the same tale of aimless strife, expatriation, and extinction. The history of the Indian nations found in occupation of a wide range of country on the northern and southern shores of the great lakes, including the whole of Upper Canada and Western New York, will most clearly suffice to illustrate this phase of savage life. When Cartier first explored the St. Lawrence, in 1535, he found large Indian Settlements at Quebec and on the the Island of Montreal, where Champlain, little more than half a century after, met with few or none to oppose his settlement. We can only surmise who the Indians at the period of Cartier's arrival were ; but it is most probable that they belonged to the same Wyandot stock, who were then withdrawing into the western parts of Upper Canada to escape the fury of the Iroquois, after having nearly desolated the Island of Montreal. At the era of Champlain's visit, and throughout the entire period of French occupation, the country to the south of the St. Lawrence, and along the whole southern shores of Lake Ontario, was occupied by the nations of the Iroquois confederacy, whose uncompromising hostility to the French materially contributed to confine their colonies to the limits of Lower Canada. The country immediately to the westward of the River Ottawa, and along the northern shore of Lake Ontario, was found unoccupied when first explored by Champlain ; but it was marked with abundant traces of cultivation, and of recent occupation by the tribes who had retreated westward from the violence of the Iroquois. The region to the north of the Wyandot or Huron territory, and the islands and northern shores of Lake Huron, were in the occupation of the Mississagas, the Ottawas, the Nippisings, and other Algonquin nations, who, though belonging to an entirely distinct stock, are repeatedly found in alliance with the Hurons against their common Iroquois foe, and to some extent shared their fate. The Hurons on the contrary, and all the nations lying between them and the Iroquois country, appear to have belonged to the same stock with the confederate nations to the south of the great lakes ; by whom they were pursued with such uncompromising hostility till their once populous regions were abandoned to the wild beasts of the forest. At the period when the Huron tribes became the special objects of missionary zeal by the Jesuit Fathers, in the seventeenth century, they were established along the great bay, once populous on all its shores with that extinct nation whose name alone survives in the Lake of the Hurons. The region lying around Lake Simcoe, and Georgian Bay, is marked on every favourable site with the traces of their agricultural industry, and crowded with their graves. They presented traits of superiority to the more northern nations of the Algonquin stock ; and equalled in fierce daring, and all the wild virtues of the savage warrior, the Iroquois by whom they were unrelentingly exterminated. Father Sagard estimated the population of the limited region occupied by the four Huron tribes at the close of their national history, at between thirty and forty thousand souls. But to the south-west lay the villages of the Tiontonones, or Petuns, another nation of the same stock, also a populous and industrious agricultural community ; and beyond this, in the territory embracing the beautiful valley and the great falls of the

Niagara River, where are now the sites of the finest orchards of Canada, and some of the most fruitful counties of the State of New York, a nation belonging to the same Huron-Iroquois family was found by the first French missionary explorers, in 1626. By the Hurons they were designated the Attiwendaronk, expressive of the mere dialectic difference between the languages of the two;[1] but from the French they received the name of the Neutral Nation, from the friendly relations thay maintained with both parties during the great struggle between the Iroquois and the allied Huron and Algonquin nations. At the close of their history their population was estimated at twelve thousand souls; but a position of neutrality between hostile rivals was rendered all the more difficult by the ties of consanguinity : though this appears to have been also shared by the Eries who occupied the broad fertile regions along the southern shores of the great lake which bears their name.

The fate of the Attiwendaronks and the Eries is certain, but the history of both is obscure, for they lay beyond the reach of the French traders and missionaries. In the earlier half of the seventeenth century the Jesuit Fathers planted their stations throughout the Huron country, amid populous walled villages and cultivated fields, and reckoned the warriors of the tribes by thousands. In 1626, Father Joseph de la Roche d'Allyon penetrated into the country of the Neutral Nation, and sought to discover the Niagara at its junction with Lake Ontario. After a journey of five days through the unbroken forest which lay between the Tiontonones, and the Attiwendaronks, he reached the first settlement of

---

[1] By this name, according to Brebœuf, the Hurons signified that they were a "*people of a language a little different.*" They applied that of Akwanake as the general name of nations speaking languages unintelligible to them.

the latter, and passed through six towns before arriving
at that of the chief Sachem. Twenty-two other towns
and villages were embraced within his jurisdiction; and
tobacco was largely cultivated along with maize and
beans. The country of the Eries was greatly more
extensive, and probably not less populous. But within
less than thirty years from this mission of Father de la
Roche, the whole region occupied by those nations, from
the Georgian Bay to the southern limits of the Eries, far
beyond the shores of the lake which perpetuates their
name, was a silent desert. Tradition points to the
kindling of the council-fire of peace among the former
nation, before the organization of the Iroquois confederacy; and to the artistic skill of the Eries are ascribed
several interesting remains of aboriginal art, among
which the pictorial inscription on Cuningham's Island
in Lake Erie is described as by far the most elaborate
and well-sculptured work of its class hitherto found on
the continent.[1] But they perished by the violence of
kindred nations before the French or English could
establish intercourse with either. In the French maps
of the middle of the seventeenth century the very existence of Lake Erie is unknown; and the first of the
Jesuit missionaries had scarcely penetrated to its shores,
when the ancient nation whose name it preserves was
swept away. Within a year or two of their destruction
the Neutral Nation experienced the same fate at the
hands of the Mohawks, under the leadership of Shori-
kowani, a famous chief of that nation; and the Attiwendaronks utterly disappeared from the Valley of
Niagara. Charlevoix assigns the year 1655 as the date
of their extermination. Their council-fire was extinguished, their name was blotted out; and the few
survivors were subsequently found by one of the French

---

[1] *History of the Indian Tribes*, vol. ii. p. 78, plates xli. xlii.

missionaries, living in degrading serfdom in the villages
of their conquerors.   All this was the result of conflict
among native tribes, and so entirely uninfluenced by the
white man that it is with difficulty we can recover some
trustworthy glimpse of the Eries or the Neuters from
the notes of one or two dauntless missionaries, whose
zeal for the propagation of the faith carried them into
the country of those extinct nations, long before the
enterprise of the *coureurs des bois* had led them within
the hearing of Niagara's voice of many waters.   It reveals to us glimpses of what had been transpiring in
unrecorded centuries throughout the vast forest ranges
and prairies of the American continent ; and may help
to reconcile us to the fate of the conquering Iroquois
by whom such wide-spread desolation was wrought.
Their remarkable confederacy was broken up by the adherence of the Mohawks to the British side, when the
colonists rose in arms against the mother country.   The
beautiful Mohawk Valley which was once their home,
is now crowded with towns and villages, and interlaced
by railways and canals ; but the remnant of the once
powerful Mohawk tribe, with a small band of the Senecas, amounting together to about seventeen hundred
souls, have found a home in the country they depopulated two centuries before.   " I have been told," says
Colden, " by old men in New England, who remembered
the time when the Mohawks made war on their Indians,
that as soon as a single Mohawk was discovered in their
country, their Indians raised a cry from hill to hill, A
Mohawk ! a Mohawk ! upon which they fled like sheep
before wolves, without attempting to make the least
resistance."   The traditional terror of their name still
survives, though they have been settled for generations
peaceably on the Canadian reserves, granted by the
British Government to them, along with other loyalist

refugees from the revolted colonies. The cry of a Mohawk still fills with dread the lodges of the Algonquin
Indians in the Canadian settlements; and they have
been repeatedly known to desert their villages on Lake
Couchiching, and Chemong and Rice Lakes, and to camp
out on islands in the lakes, from the mere rumour of a
Mohawk having been seen in the vicinity.

The pure-blood Mohawks still exhibit traces of the
superiority which once pertained to all the members of
the Iroquois league; and the same traits are discernible
in survivors of the other confederate nations. The Onondagas, who claimed to be true autochthones, alone of all
the six nations retain their hold on their native spot of
earth, and still dwell in the beautiful and secluded valley
of Onondaga, with sufficient territory for the maintenance of the surviving remnant. But Mohawks and
Onondagas alike betray, in the assemblies of the tribes,
many traces of mixed blood as well as of diminishing
numbers, and the same fact is manifest with the representatives of the other nations. Of the Oneidas, a portion lingers on their ancient site, but the main body of
the survivors are scattered : one band in Canada, and
another and larger one in Wisconsin. The Senecas and
Tuscaroras have their few living representatives near the
Niagara river, on a portion of the land which their fore-
fathers wrested from the denationalized Eries; and even
the Cayugas, the least fortunate among those unfortunate
inheritors of a great name, have found shelter for a little
handful of their survivors on the Seneca reserves in
western New York.

Such is the history of the aboriginal population which,
in the seventeenth century, occupied the valley of the
St. Lawrence, and stretched away on either bank and
along the shores of the great lakes westward to Lake
Huron and St. Clair. La Houtan estimated the Iroquois,

when first known to Europeans, at seventy thousand ;
at the present time they number altogether, in Canada
and the States, about seven thousand. They have passed
the most critical stage in the collision between savage
and civilized man ; and, settled on their little farms
apart from the populous centres of trade and commerce,
they are improving both socially and morally. Nevertheless, kept apart in detached little communities in a
state of pupilage, and forced into constant intermarriage,
their fate is inevitable. Better far would it be for them
to accept the destiny of the civilized half-breed, and
mingle on equal terms with settlers, many of whom have
yielded up a nationality not less proud than theirs, and
forsaken the homes and the graves of their fathers to
share the fortunes of the New World's heirs. It is as
impossible for the civilized Indian to live in a community, yet not of it, as for any other of the nationalities
whose members merge into the nation with whom their
lot is cast. By such a process the last visible remnants
of the famous Iroquois league would indeed disappear,
absorbed, like all other foreign nationalities, into the new
leagues which growing empires are forming in the West.
But each survivor of the old Indian confederacy would
be the gainer by the abandonment of what is worse than
an empty name ; while the Euroamerican race would take
once more into its veins the red blood of the ancient and
haughty aristocracy of the forest.

In the second volume of the *Archæologia Americana*,
a synopsis is given of the Indian tribes of the continent
to the east of the Rocky Mountains, and of those in the
British and Russian possessions in North America, from
the pen of Mr. Albert Gallatin, which may be said to
constitute the true basis of all native American ethnology. Its value has been fully recognised by subsequent
writers on the subject, and reference has already been

made to it in previous pages. To him we owe the determination of the elements of philological affinity by which
we classify the great families or stocks of the Algonquin-
Lenapé and the Iroquois as occupying the whole region
to the east of the Mississippi, from the fifty-second to
the thirty-sixth degree of north latitude. But to the
south of this lies a country in which Gallatin recognised
the existence of at least three essentially distinct languages of extensive use : the Catawba, the Cherokee,
and that which he assumed to include in a common
origin both the Muskhogee and the Choctaw. But besides those, six well-ascertained languages of smaller
tribes, including those of the Uchees and the Natchez,
appear to demand separate recognition. Their region
differs essentially from those over which the Algonquin
and Iroquois war-parties ranged at will. It is broken up
by broad river-channels, and intersected by impenetrable
swamps ; and has thus afforded refuge for the remnants
of conquered tribes, and for the preservation of essentially distinct languages among comparatively small
bands of refugees. There also the Cherokees were the
first to settle, as a comparatively civilized agricultural
nation, under very peculiar circumstances. In their
predatory inroads they carried off slaves from Carolina ;
and speedily recognising the advantages derived from
enforced service, they have gradually settled down in
the remarkable condition of a civilized nation of Red
Indian slaveholders. In 1825, they numbered 13,783,
and held 1277 slaves of African descent. But the fact
that at the same time they possessed 2923 ploughs, suffices to prove that agricultural labour must be carried on
to a great extent by other than the slave population.
Meanwhile the admixture of white blood has largely
affected the dominant race. The true test of equality of
races is when the civilized Indian marries a white woman,

and this has already taken place to some extent among the Cherokees. The census of 1825 included, among the numbers of that nation, sixty-eight Cherokee men married to white women, and one hundred and forty-seven white men married to Cherokee women. This alone, exclusive of all previous hybrid elements, must rapidly tend to efface the predominant characteristics of Indian blood. When the last census was taken, in 1852, the Cherokees numbered 17,530 ; and the commissioner remarks in reference to their growing numbers : "A visible increase is discernible especially among the half-breeds," but they view with extreme jealousy the inquisitorial visits of the statist, and yield all such information very reluctantly, so that the latest returns do not admit of comparison with the older census.

In so far as the employment of the African race as slaves is to be regarded as an evidence of the civilisation of the Red Indian, it is by no means confined to the Cherokees. Mr. Lewis H. Morgan writes me thus : " I have visited all the emigrant Indian nations in Kansas and Nebraska, with two or three exceptions. I saw instances among the Shawnees and Delawares, and the Wyandots in Kansas, where white men who had married half-breed Indian women were living genteelly among them, and had slaves to cultivate their land ; and also instances where half-breed Indians had married white wives and lived in good style." Moreover, among recent accounts of the revolutionary struggle between the northern and southern States, the *Texan News* of April 27, 1861, reports the contents of a letter from the Indian nation giving assurances of the friendly reception of the commissioners of the State Convention by the Choctaws, Chickasaws, Cherokees, Seminoles, and Creeks. " All the tribes," it is added, " are to hold a general council on the 8th of May. These tribes are slaveholders, and are

for secession and the Southern Confederacy. The Chickasaws wished to secede at once ; but the Cherokees desire
to wait until the return of a delegation they have sent
to Washington to see about their funds held in trust by
the United States Treasury." But meanwhile the editor
of the *Kansas News* adds, in proof of the soundness of
the worldly-wise Cherokees, notwithstanding their prudent desire to ascertain the safety of their funds before
committing themselves to secession : "The Cherokees
have cleared out the abolition emissaries among them.
Parson Jones, the secretary of Ross their chief, and an
abolition agent, has been in danger of his life. He will
have to leave the country." The evidences of progressive civilisation are very various ; and as the wanderer
who, on landing on an unknown shore, discovered a
gallows set up there, blessed God that he was once more
in a civilized country : so we may unhesitatingly accept
the revolutionary convention of the Chickasaws, Choctaws, and the other slaveholding tribes, and the summary
clearing out of Parson Jones and other abolitionists by
the more cautious Cherokees, as very conclusive evidence
that the southern Indian nations are not greatly behind
their white neighbours in the march of civilisation.

In the first volume of the *History of the Indian Tribes
of the United States,* a complete census is given from
data furnished by the Indian department at Washington,
but no statistical information appears to have been collected relative to the extent of mixed blood. In 1789,
the total number of Indians within the territory of the
United States was estimated to amount to 76,000 ; but
since then, while many semi-civilized and frontier tribes
have diminished in numbers, or even become extinct, the
acquisition of new territories has brought large acces-
sions to the United States Indians. In 1825, when the
census of the Cherokees already referred to was taken,

the aggregate of the whole number of Indians within the geographical boundaries of the Union was stated at 129,366; and in 1850, owing to the acquisition of California, Texas, New Mexico, etc., it had risen to 400,764.

Mr. Lewis H. Morgan, the historian of the Iroquois, who has devoted much attention to the history and condition of the Indian tribes, and has enjoyed many opportunities of personal observation, thus writes in reply to my queries relative to the amount of mixed blood traceable among the Indians of the United States: "I doubt whether there is any statistical information upon the subject in the possession of the Government. I know of none. Actual observation would throw some light upon the question; but even this would be met with the difficulty that some of our native races of pure blood are darker than others. The Kaws of Kansas are unmixed. They are also prairie Indians, and very dark skinned, nearly as much so as the negro. The Sauks or Foxes are adulterated somewhat, yet I have seen some of them as dark as the Kaws. The Pawnees of the upper Missouri are also prairie Indians, and the pure-bloods are nearly as dark-skinned as the Kaws. I have seen their bare backs many times, and examined them closely. It is slightly mottled, with a bronze colour, and is a truly splendid skin. On the other hand the Sioux, or Dakotas, are much lighter. So are the Chippewas and Potowattomies when pure. But all of these have taken up white blood in past generations, and the rapidity of its dissemination after a few generations needs no proof. I think they have taken up enough, through the traders and frontier men, since 1700, to lighten their colour from one-sixth to one-fourth. The pure-blood Iroquois are light. I have seen them nude to the waist in the dance very many times. Their skin is splendid, of a rich coffee and cream colour. But it must be remembered that all of these are forest tribes except the Dakotas, and even they have been forced back on the prairies, from Lake Superior and the east side of the Mississippi, since the period of colonization. Indians of the same stock grow much darker on the prairie if far south. I tried, when in Nebraska, to ascertain the number of half-breeds and quarter-breeds around our forts in the Indian territory. The number is large, but I could gain no satisfactory information." The observations thus noted have a very comprehensive bearing on the general question of hybridity ; for so far from implying any tendency to deterioration or extinction as the result of an intermixture of the white and red races, they point to such admixture of blood already affecting whole tribes of wild Indians still roaming the forests and the prairies; in so much that the term "pure-breed" is perhaps only partially applicable to any of them, and it may even be a question how far the physical form, as in the features and the shape of the head, may have been modified by such influences.

Through the aid of the officers of the Indian Depart ment of Canada, I have succeeded in obtaining statistical information of a more precise and definite kind relative to some at least of the settled tribes. In Lower Canada, no detailed system of superintendence has been organized, so that information relative to the Indians of that portion of the province is much less accessible. The Indian Department affords aid to them upon the representation of the priests or other white residents in their neighbourhood ; but, in 1856, his Excellency, Sir Edmund Head, appointed a Commission to inquire into the best means of securing the future progress and civilisation of the Indian tribes in Canada, and, from their Report rendered in 1858, the following facts relative to

the Indians of Lower Canada are chiefly derived. The
numbers of the settled tribes, at the date of the Report,
were as follows :—

Iroquois of the Sault St. Louis, . . .		1342
Iroquois of St. Regis, ...		658
Indians at the Lake of the Two Mountains :—		
Iroquois, ...	375 ⎫	
Nipissings, ...	176 ⎬	889
Algonquins, ...	338 ⎭	
Abenakis of St. Francis, ...		387
Abenakis of Beçancour, ...		172
Hurons of La Jeune Lorette, . . .		282
Amalicites of Viger, ...		171
Micmacs of the Restigouche, . . .		473
		4374

There are thus upwards of four thousand Indians of
various tribes settled on lands secured to them by the
provincial government, and all more or less brought
under the same influences as the white settlers around
them. But in some of those bands not a single pure-
blood Indian now remains. They have all abandoned
paganism, and the greater number adhere to the Roman
Catholic Church ; but their condition varies considerably
in different localities. The Iroquois of St. Regis are
specially noticeable as having blended some of the healthful elements of European civilisation with the self-
reliance and vigour which once rendered them the most
formidable enemies of the colonists of Louis XIV. They
are now conspicuous among the settled native tribes for
their temperate and orderly lives, and the great progress
they have made as a settled community. They raise
wheat, oats, Indian corn, potatoes, and other agricultural
products, to a considerable extent ; and when the last
census was taken, they possessed 126 cows, 17 oxen,
114 horses, and 250 swine. A considerable number of
them are of mixed blood, but they still manifest a pre-

dilection for employments more in accordance with the hereditary instincts of forest life. The able-bodied men reluctantly expend the summer months on their farms. They prefer entering on engagements as raftsmen and pilots for the river, or engaging in the service of the Hudson's Bay Company. They appear, however, to have acquired provident habits, along with other virtues of civilisation. Their numbers have increased more rapidly than any other tribe in Canada of late years, notwithstanding a severe mortality in 1832, when 336 persons died of cholera.

In their industrious and provident habits, the Iroquois of St. Regis present a striking contrast to other tribes, such as the Abenakis of Beçancour, whose whole live stock in 1857 consisted of a single horse. The band of Abenakis settled on the river St. Francis, has, however, attained to a condition of higher advancement; though some of the evidences of its progress in civilisation are not productive of the most beneficial results. Its further improvement is reported to have been greatly retarded by the divisions and jealousies consequent on the adoption of the Protestant faith by a portion of the tribe, while the remainder hold fast to that of the Roman Catholic Church. They include among their numbers a few of the descendants of the once famous Mohegans, and their warlike allies, the Sokokis, but the report of 1858 states that there was not then a single pure-blood Indian surviving. The Rev. J. Maurault, Roman Catholic missionary at St. Francis, remarks:—" Our Indians are, with but very few exceptions, *Métis*, or half-breeds. Here, I do not know one Abenakis of pure blood. They are nearly all Canadian, German, English, or Scotch half-breeds. The greater part of them are as white as the Canadians, and the dark complexions we see with many are owing, in most cases, to their long voyages, exposed, as they frequently are, for two and three months at a time, to the burning rays of the sun. Many suppose that our Indians are intellectually weak and disqualified for business. This is a great mistake. Certainly, so far as the Abenakis are concerned, they are nearly all keen, subtle, and very intelligent. Let them obtain complete freedom, and this impression will soon disappear. Intercourse with the whites will develop their talents for commerce. No doubt some of them would make an improper use of their liberty, but they would be but few in number. Everywhere, and in all countries, men are to be found weak, purposeless, and unwilling to understand their own interests ; but I can certify that the Abenakis generally are superior in intelligence to the Canadians. I have remarked, that nearly all those who have left their native village to go and live elsewhere free, have profited by the change. I know of several who have bought farms in our neighbourhood, and are now living in comfort. Others have emigrated to the United States, where they have almost all prospered, and where several of them have raised themselves to honourable positions. I know one who is practising with success the profession of a doctor. Others have settled in our towns with a view to learn the different trades. There is one at Montreal who is an excellent carpenter ; but here we see nothing of the kind. Nevertheless, I observe a large number of young men, clever, intelligent, and gifted with remarkable talents." This experienced observer accordingly urges the emancipation of all at least of the more civilized Indians, from the condition of minors in the eye of the law ; feeling assured that if they were placed in competition with the whites, and allowed to hold and dispose of their property, they would be found fully able to maintain their place in the community.

This is remarkable testimony, alike in reference to the intelligence and the enduring vigour of a tribe already so largely affected by intermixture with the whites. But the changes wrought on the descendants of the Hurons, whom the Jesuit missionaries of the seventeenth century guided from their ravaged hunting-grounds around the Georgian Bay to their later settlements on the banks of the river St. Charles, have still more completely effaced all aboriginal traces. The author's disappointment was great on first visiting the village of La Jeune Lorette for the purpose of seeing the remnant of the warlike Hurons. Their nominal existence there still, is indeed chiefly due to the hereditary claims which they maintain to their share in the annual division of certain Indian funds. The Commissioners refer to them as a band of Indians "the most advanced in civilisation in the whole of Canada ;" but, after all, the progress has been but partial, while the interest it was calculated to awaken disappears to a great extent, when it is found admitted in the same Report, that since the migration of this band of the Huron tribe from their ancient territory in Upper Canada, "they have, by the intermixture of white blood, so far lost the original purity of race as scarcely to be considered as Indians." They are, moreover, the only band of Indian descent in Canada who have lost nearly all traces of their native language. They speak entirely a French *patois*, and, but for the care of their spiritual guardians, and the pecuniary inducements of the annual Indian grant, they would long since have intermingled and disappeared among the habitans of pure French descent, by whom they are surrounded. Here, then, is an example of the admixture of blood protracted through a period of upwards of two centuries. But so far from this practical experiment of the influence of hybridity furnishing any proof of the supposed infertility and inevitable extermination assumed as its result, the numbers of the Hurons of Lorette were found to have considerably increased in the interval between 1844, when the Indian census was taken, and the date of the Commissioner's Report. For all that now appears to the contrary, they seem likely to survive until, as a settlement of French-speaking Canadians on the banks of the St. Charles, they shall have to prove by baptismal registers, or genealogical records of the tribe, the Indian descent, of which all external traces shall have disappeared.

The Micmacs of Restigouche, numbering less than five hundred in all, including many of mixed blood, are a small though highly-civilized band of the Micmac nation, detached from the main stock owing to the intersection of their lands by the boundaries of the British provinces. Bands of the same Indian nation occupy various reserves in New Brunswick, and throughout Nova Scotia ; and small encampments of them may be met with along the shores of the lower St. Lawrence, industriously engaged in the manufacture of staves, barrel-hoops, axe-handles, and baskets of various kinds. They generally speak English, and manifest an unusual shrewdness and sagacity in making a bargain. Attracted on one occasion by a picturesque group of birch-bark wigwams on the southern shore of the St. Lawrence, below the Isle of Orleans, I landed for the purpose of sketching ; and, entering into conversation with the group of Micmac Indians, I was amused to find myself presently involved in a discussion as to the price of staves and hoops, the fluctuations of the market, and the hard bargains driven with the occupants of the wigwams by the traders of Quebec ; and all conducted with an acuteness that might have done credit to a disciple of Adam Smith or Ricardo. Nevertheless, when at parting I ventured on the improper liberty, according to Indian ideas, of asking the name of the leader of the party, with whom the conversation had been chiefly carried on, all his Indian prejudices reappeared. He was once more the native of the rude wigwam ; and I was given plainly to understand that I had encroached on the courtesies of friendly intercourse, and attempted to take advantage of him. A small purchase sufficed, however, to restore amity between us. He appeared to be a full-blood Indian. His figure was muscular and well-proportioned, and his skin presented the strongly-marked red colour, which has repeatedly attracted my attention in the pure-blood Micmacs.

Such is the condition of the settled tribes and bands of Indians occupying lands in Lower Canada. But besides those already enumerated, various unsettled tribes are to be met with on the Lower St. Lawrence, small bands of which, including a considerable number of half-breeds, have settled at different stations, and been partially brought under the influence of civilisation, chiefly by the Roman Catholic missionaries. A much greater number, however, are wild forest and hunter tribes, of whom some knowledge was formerly gained at the annual gatherings for the distribution of presents ; but since that practice was abandoned, they rarely come within the range of any civilized observers, excepting those connected with the Hudson's Bay Company. Different tracts of land have been set apart for the Montagnars tribes on the Peribonka river, on the Metabetchouan, near the Lake St. John, and on the St. Lawrence, from the River de Vases to the Des Outardes. But a large proportion of the Montagnars Indians are still nomadic ; and indeed of the wild tribes lying to the north and east of the Lower Canadian clearings, comparatively little is known. Among these may be classed the Têtes de Boule, the Algonquins of Three

Rivers, and the Nipissings, Algonquins, and Ottawas, who wander uncontrolled near the confines of the Hudson's Bay territory, towards the head-waters of the Ottawa river. The Mistassins and Naskapees, on the Lower St. Lawrence, are mostly in the same nomade condition. The latter belong to the Montagnars stock, and have been estimated at 2500, of whom fully 1500 are still wild pagans. They worship the sun and moon, or Manitous who are supposed to have their abode there. They devote to both of these deities parts of every animal slain, and annually offer up the sacrifice of the white dog. In their mythology and superstitious rites, the wild Naskapees reveal traces of the same Sabian worship which, under many varying and degraded forms, constitutes a link seeming to connect the savage tribes of North America with the ancient native centres of civilisation both in Mexico and Peru. It is not a little strange to find such pagan rites perpetuated among nomades still wandering around the outskirts of settlements occupied by the descendants of colonists, who, upwards of three centuries ago, transplanted to the shores of the St. Lawrence the arts and laws of the most civilized nation of Europe. The forest-regions occupied by those savage tribes are annually coasted by the richly-laden merchant fleets of Britain; and the Galway steamers, which have now brought them within less than six days' sail of Europe, bear weekly past them hundreds of luxurious Atlantic voyagers : few indeed reflecting on the contrast between the modern Anglo-American supplanter and those outcast descendants of the aboriginal owners of the soil. The Mistassins and Naskapees exhibit all the characteristics, and some of the most forbidding traits, of the Indian savage. They are clothed altogether in furs and deer-skins, their only weapons are the bow and arrow, and they resort to the bow and drill for the purpose of procuring fire.

Yet the wild nomades are unquestionably better off than some who wander in a partially civilized condition on the lands allotted to them on the Lower St. Lawrence. Of the Montagnars, the Indian Commissioners remark in their report of 1858 : " Where uncorrupted by intercourse with unprincipled traders, they were remarkable for their honesty ; and even now it is but very seldom that they break their word, or wilfully violate engagements which they have entered into. There are but few half-breeds among them. They are diminishing rapidly, upwards of three hundred having died within ten years, one half of whom have fallen victims to starvation." Fever and small-pox have from time to time committed terrible ravages among them ; but more fatal though less noted effects result from the destruction of their game, and the great injury to their fisheries, effected by the lumberers and white settlers. Fearful tales of cannibalism are whispered ; and I have been told of instances brought under the notice of missionaries in the lower province, in which they entertained no doubt that, in the privations incident to the long and severe winters of that region, the wretched natives have only escaped starvation by the most frightful means to which imagination can conceive a parent to resort. It seems indeed unquestionable that the privations of the Indians on the Lower St. Lawrence are frequently fully as great as those of the Esquimaux within the Arctic circle; while the resources available for them are more uncertain, and subject to greater diminution by the encroachments of the European.

The numbers of the unsettled tribes of Lower Canada within reach of direct observation and intercourse amount to about 3000, to which must be added the unascertained numbers of the wild tribes. Altogether there cannot be less than 8000 Indians still left in the lower province; and of these it is obvious that, as fast as they are brought directly into contact with the civilisation and the religious teaching of their European supplanters, they gradually disappear by a variety of processes: of which the only one it is possible to dwell upon without many painful, though unavailing regrets, is that by which, as in the case of the Hurons of Lorette, we see the descendants of the older tribes gradually absorbed into the predominant race, as the waters of the St. Lawrence merge into those of the Atlantic Ocean.

In Upper Canada a well-organized system of superintendence has been long maintained over the settled tribes; and a superintendent is also appointed to take oversight alike of the bands in occupation of reserves on the Great Manitoulin Island, and of the wild Indians who have taken refuge on the numerous islands of Lake Huron or along its northern shores. Until the recent abandonment of the practice of distributing presents to the Indian tribes, the Great Manitoulin Island was annually the scene of an assemblage, not only of Indians belonging to nearly all the tribes of British North America, but also of many from the United States. It was found, however, that no beneficial results accrued from this practice, and, after sufficient notice had been given, the last distribution took place in 1855. At this annual gathering the white traders latterly flocked, like vultures to the battle-field, and the presents, for the most part, passed into their hands in exchange for gaudy trifles, or for the deleterious fire-water. It was wisely judged, therefore, that the money could be much more judiciously expended on behalf of the settled tribes. Nevertheless the practice has not been abandoned without strong manifestations of dissatisfaction on the part of many and it is not uncommon for those who have dealings with tribes lying beyond the influence of the Indian superintendents, to find this referred to as a breach of faith, which makes them receive with suspicion any attempts at negotiation. Statements probably loosely made by government officers or interpreters, have circulated among the tribes as a perpetual pledge guaranteed by the honour of the British Crown ; and their feelings have repeatedly found expression in some such terms as these : "The Indians of the forests and the prairies were promised the annual renewal of those presents as long as the sun shone, water flowed, and trees grew. The sun still shines upon us, the rivers flow on, and we see the trees renew their leaves, but we no longer receive anything from our great mother beyond the sea." This annual distribution brought under the notice of the officers of the Indian department the representatives of many tribes only now to be met with in the far West; but encouragement has been held out to the broken tribes and scattered bands of Western Canada to settle on the Manitoulin Islands ; and all who have done so are under the efficient oversight of Captain Ironsides, the resident Superintendent, who also visits from time to time the tribes scattered along the neighbouring mainland and the north shore of Lake Superior. Three other resident Superintendents are in charge of the tribes and bands occupying the various Indian reserves in Upper Canada, including representatives of the three great divisions of Iroquois, Algonquins, and Lenapés. The Indians of Upper Canada and those of the islands and north shores of Lakes Huron and Superior, who are all brought more or less directly under the notice of the Superintendents, number upwards of 12,000, embracing representatives of the following tribes and nations :—

Indians of the Six Nations, including Mohawks, Oneidas,
Onondagas, Cayugas, Senecas, and Tuscaroras, . 2958
Wyandots, or Hurons, ... 66
Delawares, ... 652
Algonquins, including :—
  Mississagas, ... 738
  Potowattomies, ... 344
  Ottawas, ... 154
  Chippewas, ... 2867
  Chippewas and Ottawas on the Manitoulin
  Islands, ... 1226
  Chippewas on the north shores of Lakes
  Huron and Superior, . . . 3274
                         ———— 8,603

         Total, ... 12,279

It thus appears that there are still upwards of 20,000
aborigines surviving within the area claimed by the
colonists of Canada, apart from those of the eastern provinces and the great North-western wilds of British
North America. The Wyandots, now in occupation of
the Huron reserve in the township of Anderdon, obtained
confirmation of that portion of the ancient territory of
their race at the general partition of lands by the different tribes in 1791 ; but since then a considerable
number of this poor remnant of the ancient lords of the
soil have migrated to the Missouri territory in the United
States ; and the little band that lingers behind, like that
at La Jeune Lorette, is fast merging into the predominant race. In 1858, they numbered sixty-five, and the
Commissioners remarked of them : " The Indians on this
reserve are mostly half-breeds, French and English ; very
few, if any, are of pure Indian blood. They must be
looked upon as among the tribes the most advanced in
civilisation in Western Canada. Many of them speak
either French or English fluently, and all, almost without
exception, have a keen knowledge of their own interest,
and would be capable of managing their own affairs."

By returns made to me by Mr. Frome Talfourd, the Indian Superintendent of their district, they number at present sixty-six, and of these sixty are half-breeds, or of mixed blood. In their religious belief they are nearly equally divided between the Roman Catholic and the Methodist creeds. They have no resident missionary of either church among them, but attend the churches, and mingle with the other worshippers of the neighbouring town of Amherstburg, distant about three miles from their settlement. Here, therefore, is a remnant of the Canadian aborigines fully able to enter, on terms of equality, into competition with the white settlers who are acquiring possession of the hunting-grounds of their Huron ancestry; and were it not for the artificial restraints of the protective system of the Indian Department, they would inevitably merge into the general population, and disappear and be lost, only in so far as they ceased to be distinguished from other members of the civilized community.

The representatives of the once famous confederacy of the Iroquois, and the faithful allies of the English, known as the Six Nations, whose ancient territories lay entirely within the State of New York, migrated to Canada at the close of the American War of Independence; and in 1784, they were settled on a tract of land on the banks of the Grand River, purchased from its Mississaga claimants, and confirmed to them by letters-patent under the Great Seal. At the same time, one of the tribes of the Mohawk nation settled on the Bay of Quinte under like circumstances; and so recently as 1840 a band of the Oneidas crossed from the United States into Canada, and purchased with their own money a tract of 5400 acres of land on the River Thames, where they are now settled. The Mohawks on the Grand River retain among their prized heirlooms, brought with them from the

Valley of the Mohawk, the silver Communion-plate presented to their ancestors by Queen Anne, and bearing the
inscription : " A. R. 1711. THE GIFT OF HER MAJESTY,
ANN, BY THE GRACE OF GOD, OF GREAT BRITAIN, FRANCE,
AND IRELAND, AND OF HER PLANTATIONS IN NORTH
AMERICA, QUEEN : TO HER INDIAN CHAPPEL OF THE
MOHAWKS." This nation, therefore, had abandoned
Paganism long before its migration ; and since the settlement of the Iroquois tribes in Upper Canada considerable zeal has been manifested by Christian missionaries and teachers in diffusing religious and secular
instruction among them. Nevertheless, even now a large
majority of the Cayugas, and also part of the Onondagas
and Senecas, have not renounced heathenism ; and
though the Indian reserves on the Grand River have
been surrounded and encroached upon by white settlers ;
and the town of Brantford—named after the celebrated
Mohawk chief,—now numbers upwards of 8000 inhabitants, the pagan Iroquois still amount to between five
and six hundred.

The Indians of the Six Nations have now been brought
into intimate intercourse with the whites for upwards of
two centuries, and for the last seventy years have been
placed in such close contact with them that intermixture
of the races has been inevitable ; though the variations
in this respect are very remarkable, and the Mohawks
have been distinguished from all the others for the readiness with which, from the earliest date of their intercourse with the whites, they have allied themselves with
them, and adopted them into their tribes. From returns
furnished to me from the Mohawks of the Bay of Quinte,
it appears that they number in all 603, but of these 601
are reported to be of mixed blood. No specific notice
of the changes thus wrought on the Indian tribes had
previously been taken ; and the novel inquiry for returns

of the number of pure-blood Mohawks left in the tribe
appears to have startled its surviving members. The
required statistics were accordingly accompanied by the
following letter addressed to Mr. W. R. Bartlett, the
Indian Commissioner, and signed with the names or
marks of Pawles Claus, and four other Mohawk chiefs:
" We send herewith the census of our band, as required
by the letter from Toronto. All of our people, with the
exception of two, are of mixed blood. It may appear
strange to the Department that the Six Nations should
be so entirely mingled with people of other countries;
but it may be accounted for by the fact that our ancestors were allies of the British in the French and Revolutionary wars. It has always been a custom among the
Six Nations to supply the place of warriors killed in
battle by persons taken from the enemy, in the wars in
which we were engaged. Many of our people were killed
whose places were filled by prisoners. These prisoners
settled in the band, and were always acknowledged as
Mohawks. The government of that time, knowing our
old customs, received them as such, distributing presents
to all alike. This happened so long since that the blood
of the whites has almost become extinct. But since we
have been asked the question, we felt it to be our duty
to state the plain fact. No white man has, since the
period above named, been recognised as a Mohawk,
though a few of our women have married foreigners, the
children of whom we recognise." One interesting example of a different class of adopted Indians is to be seen
in the lodges of the Bay of Quinte, in an aged squaw,
reputed to be one hundred and seven years of age. The
child of white parents, she was carried off by the Indians
in one of their marauding excursions, while they still
dwelt in their native Valley of the Mohawk, and now
survives, the mother of a chief, knowing no language but

that of the tribe, as thorough an Indian in every sentiment and feeling as if the pure blood of the forest flowed in her veins.

The Mohawks, among whom the experiment of hybridity has thus been carried so far as almost to efface the last traces of pure Indian blood, betray no symptoms of inevitable decay and extermination. They are among the most civilized Indians of Western Canada, though still manifesting highly characteristic traits of the native instinct uneradicated by all the admixture of white blood in their veins. The superintendent describes them as beset with an ungovernable propensity for what they term "speculation;" "swopping" horses, cattle, and buggies; and for "trade," *i.e.*, barter: in all which the whites invariably overreach them. "The Mohawks are excellent labourers for short periods. There are in this tribe several native carpenters and shoemakers, one tailor, and one blacksmith. They have at least one hundred and forty children of an age fit to go to school; but though loud in the apparent desire to have their children educated, like other tribes, the most trifling excuse serves to keep a large portion of them idling about the streets or fields with their bows and arrows. These people, unlike the Chippewas, are not easily removed by threat or arguments from resolutions they may have formed; and they have been so much mixed up in trifling law-suits, that they consider themselves quite competent to express an opinion. In short, they have arrived at that state of semi-civilisation from which I believe nothing but their own future experience and convictions can disentangle them, and leave them open to the reception of friendly advice." There is something piquant in this phase of progressive civilisation, not without its parallel in many a European community, which thus exhibits the Mohawk growing

wealthy, opinionative, and litigious ; and vexing the
soul of his friendly superintendent by choosing to have
a will and an opinion of his own. All this, however,
will right itself. The Mohawks of the Bay of Quinte
appear to have passed the most critical transitional
stage. Their numbers have exhibited a large and steady
increase during the last fourteen years. Thomas Claus,
one of the chiefs whose name is attached to the letter
quoted above, is a skilful builder and carpenter ; and
when visited by the Commissioners in 1858, was employed in making a lectern for St. Paul's Church,
Kingston, the workmanship of which was reported to
be excellent. Like most of the Mohawks of the Bay
of Quinte, he is a member of the Church of England ;
and he frequently plays the organ during the service in
the Mohawk chapel there. In the recent returns furnished to me from the Indian Department, the children
are entered under two heads, the one as half-breeds, *i.e.*,
the offspring of Indians of mixed blood, and the other
as "illegitimate ;" and it is added, "by illegitimate
children in this return is meant the children of white
men by Indian women." The latter, as is seen, are
recognised as Mohawks, and of these twenty-three appear in their recent returns. This, therefore, points to
a source in full operation ; and the same which has
contributed in a still larger degree to produce such a
transformation on one band of the Hurons, as to render
them nearly indistinguishable from the white settlers
around them. Its influence must inevitably lead to the
same results in every tribe of Indians thus settled amid
the clearings on which the tide of European emigration
is annually pouring its thousands, while the red race
is cut off from all external sources from whence to
recruit its numbers and retard its inevitable absorption
or extinction.

The Oneidas, another of the Six Nations settled on the River Thames, have already been referred to as occupying land purchased for them with the money which they brought with them on migrating from the United States. The comparatively independent position which they occupy is accompanied by very favourable evidences of capacity for self-government. They are settled in the immediate vicinity of the Chippewas and the Delawares or Munsees on the Thames ; but the condition of the Oneidas presents a favourable contrast to either of these tribes. In 1858, the Commissioners remarked of them : "This band, without any annuity or assistance from the Government, are better farmers than their neighbours the Chippewas. Their clearings are larger and better worked, many of them are able annually to dispose of considerable quantities of grain after providing for the comfortable support of their families. Their houses are generally of a better description, and many are well furnished and neatly kept. A portion of the band are very idle and dissipated, and spend most of their time in the neighbouring villages of the whites ; but taken as a whole, the Oneidas will compare most favourably with any Indians in Western Canada. In numbers there has been a gradual increase." They appear to have kept themselves apart from the whites in a way that presents a striking contrast to the statistical disclosures in reference to some others of the Six Nations. The returns furnished to me during the present year include no illegitimate children, and specify only six half-breeds among the whole 509 representatives of that ancient people, whose traditions embody a legend that the Onondagas and the Oneidas sprang together out of the ground on the banks of the Oswego River. At a later date, though long prior to the intrusion of the white man, they separated from the Onondagas, and

grew to the rank of an independent nation on the
eastern shores of the Oneida Lake.   There a little remnant still lingers; but the nation is broken and scattered.
The larger number migrated to Wisconsin ; this other
portion survives apart on its Canadian reserve ; and
legend and national tradition are disappearing with that
old past to which they pertain.

The returns of statistics of the Algonquin tribes of
Upper Canada are less perfect than those of the Iroquois
and Hurons, owing to a considerable portion of them,
including even some of those provided with reserves,
surrounded by old and populous settlements, still leading
a half-wild gipsy life.   Of one band of Chippewas, for
example, formerly occupying lands on Point Pelé, on
the shore of Lake Erie, the Commissioners remarked in
1857 : " This band are generally dissipated, and roving
and unsettled in their habits, depending mainly as a
means of support on the fish and wild-fowl which at
certain seasons of the year are here very abundant.   The
clearings are small and poorly cultivated.   Indian corn
and potatoes are raised in small quantities.   With the
exception of the chief, they live mostly in bark shanties
or wigwams, and are poorly clothed."   In such a condition, the Indian, cut off from such advantages as pertain to the wild life of the forest, and open only to the
influence of the vices which civilisation brings in its
train, is in a peculiarly hopeless condition.   The Chippewas of Point Pelé were indeed only the deserted and
vagabond remnant of a large band, which had diminished
within a period of fifteen years, from 250 to less than
60, in part by the removal of the more civilized and
industrious Indians to other settlements.   This year the
superintendent writes to me, " The Point Pelé Indians
having for the last two years abandoned their old loca-
tion, and become scattered through the county of Kent,

living by hunting and basket-making, I have been unable with any certainty to obtain their present numbers. But from their wandering and dissipated habits I feel certain they are decreasing, having heard of several deaths during the year." The fate of such nomades in an old settled district is inevitable. A few survivors will join themselves to other bands, and the Point Pelé Indians will permanently disappear from among the Chippewas of Upper Canada.

The returns of property, farming implements, and live stock, furnish no unfair test of the progress of the Indian settlements, and several of these have been referred to in illustration of their advancement in civilisation. In the case of the smaller or the less civilized bands, such property is necessarily on a diminished scale ; but the supplementary notes appended to their tables of statistics occasionally afford curious insight into the workings of the semi-civilized Indian mind, while at other times they present a whimsical incongruity in the grouping of the common stock. In the census of the Mississagas of Chemong Lake, the public property belonging to the tribe is enumerated as "one log church, one waggon, one wood sleigh, one cow, three ploughs, and one harrow." The Snake Island Chippewas of Lake Simcoe "have, as public property, one frame school-house, occasionally used for public worship, three yoke of oxen, one plough, one harrow, two carts, one church-bell, and a grindstone." The Lake Skugog Indians, viewing with suspicion the designs of the Government agent in his too curious inquiries into their joint possessions, refused all information on the subject ; while the Chippewas of Beausoleil Island, a shrewd band of industrious farmers, possessed of six yoke of oxen, fifteen cows, twenty head of young cattle, farming implements, and other useful property in proportion, communicated to the superintendent this practical stroke of financial policy, which might supply a useful hint to the chancellor of larger exchequers : "The schoolmaster, Solomon James, has been absent, therefore no school has been kept ; and the band have resolved in council, that they will not pay any salaries to chiefs or others, except the doctor, as it is so much money taken from the general funds without any corresponding benefit." Such sagacious political economists might be safely assumed no longer to stand in need of any departmental superintendence. From minute returns furnished to me from eight of the largest Chippewa reserves, it appears that out of 1839 Indians, 312 are of mixed blood ; of the Mississagas, out of 530 Indians, 141 are of mixed blood ; of 246 Potowattomies, only 20 are returned of mixed blood ; and of 390 Delawares, only sixteen : though it can scarcely be doubted by any one familiar with the habits of frontier life, that all of those bands have taken up some considerable amount of white blood at an earlier date. In some of them the numbers are rapidly diminishing, under circumstances which could not fail to produce the same results on an equal number of white settlers ; but in other cases increasing numbers are the healthful concomitant of industrious habits and accumulating property ; and the Commissioners, in the Report of 1858, when urging the claims of the Indians to the permanent protection of the Imperial Government, add : "We cannot coincide in the opinion that the Indian service is an expiring one. The statistics in this Report militate strongly against the theory of a steady decline in the numbers of the Indians."

Such, then, are the illustrations which Canada affords of the transitional process which precedes the inevitable disappearance of the last remnants of its aborigines, including refugees from the vast tracts of extinct nations, now occupied by the restless industry of the United

States. The system of protection and pupilage under which, from the most generous motives, the Indian has hitherto been placed, has unquestionably been protracted until, in some cases at least, it has been prejudicial in its influence. It has precluded him from acquiring property, marrying on equal terms with the intruding race, and so transferring his offspring to the common ranks. While, however, we thus see that, in this transitional stage, a large proportion of the degenerate descendants of the aborigines absolutely perish in their premature contact with European civilisation, the half-breed of the frontier occupies a more favourable position. He mingles, in many cases, on a common footing with the settlers of the western clearings ; his children grow up as members of the new community ; and that inevitable process of amalgamation produces the same results there, which, it is manifest, are effacing every trait of Indian blood from the longest settled and most civilized of the survivors of the Indian nations of Canada.

The causes which have been referred to, as operating to prevent either the half-breed Indians or their posterity from being transferred in a condition of social equality to the common ranks of the New World's settlers, are neither irremediable nor of universal application. The honours of the Government House at Vancouver's Island are at present done by the daughters of an Indian mother ; the hospitalities of more than one Canadian parsonage have been enjoyed by the author, where the hostess had the red blood of the New World in her veins ; and Mr. Lewis H. Morgan, in replying to inquiries on the extent of hybridity in the United States, thus concludes : " When the Indian acquires property, and with it education, and becomes permanently settled, then honourable marriage will commence, and with it a transfer of the posterity to our ranks. I hope to see that day arrive ; for I think we can absorb a large portion of this Indian blood, with an increase of physical health and strength, and no intellectual detriment." Whether it is calculated to prove beneficial or not, this process has not now to begin ; though a change in the relative position of the civilized Indian with the occupants of the older settlements may tend greatly to increase it. The same process by which the world's old historic and unhistoric races were blended into elements out of which new nations sprung, is here once more at work. Already on the Red River, the Saskatchewan, the Columbia, and Fraser's River, on Vancouver's Island, and along the whole Indian frontiers both of the United States and British North America, the red and the white man meet on terms of greater equality ; and the result of their intercourse is to create a half-breed population on the site of every new western clearing, totally apart from those of mixed blood who are reabsorbed into the native tribes. The statistics of the more civilized and settled bands of Indians in Upper and Lower Canada do not indicate that the intermixture of red and white blood, though there carried out under unfavourable circumstances, leads to degeneracy, sterility, or extinction ; and the result of their intermingling in the inartificial habits of border life, is the transfer of a larger amount of red blood to the common stock than has hitherto, I believe, received any adequate recognition by those who have devoted attention to the comprehensive bearings of the inquiries which such phenomena of hybridity as have been discussed in this chapter involve.

CHAPTER XXIV

THE INTRUSIVE RACES.

Do races ever amalgamate? Does a mixed race exist? asks Dr. Knox :[1] himself the native of that little island-world where, favoured by its very insulation, Briton and Gael, Roman, Pict, and Scot, Saxon and Angle, Dane, Norman, and Frank, have for two thousand years been mingling their blood, and blending their institutions into a homogeneous unity. In seeking an answer to the great problem of modern science involved in such inquiries, the insular character of Britain presents some important elements tending to simplify the inquiry ; but the archæological and historical data illustrative of the process by which the island race of Britain,

> " This happy breed of men, this little world,"[2]

has attained to its present development, become of secondary importance, when compared with the gigantic scale on which undesigned ethnological experiments have been wrought out on the continent of America. Admitting, for the sake of argument, all that is implied, not only in acknowledged Asiatic affinities of the Esquimaux ; but the utmost that can be assumed in favour of an intrusive population by means of Phœnician, Celtiberian, ancient British, or Scandinavian colonizations, nevertheless it remains indisputable that the Western

---

[1] *The Races of Men*, Lect. i.   [2] *Richard II.* Act ii. Sc. i.

Hemisphere has been practically isolated from the Old
World and all its generations for unnumbered centuries. The traditions of the Aztecs told of an ancient
era when Quetzalcoatl, the divine instructor of their ancestors in the use of the metals, in agriculture, and the
arts of government, dwelt in their midst. Fancy pictured in brightest colours that golden age of Anahuac,
thus associated with the mythic traditions of some wise
benefactor and civilizer of the Aztec nation. But amid
all the glowing fancies with which tradition delighted
to clothe the transmitted memories of the age of Quetzalcoatl, a curious definiteness pertains to the physical
characteristics of this ancient benefactor of the race.
He was said to have been tall of stature, with a fair
complexion, long dark hair, and a flowing beard. This
remarkable tradition of a wise teacher, superior to all
the race among whom he dwelt, and marked by characteristics so unlike the native physiognomy, was accompanied with the belief that, after completing his mission
among the Aztecs, he embarked on the Atlantic Ocean
for the mysterious shores of Tlapallan, with the promise
to return. How far the rumours of Spanish invasion
preceded the actual landing of Cortes, and helped to give
shape to more ancient traditions, it must be difficult
to determine. Nearly thirty years elapsed between the
first insular discoveries of Columbus and the landing of
Cortes on the Mexican shores ; and many a tale of the
strange visitors who had come from out the ocean's
eastern horizon, armed with the thunder and the lightning, and with a skill in metallurgy such as the divine
teacher of the art could alone be supposed to possess,
may have shaped itself into the vague tradition of the
good Quetzalcoatl, as it passed from one to another
eager listener, ere it reached the Mexican plateau. But
the tradition seems like the embodiment of the faint

memories of an older intercourse with the race of another hemisphere, when Egyptian or Phœnician, Greek,
Iberian, or Northman, may have dwelt among the gentle
elder race of the plateau, before the era of Aztec conquest, and taught them those arts wherein lie the essential germs of civilisation. If so, however, the race
remained physically unaffected by the temporary presence of its foreign teachers, and continued to develop
all the special characteristics of the American type of
man, until Columbus, Cabot, Verrazzano, and Cartier,
Cortes, Pizarro, De Leon, Raleigh, and other discoverers
and explorers, prepared the way for the great ethnological experiment of the last three centuries, of transferring the populations of one climate and hemisphere to
other and totally diverse conditions of existence on the
New Continent.

But now we witness on the American continent the
two essentially distinct forms of migration, by means of
which the capacity of the indigenous man of one quarter
of the globe to be acclimatized and permanently in-
stalled as the occupant of another, is to be fully tested.
First we have the abrupt transport of the Spaniard to
the American archipelago, to the *tierra caliente* of the
Gulf coast, and the *tierra fria* of the plateau ; the
equally abrupt transference of the Englishman to the
warm latitudes of Virginia and the bleak New England
coast; and the attempt of the colonists of Henry IV.
and Louis XIII. to found *la Nouvelle France* between
Tadousac and Quebec, where winter reigns through half
the year, and the thermometer ranges frequently from
30° to 40° below zero. Again, we have the compulsory
migration of a population derived from the interior and
the Atlantic coasts of the African continent, to the
islands and those southern states of America, where
experience indicates that the industrial occupation of

the soil is incompatible with the healthful development
of the races of northern Europe. But on the same continent we also witness another and totally distinct process of migration, analogous to that by which the ancient
earth must first have been peopled, whether from one
or many centres of human origin. Unnumbered ages
may have elapsed after the creation of man before, on
the theory of his passage from Asia to America, the
first progenitors of those whom we call its aborigines
acquired a footing on the soil of the New World. Its
ancient forests and prairies, its lakes, river valleys, and
mountain chains, lay all before them, to be subdued,
triumphed over, and, with their wild fauna, to be made
subservient to the wants and the will of man. From
one or many points the ever-widening circle of migration enlarged itself, until, throughout the broad territories of the Western Hemisphere, from the Pacific to
the Atlantic, every region had passed to its first rightful
claimants. Thus secured in full possession of the soil,
the American Mongol made of it what he willed through
all the centuries of his race's destiny, till that memorable year when, according to the traditions of the Mexican plateau, the race of Quetzalcoatl came to fulfil the
doom of Montezuma's line, and to accomplish the pro-
phecies of the Aztec seers. Then followed the second
migration to the New World, which is still in progress,
and only differs from the primary migration in this, that
the forest and the prairie are already in occupation ;
and, with their wild fauna, the scarcely less wild aborigines have to be subdued, supplanted, or embraced
within the conquests of nature to the uses of civilized
man. Once more, from many single points, as from the
Pilgrim Rock of Plymouth Bay in 1620, the new population has diffused itself continuously in ever-widening
circles. It has been estimated that, under the combined

influences of natural increase and constant augmentation by immigration, the outer circle of the great western clearings encroaches on the unreclaimed West at the rate of about nine miles annually throughout the whole extent of its vast border. We know that the New Englander, abruptly transplanted to South Carolina or Alabama, is as incapable of withstanding the climatic change as the Old Englander. But if we suppose the first settlers of New England to have been left to themselves, with their indomitable industry and earnest enterprise, to build up a well-consolidated community, to frame laws for the government of the growing society, and to send out hardy young pioneers to win for themselves the needful widening area, we can see how, in the lapse of centuries, younger generations would at length reach the Gulf of Florida and the Rocky Mountains, without any one of them having travelled beyond the circumference of its previously acclimated region ; unless indeed we believe, with the extreme sticklers for the well-defined habitats of indigenous races of men, that such an intrusive exotic race, however much it may seem for a time as though it were begetting native inheritors of the territorial acquisition, is in reality only

> "Like a circle in the water,
> Which never ceaseth to enlarge itself,
> Till, by broad spreading, it disperse to nought."[1]

This is the actual question which has to be solved by means of the dual migration of the fair and the dark races of the ancient world, who have become the supplanters of the indigenous tribes of America. And by means of such migration many questions besides this have already been at least provisionally answered. Are subdivisions of the human family indigenous in certain

[1] *Henry VI.* Part I. Act i. Scene ii.

geographical habitats, and incapable of permanent trans-
lation to other regions? Are the indigenous types of
such distinct habitats capable of innocuous amalgamation? In other words, do the subdivisions which ethnography clearly recognises in the human family, partake
so essentially of the characteristics of distinct races
among the inferior orders of creation, as to be incapable
of permanently perpetuating an exotic life, or transmit-
ting fertility to a mixed breed? To the different questions involved in this inquiry, one school of American
and British ethnologists has replied with a distinct and
strongly asserted negative; and the strength of the convictions of American ethnologists is shown by their
adoption of a view so inimical to the theory of permanent triumph as the destiny of the Anglo-American
colonists of the New World.

The African, as has been already remarked, owed his
involuntary migration to the Western Hemisphere to the
belief, which the experience of centuries has confirmed,
that this distinct type of man, transported to an entirely
different geographical area, and to a diverse climate,
would nevertheless prove more enduring than the indigenous Red Man of the soil. The whole instincts of an
essentially unmaritime race were outraged by the trans-
portation of the African to the New World. The cara-
van, and the patient assiduity of overland commerce and
interchange of the commodities of countries separated by
burning tropical regions and waterless deserts, have been
the characteristics of Africa in every age. The camel is
her ship of the desert, and maritime enterprise pertained
there only to the era of her Punic colonies. No test
could therefore seem more completely to satisfy all requirements, relative to Agassiz's postulate of the natural
relations inherent in the different types of man, and the
animals and plants inhabiting the same regions. A sub-

division of the human family most strongly marked in type, in opposition to all its natural or acquired instincts, was forcibly transported to another continent, inhabited by indigenous tribes essentially diverse in all their physical characteristics. Ethnologists are not quite agreed as to all the results; for it is difficult for the American writer to separate the consequents of this great, though undesigned scientific experiment, from its incidental political and social bearings. This, however, is beyond dispute, that the African, under all the disadvantages of transference to a new geographical region and diverse climatic influences, has held his ground where the indigenous Red Man has perished. The difficult question of hybridity complicates the further bearings of the experiment; for a hybrid race like the "coloured people" of the United States, intermingling with a diverse white race, especially under relations which preclude them from a free agency and voluntary isolation, such as pertain to the half-breed Indians of British America, is necessarily in an unstable condition.

There are upwards of four millions of people of African blood in the United States, and certainly not less than ten millions throughout the continent and islands of North and South America;[1] but of these the larger proportion consists of hybrids. Their numbers are still increased to a small extent by direct, though illicit transmigration of the pure stock from Africa; still more they are largely augmented by the intermixture of white and black blood, under circumstances least accordant with

---

[1] The numbers have been estimated as high as fourteen millions. That given in the text is based on the following estimate: the United States, 4,200,000; Brazil, 2,000,000; Hayti, 950,000; South and Central America, 900,000; Cuba, 900,000; British Possessions, 700,000; French Possessions, 230,000; Dutch, Danish, and Mexican, 120,000. The data for some of the statements are very imperfect, but in such cases I believe the numbers are understated.

the natural instincts of man, and which place them beyond the reach of the statistician. All this complicates the question. It is impossible to determine with certainty how far the hybrid coloured population of the United States is capable of permanency, either by the development of a fixed hybrid type, or by continuous fertility, until the predominant primary type reasserts its power, by their return to that of the original white or black parent ; so long as the mixed breed is constantly augmented in the Southern States by means at variance with the natural and moral relations of social life.

In Canada the coloured population numbered about 8000 in 1852, and by the census of 1861 they are shown to have increased—doubtless to a great extent by immigration,—to 11,395, including 190 settled in Lower Canada. The number is no doubt understated, as the older coloured settlers are unwilling to return themselves as such in the census papers. But the Canadian settlers of African blood are chiefly congregated in a few localities, as at St. Catherine's, Chatham, and on the Buxton settlement in Western Canada. Admitted as they are to a perfect political equality, with access to the common schools, and other educational institutions of the province, they are placed under circumstances calculated to afford some fair test of their fitness for bearing a part in the progress of a free community, and of their capacity for acclimatization in a region essentially diverse either from the native continent of the African race, or the American States which have become, in a secondary sense, the native centres of the coloured population of the New World. But too brief a period has elapsed to furnish any fair data for judging of the fruits of this experiment ; and systematic inquiries instituted for the purpose of testing the results already noticeable, have led

to no very precise or reliable returns.[1]   This, however, is
to be observed, that, whether from habits already acquired
under a different social condition, or from causes specially
pertaining to their own physical and intellectual type,
the coloured population of Canada voluntarily perpetuate
social distinctions which separate them as a class from the
general community.   They have their distinct places of
worship, their special societies, assemblies, and festivals ;
and thus throw obstacles of their own creating in the
way of amalgamation.   This is probably mainly to be
accounted for by the prejudices of caste meeting them with
little less force in Canada than the neighbouring Union ;
and by the fact that they necessarily belong, with few
exceptions, to the poorer classes, and have therefore a
keener sense of social equality among themselves, alike
in religious and festive assemblies, than when asserting
their claims to such among the general community.

But the experiment of a population of African origin
transferred to a region essentially different from its
native habitat, and after mingling its blood alike with
that of the native and the European, being at length left
to its own resources for self-government and the perpetuation of the race, has been tried, and is still in
progress, under very remarkable circumstances, in the
Island of Hayti.   The island is nearly as large as Ireland,
and, with a surface of about twenty-five thousand square
miles, presents a remarkable diversity of soil and climate.
The central mountain group rises to an elevation of some
eight thousand feet above the level of the sea, and from
this mountain-ranges branch off in various directions,
dividing the island into broad valleys and extensive
savannahs or meadows.   With the surface thus broken
up by lofty elevations, it is generally well watered in the

[1] For printed Queries circulated by the author, relative to the coloured
population in Canada, *see* Appendix C.

valleys and plains, and is considered to be the most fertile as well as one of the most healthy islands of the Antilles. It has a coast line of about twelve hundred miles in extent, indented with bays, and with many harbours, some of which are spacious, well sheltered, and offering accommodation for a numerous fleet. The climate is peculiar, with a rainy season occurring at different periods on its northern and southern coasts, and a temperature modified by the prevalence of northern winds, land breezes, and the varying elevations of the surface. The winter is equable and cool, and the heat of the summer is moderated by the prevailing winds, so as to present little climatic correspondence to any region of the African continent, and even to contrast strikingly in this respect with the other Antilles.

The history of this beautiful island is full of interest for us. When Columbus, during his first voyage among the earliest discovered islands of the New World, was perplexed amid the varied and deceptive allurements which hope and fancy conjured up for him on every side, the lofty mountains of Hayti rose on his view above the clear horizon, and gave evidence of a region of wide extent. The mountains were higher and bolder in their rocky outlines than any he had yet seen, and swept down, amid rich tropical forests, into luxuriant savannahs ; while the cultivated fields, the canoes along the shore, the columns of smoke by day, and the fires that lighted up the island coast at night, all gave promise of a numerous population. Wandering amid the shades of its tropical vegetation, in the month of December, under trees laden with fruit, and listening to the melody of birds, among the notes of which they fancied they recognised the sweet voices of the nightingale and other songsters familiar to them in the far distant groves of Andalusia, the voyagers gave to the

new-found island the name of Española, or Little Spain.
Among all the beautiful islands of the newly-discovered
archipelago, none impressed the first voyagers so strongly
with its natural charms, or with the virtues of the gentle
race who lived amid the luxuriance of their favouring
climate in a state of primitive simplicity. None, among
all those who welcomed the strangers as heavenly visit-
ants, were doomed to look back with more mournful
bitterness on that fatal hour when the white sails of the
"Santa Maria" first rose on their horizon. They are
described by Las Casas as a well-formed race, fairer and
more perfect in figure than the natives of other islands;
but gentle, careless, and altogether indisposed to toil.
Experience, indeed, soon revealed to the Spaniards the
presence of the fierce Carib, as well as of the docile
Indian native on the island. But he was an intruder
like the Spaniard; and Carib and Haytian shared alike
in the exterminating violence of the Spanish lust for
gold. They perished, toiling in the mines, in vain resistance to oppression, or despairingly, by their own
hands; so that, according to the venerable Las Casas,
who witnessed many of the horrors he describes, before
twelve years had elapsed from their first friendly welcome of the Spaniards as celestial beings, several hundred
thousands of the Indians had been exterminated. The
original population of Hispaniola can only be a subject
of conjecture; but in 1507 it had been reduced to
sixty thousand : in 1535 only five hundred remained,
and the last survivors of the aboriginal race died out in
the early part of the eighteenth century. But it was at
the earliest stage of this exterminating process that the
idea was suggested, of substituting for the weak and
indolent islander the robust and patient African. The
first negroes were transported to the Antilles, in 1503,
only eleven years after the discovery of Hispaniola by

Columbus ; and for three centuries thereafter the nations
of Europe made merchandise of the African race, and
transplanted them yearly by thousands to the islands
and the mainland of the Western World. By such
means were the aborigines displaced and supplanted by
a totally different race ; though they have not even now
so totally disappeared, but that the traces of Indian
blood, intermingled with that of both intruding races,
are discernible. Their characteristic features and luxuriant hair contrast strikingly with those of the predominant African type, and such mixed descendants of
the native stock are still called Indios. The modern
name of Hayti is a revival of a native term signifying
" the mountainous country," and implying in its adoption
the rejection of all foreign interference with its later
native race.

The French acquisition of the Haytian territory, which
contributed so largely to its ultimate emancipation and
independence, dates from the reign of Louis xiv. Towards the close of the eighteenth century, it was regarded as the most valuable of all the foreign settlements
of France. But the Revolution, in which the descendants
of the Grand Monarque perished on the scaffold, extended its influence to the remotest French possessions.
In 1794, the negro slaves of Hispaniola were, by a vote
of the National Convention, declared equal participators
in the liberty and equality which France had proclaimed
to all her citizens, and they hastened to imitate the example of Paris. A general insurrection of the coloured
population ensued. All the white inhabitants who
escaped massacre were compelled to emigrate, and Tous-
saint L'Ouverture, a black chief, established the first
Haytian Republic in 1801. The subsequent history of
Hayti, if compared with the neighbouring continental
republic, is not very favourable to the capacity of the

coloured race for self-government. Presidents, military dictators, emperors, and other changing phases of supreme rule, have marked the unstable constitution of the black Republic. After the whole island had been united for a time, it divided once more into an empire and republic, parted by the same boundaries which formerly separated the French and Spanish divisions of the island ; and Spain, taking advantage of a favourable opportunity, has since reasserted her title to her ancient possessions. Meanwhile, the Emperor Soulouque has been driven into exile ; his marshals, dukes, barons, and knights have vanished with the fountain of such questionable honours ; and by a recent enactment of the Legislative Chambers of Hayti, the chief portions of the extensive forfeited estates of the ex-emperor have been converted into rewards for prolonged military service. The instability of a government founded on insurrection and revolution has marked the varying phases of the Haytian Constitution. But the Government of France, since the reign of liberty and equality was proclaimed in Hayti, has not been so stable as to justify any contrast between it and its insular offshoot ; whilst a comparison with the neighbouring Spanish republics of the New World tells even less in favour of the capacity for self-government of the colonists of southern European blood. In the Haytian Republic complete religious toleration is established, education is encouraged, and the emigration of "the blacks, men of colour, and Indians in the United States and the British North American provinces," is invited by the offer of free grants of land, and all rights of citizenship.[1] Hundreds of the coloured people of Canada and the United States, including industrious farmers, tradesmen, and mechanics, have already embraced the advantages thus held out to

[1] *Emigration to Hayti,* Appendix D.

them, and added to the strength and vigour of the young republic. Meanwhile, a concordat between the Pope and President Geffrard has been published at Port-au-Prince, creating an archbishop and four bishops; and by a special article, his Holiness is not limited in the choice of these Haytian ecclesiastics, to the dark race. Time, therefore, must be allowed the Haytian before we infer from the history of this black Republic, that the men of mixed African blood are incapable of self-government, or of permanent independent existence.

In truth, this view of the great ethnological experiment forces us back on the question of inherited progress, and the physical and intellectual development of whole races by the protracted influences of civilisation. In the eighth and ninth centuries the insular Anglo-Saxon was among the least civilized of all the nations of Christendom. He was far inferior to the Irish Celt in arts and learning, though even then displaying a greater capacity for self-government. Danish conquest and rule did something for him ; Norman conquest accomplished a great deal more. Slowly, through successive generations, the Saxon helot of the Conquest grew into the sturdy English freeman of the Reformation era ; and then in the marvellous Elizabethan age that followed, while the principles of free government were still very partially defined or understood, but when the intellect of the nation was at its ripest, the Anglo-Saxon colonization of the New World began. The Roman Catholic sought freedom there from Anglican intolerance ; the Puritan found a refuge from ecclesiastical and political tyranny ; and the schooling of England's Commonwealth, the Covenanters' struggle in Scotland, and the crowning Revolution settlement, all guided the little detached communities of exiled Englishmen scattered along the clearings from Cape Cod to the Gulf of

Florida, and trained them, through a protracted minority, for independent self-government. Can a grosser injustice be conceived of, than to place a government thus built on the foundations of a thousand years, by free sons of the freest nation in the world, in comparison with the hasty improvisation of a nation of slaves? In 1795, the whole educated, civilized, and governing class disappeared from Hayti; and a people far below the standing of the Saxon helot of the Conquest, galled with the recent chains of slavery which so peculiarly unfit man for moderation as a ruler, without education and without experience, were suddenly summoned to govern themselves. It is something to say of such a people that their government has not proved less stable, nor less compatible with the progress of the community, than the republics established by the descendants of the Spanish discoverers and depopulators of Hispaniola.

The statistics of the Haytian Republic furnish some important contributions towards the desiderated answers to ethnological inquiries. So far as the material returns of the political economist are concerned, the response is anything but satisfactory. Seventy years ago Hispaniola was noted for its rich plantations of sugar, coffee, and cotton. Three years before the memorable declaration of the National Convention of Paris, the agricultural produce of that portion of the island which then belonged to France was valued at eight millions sterling. Sugar no longer reckons among the Haytian exports; the cotton plantations yield little more than one million pounds' weight per annum; the coffee plantations have been greatly reduced; and the whole annual exports little exceed one million pounds sterling. The principal commercial wealth of the island is now derived from the magnificent forests of mahogany and fine dye-woods with which its mountains are clothed, and the hides and jerked beef of numerous herds of cattle pastured on its verdant plains. The island aristocracy disappeared in the insurrection and emigrations of 1795, and with them the luxurious demands which the artificial wants of a highly civilized community create. The gardens and forests produce almost spontaneously cocoa-nuts, pine-apples, and the fruits introduced by the Spaniards from southern Europe, such as figs, oranges, pomegranates, and almonds. Maize, millet, cassava, plantains, and sweet potatoes are raised with little labour; and the Haytian race of African blood have to a great extent resumed the life of ease and careless indolent enjoyment in which the aborigines passed their days under the rule of their native caciques. The Spaniards, who broke in upon that enviable scene, described the very social existence which they so ruthlessly destroyed, as seemingly realizing the golden age of poets' dreams. Doubtless it had its full share of the evils inseparable from the most favoured savage life; but the worst of these were of little moment when compared with the pandemonium which the presence of Europeans created; and perhaps the unproductive life of the modern Haytian, while supplying all his moderate wants, contrasts as favourably with the productive era prior to the declaration of independence, as did that of the gentle indigenous race before the Spaniards explored their mines for gold, and made the island productive alike to the colonist and the crown by the fatal system of *repartimiento.* The present population is said to employ only about two hours a day in productive labour, and to seek its enjoyment in the pleasant ease to which the perpetual summer of the island climate invites. But conflicting parties and political revolutions, no less than the frequent hurricanes and occasional earthquakes of Haytian latitudes, disturb the reveries of such indolent dreamers, and recall them to some of the stern realities of life. The moral tone of the community, moreover, is reputed to be fully as low as might be anticipated among a people so recently emancipated from slavery; and thus it appears that neither the Indian Arcadia nor its African successor, amid all the unequalled advantages of soil and climate, could escape the malign elements by which man mars every paradise into which he is admitted.

But these are incidents apart from the real question: which is not whether an intrusive exotic race of pure or mixed African blood will raise any given quantity of sugar, coffee, and cotton; but whether it can rear such young generations of its own race as shall perpetuate the intruders, and beget a native race as the permanent inheritors of the soil. Time is required for fully testing this question, but the statistics of the Haytian empire and Republic seem so far to render a very satisfactory reply. Before 1791 the population is believed to have been about 700,000 souls. Since then the commerce of the island has greatly decreased, but its population meanwhile has gone on steadily advancing. According to the census of 1824, it amounted to 935,000; in 1852, Sir Robert H. Shomburgk estimated it, including the empire and republic into which the island was then divided, at 943,000; and with the additions by recent immigration, besides the ordinary increase, it cannot now be less than 950,000 souls. This progressive increase in the population of Hayti has taken place under circumstances far from being favourable to such results. Revolts, expatriations, wars, and revolutions have all contributed to retard its progress; and in 1842 a terrible earthquake overthrew several towns, and destroyed thousands of lives. Nevertheless, during its brief term of independent existence, whatever other elements have

tended to arrest its advancement, no indications hitherto
suggest any proof of that inherent tendency towards
degeneracy and sterility which have been affirmed to involve the inevitable extinction of such a hybrid race.
The evidence derivable from the four millions of
coloured people in the United States, in reference to the
subjects under consideration, is complicated, and dete-
riorated by various elements of uncertainty inseparable
from the peculiar social condition in which they are
placed, especially in the Southern States. Nevertheless,
the American coloured race offers to the ethnologist a
highly interesting subject for investigation; and present
materials from which to gather data for future deductions of a more determinate character. Among American writers, Dr. J. C. Nott has given this subject the
most systematic attention, and has enjoyed peculiarly
favourable opportunities for its study, during a residence
of half a century among the mingled white and black
races of South Carolina and Alabama, and twenty-five
years' professional intercourse with both. The conclusions he arrives at, it cannot be doubted, have been
affected in some degree by opinions and prejudices inseparable from observations made on the two races placed
on so unequal a footing as they are in the States referred
to; and his deductions from the evidence he reviews,
must be considered along with the fundamental theory
he entertains, that the genus *homo* includes many primitive species, and that these species are amenable to the
same laws which govern species in many other genera.
He regards such species of men as all *proximate, i.e.,*
producing with each other a fertile offspring, in contradiction to *remote species,* which are barren, and *allied
species,* which produce *inter se* an infertile offspring.
But along with this, he maintains that while some are
perfectly prolific, others are imperfectly so, possessing a

tendency to become extinct when their hybrids are bred together.[1] More extended opportunities of observation have also led Dr. Nott to the conclusion that certain *affinities* and *repulsions* exist among various races of men, which cause their blood to mingle more or less perfectly. Contrary to deductions published before his opportunities of observation were extended to Mobile, New Orleans, and Pensacola : he acknowledges having witnessed there many examples of great longevity among mulattoes, and sundry instances where their intermarriages, contrary to his antecedent experience in South Carolina, were attended with manifest prolificacy. He accordingly recognises an essential distinction between mulattoes of the Atlantic and Gulf States. The former he regards as the offspring of intermixture between the negro and *fair-skinned* European races, Teutonic and Celtic, between whom no natural affinity exists, and who are consequently destined to speedy extinction. The latter owe their white blood to French, Italian, Spanish, Portuguese, and other *dark-skinned* European races, with whom he conceives certain affinities to the dark races of Africa exist. The classification of France in this latter group is manifestly suggested more by the actual history of the white colonists of the Gulf States, than by any preconceived ethnic characteristics ; and it can only be detached from the Celtic nations of Europe by an exaggerated estimate of the very limited Basque element of its south-western provinces. But to this dark-skinned, black-eyed, black-haired Basque race of southern Europe, an approximation to the African Berber, both in physical and moral traits, is suggested ; and thus sufficient ethnic affinities between the essentially distinct European and African "species" of man are

---

[1] *Hybridity of Animals viewed in connexion with Mankind*, p. 379, *Types of Mankind*, p. 81.

recognised to account for the phenomena resulting from
their intermixture. "Such races, blended in America
with the imported negro, generally give birth to a hardier,
and therefore more prolific stock than white races, such
as Anglo-Saxons produce by intercourse with negresses."[1]

In pursuing this inquiry, Dr. Nott has followed the
example of Jacquinot, Hamilton Smith, and other ethnologists, in assuming that, "zoologically speaking, mankind and *canidæ* occupy precisely the same position,"
and that, in reference to the influences of climate, domestication, and hybridity, mankind is governed by the same
zoological laws which regulate animals generally.[2] But
these are propositions I am by no means prepared to
admit. Apart altogether from the question of unity or
multiplicity of species, this fact is entirely overlooked,
that man's normal condition is that of domestication,
while for all other animals it is an essentially artificial
condition. Take man in what is popularly called a
state of nature, such as the Red Indian of the American forests or prairies. He lives in a community controlled by many binding, though unwritten laws ; he
selects his food, and modifies it by artificial means, with
the aid of fire, and various preparatory and conservative
processes ; he clothes himself with varying coverings
according to the changing climate, and also according to
fashion, taste, and prescriptive usage. His marriage, the
treatment of his wife or wives, the physical nurture and
training of his offspring, and the choice of the locality
for their permanent residence, are all regulated in a very
arbitrary manner, by motives and influences resulting
from his social condition. The very shape of the head,
the scarification and deformation of the body, and the
rites and practices accompanying birth, puberty, marriage, sickness, and death, are all determined by complex

---

[1] *Hybridity of Animals,* p. 374.   [2] *Ibid.* pp. 376, 394.

influences; to which there is nothing analogous among the lower animals, until man superinduces upon them artificial conditions of life which are natural to him. The hunted savage, driven forth into the wilderness, still manifests the " instincts" of domestic and artificial life. He, and he alone, is a clothing, cooking, fire-making, tool-using animal. In his most savage condition he is distinguished from all other animals by certain characteristics which point to civilisation as his normal condition. Accordingly, the civilized man is the most fully developed physically as well as intellectually. The white hunter and trapper soon surpasses the Indian even in the skill and endurance of forest life. The civilized man endures most easily sudden changes of climate, and withstands longest the privations to which previous training would seem calculated to render him most sensitive. The very opposite of all this is true of the domesticated animal. Domesticated cattle, housed, artificially fed and tended, are superior to the wild cattle in the milk they yield, the supply of animal food they furnish, and the specialities of breed for the conditions best adapted for the uses to which man has diverted them. But their natural instincts have disappeared. They are less sagacious, less hardy, and have become altogether dependent on an artificial condition of existence which they cannot beget for themselves. And this domestication of the inferior animals is one of the artificial changes natural to man, and to man alone. The germ of it is seen in the savage with his dog and his horse. It constitutes the special characteristic of the next stage of social progress, the pastoral state ; and in its full development man becomes in a peculiar sense a modifier of creation, a subordinate creator. As the result of this lordship over the inferior animals, we see the horse, the ox, the sheep, the hog, the ass, and the dog transplanted to the continents

of America and Australia, to the Cape, and to every
island where the civilized European has found inducements to effect a settlement. His wishes and necessities
require it, and forthwith animal life multiplies in specific
forms, on spots where nature had placed otherwise insur-
mountable barriers to its introduction. One man, Robert
Bakewell of Diskley, originated the Leicester breed of
sheep ; to another, Arthur Young, is ascribed the South-
down breed ; so also, short-horn and long-horn, Durham,
Devon, and Ayrshire cattle have been successively called
into being, and perpetuated or abandoned at the will of
man. The favourite form, colour, or breed has been
transferred to the remotest regions of the earth, and
multiplied as the supplanters of their indigenous fauna.
The hybrid mule is annually produced by thousands;
developing peculiar attributes and instincts, of singular
value to man. Even fashion has exercised its influence ;
and with the demand for black, bay, chestnut, or grey
horses, the stock breeder has modified his supply.
Butchery, reduced to an accredited craft in the shambles
and markets of civilized man, has shocked the sensibili-
ties of many ; but it must not be overlooked that the
droves of Smithfield owe their existence, no less than
their destruction, to his will ; and if it were possible
that " vegetarian " enthusiasts could convert the civilized
world to their herbivorous diet, the extinction of domesticated animal life would only be prevented in so far as
the milk of the cow and the wool of the sheep still supplied a motive to man for their perpetuation.

The existence and condition of the coloured population
of the Western Hemisphere most nearly approximate to
those of the wild animals which have been domesticated,
and modified in form and habits to meet the wants
of civilized man. The African transported to America
was as little a free agent as the horse or the hog, which

have multiplied there even beyond the wants of their transplanter. It is indisputable, moreover, that the coloured race is purposely multiplied for sale. But the horse, which has run free, has returned to the broad pampas, and resumed the wild life of his Asiatic sire; while the African of Hayti, instead of resuming the savage life of his fatherland, has set up republics and empires, instituted ranks and titles, established churches and schools, and is even now striving towards law, order, and a more perfect civilisation. In truth, though the ethnologist does regard man as an animal, he must never lose sight of the fact that that animal is man. He cannot divest man, as an animal, of his moral nature, his reasoning faculties, his use of experience, his power of communicating knowledge by speech and writing, or his natural use of artificial appliances at every stage of his being, from the rudest stone or flint tool of the savage, to the telescope, the steam-engine, the electric telegraph. On all those grounds, therefore, may we demur to the assumption that, even in relation to the laws affecting hybridity and the perpetuation of species, the principles applicable to animals generally, or to any specific species of animals, are therefore applicable to man.

The following are the conclusions apparently deducible from the opinions arrived at by Dr. Nott in relation to the mixture of white and Negro blood in the United States:—

1. The mulattoes and other grades of the coloured race may be assumed as the invariable offspring of white paternity. "It is so rare in this country," Dr. Nott remarks, "to see the offspring of a Negro man and a white woman, that I have never encountered an example; but such children are reported to partake more of the type of the Negro than when the mode of crossing is reversed."

2. The offspring of the Spanish or other dark-skinned

European race and the Negro is hardier, more prolific, and therefore more likely to be permanent than that of Anglo-American paternity.

3. Mulattoes are less capable of undergoing fatigue and hardship than either the blacks or whites, and are the shortest-lived of any·class of the human race.

4. Mulatto women are peculiarly delicate, and subject to a variety of chronic diseases. They are bad breeders, bad nurses, liable to abortions, and their children generally die young.

5. Mulattoes, like Negroes, although unacclimated, enjoy extraordinary exemption from yellow fever when brought to Charleston, Savannah, Mobile, or New Orleans.

6. When Mulattoes intermarry they are less prolific than when connected either with the white or Negro stock; and all Mulatto offspring, if still prolific, are but partially so, and acquire an inherent tendency to run out, and become eventually extinct when kept apart from the parent stocks.

Assuming, for the sake of argument, that these conclusions are indisputable, they reveal a very remarkable series of results, when brought into comparison with the data which the census supplies. The Superintendent of the Census of the United States for 1850 appears to incline towards very different conclusions when estimating the progressive increase of the slave and coloured population. Deriving his information from various sources, he sets down the whole number of Africans imported at all times into the United States prior to 1850 at from 375,000 to 400,000.[1] At present the number of their descendants, including those of mixed blood, exceeds 4,000,000. With every deduction for the influence of the pure stocks on such increase, in a country where intermarriage between the white and coloured races is almost

---

[1] *Compendium of the Seventh Census of the United States,* p. 13.

unknown, it seems scarcely possible to reconcile such results with the idea of a race having within it the elements of disease, sterility, and inevitable extinction. Moreover, in estimating the full value of the previous summary of conclusions deduced from observed facts, one important admission must be taken into account. " I have found it impossible," observés Dr. Nott, ." to collect such statistics as would be satisfactory to others, and the difficulty arises solely from the want of chastity among mulatto women, which is so notorious as to be proverbial." This, and further remarks illustrative of the same statement, go far to neutralize the value of Nos. 3, 4, and 6 ; and to suggest totally different causes for the liability to disease, physical weakness, and sterility, of a race placed under such unfavourable circumstances either for moral or physical development. Sir Charles Lyell, in commenting on the affirmed relative intellectual capacity of the coloured race according to the predominance of white or black blood, adds : " It is a wonderful fact, psychologically considered, that we should be able to trace the phenomena of hybridity even into the world of intellect and reason." Yet it is not more wonderful than the familiar examples of transmitted intellectual characteristics from one or other parent of the same race, or the supposed influence of a superior maternal intellect on the corresponding mental faculties of distinguished sons. But it may be presumed that no one is prepared to maintain the monstrous doctrine that the profligacy of the southern mulattoes is the inevitable result of hybridity. Yet, unless such can be proved, the weakness, disease, and sterility of. the mixed race is produced by the very same causes which have degenerated and brought to an ignoble end some of the royal lines and the most ancient blood of Europe. Again, Dr. Nott discusses the possibility of gradual amalgamation merging the coloured into the predominant white race. It is admitted that, according to the assertion of both French and Spanish writers, when the grade of *quinteroon* is reached the Negro type has disappeared. So thoroughly has this been recognised that, by the laws of some of the West India Islands, this grade of descent was free. But, in commenting on this, Dr. Nott adds : " It must be remembered that the Spaniards and a certain portion of the population of France are themselves already as dark as any quinteroon, or even a quadroon, and thus it may readily happen that very few crosses would merge the dark into the lighter race." Sir Charles Lyell speaks of having met in South Carolina some " mulattoes" whom he could not distinguish from whites. But against this Dr. Nott sets his experience of half a century, and adds : " I am not sure that I ever saw at the South one of such adult mixed-bloods so fair that I could not instantaneously trace the Negro type in complexion and feature." He accordingly affirms as the only rational explanation, that " the mulattoes, or mixed breeds, die off before the dark stain can be washed out by amalgamation." But against opinions founded on such long experience, it may still be permissible to say that, supposing the descendant of mixed blood, quinteroon, sexteroon, or octoroon, to have reached that condition which, in the West India Islands at least, is no abstract theory, of being no longer distinguishable from the white race, how is such descent to be detected ? The freed man thus emancipated from a degraded caste is not likely to blazon the bend-sinister on his escutcheon. In my own experience I have seen in Canada several descendants of such mixed blood, who, still perhaps retaining such minute traces as the experienced eye of the author referred to would detect, yet could mingle without observation in any white assembly. In one case I have observed the eldest son of a white father and a mulatto mother in whom no casual observer could detect the slightest traces of the maternal blood; and who only betrays such in a complexion not darker than many of pure white descent. But this, it must be admitted, is not strictly an example of amalgamation, but an illustration of the predominance of the original pure stock; as is further shown by the return, in the case of younger members of the same family, not only to the true mulatto complexion, but to the crisp woolly locks of the African type. Nevertheless this white descendant of mixed blood, having married a white wife, has healthy offspring, betraying no traces of African blood. Another and more conclusive case which has come under my observation in Canada is that of a young woman descended of white and coloured parentage, the mother being probably a quadroon, from her appearance. Her hair is long and flowing, her complexion good, and the only trace of Negro blood is in the eye, which I have observed both in the red and black hybrid is one of the most enduring traits of the darker blood.

Intellectually the mulattoes are declared to be intermediate between the blacks and the whites; and Sir Charles Lyell was informed in Boston, that the coloured children were taught there separately from the whites, not from an indulgence in anti-Negro feelings, but because ".up to the age of fourteen the black children advance as fast as the whites; but after that age, unless there be an admixture of white blood, it becomes in most instances extremely difficult to carry them forward." But this is manifestly a mere evasion of distinctions traceable to the spirit of caste, which has led to separate coloured schools in Canada as well as in New England. If the Boston coloured children advanced with average intellectual capacity up to the age of fourteen, they must have completed their common school education ; and only those who aimed at the Central High School, or Harvard College, could remain to compete with their white rivals. There need be no hesitation, however, in allowing *à priori* probabilities in favour of the intellectual inferiority of the coloured people of America as a class, notwithstanding striking exceptional examples of the reverse. So far as their blood is African, they are the descendants of an unintellectual and uncultured race ; and in so far as they are the offspring of southern coloured blood, they are sprung from a people excluded from every source of intellectual or moral development ; so that to expect the coloured American to stand up at once on a par with the Anglo-American—

"The heir of all the ages in the foremost files of time,"

is simply to expect grapes of thorns, and figs of thistles.

Before passing on to another subject, it may not be superfluous to notice the use made here of the convenient term, *race.* It will be apparent to all who are familiar with such inquiries, that it is employed throughout this work in its popular sense : not as equivalent to *species,* though that also has become a term of vague and variable import ; but as a convenient designation for existing varieties of the human family, of which the origin of some, and the permanency of others are still undetermined. The language and the science are indeed both imperfect, in this respect ; and it is more from necessity than choice that the same term is used in speaking of the coloured race, the half-breed race, the Indian race, and the human race. It is perceived that the word is employed in such collocations, as the symbol of different values ; and an attempt is made in the Appendix to supply some of the most familiar deficiencies of ethnographic terminology.[1] But looking to the

[1] *Vide* Appendix B.

well-understood significance of the distinctions of race, whatever be the theory of their origin, the whole history of the last two centuries seems to affirm the strongly asserted conclusion of Dr. Knox,—however much it may conflict with his other deductions,—that race is everything : literature, science, art, in a word, civilisation depends on it. As to the origin of new varieties, the Anglo-Saxon himself is one of the most striking illustrations of such, however many elements we recognise as compounded into the so-called race ; and, to those who still see no necessity for abandoning their belief in the descent of all the varieties of mankind from one common origin, the development of a new and permanent type, either from the half-breeds of the Red River, or the coloured people of Hayti or the States, is an altogether conceivable thing, and would be no more than is assumed to have already occurred in the Magyars of Hungary, the European Turks, the Lombards of Northern Italy, or even the mingled race designated in no strictly scientific sense Anglo-Saxons. The latter, however, were the results of the admixture of proximate, if not of cognate races ; while the modern hybrids of the New World have sprung from an extreme and abrupt union of some of the most diverse varieties. Time alone can determine whether, placed under the peculiar circumstances they now occupy, in contact with a predominant and numerically superior white race, either of them will develop a permanent variety ; or whether they are destined to extinction by absorption into the predominant stock, or from inherent elements of decay and sterility.

But the ethnological phenomena of the American continent invite to the consideration of other and totally distinct questions from that of the mixed races which have resulted from the policy of the European colonists

of the New World. That the admixture of European
or African with Indian blood, must result in the development of new and intermediate varieties, is a conclusion
which all previous experience rendered probable. But
the further propositions, bearing directly on the whole
question of man's migrations, are also offered here for
solution : whether the mere climatic and other changes
consequent on the transference of Europeans from the
Eastern to the Western Hemisphere, have tended to
develop new and permanent varieties ? or whether the
geographical range of distinct types of man is so absolutely determined as a law of nature, that the mere transference of such to another region involves their ultimate
extinction ? Both propositions have already found their
supporters, from evidence derived from the data which
the phenomena attendant on the colonization of America
have supplied.

Among those who have maintained that the great
experiment of transferring a population indigenous to
one continent, and attempting to make them the colo-
nizers and permanent occupants of another continent,
must inevitably end in failure, Dr. Knox takes a foremost part. After questioning the perfect acclimation
of the horse, the ox, and the sheep, he proceeds to ask :
" How is it with man himself ? The man planted there
by Nature, the Red Indian, differs from all others on
the face of the earth. He gives way before the European races, the Saxon and the Celt : the Celtiberian
and Lusitanian in the south ; the Celt and Saxon in the
north. Of the tropical regions of the New World I
need not speak ; every one knows that none but those
whom nature placed there can live there ; that no Europeans can colonize a tropical country. But may there
not be some doubts of their self-support in milder regions ? Take the Northern States themselves. There

the Saxon and the Celt seem to thrive beyond all that
is recorded in history.   But are we quite sure that this
success is fated to be permanent?   Annually from
Europe is poured a hundred thousand men and women
of the best blood of the Scandinavian, and twice that
number of the pure Celt ; and so long as this continues
he is sure to thrive.   But check it, arrest it suddenly,
as in the case of Mexico and Peru ; throw the *onus* of
reproduction upon the population, no longer European,
but native, or born on the spot ; then there will come
the struggle between the European alien and his adopted
fatherland.   The climate, the forests, the remains of the
aborigines not yet extinct ; last, not least, that unknown
and mysterious degradation of life and energy which in
ancient times seems to have decided the fate of all the
Phœnician, Grecian, and Coptic colonies.   Cut off from
their original stock, they gradually withered and faded,
and finally died away.   Peru. and Mexico are fast re-
trograding to their primitive condition ; may not the
Northern States, under similar circumstances, do the
same ?"[1]   Such are the ideas formed on this subject by
an English anatomist and physiologist ; nor are they
without support among those whose national predilec-
tions might have been presumed to be sufficiently strong
to preclude them from readily giving currency to such
opinions.   Dr. Nott, after affirming that negroes die out
and would become extinct in New England, if cut off
from immigration, adds : "It may even be a question
whether the strictly white races of Europe are perfectly
adapted to any one climate in America.   We do not
generally find in the United States a population constitutionally equal to that of Great Britain or Germany ;
and we recollect once hearing this remark strongly en-
dorsed by Henry Clay, although dwelling in Kentucky,

[1] *Races of Men*, p. 71.

amid the best agricultural population in the country."[1]
Such an opinion must be the result of deep conviction
before it could be thus published by an American writer,
even though a necessary corollary from the general proposition he asserts relative to the origin and geographical
distribution of animals and man. The English anatomist, freed from all national sympathies or prejudices,
deals with this idea of the degeneracy of the Transatlantic European, or the Euromerican as it may be
convenient to call him, in still more uncompromising
fashion : "Already," he exclaims, "the United States
man differs in appearance from the European. The
ladies early lose their teeth ; in both sexes the adipose
cellular cushion interposed between the skin and the
aponeuroses and muscles disappears, or at least loses its
adipose portion ; the muscles become stringy, and show
themselves ; the tendons appear on the surface ; symptoms of premature decay manifest themselves ;"[2] and
the conclusion he deduces is that these indicate "not
the conversion of the Anglo-Saxon into the Red Indian,
but warnings that the climate has not been made for
him, nor he for the climate." The latter remark is the
more noticeable from the singular though undesigned
contradiction offered to it by another distinguished physiologist. Dr. Carpenter remarks, in his *Essay on the
Varieties of Mankind,*[3] "It has not been pointed out, so
far as the author is aware, by any ethnologist, that the
conformation of the cranium seems to have undergone
a certain amount of alteration, even in the Anglo-Saxon
race of the United States, which assimilates it, in some
degree, to that of the aboriginal inhabitants ;" and after
noting the peculiarities of New England physiognomy,

---

[1] *Distribution of Animals and the Races of Men, Types of Mankind,* p. 68.

[2] *Races of Men,* p. 73.

[3] Todd's *Cyclopædia of Anatomy and Physiology,* vol. iv. p. 1330.

he thus proceeds : " There is especially to be noticed an excess of breadth between the rami of the lower jaw, giving to the lower part of the face a peculiar squareness, that is in striking contrast with the tendency to an oval narrowing which is most common among the inhabitants of the old country. And it is not a little significant, that the well-marked change which has thus shown itself in the course of a very few generations, should tend to assimilate the Anglo-American race to the aborigines of the country : the peculiar physiognomy here adverted to, most assuredly presenting a transition, however slight, toward that of the North American Indian." Were the opinions thus confidently affirmed, borne out by my own observations, I should be tempted to assign to some admixture of red blood, as already adverted to in a former chapter, a share at least in so remarkable a transition from the European to the American type of man. But I can scarcely imagine any one who has had abundant opportunities of familiarizing himself with the features of the Indian and the New Englander, tracing any approximation in the one to the other. Nevertheless the physiognomical and physical characteristics of the New Englander are subjects of study of the highest importance to the ethnologist.

The evidence supplied by ancient monuments, and especially by the sculptures and paintings of Egypt, of the constant and undeviating character of some of the most remarkable existing types of man, has been frequently employed as an argument in favour of the permanency of types, and consequently of the essential diversity and multiplicity of human species ; and it has been confidently asked,—" If all the different races of man are indeed only varieties of one species, how is it that no well-ascertained variety has originated within

historic times?" It is, therefore, a fact of the utmost
value, that in the New Englander or Yankee, we have
such a variety unmistakably presented to us. His
history is well known. Two hundred and forty years
ago, the little "Mayflower" landed on the bleak shores
of New England the pioneers of civilisation. They
came of a noble old stock, and brought with them the
sturdy endurance of the Saxon, and the lofty spirit of
the Christian patriot; and the self-denial, the daring,
and the stern endurance of the Pilgrim Fathers were
needed on that bleak November day of the year 1620,
when the little band were landed on Plymouth rock, to
make for themselves a home and a country in the forest
wilderness. Now, after an interval of nearly two and
a half centuries, it is acknowledged on all hands that the
New Englander differs in many respects very unmistakably from the Old Englander. Dr. Knox, whilst admitting it, solves the difficulty by classing him with the
degenerate Spaniard of Mexico and Peru, already hasten-
ing, as he conceives, to speedy extinction. But the
Mexican of Spanish descent scarcely differs more widely,
in his degeneracy, from the conquistador of Cortes, than
does the modern Spaniard from the proud subject of
Charles v. The causes of the degeneracy of both are
patent to all, and lie to a great extent apart from questions of climate or geographical distribution; but, as we
have seen, Dr. Knox further affirms that the New Englander already manifests symptoms of premature decay;
and Dr. Nott, a native American, admits that his country-
men are constitutionally inferior to those of Germany or
Great Britain. The latter statement is consistent with
every probability, on a continent which, in the Northern
States, combines the extremes of temperature of Rome
and St. Petersburg. But even in this respect the New
Englander is unusually favoured with the cooling breezes

and the equalizing temperature of the Atlantic, tempering his northern latitudes, and exposing him to less violent extremes of heat or cold ; and all experience disproves this theory of degeneracy and decrepitude. He is proverbial for his energy, acuteness, and physical and intellectual vigour. The homes of New England approximate to those of the mother country in their genial, domestic attractions ; and yet the enterprising Yankee is as indefatigable a wanderer as the sturdy Scot. So thoroughly is he the type of American enterprise, that even among the Indians on the North Pacific coast, where a strange *lingua Franca* has been developed as the means of intercourse between natives and whites, the designation for an American is *Boston,* derived from the capital of the State of Massachusetts. And, while he is thus known on the remote Pacific shores, the New England States reveal everywhere the evidence of indomitable perseverance, successful industry, and the proofs of old settlements progressing under the same energy and patience which have united to make old England what she is. Nevertheless, it is most true, that it is easy for any one familiar with the New England physiognomy to point out the Yankee in the midst of any assemblage of Englishmen. He furnishes the indisputable example of a new variety of man produced within a remarkably brief period of time, by the same causes which have been at work since man was called into being, and scattered abroad to people the whole earth. If intermixture of blood has contributed any share in the development of such a physical change, that has been the invariable consequent of all colonization of previously peopled regions. If it is further ascribed to changes of climate, diet, habits, occupation, and intellectual training, all these have been in operation wherever man has wandered forth to seek

a new and distant home in the wilderness. And if two
centuries in New England have wrought such a change
on the Englishman of the seventeenth century, what
may not twenty centuries effect? or, what may be the
ultimate climatic influences of Canada, the Assinaboine
Territory, or Fraser's River ; of Utah, California, or the
States on the Gulf? It is only some twelve centuries
since the Angle and Saxon migrated as foreign intruders
to England, where the remnant of the elder native race
still speak, in a language unintelligible to him, of the
Saesonach as strangers. The transmigration, though
from a nearer coast than that of his New England
descendant, was a maritime one, and the climatic change
involved in the transfer to the peculiar insular climate
of England was not inconsiderable. The Englishman of
the present day is distinguishable from all his continental Germanic congeners, and is himself a type of
comparatively recent origin. Moreover, the Englishman
of the genuine Angle and Saxon districts, to the south
of the Humber, is a markedly distinct type from the
northern race, from the Humber to the Moray Firth ;
while again, in the Orkney Islands, the descendants of
its Norse colonists of the ninth and tenth centuries, not
only retain distinctive physical characteristics, but their
inherited maritime instincts and enterprise are so universally recognised, that the English as well as Scottish
Greenland fleets annually strive to complete their crews
at Kirkwall, before proceeding to the whale fishery in
the northern seas. The Orkney mariner and fisherman
is surrounded in his island home by seas peculiarly exposed, and in navigating the Pentland Firth, has to cross
an arm of the sea swept by the currents and subject to
the tempests of the Atlantic and German oceans. But
that this alone would not make a seaman of him, is proved
by the proverbial disinclination to all maritime daring

of the hardy Celtic population of the Hebrides and the
west of Ireland.

It is in such minute ethnology that the truths of the
science must be sought. The simplicity of such systems
as that of Blumenbach, with his five human species; of
Pickering, with his eleven races of men ; or of Borey de
St. Vincent, with his fifteen species ; or again of Virey,
who can overcome all difficulties if allowed two distinct
human species ; and of Morton, who, for the whole American continent, from the Arctic circle to Cape Horn,
admits of only one type of man : is exceedingly plausible
and seductive. When we place alongside of each other
Blumenbach's typical Caucasian, Mongolian, Malay,
Ethiopian, and American, the physical differences are
striking and indisputable ; but when we come to examine more minutely, the Caucasian region of Europe
has its fair and its dark-skinned races ; the little island
of Britain has its three, four, or five distinct types; and
it seems probable at last, that if we must divide mankind into distinct species, we may find that not five, but
five hundred subdivisions, will fail to meet all the demands of extended observation. Well-defined types have
perished, and new ones have appeared within the historic
period ; and if all the intermediate links between one
and another of the great subdivisions of the genus *homo*
cannot now be found, the causes for their disappearance
are sufficiently manifest. Nevertheless, the science has
still many difficult questions to solve. The essential
physical differences between the dark, woolly-haired
negro and the blue-eyed, fair-haired Anglo-Saxon, are
not greater than those others which distinguish the Indo-
European and monosyllabic languages. On the most
ancient historic sites along the shores of the same Indian
Ocean, have been recovered the highly-inflected Sanscrit,
with its wonderful richness of grammatical forms, its

eight cases, its six moods, and its numerous suffixes ;
and the monosyllabic Chinese, entirely devoid of inflexions, or even what seem to us grammatical forms.
But in the history of the Romance languages, we see
how curiously, first by a process of degradation, and
then of reconstruction, a whole group of new languages has sprung from the dead parent stock, presenting diversities so great as those which distinguish the
ancient Latin from the modern French.   Moreover, we
witness, on the native area of the monosyllabic Chinese,
our own vernacular tongue actually passing through the
first transforming stages, in the " Pigeon English " of
Hong-Kong and Canton.   Its name *pigeon*, which may
serve as an apt illustration of its vocabulary, is the
Chinaman's pronunciation of the word *business*.   Mr.
James H. Morris, a recent Canadian visitor to China,
remarks : " This language has become a regular dialect,
and, when first heard, it would appear as though the
speaker was parading indiscriminately a few English
words before his hearer, whose duty it was to make a
meaning out of them.   A foreign resident will introduce
a friend to a Chinese merchant, as follows : *Mi chin-
chin you, this one velly good flin belong mi ; mi
wantchie you do plopel pigeon along he all same
fashion along mi ; spose no do plopel pigeon, mi flin
cum down side mi housie, talke mi so fashion mi kick
up bobbery along you.*   To which the Chinaman will
reply :—*Mi savey no casion makery flaid ; can secure
do plopel pigeon long you flin all same fashion long
you.*"   This language is as simple as it seems absurd ;
but the words must be arranged as the Chinaman has
been accustomed to hear them, or he will not understand
what is said.   It is spoken in all the ports of China open
to foreign trade, and there is no disposition to adopt a
purer one.

The languages of Europe are undergoing the very same process of degradation and reconversion into new dialects and languages, on the American continent. The Negro-French is stripped of all its grammatical richness, and simplified into a dialect scarcely intelligible to a Parisian ; and Negro-English, though checked in its progress of degradation by constant contact with the vernacular tongue, has dropped many of its inflexions, altered the irregular tenses in defiance of euphonic laws, and modified the vocabulary in a manner that only requires complete isolation to beget a distinct dialect, and ultimately a new language. Mr. William H. Hodgson, of Savannah, Georgia, showed me a remarkable illustration of this. It consisted of portions of the Scriptures written by a native African slave, in Negro *patois* and in Arabic characters. The writing was executed with great neatness, but a more puzzling riddle could scarcely be devised to tax the ingenuity of the Shemitic scholar. In Lower Canada, also, French is already written and spoken with many English idioms, and with modified terms of English or Canadian origin. But it is on the North Pacific coast that the most remarkable example of the development of an entirely new language out of the commingling English and native vocabularies, is now in progress. Mr. Paul Kane, during his travels in the North-west, resided for some time at Fort Vancouver, on the Columbia river, and acquired the singular *patois* which is there growing into a new language. The principal tribe in the vicinity is the Chinook, a branch of the Flathead Indians, who speak a language which so entirely baffles all attempts at its mastery, that it is believed none have ever attained more than the most superficial knowledge of its common utterances but those who have been reared among them. Pickering remarks, on his approach to the straits of De Fuca,

" after the soft languages and rapid enunciation of the
Polynesians, the Chinooks presented a singular contrast,
in the slow, deliberate manner in which they seemed to
choke out their words, giving utterance to sounds some
of which could scarcely be represented by combinations
of known letters." Having heard its utterances as spoken
for my behoof by more than one traveller, I can only
compare them to the inarticulate noises made from the
throat, with the tongue against the teeth or palate, when
encouraging a horse in driving. Mr. Kane states in
reference to it, " I would willingly give a specimen of
the barbarous language were it possible to represent by
any combination of our alphabet the horrible, harsh,
spluttering sounds which proceed from the throat, apparently unguided either by the tongue or lip." Fort
Vancouver is the largest of all the posts in the Hudson's
Bay Company's Territory, and has frequently upwards
of two hundred voyageurs with their Indian wives and
families residing there, besides the factors and clerks.
A perfect Babel of languages is to be heard amongst
them, as they include a mixture of English, Canadian-
French, Chinese, Iroquois, Sandwich Islanders, Crees,
and Chinooks. Besides these the Fort is visited for
trading purposes by Walla-wallas, Klickatats, Kala-
purgas, Klackamuss, Cowlitz, and other Indian tribes ;
and hence the growth of a *patois* by which all can hold
intercourse together. The English, as it shapes itself on
the lips of the natives, forms the substratum ; but the
French of the voyageurs has also contributed its quota,
and the remainder is made up of Nootka, Chinook, Cree,
Hawaiian, and miscellaneous words, contributed by all
to the general stock. The common salutation is *Clak-
hoh-ah-yah,* which is believed to have originated from
their hearing one of the residents at the Fort, named
Clark, frequently addressed by his friends : " Clark, how

are you ?" The designation for an Englishman is *Kin-*
tshosh, i.e., King George ; while an American is styled
Boston.   Tala, i.e., dollar, signifies silver or money ;
oluman, i.e., old man, father, etc. The vocabulary as
written, shows the changes the simplest words undergo
on their lips : *e.g.,* fire, *paia ;* rum, *lum ;* water, *wata ;*
sturgeon, *stutshin ;* to-morrow, *tumola.* And the French
in like manner : la médecine becomes *lamestin;* la grasse,
lakles; sauvage, *savash, i.e.,* Indian; la vieille, *lawie,* etc.
The formation of the vocabulary appears to have been
determined to a great extent by the simplicity or easy
utterance of the desired word in any accessible language.
As to the grammar : number and case have disappeared,
and tense is expressed by means of adverbs.   Nouns
and verbs are also constantly employed as adjectives or
prefixes, modifying other words ; and are further increased, not only by borrowing from all available sources,
but by the same onomatopœic process to which has
already been assigned the growth in some degree of all
languages.   Thus we have *moo-moos,* an ox, or beef ;
tiktik, a watch ; *tingling,* a bell ; *hehe,* laughter ; *tum-*
tum, the heart ; *tum-tumb,* or *tum-wata,* a waterfall ;
pah, to smoke ; *poo,* to shoot ; *mok-e-mok,* to eat, or
drink ; *liplip,* to boil.   Nor is this patois a mere collection of words.   Mr. Kane informs me, that by means
of it he soon learned to converse with the chiefs of most
of the tribes around Fort Vancouver with tolerable ease.
The common question was : *cacha-mikha-chacha,* where
did you come from ? and to this the answer was : *sey-*
yaw, from a distance ; but in this reply the first syllable
is lengthened according to the distance implied, so that
in the case of the Canadian traveller he had to dwell
upon it with a prolonged utterance, to indicate the
remote point from whence he had come.   *Mikha* is the
pronoun you ; *neiki,* I ; as : *neiki mok-e-mok tschuck,* I

drink water. But accent and varying emphasis modify
the meaning of words, as is the case to a great extent
with the Chinese. Mr. Hales, the philologist of the
United States Exploring Expedition, remarks in reference to the Indians and voyageurs on the Columbia
river : " The general communication is maintained
chiefly by means of the *jargon*, which may be said to
be the prevailing idiom. There are Canadians and half-
breeds married to Chinook women, who can only converse with their wives in this speech ; and it is the
fact, strange as it may seem, that many young children
are growing up to whom this factitious language is
really the mother-tongue, and who speak it with more
readiness and perfection than any other."

Thus in all ways are the emigrants from the Eastern
Hemisphere making a new world of the West. The
face of the country, the life native to its soil, the autochthones by whom it is claimed, and the languages
in which such is uttered, are all being modified, effaced,
displaced. Whatever be the future fate of the intrusive
races, they have wrought mightier changes in two centuries, than it is probable the American continent witnessed for twenty centuries before. The rapidity, indeed,
with which such changes now take place strikes the on-
looker with astonishment ; and it is inconceivable to those
who have not witnessed it for themselves. In 1841, the
" Vicennes," fresh from exploring the islands and coasts
of the Southern Ocean, entered the Straits of De Fuca,
and Dr. Pickering describes his impressions on landing.
The maritime skill of the Chinooks, their eagerness for
traffic, and the striking quietness of their movements,
all excited his interest. They had some of the usual
forbidding habits natural to savage life ; but he adds,
" they appeared to live, as it were, on a good understanding with the birds and beasts, or as if forming part

and parcel of the surrounding animal creation ; a point
in correspondence with an idea previously entertained
that the Mongolian has peculiar qualifications for re-
claiming, or reducing animals to the domestic state."
But all was strange, wild, and savage. The broad continent lay between those Pacific coasts and the seats of
civilisation on its eastern shores ; and standing in the
midst of a temporary Indian encampment, and surrounded by all the rude details of savage life, he exclaims : " Scarcely two centuries ago, our New England
shores presented only scenes like that before me ; and
what is to be the result of the lapse of the third?"
Twenty years have elapsed since then. The town of
Victoria is rising on Vancouver's Island, and that of
New Westminster, in British Columbia. And the *British Colonist*, the *New Westminster Times*, and other
broadsheets of the North Pacific coast already tell of
the printing-press in full operation, where so recently
the Indian trail and the rude wigwam of the savage
were the sole evidences of the presence of man. The
mineral wealth of Fraser's River has attracted thousands
to the new province. The clearing, the farm, and the
industrious settlement, have displaced the ephemeral
lodges of the Indian ; and are rapidly superseding the
no less ephemeral shanties of the gold diggings. The
Customs' receipts of the colony of British Columbia for
the year 1860 exceeded £32,000 ; and the proceeds are
being chiefly expended on public works. The progress
of a single year outspeeds the work of past centuries.
Amid the charred stumps and the rough clearings of the
young settlement, fancy traces, not obscurely, the foundations of future states and empires, and the ports of
the merchant navies of the Pacific that shall unite
America to Asia, as America has been united to Europe.
Already the indomitable enterprise of the intruding races

has planned the route of overland travel, and even now the railways are stretching westward towards the Rocky Mountains. Explorers are surveying their defiles for the fittest passage, through which to guide the snorting steam-horse, and all the wonderful appliances by which the triumphs of modern civilisation are achieved. If such victories were only to be obtained, like those of the first Spanish colonists of the New World, by the merciless extermination of the Indian occupants of the soil, it would be vain to hope for the endurance of states or empires thus founded in iniquity ; but if, by the intrusion of the vigorous races of Europe, smiling farms and busy marts are to take the place of the tangled trail of the hunter and the wigwam of the savage ; and the millions of a populous continent, with the arts and letters, the matured policy, and the ennobling impulses of free states, are to replace the few thousands of the scattered tribes living on in aimless, unprogressive strife : even the most sensitive philanthropist may learn to look with resignation, if not with complacency, on the peaceful absorption and extinction of races who accomplish so imperfectly every object of man's being. If the survivors can be protected against personal wrong ; and, so far as wise policy and a generous statesmanship can accomplish it, the Indian be admitted to an equal share with the intruding colonizer, in all the advantages of progressive civilisation : then we may look with satisfaction on the close of that long night of the Western World, in which it has given birth to no science, no philosophy, no moral teaching that has endured ; and hail the dawn of centuries in which the states and empires of the West are to claim their place in the world's commonwealth of nations, and bear their part in the accelerated progress of the human race.

CHAPTER XXV.

ETHNOGRAPHIC HYPOTHESES : MIGRATIONS.

THE ethnology of the New World is unquestionably simpler than that of Europe or Asia, in its freedom from complicated elements which retard our study of the latter alike in their ancient and modern aspects. Nevertheless, this may be more apparent than real. Our knowledge of history prevents our under-estimating Pelasgian or Etruscan, Basque, Magyar, or Celtic elements of diversity. Ignorance may be the cause of our overlooking or under-estimating diversities among American languages as great as the German and Eus-. kara, or the Sanscrit and the Chinese. America, indeed, appears to have its monosyllabic Otomi and Mazahui, with their analogies to the Chinese, and their seemingly radical contrast to that polysynthetic structure which appears to be as predominant throughout the New World as Indo-European affinities are characteristic of the languages of Europe. But we scarcely know yet how justly to estimate the amount of difference ; for Mr. Schoolcraft affirms, as a conclusion to which his intimate familiarity with the Algonquin dialects had led him, that they betray evidence of having been built up from monosyllabic roots. If this be indeed demonstrable in any other than the vague sense in which it may be stated of every tongue, the same conclusion will apply to other American languages. Nearly all the Chippewa root-

words, he observes, are of one or two syllables; and
Gallatin has shown that the same may be affirmed to a
great extent of the Mexican, if the pronominal adjuncts
and the constantly recurring terminations are detached
from the radix. But the polysyllabic characteristics
of the Algonquin exceed even those of the Esquimaux.
Holophrasms are common in all its dialects, compounded
of a number of articulations, each of which is one of the
syllables of a distinct word; and the whole undergoes
grammatical changes as a verbal unit. This, therefore,
is a condition widely diverse from that of the monosyllabic languages, even where, as in the Otomi, many
compounded words occur in the vocabulary. But after
making every allowance for unknown nations and
tongues, and misinterpreted or unappreciated elements
of difference among the varieties of man in the New
World, the range of variation appears to extend over a
smaller scale than that of Europe or Asia, or even of
Africa; while he is everywhere found there under
much less diversified modifications of civilized or savage
life than on the old historic continents. The original
centres of population may have been manifold; for the
evidence of the lengthened period of man's presence in
America furnishes abundant time for such operations of
climatic influences, direct or indirect intercourse, or even
positive intermixture, to break down strongly-marked
elements of ethnic diversity. Nevertheless, after carefully weighing the various kinds of evidence which have
been glanced at in previous chapters, they all seem to
resolve themselves into three great centres of propagation, of which the oldest and most influential belongs to
the southern and not to the northern continent. The
routes originally pursued in such immigrations may
have been various, and it is far from impossible that
both southern and northern immigrants entered the con-

tinent by the same access. Such, however, is not the conclusion to which the previous investigations appear to me to point. If we adopt the most favoured theory, that the New World has been entirely peopled from Asia, through Behring Straits, then the Patagonian should be among the oldest, and the Esquimaux the most recent of its immigrant occupants. But that which seems theoretically the easiest is by no means necessarily the most probable course of migration ; and many slight indications combine to suggest the hypothesis of a peopling of South America from Asia, through the islands of the Pacific.

The tendency of philological inquiry, as directed to the peculiar grammatical structure and extreme glossarial diversities of the American languages, was at first to isolate them entirely, and to exaggerate their special phenomena into widely prevalent linguistic features, common to the New World and utterly unknown elsewhere. In this the philologist only pursued the same course as the physiologist, the attention of each being naturally attracted chiefly by what was dissimilar to all that had been observed elsewhere. But as physiological investigations have extended, their disclosures prove less conclusive in the support they yield to the favourite theory of an essential isolation and ethnic diversity for the American man. Increasing knowledge of his languages tends rather to diminish the proofs of that radical difference from all other forms of human speech which was at first too hastily assumed. The synthetic element of structure, though very remarkable in the extent of its development, has many analogies in ancient languages, and is embraced in the grammatical process of all inflectional tongues. But beyond this, important elements of relationship appear to be traceable between languages of America and those of the Polynesian family.

Gallatin early drew attention to certain analogies in the structure of Polynesian and American languages as deserving of further investigation; and pointed out the peculiar mode of expressing the tense, mood, and voice of the verb, by affixed particles, and the value given to place over time, as indicated in the predominant locative verbal form. The peculiar substitution of affixed particles for inflections, especially in expressing the direction of the action in relation to the speaker, is common to the Polynesian and the Oregon languages, and also has analogies in the Cherokee.[1] Subsequent observations, though very partially prosecuted, have tended to confirm this idea, especially in relation to the languages of South America, as shown in their mode of expressing the tense of the verb ; in the formation of causative, reciprocal, potential, and locative verbs by affixes ; and the general system of compounded word structure. The incorporation of the particle with the verbal root appears to embody the germ of the more comprehensive American holophrasms. But here again, while seeming to recover links between Polynesia and South America, we come on the track of affinities no less clearly Asiatic.   Striking analogies have been recognised between the languages of the Deccan and those of the Polynesian group, in which the determinate significance of the formative particles on the verbal root equally admits of comparison with peculiarities of the American languages.   On this subject the Rev. Richard Garnett remarks that most of the languages of the American continent respecting which definite information has been acquired, bear a general analogy alike to the Polynesian family and the languages of the Deccan, in their methods of distinguishing the various modifications of time ; and he adds : " We may venture to assert in general terms that a South American

---

[1] *American Ethnological Transactions,* vol. ii. p. cliv.

verb is constructed precisely on the same principle as those in the Tamul and other languages of Southern India; consisting, like them, of a verbal root, a second element defining the time of the action, and a third denoting the subject or person."[1] Such indications of philological relation of the islands of the Polynesian archipelago and the American continent to Southern Asia, acquire an additional interest when taken in connexion with remarkable traces of megalithic sculpture and of ancient stone structures in the Pacific, long ago noted by Captain Beechey on some of the islands nearest to the coasts of Chili and Peru, and more recently observed on Bonabe and other islands lying off the Asiatic shores. Some of those have already been referred to in their general bearings on oceanic migration, and on the probability of an era of insular civilisation, during which maritime enterprise may have been carried out on a scale unknown to the most adventurous of modern Malay navigators.

The affinities recognisable between Polynesian and American arts manifestly belong to a remote past; and the character of such philological relations as have been indicated fully accord with this. The direct relationship of existing Polynesian languages is not Mongol but Malay; and this is for the most part so well defined as to indicate migrations from the Asiatic continent to the islands of the Pacific at periods comparatively recent; whereas the diversity of those of America, and their essentially native vocabularies, prove that the latter have been in process of development from a remote period free from all contact with tongues which, as we see, were still modelling themselves according to the same plan of thought in the clustering islands of the Pacific. But the American languages present a widely

---

[1] *Proceedings of the Philological Society,* vol. i. p. 271.

diversified field of study scarcely yet fairly entered
upon; while their peculiar complexities, when considered
in relation to nations broken up into numerous unlettered and nomade tribes, and with no predominant
central nationality, seem to afford such facilities for ever-
changing combinations, that the difficulty of determining
their radical elements is greatly increased in any attempt
to compare their old and modern forms.   Two languages, however, seem to invite special study, in addition to that of Mexico.   The Maya, which presents
striking contrasts to it in its soft, vocalic forms, has
already been referred to as that to which we are attracted
by some apparent relations to the remarkable antiquities, and the possible surviving civilisation, of Central
America; while the Quichua was the classical language
of South America, the richly varied and comprehensive
tongue, wherein, according to its older historians, the
poets of Peru incorporated the national legends, and
which the Incas vainly strove to make not only the Court
language, but the medium of all official intercourse, and
the common speech of their extended empire.

From some one of the early centres of South American population, planted on the Pacific coasts by Polynesian or other migration, and nursed in the neighbouring valleys of the Andes in remote prehistoric times, the
predominant southern race diffused itself, or extended
its influence through many ramifications.   It spread
northward beyond the Isthmus, expanded throughout
the peninsular region of Central America, and after
occupying for a time the Mexican plateau, it overflowed
along either side of the great mountain chain, reaching
towards the northern latitudes of the Pacific, and extending inland to the east of the Rocky Mountains,
through the great valley watered by the Mississippi and
its tributaries.   It must not, however, be supposed that

such a hypothesis of migration implies the literal diffusion of a single people from one geographical centre. I should no more think of designating either the Toltecs or the Mound-Builders Peruvians, than of calling the Iranian Indo-Germans Greeks. But many archæological traces seem to indicate just such affinities between the former as have been suggested by the philological relations of the latter.

Thus far we have chiefly regarded the traces of oceanic migration by the southern Pacific route; but while its island groups appear to furnish facilities for such a transfer of population to the New World as evidence of various kinds tends to confirm, it seems scarcely to admit of doubt that the Canary Islands were known to the ancients, and that by Madeira and the Azores, on the one hand, and by the Cape Verde Islands, on the other, the Antilles and Brazil may have become centres of diverse ethnological elements, and also of distinctive arts and customs of the western hemisphere. The Carib race, which was the predominant one in the Lesser Antilles, and occupied extensive regions of the mainland toward the southern Atlantic seaboard, differed very strikingly, alike in mental and physical characteristics, from the races of Central and of North America, and still more so from those with whom they came in contact in the larger islands. Traces of words common to the Colfachi of Florida and the insular Caribs are probably the sole grounds for the tradition of a North American origin for the latter; though in cranial conformation their analogies are with the northern dolichocephalic nations. Greatly more interesting is the fact that, while their continental habitat belongs to the southern and not to the northern hemisphere, they also disclose Polynesian affinities in language and customs. Dr. Latham remarks in his *Varieties of Man:* "In the ethnography of Polynesia certain peculiar customs in respect to the language of caste and ceremony were noted. The Carib has long been known to exhibit a remarkable peculiarity in this respect. The current statement is that the women have one language and the men another. The real fact is less extraordinary. Certain objects have two names; one of which is applied by males, the other by females only." The explanation offered attempts to trace the female terms to the language of the Arawaks, the older inhabitants of the islands, the males among whom are assumed to have been exterminated, and the women adopted by the conquering Caribs as wives. But such an admixture of races has occurred in every age of the world, with no such results; and the theory very unsatisfactorily accounts for a philological phenomenon by no means limited to the Carib among the languages of America. In our modern English language grammatical gender has to a great extent disappeared; in the ancient Saxon, as in the Latin, it affected noun, pronoun, and adjective, and modified them through all their declensions; in the peculiar laws thus found as an analogous feature of Polynesian and South American languages, gender is carried to the utmost extent, and not only modifies the forms of speech applicable to the sexes, but those in use by them. It is in this direction that the peculiarities analogous to true gender have been developed in widely different American languages. The general mode of expressing sex for the lower animals, alike among the northern Indians, and in the languages of Mexico and Central America, is only by prefixing another noun to their names, equivalent to our "male" and "female," or "he" and "she." But the use of distinct terms expressive of difference of sex in the human species is carried to an extent unknown in ancient or modern European languages; and separate adjectives are employed to express qualities, such as size, form, proportion, etc., from those which define the same attributes of inanimate objects, and even of the lower animals. In closing his analysis of the Huasteca language, along with others spoken in Central America, Gallatin remarks on an abbreviated mode of speech noted by Father Tapia Zenteno as in use by the women, and adds, " Here, as amongst all the other Indian nations, the names by which they express the various degrees of kindred differ from those used by men."

The cranial affinities of the Caribs have already been referred to. They are essentially dolichocephalic; and the predominance of such configuration throughout the American Archipelago has been made the basis of important ethnological deductions. Retzius especially has recorded the opinion that, while he conceives the Tongusian skull to form a clearly recognised link between those of the Chinese and the Esquimaux; the other primitive dolichocephalæ of America are nearly related to the Guanches of the Canary Islands, and to the populations of Africa, comprised by Dr. Latham under subdivisions of his Atlantidæ. The migrations which such affinities would indicate have already been referred to as altogether consistent with the probabilities suggested by the course of ancient navigation; and if early Mediterranean voyagers found the Antilles uninhabited, the genial climate and abundant natural resources of those islands peculiarly adapted them as nurseries of such germs of colonization for the neighbouring continent.

But independent of all real or hypothetical ramifications from southern or insular offsets of oceanic migration, many analogies confirm the probability of some portion of the North American stock having entered the

continent from Asia by Behring Straits or the Aleutian
Islands; and more probably by the latter than the former, for it is the climate that constitutes the real barrier.
The intervening sea is no impediment. In a southern
latitude, such a narrow passage as Behring Straits would
have been little more interruption to migration than the
Bosporus between Asia and Europe; and in its own
latitude it is annually bridged by the very power that
guards it from common use as a highway of the nations,
and is thus placed within easy command of any
Samoyed or Kamtchatkan sleighing party. It is, indeed, a well-authenticated fact, that the Russians had
learned from native Siberians of a great continent lying
to the east of Kamtchatka, long before Vitus Behring
demonstrated that the western and eastern hemispheres
so nearly approached, that the grand triumph of Columbus could be performed by the rudest Namollo in his
frail canoe.

By such a route, then, a North American germ of population may have entered the continent from Asia, diffused
itself over the North-west, and ultimately reached the
valleys of the Mississippi, and penetrated to southern
latitudes by a route to the east of the Rocky Mountains.
Many centuries may have intervened between their
first immigration, and their coming in contact with the
races of the southern continent; and philological and
other evidence indicates that if such a north-western
immigration be really demonstrable, it is also one of
very ancient date. But so far as I have been able to
study such evidence, much of that hitherto adduced
appears to point the other way; and while, theoretically,
the northern passage seems so easy, yet so far as any
direct proof goes, the Polynesian entrance into the south,
across the wide barrier of the Pacific, is the one most
readily sustained.

Mr. Lewis K. Daa, a learned Norwegian, has traced out certain curious affinities between the Samoyed languages of northern Asia and some of those of America; and through the other dialects of Siberia, and the relations of both to those of the Finnic and Altaic stock, completes, as he conceives, a chain of connexion, eastward from North Cape to Behring Straits, and thence to the related American stocks beyond the Pacific. But the comparison is chiefly based on a parallelism of vocabularies, and not on any reappearance of the peculiar constructive elements of the American languages. It does not, therefore, lead us very far; for the determination of the true form of the radical, for the purpose of useful comparison, in the unwritten languages of nomade tribes, is exceedingly difficult. But it does furnish some guidance, though not, as I conceive, in the direction its author imagines. He has demonstrated, as he believes, certain striking Asiatic affinities in the Athabaskan and Dakota tongues; and has shown a series of very suggestive similarities between words in the Asiatic and North American languages, relating to primitive arts, customs, and the rudimentary terms of religious belief. These include *God, priest, slave, dog, fire, metal, copper, knife, axe, awl, boat, house, tent, village, door, spin,. bag*: terms for the most part relating to arts, institutions, and opinions, common to the rudest tribes of Asia and America. Following out the idea founded on such evidence, Mr. Daa is disposed to trace the entire peopling of the western hemisphere to successive waves of migration flowing on in a continuous stream across Behring Straits, and he pushes his theory far beyond its legitimate bearings by affirming: "That the lowest savages, unacquainted with houses and garments, are found in South America only, in Brazil and Guyana, furthest off from Asia; and that the fishing tribes that border the Arctic and Pacific Oceans, from Labrador to Oregon —the Esquimaux, the Athabaskans, and their kindred,— being in the closest contact with Asia, are also the most improved, if we take into account their hard climate."[1] "Does not this," he asks, "point out the beginning and the end of the immigration?" But, in so far as any such difference really exists, it is altogether the product of climate, and furnishes no gauge of the relative age of nations. Whatever may have been the original direction of the current of migration, such evidence as philological comparisons with Northern Asia reveal, when viewed along with the more comprehensive analogies indicated to Southern Asia, appears to point rather to the ebb than the flow of such a tide, and discloses elements contributed by America to the older world of Asia. It is worthy of notice, in connexion with this view of the subject, that Charlevoix, in his essay on the Origin of the Indians, states that Père Grellon, one of the French Jesuit Fathers, met a Huron woman on the plains of Tartary, who had been sold from tribe to tribe, until she had passed from Behring Straits into Central Asia. By such intercourse as this incident illustrates, it is not difficult to conceive of some intermixture of vocabularies ; and that such transmigration has taken place to a considerable extent is proved by the intimate affinities between the tribes on both sides of Behring Straits.

The Esquimaux occupy a very remarkable position as a double link between America and Asia. Extending as they do in their detached and wandering tribes across the whole continent, from Greenland to Behring Straits, they appear, nevertheless, as the occupants of a diminishing rather than an expanding area. When the first authenticated immigration from Europe to America took place in the eleventh century, it was with the Esquimaux

---

[1] *Transactions of the Philological Society,* 1856, p. 293.

that the Scandinavians of Greenland, and apparently even the discoverers of Vinland, were brought in contact. If the Scraelings of New England at that comparatively recent date, were indeed Esquimaux, it is the clearest evidence we have of the recent intrusion of the Red Indians there. When the sites of the ancient Norse colonies of Greenland were rediscovered and visited by the Danes, they imagined they could recognise in the physiognomy of some of the Esquimaux who still people the inhospitable shores of Davis Straits, traces of admixture between the old native and Scandinavian or Icelandic blood. Of the Greenland colonies the Esquimaux had perpetuated many traditions, referring to the colonists under the native name of *Kablunet*. But of the old European language that had beer spoken among them for centuries, the fact is a highly significant one that the word *Kona*, used by them as a synonym for woman, is the only clearly recognised trace. But the Esquimaux, who thus took so sparingly from the languages of the old world, have contributed in a re-markable manner to them. The Tschuktschi, on the Asiatic side of Behring Straits, speak dialects of the Arctic American language. The Alaskan and the Tshugazzi peninsulas are peopled by Esquimaux ; the Konegan of Kudjak island belong to the same stock ; and all the dialects spoken in the Aleutian Islands, the supposed highway from Asia to America, betray in like manner the closest affinities to the Arctic Mongolidæ of the New World. Their languages are not only un-doubted contributions from America to Asia, but they are of recent origin, as compared with the traces of rela-tionship between those of the western hemisphere and the languages of Asia to which these bear any analogy. This is shown by the close affinities between the Esquimaux dialects of both continents, when contrasted with any recognisable evidence of some mutual but remote relationship, by which the Samoyede and the Finn are linked to the nations of the New World. Of such links, some of the most important art-words, such as *fire, metal, copper, tools* under their various forms, *boat,* and *house* or *temple,* have already been discussed in their relation to the growth of indigenous American arts. In respect to those, America had more to give than to borrow from the hyperborean Asiatics. With the Asiatic Esquimaux thus distributed along the coast adjacent to the dividing sea; and the islands of the whole Aleutian group in the occupation of the same remarkable stock common to both hemispheres; the only clearly recognisable indications are those of a current of migration setting towards the continent of Asia, the full influence of which may prove to have been greatly more comprehensive than has hitherto been imagined possible. While thus groping our way after remote ethnic and philological genealogies, it may be worth recalling that, along with the older and more obscure traces of linguistic affinities which lie beyond and within the discontinuous Ugrian area, analogies with the polysynthetic element of the American languages have been long sought in the peculiar agglutinate characteristics of the Euskara or Basque. It would be a remarkable and most unlooked for result of the ingenious hypothesis of Arndt and Rask, if it were found to resolve itself into ancient tide-marks of two great waves of population : the one the broad stream of Indo-European migration setting north-westward towards the shores of the Atlantic, and the other an overflow from the western hemisphere, also › setting westward, but within those higher latitudes of which history has taken no account, and only coming within the range of observation as it breaks and disperses in the shock of collision with the world's later historic stock. Yet such is not utterly improbable. The shores of the Indian Ocean were doubtless reached by an early wave of aboriginal population. Prof. H. H. Wilson points out in his edition of the *Rig Veda Sanhita*, as specially worthy of notice, that at the remote epoch of the earliest of the Vedas, the Indo-European Asiatics were already a maritime and mercantile people. With the development of skill and enterprise, maritime wanderers must have speedily passed over into the nearer island groups. From thence to the remoter islands was as easy at an early as at any later date ; and a glance at a hydrographic chart of the Pacific will show that a boat, driven a few degrees to the south of Pitcairn, Easter, or the Austral Islands, would come within the range of the Antarctic drift current, which sets directly towards the Chili and Peruvian coasts. It is, moreover, among the easternmost of those Polynesian islands that Captain Beechey noted the occurrence of colossal statues on platforms of hewn stone, or frequently fallen and mutilated : objects of neglectful wonder only, and not of worship, to the present inhabitants, who appear to be incapable of such workmanship. Similar sculptures, indeed, were observed on other islands, now uninhabited, and many traces indicate an ancient history altogether distinct from that of the later island races. Wanderers by the oceanic route to the New World may therefore have begun the peopling of South America long before the north-eastern latitudes of Asia received the first nomades into their inhospitable steppes, and opened up a way to the narrow passage of the North Pacific. At any rate, the north-eastern movement of the tide of migration, and its overflow into America, have been too absolutely assumed as the chief or sole means by which the New World could be peopled from an Asiatic centre.

In other respects also the tendency has been to read
the record backwards. Among the Atnahs, Chinooks,
Nasquallies, and other rude tribes on the Oregon coast,
the uncouth clicking sounds, equally harsh and undefined
to European ears, resolve themselves, when reduced to
writing, into the *tli, txl, atl, iztli,* and *yotl,* of the most
characteristic Mexican terminations. But looking at
such traces as analogous to one of the old Mexican
migration-pictures, the important question is, What is
the direction of the footprints? Do they reveal the trail
of the advancing Mexicans, as tracks left behind them
on their way towards the plateau of Anahuac, or are
they the mere reflex traces of later and indirect Mexican
influence? The latter I conceive to be most probable
by all just estimate of the very partial nature of the
traces. And yet they are curiously suggestive, and full
of interest, affecting as they do both the languages
and arts of the North-west. In this direction, however,
while facilities for intercourse between America and
Asia are obvious enough, the only well-defined indications of their use are by those hyperborean nomades
who have sought a new home in old Asia.

But confining our view to the American continent,
the north and south tropics were the centres of two very
distinct and seemingly independent manifestations of
native development; and many points of contrast between them tend to confirm the idea of intimate relations between the immature north and such matured
progress as Mexican civilisation had achieved. But also
this idea receives confirmation from equally clear indications of an overlapping of two or more distinct migratory trails leading from opposite points. The ebb and
flow of the northern and southern waves of migration
within the area of the northern continent have left
many tidal marks, with evidence of some interchange

of arts, and a considerable admixture of blood. These have already been sufficiently referred to in considering the physical and intellectual characteristics of the Mound-Builders. But this further may be admissible here in the form of suggestive hypothesis. The dolichocephalic form of cranium predominates among the northern tribes, as well as the Esquimaux. That of the Mound-Builders appears to have been very markedly brachycephalic. The tribes lying between the country of the Mound-Builders and Mexico presented an intermediate type,· and were superior in artistic skill to the northern nations. May it not be that we have here traces of an irruption of northern barbarians on the semi-civilized Mound-Builders, an extermination of the males, an extensive intermarriage with the females, and the usual results, of which the history of European nations furnishes many illustrations?

The Central American civilisation, the most matured of all that the New World gave birth to, was, I conceive, mainly of southern origin. Much that pertained to Mexican arts and polity was still more clearly derived from the north. But there are also evidences of mutual interchange. It must be borne in remembrance that we have in reality no such thing as a pure race among the historic nations of the old world. Admixture, not purity, seems the essential element of progress. The Greeks were no pure race, still less were the Romans ; and neither are the Spaniards, the French, the English, nor the Anglo-Americans. If we want pure, that is, unmixed blood, we must seek it in the hut of the Fin, the tent of the Arab, or for the New World in the Indian wigwam. There is abundant evidence that the races of Peru, Yucatan, and Anahuac were the products of great intermixture : it may have been of closely allied races, but also, and more probably, of widely diverse ones. In

Central America especially we are tempted to conceive of the possible meeting of immature South American civilisation with that which an essentially distinct migration had borne across the Atlantic, it may be, in accordance with the fondly-cherished dream of the modern American, while yet the fleets of Tyre and Carthage swept fearlessly beyond the Pillars of Hercules into the great engirdling ocean of their ancient world. Here, at any rate, are such indications of intermixture and interchange as investigation helps us to recover. South America had her immature picture-writing, her sculptured chronicles or basso-relievos, her mimetic pottery, her defined symbolism and associated ideas of colours, and her quipus. North America had her astronomical science, her more developed though crude picture-writing, her totems, pipe-sculpture, and wampum ; and her older Mound-Builders, with their uniform standards of weight and mensuration. Each had a nearly equally developed metallurgy. In Central America we seem to look on the mart of intellectual interchange, and the centre towards which all elements of progress converge into the grand product of that civilisation still so wonderful in its ruins. The idea may be intelligibly presented to the eye thus :—

South America.	North America.
The Quipu.	The Wampum.
Picture Writing.	The Totem.
Bas-relief Chroniclings.	Picture Writing.
Mimetic Pottery.	Mimetic Pipe-sculpture.
Metallurgic Art.	Metallurgic Art.
The Balance.	Standard Weights.
Agricultural Science.	Geometrical Mensuration.
Beasts of Burden.	Metallic Currency.
Peruvian Azimuths.	The Astronomical Calendar.

CENTRAL AMERICA.

Architecture.
Fictile Art.
Portrait Sculpture.
Hieroglyphics.
Numerals.
Letters.

To the characteristics thus distributed among the more civilized nations of the New World, have to be added that strange custom of cranial deformation, ancient Asiatic as well as American, and not unknown to the islanders of the Pacific. It is common to nations north and south of the Isthmus of Panama, yet seemingly more truly indigenous to the southern than the northern continent; and it is fully more probable that it was derived by the Asiatic macrocephali, than originally contributed from their Eastern steppes to the prairies and forests of what we style the New World.

The idea which seems best to harmonize with the varied though still imperfect evidence thus glanced at, when viewed in connexion with a supposed Asiatic cradle-land, conceives the earliest current of population destined for the New World to have spread through the islands of the Pacific, and to have reached the South American continent long before an excess of Asiatic population had diffused itself into its own inhospitable northern steppes; that by an Atlantic oceanic migration, another wave of population passed by the Canaries, Madeira, and the Azores, to the Antilles, Central America, and probably by the Cape Verdes, or, guided by the more southern equatorial current, to Brazil; and that, latest of all, the Behring Straits and the North Pacific Islands may have become the highway for a northern migration by which certain striking diversities of nations

of the northern continent, including the conquerors of
the Mexican plateau, are most easily accounted for. But
of this last especially, the evidence is chiefly inferential ;
and the more obvious traces rather indicate the same
current which set from Southern Asia to the Pacific
shores of South America, moving onward till it overflowed by Behring Straits and the Aleutian Islands, into
the continent from whence it was originally derived.

But such are only guesses at truth, suggestive it may
be of definite views, and permissible in gathering up the
last stray links of such accumulated, though still very
imperfect evidence ; but not to be confounded with its
more obvious teachings.

CHAPTER XXVI.

GUESSES AT THE AGE OF MAN.

In previous chapters are embodied the impressions produced by personal observation and direct intercourse with a people in the primitive condition of the Red Indians of the American forests, after years devoted to the study of the traces of an aboriginal population in the British Islands. So much that is natural to the habits and simple arts of savage life, as seen among the Indians of the New World, has presented itself to my eye and mind as the realization in a living present of what I had already conceived of amid the relics of Britain's allophylian tribes, that I am led to believe such archæological researches may be found to have constituted a useful preparative for the study of American ethnology, and the solution of some of the deeply interesting problems which are suggested by the phenomena it discloses ; nor can I now doubt that the observation of man in such primitive stages of social development furnishes important aid towards the true interpretation of some of the first traces of human history which so curiously underlie the later records of his presence in Europe. The prehistoric glimpses recorded in previous chapters refer, accordingly, fully as much to the Old World as the New. The latter has furnished not only a novel field of study, but an entirely new point of view, even for those researches into the history of the primeval man of Britain and Europe, which had already been minutely pursued. Some old views have been modified, while others are confirmed and rendered even more clear. But confined as my former researches were to an area so limited, and dealing with results which claimed some of their peculiar interest from the very insulation of the microcosm within which they were embraced : I feel the more at liberty, when attempting to deal with similar traces pertaining to a continent, to range even beyond its confines, and to follow out the seductive leadings of the younger science into some questions affecting the whole compass of ethnology.

In thus reviewing the evidence elicited by the disclosures of American archæology and ethnology, I have pursued the previously recorded researches with no favourite theory to maintain, but have anxiously striven to arrive at an impartial decision as to what are the legitimate deductions from the evidence. The determination of the relations which the man of America bears to the European or Asiatic man is felt to involve such important results, that this very fact has helped to impede the progress of truth. The assailant has, perhaps, felt emboldened at times by the very gravity of the issues imperilled by his attack ; while the adherents to a faith in the all-comprehensive brotherhood of man, have rather entrenched themselves in their own strongholds than fairly met their opponents on the open field of scientific inquiry. Scientific truths, whatever be the interests they involve, can only be determined on scientific grounds ; and on such only has any attempt been made to base them in this work. But if an inquiry thus honestly and impartially pursued—like a problem wrought out by algebraical notation,—brings out a result precisely corresponding to conclusions already determined by wholly independent proof, it cannot be unacceptable even to those who stand in no need of its confirmation. Such has been my experience in the present inquiry. The subject presented itself in novel aspects : the results, whatever they should prove to be, were welcome, since I had no preconceived theory at stake ; but, as the subject has expanded before me, I have more and more been convinced how needless a thing it is to supplant ancient belief, from too ready a yielding to the seductive temptations of novel and seemingly simple hypotheses, which commend themselves to the judgment by their apparent solution of difficulties. It is little more than three and a half centuries since the men of the Old and the New World met face to face. For unknown ages before that America had been a world within herself, with nations, languages, arts, and civilisation all her own ; and the whole tendency of that later American science, which also claims to be native, though the product of a race of European descent, has been to make of the red man a distinct race and species. I have approached the inquiry pursued in the previous chapters with an earnest desire to avoid prejudging this question, or testing it on other than purely scientific evidence. But the result has been to satisfy me that there is no ground for separating the American from the Asiatic man ; but that, on the contrary, greater difficulties exist in reconciling our belief in the descent of all men from a common stock, when we proceed to compare some of the diverse tribes and nations of the Asiatic continent, than any that interfere with our acceptance of the dogma that the Mongols of Asia and America are one.

In the ingenious speculations on the origin of species by which Charles Darwin has startled the scientific world, he remarks, as he draws his first abstract to a close : " The whole history of the world, as at present

known, although of a length quite incomprehensible by
us, will hereafter be recognised as a mere fragment of
time, compared with the ages which have elapsed since
the first creature, the progenitor of innumerable extinct
and living descendants, was created.   In the distant
future I see open fields for far more important researches.   Psychology will be based on a new foundation, that of the necessary acquirement of each mental
power and capacity by gradation.   Light will be thrown
on the origin of man and his history." Already the
speculations of Darwin have done good service to the
ethnologist, though not in the way he intended or
imagined they should.   They will not persuade him
that the universe is a product of measured and beautiful
motion, within which this earth-planet has gone cycling
on according to fixed laws, until, from the simplest
monad or life-germ, endless forms of wonder and beauty
have been evolved, closing at length with the evolution
of man, as the latest and crowning work of such development ; but they may give a new force to the
persuasion of many, that time and external influences
supply all the requisite elements for the evolution of
varying tribes of mankind from a common stock.   Mr.
Darwin has not succeeded, in the whole course of his
ingenious argument, though returning to it again and
again, in tracing the slightest indications of that favourite
illustration of the instability of species, the pigeon,
being developed out of any essentially distinct form.
But he has shown that pigeons have been subjected to
the influences of domestication and of civilisation for
thousands of years ; that one of the most favourable
circumstances for their production of distinct breeds is
to be traced to the fact, that male and female pigeons
can be easily mated for life ; and that they have been
found capable of domestication alike in Northern Europe,

in Egypt, and in Southern India. Selecting some of
the greatest of known extremes within the natural
family of *Columbidæ* subjected to such influence, he
remarks : " Although an English carrier or short-faced
tumbler differs immensely in certain characters from the
rock-pigeon, yet, by comparing the several sub-breeds
of these breeds, more especially those brought from
distant countries, we can make an almost perfect series
between the extremes of structure." In so far as these
are well-accredited facts, entirely independent of the
theory they are advanced to maintain, they furnish interesting analogies readily applicable to the so-called
races of men. It is easy to subdivide the human family,
as Blumenbach has done, into Caucasian, Mongolian,
Ethiopian, Malay, and American ; nor is it difficult to
select a typical example of each, presenting very striking
elements of contrast to all the others. But, meanwhile,
research tends only to the multiplication of species.
Pickering makes eleven, and Borey de St. Vincent,
fifteen. Gliddon and Nott, following out the sugges
tive idea of Agassiz as to the correspondence of diverse
species of man with the natural geographical areas of
the animal creation, have divided the globe into eight
zoological realms. Through these they distribute their
human fauna under forty-three different heads ; and it
is by no means apparent that this is a sufficiently liberal
apportionment to exhaust the requirements for such
primary human species as this theory demands. But,
meanwhile, as the species multiply, the elements of
diversity diminish. The intervals between seemingly
primary typical forms, such as those of Blumenbach,
are rapidly filled up. Instead of isolated and diverse
forms, we have a nearly continuous chain, passing by
slightly varying links from one to the other form ; and
here once more we realize what Darwin has observed of

his *Columbidæ,* that we can make an almost perfect series between the extremes of structure.

It may, perhaps, be legitimately objected that some of the problems most strenuously forced on the notice of the ethnologist, at the present time, lie entirely beyond the province of science. It cannot, certainly, establish the unity of the human race, the source of its origin, or the term of its existence. Nevertheless, it may contribute important confirmatory evidence for those who have already accepted, on higher authority than scientific induction, the story of Edenic creation, and of the division of the earth among the descendants of a common stock. Some of the grounds on which we may hope to establish, with reasonable probability, such scientific guesses at the origin and age of the human race, in so far as they are suggested by the present inquiry, have already been noticed, and may here be recapitulated, in conclusion, under their different heads. And first of LANGUAGE. To those who can accept of a theory which would make man the mere latest development of the same life-germ out of which all organic being has been evolved by a process of natural selection, it is as difficult to place limits to his possible existence, as to determine where the ape or the faun ended and man began. But to those who still believe that God made man in his own image, the limits which must be assigned to the existence of the race lie within moderate, if undefined bounds. We are as yet only on the threshold of philological disclosures ; but the tendency of all investigation into the analogies discernible in the structure of ancient and modern, of living and dead languages, points towards the discovery of relations, heretofore undreamt of, even between languages seemingly most dissimilar. Iceland, we know, was colonized by Northmen in the ninth century, and has ever since been in the occupation of a people of Scandinavian descent, and speaking and writing a language which in that ninth century was common to them and to the occupants of the European fatherland. But during the intervening centuries the Icelander has been isolated, and to a great extent excluded from intercourse with any other race ; while the Dane has bordered on Germany, and been carrying on intimate commercial and diplomatic relations with the other nations of Europe. Hence the slight change of the Icelandic tongue, compared with that wrought on the Danish in the same period, during which the dialects of the Scandinavian colonies, provinces, and kingdoms have been developed into separate and mutually unintelligible languages. Here, then, we have some clue to the causes and the rate of development of the dialects of a common language into separate tongues. But in the same ninth century the Northmen acquired and colonized the region of Northern France, ever since known as Normandy, and there, instead of creating a new offshoot from the common mother-tongue, they adopted the Romance dialect of the district, and made of it the vehicle of the most remarkable and influential literature of mediæval Europe. There were then already in independent though immature existence the six Romance dialects : the Italian, Wallachian, Provençal, Spanish, Portuguese, and French, all acknowledging their descent from the common Latin mother-tongue, within an era so recent as the decline of the Roman Empire. But the Latin itself is no primary root-language, but bears within its vocabulary and grammatical structure as unmistakable evidences of a derived and composite character, as any mass of conglomerate does to the geologist ; and as the philologist pursues his investigations, it becomes apparent to him that not only the Latin and Greek, the Germanic, Scan-

dinavian, and Slavonic, but also the Zend, Sanscrit, and
Celtic tongues, all embody modifications of some antecedent parent language. So also the scattered members
of the Shemitic group have been gathered up towards
a common centre ; and the influence of Mohammedan
aggression within comparatively modern times, is seen
to have done for the Arabic what the ambition of Imperial Rome did for the Latin. The affinities of the
other languages of Asia and Africa, of the Australasian
archipelago, and of America, are as yet very partially
determined ; but many glimpses of analogous truths
are already discernible ; and in this direction lies the
reasonable anticipation of important revelations as to
the relations of the tribes and nations of mankind to
one original centre, and the determination of the probable lapse of time requisite for such a subdivision and
migration of the common stock as meets the eye of the
inquirer at the present day. The number of languages
spoken throughout the world at the present time has
been computed to exceed four thousand. The number
of dead and extinct languages is an unknown quantity
which may be slighted or exaggerated according to the
tendencies of the theorist and investigator. But the
proposition which such facts as have already been indicated suggest to the mind, assumes a shape which may
be stated in this form : ˙If six independent and mutually
unintelligible languages, such as the Romance tongues,
have been developed out of the common mother Latin
tongue in five centuries, how many centuries are required for one common language to have begotten four
thousand ? The diverse circumstances tending to ac-
celerate or retard the rate of progress, dependent on
culture, isolation, and settled or migratory habits, no
doubt complicate the question ; and the possible, and
indeed ascertained disappearance of languages, without

leaving any trace of their vocabulary or grammar, detracts from the absolute value of conclusions thus determined. But with every allowance for the elements of doubt or error, we perceive in this direction one means whereby we may gauge the probable duration of the human race, and determine for it an existence commensurate with the date of man's origin as the latest of all created beings over which he has been placed with so ample a dominion.

Full value has already been attached by the philologist to the fact that the remarkable relations subsisting between the modern languages of Europe and the ancient dead language of the Indian Vedas, carry us back by the radiations of the different members of the Indo-European group to some probable Asiatic centre, according in so far with the history of the dispersion of the human race. But other elements contributing to the same source of approximate determination of the origin and age of man, point even still more unmistakably to a common Asiatic centre ; as is the case with the next to which I refer, THE DOMESTICATION OF ANIMALS. Geoffroi St. Hilaire estimated the animals reduced to a state of domestication at forty species, of which thirty five, such as the horse, ox, dog, sheep, goat, and pig, may be characterized as cosmopolitan. Out of these thirty-five domesticated species possessed by Europe, thirty-one appear to originate in Central Asia, or in Northern Africa, in the vicinity of the Mediterranean Sea, where, as in Southern Europe, the tribes of the dispersion were scattered at the earliest dates. Almost the whole are derived from warm climates, and thus indicate that civilisation pertained to the primeval Asiatic man ; that he brought with him to Europe the animals he had already domesticated ; and introduced there the pastoral life which is associated with the patriarchal history of the infancy of Asiatic nations. The monuments of Egypt and Assyria illustrate the early domestication of cattle and fowls; while in special localities peculiar additions supply the wants of particular regions : such as the elephant, the camel, and ostrich, of tropical climates, and the rein-deer of the Arctic north. Whilst, however, from the era of Athenian independence, Europe has been the centre of human progress, and the traces of its progressive civilisation reach far behind that, into the heroic ages of Grecian story : it is an important fact that nearly all the domesticated animals of Europe appear to be of exotic origin, and belonged originally to warmer climates, where it was possible for man to have subsisted on fruits and the vegetable products of the soil, and to have dwelt indifferent to the protection from the elements, which engrosses so much of labour in less genial climes. The latter condition forces him to develop the resources which supply the necessities of food, clothing, and shelter from an inclement sky; but the former is the state that leaves him at leisure to turn his intellectual powers to account, and achieve those victories of civilisation which have not necessity, but progress and a higher utility in view.

In relation to America, the history of its domesticated animals is intimately connected with the next phase in the present argument, THE ORIGIN OF CIVILISATION. The whole evidence of history places beyond doubt that the seats of early civilisation lay in warmer climates, on the banks of the Nile, the Euphrates, the Tigris, the Indus, and the Ganges. The shores of the Mediterranean succeeded in later centuries to their inheritance, and were the seats of long-enduring empires, whose intellectual bequests are the life of later civilisation. But transalpine Europe is entirely of modern

growth, and much of it even now is but in its infancy.
Here, then, we trace our way back to the beginnings
of our race. There is no endless cycle in which the
nations could revolve. Man primeval in a state of
nature, and in the midst of the abundance of a tropical
region, employing his intellectual leisure, begins that
progressive elevation which is as consistent with his
natural endowments as it is foreign to the instincts of
all other animals. He increases and multiplies, spreads
abroad over the face of the earth ; and slowly, in the
wake of the wandering nations, follow the brightening
rays of that civilisation which was kindled at the central
cradle-land, and could burn brightly only amid the
fostering influences of settled leisure.

America has no domesticated animals common to the
other quarters of the globe, excepting such as have been
introduced by her modern European colonists. The
llama and the alpaca remain in their native regions, on
the tropical plateaus of Bolivia and Peru ; and these,
with the dog, constitute the domesticated animals of
the New World. They indicate that man, if, as we
believe, he migrated from Asia to America, brought
with him no evidences of progress such as the domesticated animals of Asiatic origin prove to have pertained to the early colonists of Europe. The parrot,
the toucan, and other native birds are tamed by some
of the tribes of South America, though, like the sacred
ibis of Egypt, rather for amusement than utility ; and
all the domesticated animals of the New World are of
native origin, and, with the exception of the dog, of
tropical character. But herein we once more see reproduced in the New World the same phenomena which
appear to have attended the birth of civilisation in
the Old World. The shores oì the Western Hemisphere
were reached at one or more points, by wanderers from

the birth-land of the nations. Slowly its forests and
prairies, its river valleys and great plateaus were occupied ; and then in the tropical regions, under skies
rendered genial by the elevation of the Andes, and surrounded by the luxuriance of a perpetual summer, man
found leisure to develop arts, letters, science, and to
start on the career of human progress. Had the seats
of indigenous American civilisation been found on the
coast of New England, or on the shores of the Great
Lakes, it would have been proof enough that it was
borrowed ; and we might then have turned with propriety to Phœnician, Egyptian, or Scandinavian theories
of colonization. But the vale of Anahuac, and the
plateaus of the southern Cordilleras, are the very centres
provided by nature for the birth of a self-originating
American civilisation. That when thus developed it
is found to present so many points of correspondence
with the primitive civilisation of the Old World, only
proves that both are alike the work of man, endowed
with the same instincts, capacities, and faculties ; and
the amount of development in both cases is, I believe,
no less surely a true gauge of the lapse of time, the
significance of which we are in the fair way of determining.

AGRICULTURE, which is another branch of early civilisation, following closely in the wake of the domestication of animals by pastoral man, points to the same
conclusions as the previous evidence. We have made
very slight and unimportant additions to our domesticated animals since the eras of human civilisation recorded on the monuments of Assyria and Egypt. It is
otherwise with our domesticated plants ; though even
of these the most important cereals date beyond all
definite chronicles, and belong in all probability to the
Asiatic birth-land of the race. Less importance is

perhaps due to the tropical origin of domesticated plants than of animals ; since in warm climates the most useful vegetable products were most likely to be found. But taken in conjunction with the previous arguments it has considerable weight; and when we turn to the New World we see there clearly that the maize, the bean, cocoa, tobacco and such other plants, including the potato, as have been brought under cultivation and disseminated among the northern tribes, are all traceable to the tropical seats of a native civilisation. Their general diffusion adds another proof of the protracted occupation of America by its aboriginal tribes; the fewness of their number, and the uniformity of their diffusion reduces the length of that period within limits readily compatible with all other evidence of the duration of the race.

So also is it with LETTERS. They lie at the foundation of all high and enduring civilisation. Yet we can trace them back to a rude origin, consistent with the most rudimentary elements of human intelligence ; and even in the late Ptolemaic era of that strange Egyptian cradle-land of the world's civilisation, we find its written and graven records betraying unmistakable traces of the infancy of letters, as the offspring of the same primitive pictorial art, which we recover anew in the picture-writing of Mexico and the symbolic totems of the American Indian. The visible progress is so slow that we stand in no need of vague geological periods to embrace the history of man. Within the interval between the rudest archaic monument of Egypt and her trilingual Rosetta Stone of the era of Ptolemy Epiphanes, we see man laboriously work out for himself a crude and very imperfect alphabet, the parent of all later and better ones ; and can trace each progressive step. We witness the whole process, from its very beginning in a picture-writing as simple as that with which the Indian savage records his deeds of arms on his buffalo robe, or engraves the honours of the warrior of his tribe on his grave-post. We need not therefore seek for older periods than by reasonable concessions of the chronologist may be already assigned to man ; and by the help of such indications as the birth of letters supply, we can trace back his intellectual history to its very birth-time, and frame a shrewd guess at the age of mind. And when we pass from the Old to the younger world of the West, its revelations amply bear out such inductive reasoning. There letters had only reached the stage of an abbreviated picture-writing, perhaps approximating to a word-alphabet, like that of the Chinese, but with no trace of pure phonetic signs. The continent was peopled from Asia, and therefore by younger nations. Its civilisation was not borrowed, but of native growth, and therefore was far younger than that of Egypt ; and in full accordance with this we find writing, first in the most infantile stage of rude Indian picturing ; next in the progressive stage of Mexican picture-writing, with abbreviation, symbols of thought, and signs relating to the details of the calendar ; and in its highest stage in the hieroglyphic holophrasms of the Central American inscriptions and manuscripts, which only required time to have produced a native demotic writing, an alphabet pregnant for the New World as that of Phœnicia has proved for the Old, and a literature embodying the reflex of the native mind.

So also with NUMERALS. We can trace back Arabic notation without question to the hieratic forms of primitive Egyptian numerals, which had no value of position, rendered the numbers by a mere multiple of the simplest signs for units, tens, and hundreds ; and only by abbreviating their combinations into a distinct set of numerical symbols for the days of the month, made the first approach to those arbitrary signs which were adopted by the Arabian mathematicians, and have become the universal arithmetical language of civilized nations. The idea of number is one of the earliest presented to the human mind, and may indeed be regarded as coexistent with the intelligent exercise of the human faculties. But, except when dealing with very small numbers, it is only the educated mind that is able to realize any definite conceptions associated with computation ; and so soon as this was called into general use, for purposes of commerce, tribute, or the calculations of science, written signs became indispensable. The appreciation of numbers is accordingly frequently made a test of intellectual development, as in the case of a Ceylonese, referred to by Mr. Lushington, who was accused of murder, but was acquitted by the English judge, from his being found incapable of counting three. So also Mr. Francis Galton, in an amusing account of the Damaras, in his *Narrative of an Exploration in Tropical South Africa,* remarks of them : "In practice, whatever they may possess in their language, they certainly use no numeral greater than three. When they wish to express four they take to their fingers, which are to them as formidable instruments of calculation as a sliding-rule is to an English schoolboy. They puzzle very much after five, because no spare hand remains to grasp and secure the fingers that are required for units." Such is no uncommon condition of the savage mind ; and I suspect the dual forms existing in certain languages, as in the most cultured of all, the Greek, preserve to us the memorial of that stage of thought when all beyond two was an idea of vague number. We can discern the various stages which have, in certain nations, marked the passage from the vague idea of multitude to the definite one of number. This

is seen, for example, in repeated passages of the Old
Testament, as in that of Jeremiah : "As the host of
heaven cannot be numbered, neither the sand of the sea
measured ; so will I multiply the seed of David my
servant, and the Levites that minister unto me."[1] Assuming the Hebrew prophet to refer to the visible
heavens as seen by the naked eye, the stars are very
far short of innumerable ; though to a pastoral people,
dealing in no elaborate computations, the simile was as
expressive of multitude as the numberless sand-grains on
the sea-shore. The same idea is illustrated by the manner in which the term μυρία is always used by Homer in
its primary sense of an indefinite number.

Many of the languages of America are found to present the singular feature of a complete decimal vocabulary of numerals, with the power of combination in some
of them sufficient to adapt them to elaborate computations. This is remarkable among rude hunter tribes
standing as little in need of a system of arithmetical
notation as the African Damaras ; and it is deserving of
consideration, whether there may not be in this some
lingering trace of the civilisation which has left its
memorials in the elaborate geometrical structures of the
Ohio Valley. Practically, however, on entering into
conversation with the Indian, it becomes speedily apparent that he is unable to comprehend the idea of
abstract numbers. They exist in his mind only as associated ideas. He has a distinct conception of five dogs
or five deer; but he is so unaccustomed to the idea of
number as a thing apart from specific objects, that I
have tried in vain to get an Indian to admit that the
idea of the number five, as associated in his mind
with five dogs, is identical, so far as number is concerned, with that of five fingers. Abstract terms and

---

[1] Jer. xxxiv. 22 ; *vide* also Gen. xv. 5 ; xxii. 16-18.

ideas are equally absent from the language and thought
of the Indian ; and indeed, as we see in our own English
speech, are of very late growth in any language. But
the concrete form of thought controls the whole American vocabularies. The different directions in which
they have expanded to embrace the novel ideas consequent on European intercourse, illustrate its influence
on the multiplication of mutually unintelligible dialects
among unlettered tribes ; and this is specially noticeable
in the singular contrast in the names of numerals in American languages, otherwise disclosing striking affinities,
as compared with the uniformity of numerical nomenclature pervading the whole Indo-European tongues.
But no corresponding variety of symbols meets the eye.
In the most perfect of the native systems of notation
the signs have advanced little beyond that primitive
repetition of units which betrays itself as the natural
form of numeration, even in the matured hieroglyphics
of the Rosetta Stone.

Thus once more we appear to reach an infantile stage
of human thought in this direction also, tracing back the
associated ideas and signs of number so nearly to their
beginning, that we seem to stand in need of no great
lapse of centuries between that and the beginning of
man himself. And so is it with his ARTS : his architecture, sculpture, weaving, pottery, metallurgy ; and his
SCIENCE : his astrology, astronomy, and geometry ; the
beginnings of all of them lie within our reach. Egypt
has her vague year, the evidence of the beginning of the
recognition of solar time in a year of 365 days, but
which could only remain in use unmodified for a few
generations ; and in the greater and lesser cycles of
Egypt, Mexico, and Peru, we equally recognise divisions
of time which could not have been perpetuated through
many centuries without a manifest discordance with

actual astronomical phenomena, and the changing seasons, to which they always bore an intimate relation. Seed-time and harvest are inevitably bound up with all national and religious festivals. We can trace back man's progress in the history of his calendars: in the "New Style" of England, with her lost eleven days, still religiously preserved in the unreformed calendar of Russia; in the French calendar of the Great Year, anno 14, when the Republic, with far-seeing forethought, enacted that A.R. 3600, A.R. 7200, and A.R. 10,800 shall not be leap years; while the very first year of this comprehensive system did not live out half its days! Backward we trace our way amid the conflicting dates consequent on the independent adoption of the Gregorian Calendar at various successive periods, from its first enactment by the Council of Trent in 1582, to its tardy adoption by Protestant Sweden in 1753. As we retrace our steps, we find the Church divided from the second to the fourth century, until another Council, that of Nice, determined for her the true period of keeping Easter. Then behind this, and before the Christian era, we come to the determination of the Julian Year, and the correction of the accumulated errors of previous divisions of time, in the year B.C. 47   The names of Ptolemy, Hipparchus, Meton, and Euctemon, carry us back by further steps; until in the Nile Valley we seem to reach the beginnings of calendars, and recognise, in the sacred Vague Year of the Egyptians, the first definite determination of solar time, with its unmistakable relations to a beginning of time for man himself.

Astronomy has had its rise, alike in the Old World and the New, in elevated tropical table-lands, and fruitful valleys and plains, such as those through which the Euphrates and the Tigris roll their ample floods, or that strange river-valley which the Nile fertilizes with its annual overflow. In those favoured regions agriculture involves little toil, and the harvest ripens almost spontaneously for the reaper's sickle. There, also, flocks and herds were tended and trained for the use of man ; and, in the pastoral life of their earliest communities, the herdsmen watched their flocks under the mild beaming stars, and acquired an intelligent familiarity with the constellations, and the planets that wander through the spangled dome of night. In the infancy of our race, men studied the stars, bringing to the aid of their human sympathies the fancies of the astrologer, to fill the void which their imperfect science failed to satisfy. The Chaldean shepherds, who had never travelled beyond the central plain of Asia, where in fancy we recognise the cradle of the human race, began the work of solving the mystery of the heavens ; and what the Scottish shepherd-astronomer of the eighteenth century, James Ferguson, accomplished, proves what lay in their power.

> " O honoured shepherd of our later days,
>   Thee from the flocks, while thy untutored soul,
>   Mature in childhood, traced the starry course,
>   Astronomy, enamoured, gently led
>   Through all the splendid labyrinths of heaven,
>   And taught thee her stupendous laws."[1]

It was impossible that intelligent man could look forth, night after night, on the constellations, as they varied their place with the change from twilight to the dawn, and from moon to moon, and on the planets that moved in timely courses amid the twinkling stars, without discovering some of their relations to the seasons of the revolving year. But amid the same scenes of mild pastoral life, empires and populous cities first arose ; forms of worship, and periodical festivals and sacrifices, marked the annual return of the seasons, when the firstlings of the flock, and the first-fruits of the harvest-home, were

---

[1] *Eudosia, a Poem on the Universe,* by Capel Lofft.

offered bv priests on national altars. The herdsman and
the tiller of the soil traced to the warm beams of the
bright god of day the sources of fertility in flock and
field. They beheld the sun when it shined, and the
moon walking in brightness, and their heart was secretly
enticed, and their mouth kissed the hand.[1] Alike in the
tropical seats of primitive Asiatic empire, in the African
Nile-Valley, and on the plateaus of the Andes, the early
astronomers became Sabians, and worshipped the hosts
of heaven, while striving to solve their mysterious relations to the earth. But if we follow them in their first
division of solar time; and conceive of an annual festival, with sacrifices of the firstlings of the flock, such as
we recognise in the most ancient religious rites, with a
calendar founded on a year of 365 days: only a very
few generations, at most, could pass away, before altogether irreconcilable and ever-increasing discrepancies
would occur between the appointed festival and the
actual season with which it was originally designed to
harmonize. The lambs would be wanting for the burnt-
offering; the festival of harvesting would return while
the wheat was still green in the ear, or the bright tassel
of the maize was unformed; and the incensed god would
be assumed to look down on his worshippers with wrath,
and tardily to withhold the increase of their flocks and
the yield of their early seed-time, until the calendar was
readjusted, and the sacred and solar years were restored
to harmony. Here, also, as we retrace our way, and
seek to follow up the stream of time, the way-marks
are no less continuous and definite. Names memorable
among the intellectual leaders of the human race, stand
out as symbols of the progress of knowledge. Leverrier,
Rosse, Herschel, Newton, Huygens, and Galileo; Kepler,
Tycho Brahe, Al Batani, and Copernicus; Ptolemy, Hip-

---

[1] Job xxxi. 26, 27.

parchus, Eratosthenes, Autolycus, and Meton ; Manetho,
and the elder astronomers of Egypt ; Berosus, and the
Chaldean astrologists : each mark successively one or
more steps of progress, from the dawn of astronomical
science on the Assyrian plains, where the first shepherds
were abiding in the fields, keeping watch over their flocks
by night.   Here it is obvious we are dealing with no
incomprehensible series of cycles of time.   There are,
indeed, difficult questions still requiring the illumination
which further observation and discovery may be expected to supply ; nor have such been evaded in those
researches ; but the present tendency is greatly to exaggerate such difficulties.   The first few steps in the
progress thus indicated cannot be reduced to a precise
chronology.   The needful compass of their duration may
be subject of dispute, and the precise number of centuries that shall be allowed for their evolution may vary
according to the estimated rate of progress of infantile
human reason ; but I venture to believe that to many
reflecting minds it will appear that, by such a process of
inquiry, we do in reality make so near an approach to a
beginning in relation to man's intellectual progress, that
we can form no uncertain guess as to the duration of the
race, and find, in this respect, a welcome evidence of
harmony between the disclosures of science and the dic·
tates of Revelation.

APPENDIX.

APPENDIX A.—Vol. ii. p. 347.

QUERIES CIRCULATED BY THE AUTHOR WITH A VIEW TO OBTAIN
ACCURATE INFORMATION ON THE RESULTS OF THE ADMIXTURE
OF RACES IN THE NEW WORLD.

INDIAN HALF-BREEDS.

1. What is the number of the half-breed Indians? and from
what tribe, or tribes, are they chiefly or wholly derived by
their Indian parentage?

2. In what respects do the half-breed Indians differ from the
pure Indians, as to habits of life, courage, strength, increase of
numbers, etc.?

3. Do marriages ever take place between an Indian husband
and white wife? If so, does the offspring differ in any noticeable degree from that of a white husband and Indian wife?

4. Is any difference discernible in half-breeds descended on
the one side from French, and those on one side from British
parentage? If so, what is the difference?

CIVILIZED INDIAN HALF-BLOOD.

1. What is the number of the settled population, either half-
breed, or more or less of Indian blood?

2. What Indian characteristics, physical and mental, are
longest traceable in successive descendants of Indian and white

blood ? *e.g.*, hair, form of head, of mouth, of cheek-bones, colour and character of eyes, and any other features ?

3. Are those of partial Indian blood liable to any diseases which do not affect the whites or the pure Indians ?   Or, Are they more or less liable to such diseases ?

4. Are the families descended from mixed parentage noticeably larger or smaller than those of whites or of Indians ?

5. State any facts tending to prove or disprove, that the offspring descended from mixed white and Indian blood fails in a few generations.

APPENDIX B.—Vol. ii. pp. 354, 418.

ETHNOLOGICAL NOMENCLATURE : AMERICAN HALF-CASTES.

In all the departments of ethnology, the want of a generally recognised terminology is a serious impediment.   Such words as *race, stock, family,* etc., are excluded, because their use in any strictly defined sense involves the affirmation of opinions most keenly disputed; and nearly the same objection lies against the adoption of such scientific terms of natural history as *order, class, species,* etc.   In relation to hybridity, however somewhat has been already done by means of popular designations of the more noticeable varieties of mixed blood.   Dr. Tschudi, after noticing the diverse characteristics of the pure-blood population of European, Asiatic, African, and American descent to be met with in Peru, gives a list of the very varied degrees of mixed blood, with the names by which they are there designated.   Of the term *Creole,* he observes, "The designation properly belongs to all the natives of America born of parents who have emigrated from the Old World."   The children of pure-blood African parents are accordingly Creoles, as much as those of unmixed European blood.   The Spaniards do not even limit the term *Criollo* to the human race, but apply it to all animals propagated in America of pure European parentage.   They have, accordingly, Creole horses, bullocks, asses, poultry, etc.

The following is Dr. Tschudi's list of half-castes, with a few additions from other sources :—

Father.	Mother.	Half-caste.
White,	Negro,	Mulatto.
White,	Indian,	Mestizo.
Indian,	Negro,	Chino.
White,	Mulatta,	Cuarteron.
White,	Mestiza,	Creole, only distinguished from the white by a pale brown complexion.
White,	Chinese,	Chino-blanco.
White,	Cuarterona,	Quintero.
White,	Quintera,	*White.*
Negro, N.A.,	Indian,	Zambo, or Cariboco.
Negro, S.A.,	Indian,	Mameluco.
Negro,	Mulatta,	Zambo-Negro, or Cubra.
Negro,	Mestiza,	Mulatto-oscuro.
Negro,	Chinese,	Zambo-Chino.
Negro,	Zamba,	Zambo-Negro (perfectly black).
Negro,	Cuarterona,	Mulatto (rather dark).
Negro,	Quinterona,	Pardoc.
Indian,	Mulatta,	Chino-oscuro.
Indian,	Mestiza,	Mestizo-claro (frequently very beautiful).
Indian,	China,	Chino-cholo.
Indian,	Zamba,	Zambo-claro.
Indian,	China-cholo,	Indian (with short frizzly hair).
Indian,	Cuarterona,	Mestizo (rather brown).
Indian,	Quintera,	Mestizo.
Mulatto,	Zamba,	Zambo.
Mulatto,	Mestiza,	Chino (of rather clear complexion).
Mulatto,	China,	Chino (rather dark).

The above deals with the results of hybridity with considerable minuteness. Nevertheless, it makes no distinction between Spanish, Portuguese, and English blood, and only once discriminates among the equally strongly marked diversities of red and black blood. But we want a no less comprehensive series of distinctive names to indicate the offspring of intrusive races of pure blood. Lieber suggests the term *Europidian* for the American of pure European descent ; but something much more minute is required to supply the want of definite terms constantly felt. The following suggests a series of terms, including some already in use, which admits of indefinite extension :—

> Europidian : of parents of European origin, born in any other quarter of the globe.
> Euromerican : of parents of European origin born in America.
> Eurasian,   ,,   ,,   ,,   Asia.
> Eurafrican,   ,,   ,,   ,,   Africa.
> Euraustralian,   ,,   ,,   ,,   Australia.
> Eurindian,   ,,   ,,   ,,   India.
> Anglo-American : of parents born in America of English descent.
> Gallo-American,   ,,   ,,   ,,   French   ,,
> Anglo-Canadian,   ,,   ,,   Canada of English   ,,
> Gallo-Canadian, or Habitant,   ,,   French   ,,
> Anglo-Australian.
> Anglo-Indian, etc., etc.

Yankee, popularly applied by foreigners to the people of the United States, properly signifies a New Englander ; but its generic use originates in the confusion created by their appropriation of the term *American,* which has a totally distinct ethnological significance, while the equally vague name of *Statesman* is already preoccupied ; and those of *Federal* and *Confederate* are as yet mere party names.

There is still wanted a further nomenclature for the descendants of mixed blood, resulting from this recolonization of the world by the European stock ; but as it is intimately blended with the foregoing, it may be best met by a less amalgamate modification of the same terms, *e.g.*

> Euro-american : of mixed European and Indian blood.
> Euro-asian,   ,,   ,,   Asiatic   ,,
> Euro-african,   ,,   ,,   African   ,,
> Euro-chinese,   ,,   ,,   Chinese   ,,
> Euro-hindoo,   ,,   ,,   Hindoo   ,,
>   Etc. etc.

APPENDIX C.—Vol. ii. p. 399.

QUERIES ON COLOURED POPULATION IN CANADA.

1. What is the number of coloured population in the district?

2. What proportion of the coloured people are of pure African blood?

3. Is there any difference in the liability to disease, or in the special diseases, between the coloured and white population, either in infancy or throughout life?

4. Are there any diseases the coloured people are liable to from which the whites are exempt; or exempt which the whites are liable to? Or,

Are there any diseases more or less fatal to them than to the whites?

5. Are the families of coloured parents noticeably larger or smaller than those of whites?

6. State any facts tending to prove or disprove that the offspring descended from coloured parents fails in a few generations.

7. Does the climate of Canada effect any change on coloured emigrants from the States? If so, in what respects?

APPENDIX D.—Vol. ii. p. 403.

EMIGRATION TO HAYTI: CIRCULAR.

To the Blacks, Men of Colour, and Indians in the United States and the British North American Provinces:—

FRIENDS,—I am authorized and instructed by the Government of the Republic to offer you, individually and by communities, a welcome, a home, and a *free* homestead in Hayti.

Such of you as are unable to pay for your passage will be provided with the means of defraying it.

Two classes of emigrants are especially invited, labourers and farmers. None of either class, or of any class, will be furnished with passports who cannot produce before sailing the proofs of a good character for industry and integrity.

To each family of emigrants five carreaux[1] of fresh and fertile land, capable of growing all the fruits and staples of the tropics, will be *gratuitously* given, on the sole conditions that they shall settle on it, and cultivate it, and declare their intention of becoming citizens of Hayti. To unmarried men, on similar conditions, two carreaux will be granted.

The Government, also, will find remunerative work for those of you whose means will not permit them to begin immediately on independent cultivation.

Emigrants are invited to settle in communities.

Sites for the erection of schools and chapels will be donated by the State, without regard to the religious belief of the emigrants.

Board and lodging, free of cost, will be furnished to the emigrants for eight days after their arrival in the island.

The same protection and civil rights that the laws give to Haytians are solemnly guaranteed to the emigrants.

The fullest religious liberty will be secured to them. They will never be called on to support the Roman Catholic Church.

No military service will be demanded from them, excepting that they shall form militia companies, and drill themselves once a month.

All the necessary personal effects, machinery, and agricultural instruments introduced by the emigrants shall be entered free of duty.

The emigrants shall be at liberty to leave the country at any moment they please; but those whose passage shall be paid by Government, if they wish to return before the expiration of three years, will be required to refund the money expended on their account. A contract, fixing the amount, will be made with each emigrant before leaving the continent.

I have been commissioned to superintend the interests of the emigrants, and charged with the entire control of the movement in America, and all persons, therefore, desiring to avail

---

[1] A carreaux is three acres and three and a third rods.

themselves of the invitation and bounty of the Haytian Government, are requested to correspond with me.

I shall at once, as directed by the Government, establish a Bureau of Emigration in Boston, and publish a Guide Book for the use of those persons of African or Indian descent who may wish to make themselves acquainted with the resources of the country and the disposition of its authorities. I shall also appoint agents to visit such communities as may seriously entertain the project of emigration.

Immediate arrangements, both here and in Hayti, can be made for the embarkment and settlement of one hundred thousand persons.

By authority of the Government of the Republic of Hayti,

JAMES REDPATH,
General Agent of Emigration.

BOSTON, *November 3,* 1860.

INDEX.

INDEX.

ERRATA.

Vol. I. p. 46, line 31, *for* applications *read* application.
   ,,   231, Title of Chapter, *for* Arts *read* Instinct.
   ,,   277, line 7, *for* have elapsed *read* must have elapsed.
Vol. II. p. 127, line 20, *for* grow *read* grew.
   ,,   138, line 21, *for* survive *read* survived.
   ,,   171, line 19, *for* But the modern *read* Both the modern.
   ,,   245, Table III. No. 10, Atacama, F.D., *for* 5·1 *read* 4·4.
   ,,   260, line 7 from foot, *dele* six.
   ,,   270, Table X. No. 9, Iroquet, F.D., *for* 4·0 *read* 5·0.
   ,,   299, line 6, *for* seventeenth *read* sixteenth.
   ,,   318, line 35, *for* of finely *read* or finely.
   ,,   321, line 12, *for* and *read* an.
   ,,   348, line 9, *for* descend *read* descended.

THE END.

EDINBURGH: T. CONSTABLE,
PRINTER TO THE QUEEN, AND TO THE UNIVERSITY